CLASSIC
CHINESE
CUISINE

CLASSIC CHINESE CUISINE

By Nina Simonds

Photography by Alan Richardson
Calligraphy by T.C. Lai
Illustrations by Kathy Bray

CHAPTERS PUBLISHING LTD., SHELBURNE, VERMONT 05482

For Sophie, Mimi and Pauline,
Who Portioned Food and Love
Most Generously

Published by
Chapters Publishing Ltd.
2031 Shelburne Road
Shelburne, Vermont 05482

Library of Congress Cataloging-in-Publication Data
Simonds, Nina
    Classic Chinese cuisine / by Nina Simonds ; photography by Alan Richardson.
    p.   cm.
    Reprint. Originally pub.: Boston : Houghton Mifflin, 1982.
    Includes index.
    ISBN 1-881527-31-X (hard) : $29.95. — ISBN 1-881527-32-8 (pbk.) : $19.95
    1. Cookery, Chinese. I. Title.
    TX724.5.C5S59 1994
    641.5951—dc20   93-48261

Trade distribution by
Firefly Books Ltd.
250 Sparks Avenue
Willowdale, Ontario
Canada M2H 2S4

Printed and bound in Canada by
Metropole Litho
St. Bruno de Montarville, Québec

Designed by Susan McClellan
Cover photograph: Shrimp With Sizzling Rice, page 41

Contents

Author's Preface

WHEN CLASSIC CHINESE CUISINE was originally published in 1982, the world was a different place. Thai, Vietnamese and Korean food had not yet enraptured the American palate. Most Chinese food enthusiasts were still experimenting with Hunan and spicy Sichuan dishes, and there was a vast audience of cooks who were uninitiated. It was a most appropriate time, at least to my mind, to publish a definitive introduction to classic Chinese cooking.

Twelve years later, even after numerous trips to China and countless return sojourns to Taiwan and Hong Kong, I am amazed at how many of the dishes I still prepare from the original version of this volume. But how many authors can turn down the opportunity to fine-tune and improve their first book? Accordingly, I have revised and adapted many of these dishes, especially where oil content is concerned, and I have added about 30 new recipes. I hope that new and old friends will be pleased with the new CLASSIC CHINESE CUISINE.

Nina Simonds
Spring 1994

Acknowledgments

THIS BOOK IS THE PRODUCT OF MORE than 10 years of study, research and experience. So many people contributed by sharing their knowledge, expertise and encouragement. I greatly regret that only a few can be mentioned by name.

My sincere thanks go to Huang Su Huei and the Chinese master chefs at the Wei-Chuan school in Taipei, who taught me so much during my years in Taiwan.

I am deeply grateful to *Gourmet* magazine for publishing my 24-part series on Chinese cuisine, thereby providing the roots for this book. In particular, Zanne Zakroff, Kemp Miles Minifie, Gail Zweigenthal, Pat Bell and Jane Montant deserve special mention.

I also must thank Debby Richards, my tireless assistant recipe tester; Linda Glick, my editor for the original edition; Sarah Flynn, my meticulous copy editor; Judy Chiu of Chiu's Garden restaurant, Boston; Stella and Pickering Lee; Andrea Lee; Laurie Murphy and Bob Somma. I am also grateful to many friends and students for their unflagging enthusiasm, which fueled my commitment to the project.

I want to thank Rux Martin, Barry Estabrook and Susan McClellan of Chapters for their hard work on the new edition. Nach Waxman at Kitchen Arts and Letters in New York City deserves special mention for his support in getting the book republished.

Alan Richardson and food stylist Anne Disrude created the beautiful photographs. T. C. Lai supplied the elegant calligraphy. Kathy Bray provided the graceful illustrations. Françoise Fetchko was a great recipe tester and food collaborator.

And thanks, as ever, to Don Rose and Jesse, who continue to delight, inspire and balance my life.

Introduction

OR A FOREIGNER IN TAIWAN whose basic Chinese vocabulary consisted of the words "hello," "good-bye," "thank you" and "no MSG," the phrase *Ni chi bao le mei you?* was extremely useful. This salutation is uttered when greeting a relative or friend, it often begins a telephone conversation, and it is frequently blurted out at acquaintances when further conversation is impossible. Although the phrase symbolizes a wish of well-being, translated literally it means, "Have you eaten yet?" For a 19-year-old woman who had grown up fascinated by all aspects of food and who had traveled to Asia to study Chinese cuisine, this sentence was a revelation. Clearly, I had come to the right place.

I grew up in New England in a family for whom food had always held a special importance. While most parents are content to read fairy tales to their children at bedtime, my father would bundle the four of us, pajama-clad and squeaky clean from our evening baths, into our beds and then describe, in mouth-watering detail, the various delicacies sampled on his latest business trips. By the age of five, we were all well versed in the subtleties of cold stone crab with mustard sauce and familiar with the heady fragrance of fried *saganaki,* a Greek specialty of fried cheese.

It was hardly surprising that after one uninspiring year in college, I decided to reassess my goals and steer myself toward a food-oriented career. An introductory course in Mandarin and a growing fascination with Chinese cuisine led me to Taiwan in 1972, where for three and a half years I apprenticed in restaurant kitchens with some of Taipei's foremost chefs. Many of these professionals were the finest of the Chinese master chefs who had fled from China after the revolution. I was overjoyed to discover that in Taiwan, all of the various regional flavors of China had been preserved, and the excellent standards of expertise and quality had been admirably maintained. The restaurants of Taipei were an ideal training ground for studying authentic Chinese cuisine.

During that time, I translated several cookbooks with Huang Su Huei, a renowned authority on Chinese food. I lived with a Chinese family and, for the first time in my life, was surrounded by a nation of people whose preoccupation with cooking outdid my own.

The Chinese fascination with food dates back to the beginning of an established culture. Ancient Chinese society held men with a refined knowledge of food and drink in high esteem. In *Food in Chinese Culture,* K.C. Chang relates that I Yin, a prime minister of the Shang dynasty (18th century B.C. to 12th century B.C.) and once a chef, apparently initiated his political career on the strength of his cooking prowess.

At a time when most other cultures regarded food solely in terms of basic survival, Chinese cuisine was well developed, and correct preparation, service and consumption were an essential part of social behavior. In his writings, Confucius placed great emphasis on food and helped to establish the refined standards of Chinese cuisine that have endured to this day. By the Han dynasty (206 B.C. to 220 A.D.), the *Li chi,* the most extensive handbook of ritual and social behavior ever compiled, was widely in use.

Some of the earliest written recipes and rules of conduct for meals appear in this volume. A section titled "Five Points to Ponder at Meals for Scholarly Gentlemen" gives guidelines for "Taking Food as a Means of Attaining Tao":

The superior person does not for one moment act contrary to virtue, not even for the space of a single meal. He first adopts the right posture, makes the proper table arrangements and reflects on his own adequacy before he takes any food.

Through the centuries, food has been the inspiration for innumerable Chinese scholars, artists and poets. One of the earliest examples is a poem written in 200 B.C. by Chü Yuan as an appeal to the departing soul of a beloved king. Culinary delicacies, in appetizing detail, are mentioned in an attempt to lure him back to life.

A modern poem, written in the 19th century, shows the same lusty appreciation of good food:

Suzhou, the good place. In summer Plump fish dart about the river Avoiding the fisherman's boat

Purple crabs and red wine dregs Make the autumn pass. When waxy meats and sturgeon appear Carp and bream leap into the pot.

Food is an international language that can provide valuable clues to the history and culture of any country. This is particularly true of China, and it is my belief that insight into the history and philosophy of food in ancient China contributes to the understanding of modern Chinese cuisine and culture. Accordingly, I have tried to acquaint the reader with the stories behind the food, relating the origin of the dishes, their symbolic importance and their significance in the contemporary Chinese diet. The recipes have been carefully selected from the repertory of classic Chinese dishes to represent a sampling of traditional specialties from all parts of China. Although refined by chefs down through the centuries and slightly adapted to modern methods, many of these dishes were originally conceived and developed in ancient China.

In China, more than in any other culture, food and civilization are synonymous. I hope this book will contribute to an understanding of both.

A Note About Romanization

THERE ARE THREE MAIN SYSTEMS OF romanization used for translating Chinese characters into English words: Pinyin, Yale and Wade-Giles. The Pinyin system, which was officially adopted by the People's Republic of China in 1979, has been used for most of the Chinese words in this book, including the recipe titles. In some cases (such as with the names of the dynasties and other notable proper nouns), the more familiar Wade-Giles spellings have been used.

*B*asics

The Regions of China & Their Flavors

CHINA IS A VAST COUNTRY, AND EACH REGION HAS DEVELOPED ITS OWN DISTINCT culinary style. Geography, climate and the availability of ingredients are just a few of the factors that influence and shape each area's cuisine.

Generally speaking, China is divided into four main culinary schools: the northern school, encompassing Peking, the northern provinces (including Shandong, Hebei and Shanxi, among others) and Mongolia; the western school, comprising Sichuan, Hunan, Guizhou and Yunnan; the eastern school, made up of Shanghai, Zhejiang, Jiangsu and Fujian (sometimes this school is divided in two, with Fujian counted as another regional school); and the southern school of Guangdon and Guangxi.

The Northern School

THIS IS PROBABLY THE MOST ECLECTIC regional cuisine; it incorporates provincial dishes of the northern provinces, Imperial Palace and Peking delicacies and Mongolian and Moslem dishes.

The vast plains that cover most of this area do little to protect it from the frigid Siberian winter winds and the arid breezes from the Gobi Desert in the summer. Accordingly, the climate for most of this region is one of extremes. Shandong, a relatively sheltered province bordering the sea, enjoys a more temperate climate. This, in addition to its fertile terrain, makes it a major agricultural area: wheat, barley, millet, corn and soybeans are staple crops. A number of vegetables, particularly of the cabbage and gourd families, and fruits (such as pears, apples, grapes and persimmons) thrive, and meat and poultry are plentiful. The long

coastline of Shandong provides the area with a wealth of seafood. Because of the somewhat cool climate, wheat rather than rice is the primary staple crop, and flour-based products such as steamed breads, pancakes and noodles grace the tables for everyday meals.

The repertory of Palace dishes (which all figure notably in the northern school) is extensive and extremely varied. These dishes are the creations of the Palace chefs, who came from all parts of China to serve the Imperial rulers. The chefs introduced ingredients and techniques from their respective regions, refining them still further for the illustrious audience. Some Palace dishes were created to suit the palates of the different ruling monarchs, and these dishes reflect the tastes and personalities of the individual emperors. Many of these recipes have survived intact and are served as they were years ago.

Since the largest concentration of

Moslems is situated in the north, the culinary style of this area has been greatly influenced by their tastes and habits. Moslems shun pork for religious reasons; as a result, there are a number of beef and lamb dishes in this cuisine. According to Kenneth Lo, an eminent authority on Chinese cooking, Peking often was called Mutton City because of the prevalence of lamb there. Mongolian influence, too, was a factor in shaping the regional style; the northern nomads introduced and popularized boiling, roasting and barbecuing. Mongolian Fire Pot and Mongolian Barbecue are two dishes that utilize these methods.

The Western School

MOVING IN A SOUTHWESTERLY DIRECTION to the provinces of Sichuan and Hunan,

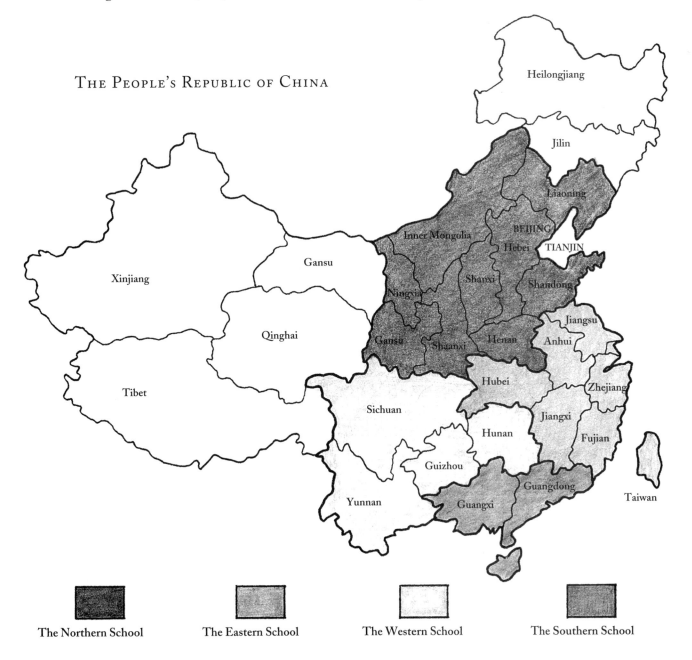

THE PEOPLE'S REPUBLIC OF CHINA

The Northern School   The Eastern School   The Western School   The Southern School

one notices that the geography changes dramatically. The northern plains give way to majestic peaks, and the arid climate is replaced by a sultry humidity. The meteorological calendar is characterized by steamy summers and mild winters. In this Land of Abundance, as it is sometimes called, subtropical fruits, such as oranges, tangerines and kumquats, thrive. This is one of the major rice bowls of China. Sichuan province is the home of the panda, which lives in the thick bamboo groves, and the people here are partial to the tender bamboo shoots. Black mushrooms, wood ears and silver tree ears are popular dried ingredients. The red chili pepper, by itself, in pastes and infused in chili oil, provides the spice for a number of fiery dishes. Other pungent seasonings include Sichuan peppercorns, garlic, onions, dried tangerine peel and gingerroot. Some theorize that the spicy cuisine developed as a result of the climate: the fiery seasonings create a natural air-conditioning effect. Others uncharitably conclude that the strong flavorings were used initially by the ancient Chinese to cover up the "off" flavors of food that had spoiled in the muggy heat. These same fiery seasonings—so the Sichuanese chefs maintain—sensitize the palate to the subtle nuances in the sauces. Flavorings and condiments are combined to create intricate blendings of hot, sour, sweet and salty in one mouthful.

Although the western school is renowned for its hot and spicy specialties, there are a number of delicately flavored dishes. These platters are mostly banquet dishes that were introduced long ago by the Imperial Palace chefs who came from other provinces; they are generally reserved for special occasions and banquets.

While all cooking methods are used in this region, stir-frying and steaming seem to be especially popular.

The Eastern School

THE NICKNAMES HEAVEN ON EARTH and The Land of Fish and Rice hint at the bounty and affluence of eastern China. The climate is basically subtropical, with warm, wet summers and cool winters, allowing a year-round growing season. Wheat, barley, rice, corn, sweet potatoes and soybeans are the major staple crops. Numerous varieties of bamboo shoots, beans, melons, gourds, squashes and leafy vegetables are found here, and peaches, plums and grapes flourish. It was in this region that Chinese vegetarian cuisine was elevated to sophisticated heights, as a result of the wealth of ingredients and the expertise of the regional chefs.

The Yangtse River threads its way inland through the eastern provinces, and innumerable streams, ponds and lakes provide the area with a host of freshwater species (crabs, shrimp, carp and shad) in addition to creating a fertile breeding ground for geese, duck and chicken. Because these provinces border the sea, saltwater products are also abundant.

Some notable ingredients and popular condiments from this region include Shaohsing wine, a high-quality yellow-grain wine; soy sauce (the area is reputed to produce the best soy sauce in China); Chinkiang vinegar, a Chinese black vinegar used as a dipping sauce and as a condiment in numerous seafood dishes; and Jinhua ham, a type of cured ham known for its smoky flavor and scarlet color.

The seasonings of this regional style are unusually light and delicate to accentuate the natural flavors of the superior ingredients. For the same reason, eastern chefs are partial to stir-frying, steaming, red-cooking (cooking in a soy-based liquid) and quick-simmering (blanching). Curing and pickling are used to preserve and flavor meat, chicken and vegetables.

The Southern School

Touted by some as the haute cuisine of China, Cantonese cooking is a subtle blending of delicate seasonings and ingenious technique. Canton, the capital of Guangdong province, has long been proclaimed a culinary mecca of China. An ancient Chinese proverb states, "If you like good food, go to Canton." Canton was an ancient trading port where wealthy Chinese merchants and foreigners resided in comfort, indulging their culinary whims. The city was said to breed gourmands with tastes for unusual foods: frogs' legs, snakes, turtles, dogs and game were popular. Ingredients and techniques from the West were incorporated into the regional cuisine.

The area is subtropical, with a lush, humid climate. The growing season extends year-round, as it does in the east, making it a major agricultural region. Vegetables grow abundantly, and fruits such as bananas, pineapples, oranges and lychees are readily available. The proximity of the sea provides a variety of fish and shellfish.

Cantonese chefs excel at a number of cooking methods: steaming, blanching, barbecuing, roasting and simmering are used in the preparation of various dishes. These chefs have an especially light touch with fresh, top-quality ingredients, and the foods are often slightly undercooked so as to accentuate the natural flavors.

Although dim sum are prepared all over China, the Cantonese are acknowledged as the true masters of this food form. These "dot-the-heart" treats (as they are known in Mandarin) include sweet and savory pastries, dumplings, soups, breads, cakes and noodle dishes. Dim sum are featured in teahouses between eleven in the morning and two in the afternoon, but they may be eaten as snacks at any time of day.

Special Ingredients

*A*FAMILIARITY WITH THE BASIC CONDIMENTS AND SEASONINGS USED in Chinese cuisine is essential. Gingerroot, scallions, garlic, star anise and red pepper are just a few of the prominent flavorings. Many of these seasonings were first utilized by the ancient Chinese for their medicinal properties. According to ancient pharmacology, certain herbs and spices were believed to help prolong youth, restore waning sexual powers and lengthen life.

The Chinese believe in harmony and balance in every aspect of life: hot must complement cold, and yin balance with yang. This philosophy applies to food as well, and seasonings play a prominent role in establishing this balance. Each food is classified as being hot (yang), meaning that the food has a stimulating effect on the body, or as cold (yin), implying a cooling or quieting effect. Chili peppers, beef and pork, for instance, are considered to be hot foods, whereas duck and most seafoods are classified as cold. Many seasonings were originally paired with foods to neutralize the effects on the body. Hence a "hot" flavoring was cooked or served with a "cold" food to create an overall balanced effect. Of course, there's no minimizing the importance of seasonings just for the flavor they impart to foods. Following is a glossary of some of the more prominent condiments, seasonings and special ingredients used in Chinese cuisine. They have been divided into three major groups: Sauces, Spirits, Oils & Pastes; Seasonings, Spices & Wrappers; and Selected Fresh, Pickled & Dried Vegetables & Starches. (See page 385 for Mail-Order Sources.)

Sauces, Spirits, Oils & Pastes

Chili Paste and Hot Bean Paste: Chili paste (or sauce, depending on the manufacturer), made with mashed chili peppers, vinegar and seasonings, and hot bean paste (a variation made with whole beans) both impart a fiery taste and a vibrant red color to dishes. A number of canned bean pastes tend to be salty; therefore, chili paste is recommended. It will keep indefinitely if refrigerated in a covered jar, but it is apt to lose its fiery intensity with age. If unavailable, substitute crushed red peppers.

Chinese Rice Vinegar: The Chinese are partial to grain vinegars, which tend to be lighter and sweeter than western vinegars. American and European vinegars are not acceptable substitutes. There are three main types of Chinese vinegar: white (clear), red and black. Clear rice vinegar is used most frequently in sauces, pickling mixtures and dressings; red vinegar is used mainly as a dipping sauce (especially for steamed crab); and Chinese black vinegar (the flavor of which resembles Worcestershire sauce) is commonly used as a dipping sauce and as an ingredient in the sauces of many seafood dishes. Although black vinegar is imported from Hong Kong, the mainland Chinese brand from Chinkiang is considered to have the best flavor. Cider vinegar has a slightly different flavor but can be used in place of clear vinegar; reduce the quantity by one-third. If black vinegar is not available, substitute equal amounts of Worcestershire sauce.

Duck (or Plum) Sauce: A fruity, thick sauce with a sweet and tart flavor made from plums, apricots, vinegar and sugar. In traditional Chinese cooking, duck sauce is primarily used as a dipping sauce in Cantonese cuisine—most notably with duck or goose. Refrigerated in a covered jar, it will keep indefinitely. Unfortunately, there is no substitute for duck sauce, but it is widely available in supermarkets.

Gaoling Wine: A fiery, distilled liquor made from sorghum, Gaoling wine is primarily used for banquet toasts and in the making of Chinese sausage. If Gaoling wine is unavailable, rice wine may be substituted.

Hoisin Sauce: This is the southern (Cantonese) variation of sweet bean sauce. It is made with fermented mashed beans, salt, sugar, garlic and, occasionally, pumpkin. The ingredients and flavor vary slightly with each manufacturer. Like its northern cousin, hoisin sauce is a thick, rich paste used as a flavoring in sauces, in marinades for roasted and barbecued meats and as a dipping sauce. It will keep indefinitely if refrigerated in a covered jar. If hoisin sauce is unavailable, substitute sweet bean sauce.

Oyster Sauce: A pungently rich concentrate made from oysters, salt, soy sauce and assorted seasonings. Once reduced to a thick paste, the sauce is cured. Oyster sauce is used primarily in Cantonese seafood dishes, where its unctuous consistency provides a richness and a delicate flavor. Oyster sauce will keep indefinitely in the refrigerator.

Rice Wine: Rice wine is a yellow-grain wine that is used in all Chinese cooking. Shaohsing, a high-quality rice wine imported from Taiwan and China, is particularly flavorful. Many Asian stores sell several types of rice wine for cooking, including mirin, a sweetened Japanese cooking wine. These are also acceptable. If Chinese rice wine is unavailable, substitute a Japanese sake, Scotch or a dry, white vermouth.

Sesame Oil: This amber-colored oil is extracted from toasted sesame seeds. Unlike the light-colored sesame oil found in many specialty shops and health-food stores, Chinese sesame oil has a strong, pungent flavor. It is used primarily as a seasoning in marinades, sauces and dressings. Because of its overpowering taste and tendency to smoke when heated, sesame oil generally is not used as a cooking oil, except in certain vegetarian, beef and lamb dishes.

Sesame Paste: A thick, pungent nut butter made from toasted sesame seeds, sesame paste is primarily used in dressings in cold salads and noodle dishes. Peanut butter may be substituted. Sesame paste will keep indefinitely in the refrigerator.

Soy Sauce: Chinese soy sauce is available in three grades: light, medium and heavy. Light soy sauce is delicate and slightly more subtle in flavor than the other varieties. Consequently, it is served as a dipping sauce and used in light-colored dishes and soups, such as with seafood and chicken. Low-sodium soy may be used in all dishes, but adjust the seasonings according to taste. Medium, or thin, soy is darker and slightly thicker than light soy. This is an all-purpose soy sauce that is used for most cooking.

Heavy, or thick, soy sauce is colored with molasses and used in rich, hearty dishes, such as stews, and with barbecued and roasted meats. If Japanese soy sauce is substituted, the quantity should be increased to taste, since it tends to be lighter and sweeter than most Chinese brands.

Sweet Bean Sauce: A thick paste with a salty-sweet flavor made from a fermentation of beans, salt, flour and water. Northern Chinese are particularly partial to this condiment; they use it in sauces and meat marinades, and as a dipping sauce, particularly with Peking duck. There are a number of bean pastes made by the Chinese, including brown bean paste and yellow bean paste. The pastes may be smooth purees or contain whole beans. The various bean pastes differ in texture and flavor, but they may be used interchangeably. All will keep indefinitely stored in an airtight container in the refrigerator. If bean paste is unavailable, substitute hoisin sauce.

Seasonings, Spices & Wrappers

Azuki Beans: Small red or azuki beans are synonymous with sweets in China, since they are frequently cooked to a paste and mixed with lard and sugar. Prepared azuki bean paste is sold in cans, but the homemade version is far preferable. Azuki beans will keep indefinitely in a cool, dry place.

Chili Peppers: Chili peppers are grown in several parts of China, but the hottest varieties and the densest concentration are found in the provinces of Sichuan and Hunan. In both fresh and dried form, as well as in a paste, chili peppers are used to infuse dishes with a fiery seasoning. Chili oil, made from chili peppers, is added to dressings and used as a dipping sauce. It is sold in Asian grocery stores, but a more flavorful version can be made at home: Heat ½ cup sesame oil and ½ cup corn oil in a wok until nearly smoking. Add 1 tablespoon Sichuan peppercorns, 6 stalks smashed scallions, 6 slices smashed gingerroot and ½ cup dried chili peppers, cut into ½-inch pieces. Turn off the heat, cover the mixture, and let it sit for 30 minutes. Strain out the seasonings, and transfer the oil to a jar. Chili oil will keep indefinitely in a cool, dry place.

Chinese Cinnamon Bark: Westerners are familiar with rolled cinnamon sticks (a good substitute for cinnamon bark), but the Chinese prefer to use thin slices of bark from the cassia tree for seasoning, braising and stewing. Cinnamon bark is also ground and used in five-spice powder.

Chinese Ham: The Chinese cure ham in a manner similar to that used for Smithfield hams. The flavors are similar, and Smithfield ham may be used as a substitute. Chinese ham, with its salty, smoky flavor, is a popular seasoning in soups, as well as in seafood, vegetable and poultry dishes. Minced ham is also sprinkled on top of dishes as a garnish. When Chinese or Smithfield ham is unavailable, use an imported prosciutto.

Chinese Sausage: Two types of Chinese sausage are available in Asian grocery stores: pork and liver. Pork sausage is red in color, with a sweet, pungent flavor. (A recipe for homemade pork sausage appears on page 275.) Liver sausage, made of pork or duck liver, tends to be brown in color, is slightly sweeter than pork sausage and has an unusual texture. Both varieties will keep indefinitely, wrapped in plastic, in the refrigerator or freezer. Chinese sausage is much sweeter than western varieties, which should not be substituted.

Cilantro: A pungent, flat-leaf parsley that is used as a seasoning and garnish in soups, cold platters and hot dishes, cilantro (also called Chinese parsley) is found in most supermarkets and in Asian markets. It will keep for up to five days, refrigerated, with the stems standing in water.

Dried Chinese Black Mushrooms: Dried shiitake mushrooms provide a strong, smoky flavor in Chinese dishes. They are available in several grades, and prices vary accordingly. The more expensive black mushrooms, with thick caps and a full, rich flavor, are usually "winter" black mushrooms. These are reserved for banquet dishes or recipes calling for whole caps. The thinner, less expensive mushrooms are used in dishes in which the caps are cut up. Fresh shiitake mushrooms are not an adequate substitute for dried Chinese black mushrooms. Store dried mushrooms in a cool, dry place in an airtight plastic bag with a dried chili pepper (to prevent worms).

Dried Shrimp: Miniature shrimp are preserved in a salty brine, dried and used as a seasoning in soups and vegetable dishes. The shrimp are extremely pungent and should be used sparingly. Dried shrimp will keep indefinitely in a plastic bag in the refrigerator.

Dried Tangerine or Orange Peel: This is a pungent flavoring used as a seasoning in stir-fried and braised dishes. Usually the peel is reconstituted in hot water before being used in stir-fried dishes. The older the skin, the more prized the flavor. Homemade peel may be made by air-drying tangerine or clementine peels for several days. Store the peels indefinitely in a cool, dry place. You may substitute fresh peel for the dried in equal quantities.

Fennel Seed: This is a licoricelike seasoning used in braised dishes and stews and to lend a fragrance to tea-smoked dishes. Chinese herbalists also recommend fennel seed for stomach maladies.

Fermented Black Beans: A popular condiment made from black beans preserved in a salty brine and then dried, fermented black beans are available in plastic bags and in cans. While the beans themselves are quite salty and pungent, black bean sauce, made with fermented black beans and other seasonings, tends to be delicate and is used in seafood, poultry, meat and vegetable dishes, where it accentuates the natural flavors of the foods. Packed in an airtight container and refrigerated, the beans will keep indefinitely.

Five-Spice Powder: A fragrant seasoning made with a number of spices that may include star anise, cinnamon, fennel, Sichuan peppercorns, cloves and nutmeg, five-spice powder is used in marinades for meat and poultry and, when combined with salt, as a dipping powder for deep-fried foods.

Garlic: One finds a liberal use of garlic in many Chinese dishes. Garlic cloves and the fresh green stalks are equally popular. Garlic is also credited with prolonging life and strengthening the body.

Gingerroot: A knobby stem (tuber rhizome) that grows underground, developing knuckles or "lobes," gingerroot is usually available in two forms: spring and mature. Spring gingerroot, which is available seasonally, has a papery skin, a delicate flavor and pink tips. It is served in soups, pickled in a sweet-and-sour dressing and sprinkled on top of dishes as a garnish. Mature gingerroot, which has a thick skin and a much stronger flavor, is used mainly as a seasoning to flavor and remove strong tastes, particularly in seafood. Gingerroot is also known for its medicinal properties and is said to cure colds, aid digestion and revitalize the body. To store gingerroot, bury the unpeeled root in a pot of sand or place it, peeled, in a jar of rice wine in the refrigerator. When a slice of gingerroot is called for, it should be about the size of a quarter.

Jujubes: Jujubes, or red dates, are from northern China, where, once dried, they are popular in fillings and soups. Soften them in boiling water. They will keep indefinitely in their dried form.

Rock Sugar: Rock sugar is occasionally used in stews and braised dishes, since it is believed to produce a lustrous sauce. If unavailable, substitute granulated sugar.

Scallions: Scallions are a prime seasoning in Chinese cooking. The white part is usually reserved for flavoring, and the greens are used as a garnish. When you are directed to smash a scallion with the flat side of a cleaver, use only the white part, reserving the green part for other uses.

Shanghai Spring Roll Wrappers: In Asia, spring roll wrappers, or lumpia skins, are light and delicate, since they are lacy thin skins made from a flour-and-water dough. Once fried, they are more crisp and delicate than the egg-flour-and-water variety. They are sold frozen in all Asian markets.

Sichuan (Szechwan) Peppercorns: Reddish brown, open-husked peppercorns with a sharp, slightly numbing flavor, Sichuan peppercorns are used as a seasoning in marinades and sauces. Toasted lightly, pulverized and added to salt, they become a dipping powder for deep-fried foods. Sichuan peppercorns will keep indefinitely in a cool, dry place.

Soybeans: Most Asian markets sell two varieties of soybeans: a yellow bean, which is ground and mixed with water to make soybean milk, and a darker black bean, which is usually cooked and eaten but can be used in pastes. Fresh soybeans are also available and are stewed with meat or cooked in soups.

Star Anise: An eight-pointed star with a licoricelike flavor, this seasoning is used in marinades and in braised dishes and stews. Unlike anise seed, which is from a bush, star anise is from a tree of the magnolia family. Some Chinese use star anise as a breath freshener or a digestive aid. Anise seed and star anise are similar in flavor and may be used interchangeably.

Selected Fresh, Pickled & Dried Vegetables & Starches

Bamboo Shoots: Few Americans are aware of the delightful flavor and variety of fresh bamboo shoots. In the Far East, one has a choice of spring, summer and winter shoots, whereas in the United States, the selection is usually restricted to canned summer and winter shoots. Winter bamboo shoots are preferable, since the shoots are at their peak during that season. Because canned bamboo shoots have a very strong flavor, they should be plunged in boiling water and refreshed in cold water before being used. Store the shoots in cold water, refrigerated in a covered jar for up to a week. Some Asian markets now offer fresh bamboo shoots, which are highly preferable to the canned variety. Remove the outer skin and cook the inner meat in boiling water for 15 minutes.

Bean Sprouts: There are two main types of bean sprouts used in Chinese cuisine: those made from mung beans (which are green) and those sprouted from soybeans (which are yellow). Mung bean sprouts are thinner and more delicate in flavor, and they require little or no cooking. They are used primarily in salads and stir-fried dishes. Soybean sprouts have a yellow tip (from the soybean) and a stronger flavor, and they require a lengthier cooking time. These sprouts are used in braised dishes and soups. Canned bean sprouts are mushy and unacceptable. Unless directed otherwise, use mung bean sprouts when bean sprouts are called for. Store bean sprouts refrigerated in plastic bags. They will keep for up to three days.

Chinese Cabbage: The Chinese cabbage family is extensive, and most Asian markets carry a number of different varieties. Napa, with an oval head and full leaves, is used in a number of dishes, but it is especially fine for dumpling fillings, soups and casseroles. Another type is celery cabbage, with an elongated head and a great deal of stem, which is appropriate for stir-fried dishes and salads. Bok choy, with fat stems and flowing green leaves that look somewhat like Swiss chard, is recommended for stir-fried dishes and soups. The small, tender hearts of cabbages that are sold in most Asian markets are excellent for braised dishes and as a decorative, edible vegetable garnish. All Chinese cabbages should be wrapped in plastic and refrigerated. They will keep for up to one week.

Chinese Garlic Chives: Chinese garlic chives, with flat stalks and a pronounced garlicky flavor, are used in soups, stir-fried dishes, noodles and dumplings. There are two main types: yellow and green. Green garlic chives are available seasonally at most Asian markets (if they are unavailable, an equal amount of scallion greens and some minced garlic may be substituted). Yellow garlic chives (which may be used interchangeably with green chives in soups, stir-fried dishes and noodles) are found seasonally at selected markets.

Daikon Radish (Chinese Turnip): While daikon radishes are similar in texture to the Western radish, they tend to have a sweeter taste and are much bigger. The size of daikon radishes varies. They are a popular vegetable in Chinese cooking and are used in salads, soups, stir-fried dishes, stews and savory pastries. They will keep for up to two weeks when refrigerated in plastic wrap. Salted and dried in strips, daikon is used as a seasoning in stir-fried dishes and soups.

Lily Buds: Lily buds, or "golden needles," are, as their name suggests, the edible dried flower bud of day lilies. They have a sweet flavor and chewy texture. Soften them in hot water for 20 minutes and remove the tough knob of the stem before cooking.

Nori (Purple Laver): Nori are thin, paper-like sheets of dried seaweed used in soups and rice dishes and for wrapping foods. The color may be purple or deep green, depending on the manufacturer. They are available at most Asian markets in packages of ten. Nori will keep indefinitely when wrapped tightly in plastic and refrigerated.

Pickled Cucumbers: Pickled cucumbers have been seeded, cut into strips and preserved in a soy-sauce brine. They are crisp, slightly salty and refreshing. They are used as a seasoning in soups, stir-fried dishes and salads. They are also served by themselves as a condiment. They are available in cans and will keep indefinitely when transferred to a jar and refrigerated.

Sichuan (Szechwan) Preserved Mustard Greens: The Sichuanese preserve the central heart of a variety of cabbage greens in salt, chili peppers and assorted seasonings. Left to sit for several months, the knobby stems retain their crisp texture but acquire a hot, spicy flavor. This pickle is then used in soups and stir-fried dishes or sprinkled on top of cold platters. Sichuan preserved mustard greens are sold in cans or by weight from huge, earthenware pickling crocks in Chinese

grocery stores. They will keep indefinitely when refrigerated in a closed container.

Straw Mushrooms: Straw mushrooms, with their pointed caps and brownish yellow body, have a flavor and texture unlike any other mushroom. They are available in cans—peeled and unpeeled. (I prefer the unpeeled because of their unusual bulblike shape.) The mushrooms will keep for about a week, refrigerated in jars with water to cover. Dried straw mushrooms, which have a mild flavor, are also available. They can be stored in the same manner as dried black mushrooms.

Tapioca Starch: Derived from the cassava root or manioc plant, native to the West Indies, tapioca starch is popularly used to make dumpling skins, as well as for a thickener. Once cooked, the white powder becomes translucent. In some recipes, cornstarch may be substituted. Tapioca starch is available in Asian markets and will keep indefinitely in a cool, dry place.

Tientsin Pickled Vegetables: In northern China, cabbage is salted and dried, creating a slightly sweet but pungent pickle known as Tientsin (or Tianjin) pickled vegetable. It is used as a seasoning in soups, dumpling fillings and, most notably, in the stuffing of Beggar's Chicken. It is generally sold in clay crocks and will keep indefinitely in the refrigerator.

Water Chestnuts: The edible portion of the water chestnut is the starchy fruit of a water plant found in the tropics. The sweet, crunchy meat is covered with a tough outer skin. Fresh water chestnuts, found in most Chinese markets, are eaten raw, candied and used in sweet confections and are cooked in numerous savory dishes. For savory dishes, fresh water chestnuts should be peeled and cooked in boiling water for 15 minutes. Canned water chestnuts should always be plunged into boiling water and refreshed in cold water to remove the tinny flavor. Unpeeled fresh water chestnuts will keep refrigerated, wrapped in plastic, for one week, whereas the peeled tinned ones should be stored in water. These will keep a bit longer.

Wheat Starch: The powder remaining from flour once the gluten has been removed is known as wheat starch. Its primary use in Chinese cooking is in the making of dumpling skins, but it also may be used in batters and in preparing assorted dim sum. It should be stored in a cool, dry place and is available in most Chinese markets.

Wood Ears: Wood ears, tree ears or black fungus, as they are frequently called, are an edible form of fungus or mushroom. They are relished for their crunchy texture. Choose the smaller variety, and check for any tough stem bits. Wood ears should be reconstituted in hot water for 30 minutes, rinsed and used as directed.

Yard-Long String Beans: Although they hardly measure a yard in length, yard-long string beans tend to be about three times as long as their Western cousins. Some say that the flavor and texture of this bean is reminiscent of the French *haricot vert.* Yard-long string beans are available year-round at most Chinese markets. They will keep for up to a week wrapped in plastic in the refrigerator. If unavailable, you may substitute western string beans.

Cooking Methods

CHINESE COOKING TECHNIQUE HAS BEEN REFINED THROUGH THE CENTURIES to a high art form. Even in its earliest stages, the system of elaborately conceived cooking methods used in Chinese dishes suggested a level of sophistication that other cuisines lacked. The ancient Chinese chefs developed more than 50 different cooking processes with subtle variations in heat and technique. Obviously, it would be impossible to describe all of these methods; an explanation of those used most frequently is given below. These basic techniques serve as a foundation for all cooking, not just Chinese.

Stir-Frying
Chao

THIS IS ONE OF THE FUNDAMENTAL cooking methods used by Chinese chefs. Intensely high heat, organization and expedience are key factors. All the preparations, including steps 1, 2 and 3, should be completed before the cooking begins.

1. The ingredients (that is, the meat, poultry, fish, seafood, vegetables) are cut to the desired size. Uniformity is stressed so that the food will cook evenly. Cut meat, poultry or seafood usually is then mixed with a marinade containing rice wine, cornstarch and other ingredients and left to marinate. This tenderizes and flavors the food. The

cornstarch (potato starch, water-chestnut flour or arrowroot may be substituted) coats the food, sealing in the natural juices so that the cooked product will be tender and juicy.

2. The seasonings, such as garlic, scallions and gingerroot, are cut, and the sauce is assembled. Homemade chicken broth (see Chinese Chicken Broth on page 345) is often used as a base for sauces, but water or a good-quality canned broth may be used.

3. Any vegetables requiring partial cooking, such as broccoli, carrots and snow peas, are parboiled or steamed and immediately immersed in cold water to prevent them from overcooking and to keep their colors bright.

4. The wok is heated until very hot. This step is extremely important, as the food will stick to the wok if it has not been heated properly. The hot wok will transmit heat directly to the oil added to the pan, speeding up the process and thereby saving heat. To test the heat of the wok, a few drops of water are sprinkled on the surface. If they evaporate immediately, the wok is ready.

5. The proper amount of oil is added to the wok and heated until very hot; the oil should be swirled around the pan to lubricate the surface. Vegetable oils, such as peanut, safflower or corn oil, are recommended, since they reach a very high temperature before smoking and the flavor of the cooked oil is good. (Chinese chefs usually use quite a bit of oil in this step, but the quantity is often reduced for home use. Also, they use the oil over and over again, until it is all gone.)

6. The meat, poultry or seafood is turned in the hot oil, using the shovel (a wide spatula) to separate the pieces and keep them constantly in motion. Once the pieces of food turn color and separate, they are

removed with the shovel and handled strainer and drained. For beef, lamb and pork, the oil should be extremely hot, about 400 degrees F, to tenderize, whereas for chicken, fish and shellfish, a moderately hot (350-degree) oil is recommended. After the food is removed, the wok should then be cleaned with a stiff brush and water and dried to remove any bits that may have stuck to the bottom.

7. A little oil is added to the hot wok and heated until very hot. The seasonings are added and stirred over high heat, mixing constantly until fragrant, so that the oil will be flavored by the seasonings.

8. The cooked meat, seafood or poultry, the cooked vegetables and the sauce are all added to the wok and tossed over high heat until the ingredients are heated through and the sauce is boiling. (If the sauce does not already contain a thickener, it is added at this point.) Once the sauce has thickened, the dish is transferred to a platter and served immediately.

Deep-Frying
Jia

MOST WESTERNERS ARE SURPRISED AT the prevalence of oil and deep-frying in Chinese cooking. Deep-fried foods are popular because they are attractive and have a pleasing texture and taste. Their crispness complements wine and beer.

The green end of a scallion or a chopstick is often used to test the temperature of hot oil in deep-frying. Though this is not the most accurate method, the following signs give a fairly reliable reading: At 350 degrees, the bubbles emerging from the scallion green or chopstick are quite small and slow-moving. There is no sound. At 375 degrees, the bubbles are bigger, they appear more quickly, and there is a slight sizzling noise. At 400 to 425 degrees, the bubbles are still bigger, they emerge at a furious pace, there is a distinctive sizzling noise, and the scallion tip turns golden brown. Of course, for greater accuracy, a thermometer can be used.

Following are the steps used in deep-frying.

1. The food is cut to the desired shape and size and usually marinated to tenderize and flavor it.

2. For "dry-frying," the food is cooked without a coating. In "wet-frying," the food is dipped in a batter or coating made of cornstarch, egg whites, egg yolks, whole eggs, flour or a combination of these ingredients.

3. The wok is heated until very hot; oil is added and heated to the proper temperature. Chinese deep-frying is usually done in two stages. The oil is heated to 350 degrees, and the food is placed in the hot oil by carefully rolling it down the sloping sides of the pan, in order to prevent the oil from splashing. The food is deep-fried until pale golden, then removed and drained on absorbent paper. (Other batches of the food are then given a first frying at this point, removed and drained. This step may be completed early in the day.)

4. The oil is reheated to a very hot temperature, about 425 degrees, or until nearly smoking, and all the food is added a second time. In this stage, it is cooked until crisp and golden brown. This second frying removes any excess oil, sealing in the natural juices and leaving the food tender and juicy. The food is removed from the oil, drained on absorbent paper, arranged on a platter and served immediately. The leftover oil may be strained, cooled and reserved for another use.

Steaming
Jeng

STEAMING IS A PROCESS USED TO COOK a number of foods, including meat, poultry, seafood, vegetables, soups, buns, dumplings and sweet and savory pastries. The ingredients should be of the finest quality and as fresh as possible, since the seasonings are usually light. Steaming tends to accentuate and complement the natural flavors of foods. There are two main methods of steaming: "open steaming" and "closed steaming." In closed steaming, a refined version of steaming, the food is placed in a closed heatproof container, such as an earthenware pot, the edges are sometimes sealed with paper or a flour-and-water paste, and the container is placed in a deep steamer made of either bamboo or metal, placed over boiling water and steamed over high heat. Soups are often prepared in this manner, creating an intense flavor and unusually clear broth. You may improvise by "closed-steaming" the food in a covered pot in a 425-degree oven.

In open steaming:

1. The food is cut, scored or marinated, as directed in the recipe, and placed on a heatproof plate, in a bowl or directly on the steamer tray, which has been lined with moistened cheesecloth, muslin or parchment paper. Since bamboo has a strong flavor, food is never placed directly on the steamer tray. (Several steamer trays may be

stacked and steamed simultaneously.)

2. A wok is filled with water level with the bottom edge of the steamer tray and heated until boiling.

3. The steamer tray is placed over the boiling water in the wok, the lid is placed over the steamer tray, and the food is steamed over high heat. The water should be boiling vigorously at all times. The water level should be checked periodically to make certain that it doesn't boil away. When food is steaming for a long time, a kettle of boiling water should be kept on the stove and extra water added when necessary. When more than one steamer tray is used, the order of the trays is reversed periodically to ensure even cooking.

4. The food is steamed for the prescribed period or until slightly underdone (it will continue to cook after it is removed from the steamer), transferred to a platter and served or served directly from the steamer.

Cooking in Liquid: Blanching, Braising & Simmering

CHINESE COOKS OFTEN DIVIDE THEIR cooking methods into two major categories: cooking in oil and cooking in liquid. The cooking-in-oil methods include stir-frying, deep-frying and the like, while the cooking-in-liquid category is more extensive and varied. Poaching, braising, simmering and stewing are some of the methods. The liquid may be water, chicken broth, a salty brine or a soy-sauce-based mixture. An explanation of the more prominent cooking-in-liquid methods follows.

BLANCHING
Tang

THIS PROCESS IS SIMILAR TO SCALDING; the food is cut as directed, then immersed briefly in boiling stock or water.

BRAISING
Shao

1. The food is cut, marinated (if necessary) and seared in hot oil. This step seals in the natural juices, colors the food to a deep golden brown and gives the dish a rich flavor. The ingredients of the braising liquid are assembled and combined. The braising liquid may be dark, made with soy sauce, sugar, star anise, water and other seasonings; or light, made with salt, seasonings and water or chicken broth. (The term red-cooked refers to foods that are cooked slowly in a soy-based liquid or braising mixture. The soy sauce colors the food a rich, reddish brown—hence the name.)

2. The food is placed in a heavy pot or casserole with the braising liquid and prescribed seasonings. The liquid is heated until boiling, and the heat is reduced to low, allowing the mixture to simmer slowly. The food is cooked until tender, and the sauce is reduced until thick.

3. The cooked food is transferred to a platter and served hot with the reduced sauce spooned over the top.

The same steps are followed in two variations of this method. In the first (*men*), a longer braising period is used and more sauce is added. In the second (*wen*), a thickener is added toward the end of the braising period.

SIMMERING
Lu

THIS METHOD DIFFERS SLIGHTLY FROM braising in that the meat, poultry or seafood most often is not seared prior to stewing.

1. The ingredients of the *lu,* or cooking marinade, are assembled and placed in a pot or casserole. The mixture may consist of soy sauce or salt, rice wine, sugar, star anise, fennel seeds, tangerine peel and Chinese cinnamon bark. The *lu* is cooked for a period to allow the flavors to intensify and marry.

2. The food (whole or in large pieces) is then added to the *lu* and simmered over low heat until tender. The food picks up the pungent flavors of the marinade. Food simmered in a *lu* is also sometimes said to be red-cooked. Such dishes are often served cold or at room temperature. When the food is served hot, some of the marinade is spooned over the top. The *lu* is saved and reused, and the seasonings and liquids are replenished periodically. It is believed that the flavor of the *lu* is enhanced with each use.

Smoking
Xun

SMOKING IS NOT ACTUALLY A COOKING process; it is more a means for flavoring and coloring foods. The food is generally cooked prior to smoking (except for seafood and fish, both of which require little cooking) by boiling or steaming. Chinese chefs use two methods of smoking: tea-smoking (*xiong*), using tea leaves in the smoking mixture, and wood-smoking (*yen*), using wood chips. The smoking mixture may also include brown sugar, rice and anise or fennel seed.

1. The food is marinated either in a light mixture, consisting of salt, rice wine and seasonings; or in a dark one, made of soy sauce, rice wine, sugar and seasonings.

2. The food is cooked by boiling or steaming and left to cool.

3. The wok and dome lid are covered with several layers of aluminum foil (**a**), and the smoking mixture is placed in the bottom of the wok. A smoking rack (or crisscrossed chopsticks) is placed at least 2 inches above the smoking mixture (**b**). The food is then arranged on the rack (**c**), and the wok is covered securely with the lid.

4. The wok is placed over high heat, and when the fragrance of smoke is detected, the timing begins, and the food is smoked for the prescribed period. The wok is then removed from the heat and left undisturbed for 5 minutes. The food is removed (it

3a

3b

3c

4

should be golden brown), brushed with sesame oil, cut as directed, arranged on a platter and served.

Barbecuing & Roasting

Kao and Shao

CHINESE COOKS DO NOT USE THESE methods as often as Western chefs do because the necessary equipment and fuel are not always readily available. These two techniques are more popular in northern China and in Canton.

In barbecuing, the food is generally marinated (to tenderize, flavor and provide a coating), skewered or put on a spit and cooked over an open fire. The intense heat seals in the natural juices and cooks the outside to a crusty charcoal brown. The food is then removed, sliced and served.

In roasting, the food is usually marinated, then placed or hung in some type of oven or closed heated container. All surfaces of the food are exposed to the heat so that it cooks evenly. Once cooked, the food is removed, cut and served.

Cutting Techniques

Holding a Cleaver

GRASP THE CLEAVER FIRMLY BY THE handle with the thumb and index finger of your hand on the blade. This position will improve control and manipulation of the cleaver. Curl the fingers of the opposite hand so that the fingertips will not be exposed to the blade. Lean the cleaver lightly against your knuckles and the middle joints of the curled fingers. Cut, pushing forward with a decisive motion.

Scoring

THIS TECHNIQUE IS USED TO TENDERIZE foods, to create attractive shapes and to even out the thickness, ensuring uniform cooking.

Grasp the cleaver firmly by the handle, and lightly cut across the food, being careful not to cut completely through it.

Slicing

TO MAKE CUTTING EASIER, FOODS SUCH as meat and chicken are partially frozen before being cut into paper-thin slices. Meats may be cut directly across the grain

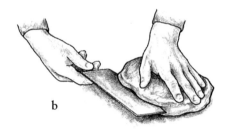

for tenderizing (**a**), or on the diagonal (slant-slicing, **b**) to extend the cooking surface and create decorative shapes.

Holding the food firmly in one hand, push the blade forward straight across the grain or on the diagonal. Let the slice fall naturally as it is cut.

Shredding

SHREDS EVOLVE FROM SLICES. SIZES VARY from a large julienne (the size of a matchstick) to as fine as a toothpick.

Holding the food firmly, slice, across the grain, cutting with a decisive motion. Let the slices fall naturally as they are cut; they should stack in an orderly fashion, domino-style. Cut several stacked slices at a time into long, thin, uniform strips.

Dicing

DICES EVOLVE FROM STRIPS. THE SIZE may vary, but it is generally about ¼ to ½ inch square. Whatever the size, uniformity is crucial.

Holding the food firmly, cut, across the grain, into thick slices. The slices should fall naturally so that they are stacked in an orderly fashion, domino-style. Cut the slices into long, uniform strips. Gather the strips together neatly, and cut them crosswise into cubes or dice.

Mincing

MINCES EVOLVE FROM SHREDS. USUALLY, two cleavers are used in the final step to speed up the process.

Holding the food firmly, cut, across the grain, into paper-thin slices, cutting forward with a decisive motion. Let the slices fall naturally so that they stack in an orderly fashion, domino-style. Cut the food into thin, uniform strips, then into smaller and smaller dice. Chop the dice repeatedly until the food is in tiny pieces.

Roll-Cutting

THIS TECHNIQUE IS USED PRIMARILY FOR root vegetables (carrots, turnips, radishes and cucumbers) to extend the cooking surface and to create decorative shapes.

Holding the food firmly with one hand, push the cleaver across the food with a decisive motion, cutting on the diagonal (**a**). Give the food a quarter turn (**b**), and slice again on the diagonal (**c**).

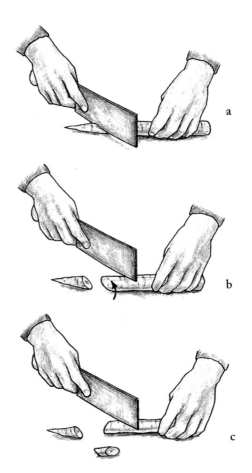

Equipment

*C*HINESE FOOD CAN BE PREPARED USING THE MOST RUDIMENTARY tools. With a bit of imagination and ingenuity, you can substitute a frying pan for a wok, and a spaghetti pot, a trivet and a pie plate can be used for a makeshift steamer. Following are brief descriptions and some suggestions concerning the more traditional tools.

Wok & Dome Lid

THIS ALL-PURPOSE COOKING VESSEL IS used for stir-frying, steaming, smoking, deep-frying, braising and poaching. The pan is designed with long, sloping sides to create an extended cooking surface and for easy tossing of ingredients. The dome lid is used for steaming, braising and as a shield to protect the cook from hot oil that can splash when the food is added to it.

Woks are available in a number of sizes and are made from various metals. Light iron woks, manufactured in Asia and available in some Asian specialty shops, conduct heat most efficiently. Rolled-steel woks, the most common type found in shops, are a very suitable substitute. These heavier pans are preferable because they conduct heat most efficiently and evenly. Stainless steel and light aluminum woks are to be avoided because both conduct heat unevenly. For most cooking, a 14- or 16-inch wok is recommended; with anything smaller, the surface area is too limited. Gas is the best kind of heat (the more powerful the fire, the better). An electric stove can be used, but a flat-bottomed wok is recommended, since it hugs the burner, preventing loss of heat.

Electric woks are available, but they are best reserved for tabletop cooking. For the most part, they do not get hot enough for proper stir-frying and deep-frying. They can be used somewhat satisfactorily for steaming and braising, however, since they maintain an even, constant temperature.

To Season a New Wok

1. Scrub the pan thoroughly to remove any lacquer or protective coating that may have been put on the surface by the manufacturer to prevent it from rusting in the store. Dry the pan thoroughly.

2. Pour a generous amount of peanut, safflower or corn oil (about 2 cups) into the wok and swirl it around to make sure the entire cooking surface is thoroughly coated with the oil.

3. Place the pan over medium heat, and heat until the oil begins to smoke, swirling occasionally to lubricate the surface with the oil. Turn off the heat, and let the pan sit until cool.

4. Swirl the oil again to coat the surface of the wok. Heat it over medium heat until the oil begins to smoke, swirling occasionally. Turn off the heat, and let the pan cool. Repeat this step two or three times. Remove the oil and wipe out the wok.

To Clean a Wok

1. Wash the pan with a bamboo cleaner or a dishwashing brush, using hot water and mild dishwashing liquid. Rinse thoroughly.

2. Place the pan over high heat until completely dry.

3. If the pan rusts, wipe the surface with an oil-soaked paper towel before storing.

Steamers

THERE ARE A NUMBER OF LAYERED steamers available—made of stainless steel, aluminum or bamboo. The traditional Chinese bamboo steamer, with two layers and lid, is recommended over the other types. Bamboo absorbs the steam so that it doesn't condense on the lid and drip back into the food, making it soggy. The efficient absorption of the steam also creates an intensely hot container, so the food cooks quickly and stays hot. Because the bamboo steamer is attractive, food may be served directly from it. If the bamboo steamer is new, it may release impurities into the water, turning the water an unattractive green. To prevent this, season the steamer before the first use by soaking it for 1 hour in cold water to cover. (A bathtub is the easiest place to do this.) If you use a 14-inch wok, a 12-inch steamer is recommended; for a 16-inch wok, use a 14-inch steamer.

An aluminum steaming tray may also be used to steam foods. The tray is placed in a wok that has been filled with boiling water. The food to be steamed is placed directly on the tray or in a heatproof bowl or plate on the tray. A dome lid is used to cover the tray, creating an airtight steamer.

Shovel, Ladle & Handled Strainer

THERE ARE THREE BASIC HAND UTENsils used in Chinese cooking. The shovel is a wide spatula designed to conform to the slanted sides of the wok, allowing greater control in handling food. The ladle is used by professional Chinese chefs to toss food and add seasonings. In the home, it is more commonly used to add or remove hot oil or water from the pan and to ladle hot oil or water over foods to ensure even cooking. Stainless steel ladles and shovels with wooden handles are recommended. The handled strainer is another multipurpose utensil used to remove foods from hot oil and water. It also works well as a colander for draining foods and as a mold for fashioning deep-fried bird's nests with shredded potatoes and noodles. In Asia, a sturdy strainer is made with a wide, steel, perforated body and a hardwood handle. In the United States, a slightly flimsier version is generally available with a woven, wire-mesh basket and a handle. Both work quite well. A slotted spoon is a fine substitute for a handled strainer.

Chinese Cleaver

A CLEAVER IS THE ALL-PURPOSE CUTTING utensil used by Chinese chefs; it is an extremely versatile tool. The sharp edge is used for all types of cutting, the blunt edge is used for tenderizing, and the flat side is used for flattening. Cleavers are available in three sizes: light, medium and heavy. The light cleaver is used for chopping vegetables and seasonings. The medium one is used for cutting all kinds of ingredients. Its weight makes it heavy enough to cut through chicken bones, yet light enough to handle most foods. The heavyweight cleaver is reserved for heavy-duty cutting, such as chopping hefty bones and tough meat.

Cleavers are usually made of carbon steel or stainless steel. Because carbon steel is a soft metal, it is easier to sharpen and holds its cutting edge better. Its one disadvantage is that it discolors when exposed to certain foods. Stainless steel, on the other hand, will not discolor, but since it is a more brittle metal, it is more difficult to sharpen and dulls easily. Some companies now manufacture high-carbon stainless steel cleavers, which contain the best properties of both metals. These cleavers are higher-priced but generally worth the additional expense.

Sandy Pot

FOR BRAISING, STEWING AND CASSEROLE cooking, a sandy pot is traditionally used. This heavy earthenware pot is made from a mixture of clay and sand and fired at an extremely high temperature. It withstands direct heat and distributes heat efficiently and evenly, making it ideal for slow cooking. Most sandy pots are glazed on the outside and unglazed inside for better heat absorption. They are available in several sizes and shapes. You may substitute a heavy Dutch oven or casserole.

Mongolian Fire Pot (or Hot Pot)

THIS SPECIALTY POT IS USED EXCLUSIVELY for Mongolian Fire Pot and Rinsed Lamb Pot—dishes that are like fondue in that each diner cooks his or her own food in the pot. Fire pots come in a variety of metals, most notably brass, copper and steel. There are two major types: one is shaped like a chafing dish with a small stand underneath for Sterno or an alcohol lamp. The other, more popular variety is a larger, more impressive-looking affair with a chamber to hold charcoal and a tall chimney attached to a tubular pan that holds the boiling broth. You may improvise with an electric wok.

Planning a Chinese Meal or Formal Banquet

TRADITIONAL CHINESE FAMILY MEAL CONSISTS OF FOUR DISHES—meat or poultry, fish or seafood, a vegetable and soup. The menu always includes a staple, such as rice, steamed breads, pancakes or noodles. In a family-style situation, all the dishes are served simultaneously, with the diners helping themselves to each. The soup is served as a beverage, and diners frequently dip their spoons into the broth to flavor their rice and quench their thirst. The main dishes are prepared in small quantities, since their purpose is to garnish the staple food—usually rice—rather than be the main filler. Once the rice bowls are emptied, they are filled with soup, signifying the end of the meal. For a simple family meal, choose a meat or seafood main dish with a vegetable, rice or noodles.

In a more formal situation (at a restaurant or banquet), the meal is a much lengthier affair, with anywhere from 10 to 14 courses. The courses follow a specific order, usually starting with a cold platter, followed by "wine-accompanying" dishes, which are often dry and crisp to complement the flavor of spirits. Most of the drinking and toasting takes place during this part of the meal. The main dishes (*da cai*) follow and may include Peking duck, roast suckling pig or a whole fish. This is the focal point of the meal. Finally, the simpler "rice-accompanying" dishes are served—vegetable, tofu and egg platters. In a traditional banquet, the courses are punctuated with sweet and savory soups or pastries, which serve to cleanse the palate and clear the stage for another type of dish.

When you plan a Chinese meal for guests, I recommend preparing a reasonably simple one. Start with a cold platter, continue with a fish (possibly steamed), meat or poultry (braised, deep-fried, stir-fried or smoked), a vegetable (steamed or stir-fried), a staple (rice, noodles, pancakes or steamed breads), a soup and sliced fruits or a fruit salad. The dishes should be selected with an eye to contrasting and complementing flavors (sweet versus salty, sour versus sweet and delicate versus spicy), textures, colors and cooking methods. The last consideration is particularly important so that you do not spend the entire evening in the kitchen.

Sample Menus

Simplified Formal Meals

Five-Treasure Seafood Fire Pot..... *page 360*

or

Mongolian Barbecue..... *page 292*

Sesame Flat Breads..... *page 64*

⌣

Fried Wontons..... *page 123*

Steamed Fish Fillets in Black Bean Sauce..... *page 228*

Stir-Fried Chicken With Cashews..... *page 186*

Moon Cakes..... *page 375*

⌣

Curry Turnovers..... *page 125*

Shredded Pork With Sweet Bean Sauce..... *page 263*

Mandarin Pancakes..... *page 62*

Stir-Fried Broccoli in Oyster Sauce..... *page 314*

Almond Cookies..... *page 371*

Formal Banquet

Hundred-Corner Shrimp Balls..... *page 206*

Spicy Lamb Kebabs..... *page 294*

Chinese Cabbage With Crabmeat..... *page 242*

Chrysanthemum Rice..... *page 40*

Steamed Chicken in Melon Soup..... *page 352*

Custard Tartlets..... *page 376*

⌣

Cantonese-Style Chicken Wings..... *page 165*

Cold Chinese Salad..... *page 308*

Red-Cooked Yellow Fish..... *page 236*

Spicy Stir-Fried Eggplant..... *page 321*

Pan-Fried Noodles With Beef & Broccoli..... *page 94*

Almond Bean Curd With Fruit..... *page 368*

ASICS

Vegetarian Banquet

Crunchy Cashews..... *page 328*
or
Vegetarian Spring Rolls..... *page 330*

Mock Abalone in Oyster Sauce..... *page 332*
Mock Sweet & Sour Pork..... *page 340*
Assorted Vegetables Over Sizzling Rice..... *page 337*
Vegetarian Lion's Head..... *page 339*
Sliced Fruit

About the Recipes

WITH ENTERTAINING IN MIND, I HAVE made sure that all the recipes in this book serve six people. All main dishes should be paired with a staple, such as rice, noodles or steamed bread. In Chinese cooking, it is especially important to read each recipe completely before proceeding with any of the preparation. The ingredients are organized into small groups (for example, Meat Marinade, Sauce, Braising Mixture,

Thickener). Before beginning to cook, you should prepare these mixtures and place them near the cooking area. In some cases, instructions for preparing the mixtures appear in the recipes. Most of the dishes, unless otherwise directed, should be served as soon as they are cooked. The Chinese believe that the guests may wait for the food, but the food must never wait for the guests.

Rice

EVERY SUNDAY NIGHT FROM THE time I was old enough to gnaw on a sparerib, my family and I would dine at a local Chinese restaurant. We prided ourselves on knowing authentic Chinese cuisine, choosing such sophisticated main courses as *mu shu* pork and sweet-and-sour yellow fish and shunning the chop suey/chow mein items on the menu. Anyone who ordered these "pseudo-Chinese" platters and was unfortunate enough to sit near our table was the target of disdainful glances. We felt very smug to be eating just like the native Chinese.

Once I had traveled to Asia and become familiar with the eating habits of the Chinese, I realized how Western we really were. We never ordered rice or any staple food to accompany the meat, fish and vegetable main courses; instead, we filled ourselves on those dishes and experienced the syndrome known to countless Americans who eat in the same manner. We, too, were hungry an hour later.

For most Chinese formal banquets in celebration of a special holiday or event, the custom is to fill oneself up on the numerous main dishes or courses. Even so, at least one type of rice, noodle or steamed bread is always served—if for no other reason than for the sake of appearance. For an everyday home-style meal, the situation is very different: rice, noodles, steamed bread or some other staple is the main filler, and the assorted meat, vegetable and fish main dishes act as garnishes. Soup is served as a beverage and also as a flavoring to be spooned over rice. In addition to being a filler, rice provides an excellent foil for the pungent seasonings, rich sauces and varied textures of the main courses. Having been weaned on processed "minute" rices, I was surprised at the delicate sweetness and pleasant texture of the cooked natural rice served to me in Asia.

Rice as a filler is a custom that has evolved from ancient times; in the *Shih ching* (Book of Songs), the earliest written text, this precedent was clearly set forth: "The meat that he eats must, at the very most, not be enough to make his breath smell of meat rather than rice."

It is believed that rice was introduced to China from the Indus Valley before 2800 B.C. Other grains, such as millet, wheat, barley, hemp and sorghum, also were cultivated and were highly regarded for their nutritional value and level of productivity. Symbolically, rice played a special role in epitomizing fertility and life.

The ancient Chinese farmers quickly learned that rice demanded a warm, moist climate and thrived in the areas where these conditions prevailed. In regions where the ideal conditions were not prevalent, experimentation in cross pollination and the natural-selection process produced hundreds of variant strains: shorter-grain rices for longer days and shorter growing seasons; lower-yield, higher-protein rices in dry areas; and salt-tolerant rices in marshy areas. Other unique varieties included rices that were yellow, pink, white, red, black, oval-grain or glutinous. Each strain had its own individual flavor and texture. So varied was this staple food in ancient China that it was treated as a delicacy; in the city of Hangzhou, reputed to be the hotbed of Chinese haute cuisine in its day, well-to-do families were known to import special, selected varieties of rice daily to their homes.

Today, the number of strains generally used for Chinese cooking is restricted to four or five: **Extra-long-grain** and **long-grain**, such as Jasmine or Basmati, used for everyday dishes, are two of the most popular, because they yield more cooked rice per cup of raw rice and because the texture of the cooked rice is very fluffy. **Short-grain**, or **Japanese**, rice is very sticky when cooked, making it ideal for sushi and other dishes requiring a sticky texture. The Japanese and many Chinese from Taiwan prefer these shorter strains for everyday eating. **Glutinous**, or **sweet**, rice is an oval-grain variety with an extremely sticky consistency. It is used primarily for sweet and savory fillings, sweet pastries and coatings for food.

A large portion of the agricultural population in China consumes **brown** rice, and for good reason. While perhaps not as aesthetically pleasing as white rice, brown rice contains much more protein, starch, fat, minerals and vitamins than white rice. Most of these nutrients are lost in the milling process, though white rice is usually enriched after it is milled to replace some of the lost nutrients and vitamins.

In addition to its role as a staple, rice is ground into powder and used in cakes and puddings and as a coating for meats and poultry. Rice powder is also used to make **rice stick noodles** (rice vermicelli).

Before cooking rice, it is important to rinse it thoroughly. This is done for three reasons: to remove any talc remaining from the polishing; to remove any impurities and excess starch; and to allow the grains to separate during cooking, creating a fluffier product.

The Chinese use two main methods for cooking rice: boiling and steaming. Boiling, which is somewhat more convenient, produces a slightly sticky rice. (We always used a pressure cooker in our Chinese household.) Steaming, the lengthier method, produces a fluffier cooked rice. Electric rice cookers are often used for steaming; they are simple to use and shut off automatically when the rice is cooked. Either of the methods on the following page will yield perfectly cooked grains of rice.

Boiled Rice

Using your fingers as a rake, rinse the long-grain rice, such as Jasmine or Basmati, thoroughly under cold running water until the water runs clear. Drain, and place the rice and the appropriate amount of water in a heavy saucepan. Cook over high heat until the water begins to boil. Cover, turn the heat to low, and simmer for 20 minutes, until the water has evaporated and craters have formed on the surface of the rice. Turn off the heat, and let the rice rest, covered, for 10 minutes. Fluff the rice with a fork or chopsticks, and serve.

Steamed Rice

Using your fingers as a rake, rinse the long-grain rice thoroughly under cold running water until the water runs clear. Drain, and place the rice and water to cover in a heavy saucepan. Heat, uncovered, until boiling; boil for 5 minutes. Drain the rice, and place it in a steamer tray lined with moistened cheesecloth. Fill a wok with water level with the bottom edge of the steamer tray, and bring the water to a boil. Cover the tray, and place the steamer over the boiling water. Steam for 30 minutes over high heat. Let the rice rest, covered, for 10 minutes. Fluff with a fork or chopsticks, and serve.

In cooking rice, the proportion of water used varies in accordance with personal taste, the type of rice and regional customs. The following chart lists the necessary amount of water and raw rice for the various strains in relation to yield per cup.

TYPE OF RAW RICE	WATER	YIELD
1 cup long-grain or extra-long-grain rice	1½ cups	3 cups
1 cup short-grain (Japanese) rice	1 cup	2 to 2½ cups
1 cup sweet (glutinous) rice	1 cup	2 cups
1 cup brown rice	1¾ cups	2½ cups

In cooking more than 2 cups of long-grain or extra-long-grain rice, the quantity of water decreases proportionally as the quantity of rice increases. Hence:

3 cups raw long-grain rice	4 cups water	9 cups cooked rice
4 cups raw long-grain rice	5 cups water	12 cups cooked rice
5 cups raw long-grain rice	6 cups water	15 cups cooked rice

Pearl Balls

Zhen Zhu Wan Zi

6 Servings ⁓ Appetizer

1½	cups sweet (glutinous) rice
6	dried Chinese black mushrooms
1	cup water chestnuts
1	pound ground beef or pork
½	cup shredded raw carrot

Seasonings

2	tablespoons soy sauce
1	tablespoon rice wine or sake
1½	teaspoons sesame oil
1	tablespoon minced scallions
1	tablespoon minced gingerroot
2½	tablespoons cornstarch

PEARL BALLS, SEASONED *meatballs coated in rice and eaten as finger foods, are so named because once they are steamed, the rice blooms into pearl-like grains. Sweet (glutinous) rice is essential to this dish, since its sticky quality allows the grains to adhere firmly to the meatballs. This famous dish originated in the province of Hunan, one of China's major rice basins. (See photograph, page 83.)*

1. Using your fingers as a rake, rinse the rice in cold running water until the water runs clear. Drain the rice, and place it in cold water to cover. Let it sit for 1 hour. Drain the rice, transfer it to a tray, and spread it in a level layer.

2. Soak the dried mushrooms in hot water to cover for 20 minutes. Remove and discard the stems. Chop the caps coarsely. Plunge the water chestnuts into boiling water for a few seconds to remove the tinny flavor. Refresh them in cold water, and chop coarsely. Chop the ground meat for a few minutes until fluffy. Place the meat in a bowl, add the chopped mushrooms, the shredded carrot, the chopped water chestnuts and the *Seasonings*. Stir the mixture vigorously in one direction to combine evenly. Roll the mixture into balls about 1 inch in diameter. Roll each meatball in the rice so that it is completely coated; lightly press the rice to make it adhere to the meatball. Line a steamer tray with cheesecloth or muslin that has been moistened with water or with parchment paper that has been punched with holes. Arrange the pearl balls on the steamer tray about ½ inch apart.

3. Fill a wok with water level with the bottom edge of the steamer tray, and heat until boiling. Place the steamer tray over the boiling water, and cover. Steam for 25 minutes over high heat, replenishing water in the steamer if necessary. Remove the pearl balls, and serve immediately, with soy sauce, if desired.

Rainbow Congee

Xian Zhou

6 Servings ⌣ Main Dish or Side Dish

To the Chinese, congee *(rice gruel) is a dish for many occasions. It is served as a breakfast cereal with side dishes of pickled vegetables, dried and salted fish or leftovers from the previous evening's meal; it is often prepared for convalescents, since it is soothing and easy to digest; and it is excellent as a filling, flavorful snack. Sweet (glutinous) and short-grain rice are both suitable substitutes for long-grain rice in this recipe.*

3	cups long-grain rice
5	dried Chinese black mushrooms
2	tablespoons peanut, safflower or corn oil
¼	cup minced shallots
3	carrots, cut into ¼-inch dice
4	Chinese pork sausages, cut into ¼-inch dice (for homemade, see page 275)

Rice Seasonings

12	cups chicken broth, preferably Chinese Chicken Broth (page 345)
2	tablespoons soy sauce
1	teaspoon salt
2	cups fresh peas, cooked for 1 minute in boiling water, or thawed frozen peas

1. Using your fingers as a rake, rinse the rice in cold running water until the water runs clear. Drain, and set aside. Soak the dried mushrooms in hot water to cover for 20 minutes, or until spongy. Remove and discard the stems. Cut the caps into ¼-inch dice.

2. Heat a wok, add the oil, and heat the oil until very hot. Add the minced shallots, and stir-fry over high heat, stirring constantly, until the shallots are soft and transparent. Add the dried mushrooms, carrots and sausage, and stir-fry for about 1 minute, until fragrant. Add the *Rice Seasonings*, and heat until boiling. Add the rice, and heat until boiling. Cook for about 2 minutes over high heat, stirring occasionally. Reduce the heat to low, cover, and simmer for about 1 hour. The mixture should be the consistency of porridge. Add the peas, toss lightly to mix, cover, and let sit for 10 minutes. Serve immediately.

Curried Fried Rice

Jia Li Fan

6 Servings ⁓ Main Dish or Side Dish

¼	cup peanut, safflower or corn oil
1	cup diced onion
1½	tablespoons curry powder
1	cup diced carrots, cooked for 1 minute in boiling water
1	cup diced cooked chicken meat
1	cup fresh peas, cooked for 1 minute in boiling water, or thawed frozen peas
6	cups cold cooked long-grain rice

Rice Sauce

3	tablespoons chicken broth, preferably Chinese Chicken Broth (page 345)
2	teaspoons salt
½	teaspoon freshly ground black pepper

Heat a wok, add the oil, and heat the oil until very hot. Add the diced onion, and stir-fry over high heat, stirring constantly, until soft and transparent. Add the curry powder, and stir-fry for about 5 seconds, until fragrant. Add the carrots, chicken and peas. Toss lightly over the heat; then add the rice. Mix thoroughly to break up the rice and combine the ingredients well. Add the ***Rice Sauce***, and quickly toss the mixture to coat evenly. Transfer the rice to a platter, and serve immediately.

THE ANCIENT Cantonese were known for their adventurous palates, utilizing foreign spices and ingredients that their country-men shunned. Gradually, these seasonings were introduced and adapted to the other regional cuisines, and by now, they have become quite popular. This is the case with curry powder; curries, once unique to southern China, are now enjoyed throughout the country. Fried rice dishes, such as this one, are often served as a staple accompanying the main courses in American-Chinese restaurants. In truth, they are more correctly served as a snack or with a light soup for a meal in itself.

Chrysanthemum Rice

Ju Hua Chao Fan

6 Servings ⁓ Main Dish or Side Dish

THE SECRET TO THIS *fried rice, as with any, is to make certain the rice is cold before stir-frying. The pink shrimp and green peas resemble the colors of a pink chrysanthemum—hence the name. Serve this dish with a soup for a light meal, or accompanied by a meat or seafood platter for a more substantial repast.*

3	tablespoons peanut, safflower or corn oil
3	large eggs, lightly beaten
1	cup scallion greens, cut into ¼-inch lengths
2	cups medium-sized cooked shrimp, diced
1½	cups fresh peas, cooked for 1 minute in boiling water, or thawed frozen peas
6	cups cold cooked long-grain rice

Rice Sauce

2½	tablespoons rice wine or sake
2	tablespoons chicken broth, preferably Chinese Chicken Broth (page 345)
1	teaspoon sesame oil
1	teaspoon salt
¼	teaspoon freshly ground white pepper

Heat a wok, add the oil, and heat until hot. Add the eggs and stir-fry over high heat, using a spatula to break them up, until hard-cooked and scrambled. Add the scallions and stir-fry for about 1 minute; then add the shrimp and peas. Stir-fry briefly to heat through; then add the rice. Stir-fry vigorously to break up the rice and mix the ingredients well. Add the *Rice Sauce* and quickly toss the mixture together to coat evenly. Transfer the rice to a platter, and serve immediately.

Shrimp With Sizzling Rice

Guo Ba Xia Ren

6 Servings ⌣ Main Dish

Sizzling Rice Cakes

1½   cups long-grain rice

1   pound medium-sized raw shrimp, shelled

Shrimp Marinade

2   slices gingerroot, the size of a quarter, smashed with the flat side of a cleaver

1½   tablespoons rice wine or sake

2   teaspoons cornstarch

½   teaspoon salt

2   cups peanut, safflower or corn oil

Minced Seasonings

2   tablespoons minced scallions

1   tablespoon minced gingerroot

Shrimp Sauce

4   cups chicken broth, preferably Chinese Chicken Broth (page 345)

3½   tablespoons ketchup

2½   tablespoons rice wine or sake

2½   tablespoons sugar

2½   teaspoons salt

Thickener

3   tablespoons water

2   tablespoons cornstarch

2   cups snow peas, ends snapped and veiny strings removed

IT HAS BEEN SUGGESTED *that a resourceful Chinese chef, ever mindful of eliminating waste of any type, invented the concept of sizzling rice so that the layer of cooked rice that often sticks to the pot would be put to good use. In this dish, shrimp and snow peas are tossed in a spicy sauce and served over the crisp sizzling rice cakes. The rice cakes should be made at least 8 hours in advance. You may store them, unfried, in an airtight container. (See photograph on cover.)*

1. To prepare the *Sizzling Rice Cakes*, rinse the rice under cold running water until the water runs clear. Drain, place in the bottom of a 9-by-12-inch lasagna pan, and add 2 cups of cold water. Spread the rice evenly over the bottom of the pan. Cover the pan with aluminum foil, and let it sit for 30 minutes. Preheat the oven to 350 degrees F. Bake the rice, still covered, for 30 minutes. Remove the

foil, flatten the rice with a spatula, and return it to the oven, uncovered. Turn the heat to the lowest setting, and bake for 8 to 10 hours, or until the rice is completely dry. Take the rice out of the pan, and break it into squares roughly 2 inches on each side. The rice cakes will keep indefinitely in an airtight container. Makes about 12 cakes.

2. Score each shrimp along the length of the back and remove the vein; the scoring will allow the shrimp to "butterfly" when it is cooked. Rinse all the shrimp, and drain thoroughly. Place the shrimp in a bowl. Pinch the gingerroot slices in the *Shrimp Marinade* repeatedly for several minutes to impart their flavor. Discard the gingerroot. Add the marinade to the shrimp, toss lightly, and let sit for 20 minutes.

3. Heat a wok, add 4 tablespoons of the oil, and heat until very hot. Add the shrimp, and stir-fry over high heat until they change color, about 1 minute. Remove with a handled strainer or slotted spoon, and drain. Wipe out the wok, reheat, add 2 tablespoons of the oil, and heat until very hot. Add the *Minced Seasonings*, and stir-fry for about 10 seconds, until fragrant. Add the *Shrimp Sauce*, and heat until boiling. Slowly add the *Thickener*, stirring constantly to prevent lumps. Add the shrimp and the snow peas. Turn the heat to very low to keep hot.

4. Heat another wok, add the remaining oil, and heat to 425 degrees F, or until almost smoking. Add a batch of the rice cakes, and deep-fry, turning constantly until puffed and golden. Remove with a handled strainer or slotted spoon, and place in a serving bowl. Repeat with the remaining rice cakes. Pour the shrimp mixture over the rice cakes immediately to create the sizzling sound. Serve immediately.

Stir-Fried Beef With Vegetables Over Rice

Good

Niu Rou Hui Fan

6 Servings ~ Main Dish

1½   pounds eye-of-round roast or top sirloin roast

Beef Marinade
- 2   tablespoons soy sauce
- 1   tablespoon rice wine or sake
- 1   tablespoon water
- 1   teaspoon sesame oil
- 1   tablespoon cornstarch

- 1   cup snow peas, ends snapped and veiny strings removed
- ½   cup peanut, corn or safflower oil
- 1   medium-sized onion, diced
- 2   green peppers, cored, seeded and diced
- 2   tomatoes, seeded and diced
- 1   cup fresh button mushrooms, rinsed lightly and quartered

Beef Sauce
- 3   cups chicken broth, preferably Chinese Chicken Broth (page 345)
- ¼   cup soy sauce
- 2   tablespoons rice wine or sake
- 2   tablespoons ketchup
- 1½   tablespoons Chinese black vinegar or Worcestershire sauce
- 3   tablespoons sugar
- 1   teaspoon salt

Thickener
- 5   tablespoons water
- 3   tablespoons cornstarch

- 1½   teaspoons sesame oil
- 6   cups hot cooked long-grain rice

1. Remove any fat or gristle from the beef, and discard. Cut the meat, across the grain, into slices that are ⅛ inch thick. (You may partially freeze the beef to

T HE SWEET FLAVOR OF *rice provides a perfect complement to any pungent dish—be it sweet, sour, salty or hot. This is a fine example of the meal–in–one-dish platters, which are combinations of meat, seafood, poultry or vegetables served over rice.*

facilitate slicing.) Cut the slices into pieces about 1½ inches square. Place the beef slices in the bowl with the *Beef Marinade*. Toss lightly, and let the beef marinate for at least 20 minutes. Blanch the snow peas in boiling water for 5 seconds. Refresh them immediately in cold water, and drain thoroughly.

2. Heat a wok, add 3 tablespoons of the oil, and heat the oil until very hot. Drain the beef, and add half the slices to the hot oil. Fry them until the color changes and the meat is cooked. Remove with a handled strainer or slotted spoon, and drain. Add 3 more tablespoons of oil, heat and add the remaining beef slices, and fry them in the same manner. Remove, and drain. Remove the oil from the wok. Wipe out the wok.

3. Reheat the wok, add the remaining 2 tablespoons of oil, and heat until very hot. Add the diced onion, and stir-fry over high heat until soft and transparent. Add the green peppers, tomatoes and mushrooms. Stir-fry for 1½ minutes over high heat, stirring constantly. Add the *Beef Sauce*, and heat until boiling. Add the *Thickener*, stirring constantly to prevent lumps. When the sauce has thickened, add the cooked meat slices, the snow peas and the sesame oil. Toss lightly to combine the ingredients, and spoon over the hot rice. Serve immediately.

Steamed Beef With Spicy Rice Powder

Fen Zheng Niu Rou

6 Servings ∽ Main Dish

1½	pounds flank steak or London broil

Beef Marinade

3	tablespoons soy sauce
3	tablespoons rice wine or sake
2	tablespoons sesame oil
1½	tablespoons sweet bean sauce
1½	teaspoons chili paste
2	tablespoons minced scallions
1	tablespoon minced garlic
1	tablespoon minced gingerroot
1½	tablespoons sugar

2	cups sweet (glutinous) rice, rinsed, soaked for 4 hours in hot water to cover, and drained
2	teaspoons five-spice powder
2	tablespoons minced scallion greens

S PICY RICE POWDER IS A *seasoned coating used frequently in chicken, duck, pork and beef dishes. The seasoned rice bits coat the meat pieces, sealing in the natural juices and producing a succulently tender and flavorful result. Seasoned rice powder is available in packages in grocery stores all over the Far East, but it seems to be scarce in the West. Preparing spicy rice powder is quite simple, and the homemade variety is far more tasty.*

1. Remove any fat or gristle from the meat, and discard. Cut the meat, across the grain, into thin slices about ¼ inch thick and 1½ inches long. (You may partially freeze the beef to facilitate slicing.) Place the beef slices in a bowl, add the *Beef Marinade*, toss lightly, and let marinate for at least 1 hour.

2. Place the soaked rice in a heavy pan (with no oil), and stir-fry over medium-low heat, stirring constantly, until the rice is very dry and light golden brown, 10 to 15 minutes. Remove, and pulverize to a coarse powder in a blender or in a food processor with a steel blade. Mix the rice powder with the five-spice powder.

3. Dredge the beef slices in the rice powder so that they are completely coated. Arrange the coated meat pieces in one layer on a steamer tray or trays lined with a sheet of parchment paper that has been punched with holes.

4. Fill a wok with water level with the bottom edge of the steamer tray, and heat until boiling. Place the steamer tray or stacked trays containing the beef directly over the boiling water, cover, and steam for 20 minutes over high heat, or until the meat is cooked and the rice is tender. Sprinkle the minced scallion greens on top, and serve immediately.

Chicken, Sausage & Rice Wrapped in Lotus Leaves

He Ye Bao

6 Servings 〜 Appetizer

THIS DISH IS A *popular selection on any well-stocked dim-sum cart. Handfuls of cooked sweet rice are blended with pieces of cooked chicken, Chinese sausage and black mushrooms, then wrapped in a fragrant lotus leaf and steamed. The leaf, which provides a tantalizing perfume to the steamed foods, is removed just before the packets are eaten. Lotus leaves are sold dried in Asian markets, but parchment paper or aluminum foil may be substituted.*

4	cups sweet (glutinous) rice
6	dried lotus leaves
1	pound boneless chicken breast, skin removed

Chicken Marinade

2	tablespoons soy sauce
1	tablespoon rice wine or sake
1	teaspoon sesame oil
1	teaspoon minced garlic
1	teaspoon minced gingerroot

Rice Seasonings

2	tablespoons soy sauce
1	tablespoon rice wine or sake
1	tablespoon sesame oil
1	teaspoon salt

3	tablespoons peanut, safflower or corn oil
½	pound Chinese pork sausage, cut into ¼-inch-thick slices (for homemade, see page 275)
8	dried Chinese black mushrooms, soaked in hot water to cover for 20 minutes, stems removed and caps diced

Chicken Sauce

¼	cup chicken broth, preferably Chinese Chicken Broth (page 345), or water
2	tablespoons soy sauce
1	tablespoon rice wine or sake
1½	teaspoons cornstarch
¼	teaspoon freshly ground black pepper

1. Using your hands as a rake, rinse the rice under cold running water until the water runs clear. Drain and place in cold water to cover. Soak for 1 hour.

Place the lotus leaves in hot water to cover for 1 hour. Line a steamer tray with wet cheesecloth or parchment paper punched with holes and transfer the rice to the steamer tray, distributing it evenly. Cover and steam the rice for 20 minutes over high heat. Remove and keep covered.

2. Trim away any fat or gristle from the chicken and cut the meat into 1-inch cubes. Place in a bowl, add the *Chicken Marinade*, toss lightly to coat, and let marinate for 20 minutes. Drain and cut each lotus leaf in half at the natural separation.

3. Transfer the cooked rice to a mixing bowl and add the *Rice Seasonings*. Toss lightly to combine.

4. Heat a wok, add the oil, and heat until very hot. Add the chicken and stir-fry over high heat until the meat changes color. Remove with a handled strainer or slotted spoon, and drain. Remove all but 1 tablespoon of the oil from the pan. Reheat the wok, add the Chinese pork sausage, and cook over low heat, stirring occasionally to render off some of the fat. Add the black mushrooms, chicken and *Chicken Sauce*. Stir-fry over high heat until the sauce has thickened, stirring constantly to prevent lumps. Remove and let cool. Separate into 12 portions.

5. Place a half of a lotus leaf on the counter, right-side down. The rounded edge should be up. Spoon some of the rice mixture in the center and using a spoon dipped in water, shape into a round circle, shaping an indentation in the center. Fill with a portion of the chicken mixture. Use more rice to cover, forming a stuffed circle. Fold in the edges of the leaf and fold down the top and bottom to form a square package. Tie securely with twine. Repeat to make 12 packages. Arrange the packages in a steamer tray. Cover.

6. Fill a wok or a pot with water level with the bottom of the steamer tray and heat until boiling. Place the steamer tray over the boiling water and steam, covered, for 25 minutes over high heat. Remove and untie the twine. Arrange the packages on a platter and serve. Before eating, open up each package and discard the leaves.

Steamed Rice Casserole

La Wei Fan

6 Servings ⌢ Main Dish

MANY AMERICANS marvel at the fluffy consistency of rice served in Chinese restaurants. (I know a student who always buys cooked rice at a nearby Chinese restaurant, rather than make it herself.) The secret behind this texture may be the fact that often the rice is steamed rather than boiled. Steaming allows each grain to cook separately, resulting in a fluffy, full texture. This tasty dish is simple, attractive and a filling meal in itself.

4	Chinese pork sausages (for homemade, see page 275)
8	dried Chinese black mushrooms
2	carrots
¼	pound fresh snow peas, ends snapped and veiny strings removed
2½	cups long-grain rice
2½	cups water
½	teaspoon salt
1	tablespoon peanut, safflower or corn oil
1	teaspoon minced garlic
2	cups Chinese cabbage (Napa), cut into 2-inch squares

Cabbage Seasonings

2	tablespoons rice wine or sake
1	teaspoon salt
½	teaspoon sugar

Rice Seasonings

1	cup chicken broth, preferably Chinese Chicken Broth (page 345)
5	tablespoons soy sauce
¼	cup rice wine or sake
2	teaspoons sesame oil

1. Cut the sausages on the diagonal into slices about ⅛ inch thick. Soak the dried mushrooms in hot water to cover for 20 minutes. Remove and discard the stems, and cut the caps in half. Peel the carrots, and roll-cut into ½-inch pieces. Blanch the snow peas for 5 seconds in boiling water. Refresh them in cold water immediately. Drain, and reserve.

2. Using your fingers as a rake, rinse the rice in cold running water until the water runs clear. Drain. Place the rice in a 4-quart casserole or Dutch oven, and add the water and the salt. Cook over high heat until the water reaches a boil. Stir the rice, and arrange the sausage slices, mushrooms and carrots in separate mounds on top of the rice. Cover, reduce the heat to low, and simmer for 20 minutes.

3. Preheat the oven to 350 degrees F. Heat a wok, add the oil, and heat the oil until very hot. Add the minced garlic. Stir-fry the garlic very briefly over high heat, and add the cabbage squares. Stir-fry until the cabbage is slightly limp,

about 3 minutes; then add the *Cabbage Seasonings*. Continue cooking for another 5 minutes, until the cabbage is tender. Spoon the cabbage over the rice, and arrange the snow peas next to the cabbage. Pour the *Rice Seasonings* over the rice. Cover the casserole.

4. Bake the casserole in the preheated oven for 15 minutes. Serve immediately.

Breads

MY MENTOR IN TAIWAN, Huang Su Huei, a noted authority on Chinese cooking, had some definite ideas about my approach to the study of Chinese cuisine. First, it was decided that I should receive a thorough introduction to the basic cooking techniques and the main regional schools. So every day, I was dispatched to her cooking school in Taipei, where I studied Cantonese, Sichuanese, northern and eastern dishes with some of the foremost master chefs of the city. After one and a half years, another conference was called, and it was agreed that I was now ready to select one or two regional styles and explore them in depth, working as an apprentice in a restaurant kitchen. "Never spread yourself too thin," my mentor admonished. "It is far better to excel in one cuisine than to be mediocre in three."

I decided to study Hunanese cooking, a cousin to the Sichuanese style but with even spicier seasonings and hotter peppers. After some persistent pleading, I convinced the Hunanese teacher to allow me to work in his restaurant kitchen as an apprentice without pay.

Once the initial uproar caused by a young Caucasian woman in an all-male Chinese restaurant kitchen had subsided and order was restored, I was able to observe firsthand the organization and routine of a professional Chinese kitchen, in addition to learning some valuable culinary skills.

The kitchen was divided into six main areas of preparation, or "stations." One station was devoted to cleaning the ingredients, with the area next to it set aside for cutting, slicing and all the other preparation work. Four or five huge woks sat in a row next to one wall on powerful gas jets that emitted heat equal to the intensity of an oxyacetylene torch. This was where most of the cooking was done, and all the cooks in this area were considered to be master chefs, a position at the highest level of the kitchen hierarchy. To one side, a smaller station was devoted to casserole cooking and braising, with several *sha guo*, or clay pots, standing at the ready. To the other side, three rows of bamboo steamer trays were stacked up 10 or 15 layers high. Away from the heat, near the sinks, was the pastry and bread corner, where the sweet pastries and savory snacks were prepared.

I spent quite some time in this corner working with a 15-year-old chef whose hands were remarkably dexterous. He would take blobs of dough and transform them into butterflies, lotus buns, snail buns, silver-thread loaves and peach buns. He would stuff dough circles with a pungent meat filling for a savory pastry and with sweet bean paste and date paste for a sweet confection. Once shaped, these pastries would be arranged in bamboo steamer trays and sent over to the next station to be cooked.

All of these pastries, both sweet and savory, are made from the same yeast dough and steamed. These foods, along with pancakes, are in the broad category of breads, and they figure prominently in the grand order of Chinese dishes. Like noodles,

Chinese breads may be served as a staple substitute for rice—particularly in northern China, where wheat reigns supreme as a staple crop—or as a dim sum (snack) or, occasionally, as a meal in themselves. Examples of these breads include Mandarin Pancakes, which are served with Peking duck and other stir-fried meat and vegetable dishes; Sesame Flat Breads (*shao bing*), which often accompany fried Chinese crullers (*you tiao*) in a Chinese breakfast and are served with Mongolian Fire Pot and Mongolian Barbecue; steamed Lotus Buns, which are served with Crispy-Skin Duck; Barbecued Pork Buns; and Scallion Pancakes. The list is endless, and the variety is extraordinary.

Like noodles, Chinese breads originated in the wheat-growing regions of northern China and became popular as early as the Han dynasty (206 B.C. to 220 A.D.). Experts have concluded that the concept probably was foreign, evolving from foods introduced from the lands to the west. Although originally received with limited enthusiasm, in time, breads and pancakes became immensely popular with both the upper and lower classes. And they came to play an important role in Chinese ritual, replacing rice on special holidays and anniversaries. On birthdays, steamed buns fashioned into peaches were served to symbolize longevity and immortality. Tinted scarlet, a color considered auspicious by the Chinese, steamed breads were presented to the gods in return for favors and were distributed on the occasion of the birth of a baby boy, an event highly regarded in China. (Boys are favored since they will continue the family name.)

Even today, these customs are still observed. On a small island near Hong Kong, thousands of Chinese annually congregate for a Buddhist celebration called the Bun Festival. There, steamed buns are presented as offerings to the gods, and several 60-foot bun mountains, each made of thousands of sweet buns, are constructed for a special race. Young men climb to the top to grab the highest bun, and those who succeed are said to be blessed with good luck for the coming year.

中式糕點類

Basic Yeast Dough

Fa Mian

CHINESE CHEFS USE two types of bread dough in making steamed breads. In both doughs, they use flour, water and lard, but the leavening agent may be plain yeast or a yeast-dough starter. One might suspect that the cooked bread would be heavy from the steaming, but quite the opposite is true. Because of the lengthy rising period and the use of baking powder, the result is a light, fluffy bread.

¼	cup sugar
2	cups warm water
1	tablespoon active dry yeast
6	cups all-purpose flour plus more if necessary
2	tablespoons peanut, safflower or corn oil plus a little more for greasing the bowl
2	teaspoons baking powder

1. Dissolve the sugar in the warm water, and add the yeast. Mix lightly, and let the mixture stand for 10 minutes, until foamy.

2. Place the flour in a mixing bowl, and add the yeast mixture and the oil. Using a wooden spoon, mix the ingredients to a rough dough. Turn the mixture out onto a lightly floured surface, and knead for 8 to 10 minutes, until the dough is smooth and elastic. If it is very sticky, knead in ¼ cup additional flour. (The dough should be soft.) Lightly grease a bowl with oil. Place the dough in the bowl, and turn it so that all sides of the dough are coated. Cover the bowl with a damp cloth, and let the dough rise for 4 hours in a warm area, free from drafts.

3. Uncover the dough, punch it down, and turn it out onto a lightly floured surface. Flatten the dough, and make a well in the center. Place the baking powder in the well, and gather up the edges around the baking powder to enclose it. Pinch the edges to seal. Lightly knead the dough to incorporate the baking powder evenly. Use the prepared dough as directed in the individual recipes. (The dough should be used immediately. If that is not possible, punch down the dough after step 2, cover with plastic wrap, and refrigerate until ready to proceed.)

Silver-Thread Loaves

Yin Si Juan

6 Five-Inch-Long Loaves ⁓ Side Dish or Snack

1 recipe Basic Yeast Dough (page 52)
6 tablespoons sesame oil or melted butter or lard

1. Prepare the Basic Yeast Dough as directed, and cut it in half. Form each half into a long snakelike roll about 1½ inches in diameter. Cut each roll into 6 pieces so that you now have 12 pieces.

2. On a very lightly floured surface, roll out 6 of the 12 pieces to rectangles that are approximately 6 inches by 4 inches. Set these rectangles aside on a lightly floured tray.

3. Roll out the remaining 6 pieces to rectangles that are 8 inches by 4 inches. Smear the sesame oil generously over the surfaces of the rectangles. Fold each one in half crosswise so that it measures 4 inches by 4 inches, and again smear the sesame oil over the surface. Fold each rectangle again so that it measures 4 inches by 2 inches, and cut it crosswise into thin shreds.

4. Lightly stretch the shreds, pulling from both ends (**a**), and arrange in the center of each of the first 6 rectangles; the shreds should run lengthwise (**b**). Fold in the closest end, then the sides and, finally, the last end so that the shreds are completely enclosed. Arrange the finished loaves about 1½ inches apart in 2 steamer trays that have been lined with wet cheesecloth or parchment paper punched with holes. Let the loaves rise for 20 minutes, uncovered.

5. Fill a wok with water level with the bottom edge of a steamer tray, and heat until boiling. Place one tray over the boiling water, cover, and steam the loaves for 20 to 25 minutes over high heat, or until the loaves are puffed and springy. Steam the remaining loaves in the same manner. Cut each loaf into 5 or 6 slices, and serve. To reheat, steam the loaves for 10 minutes over high heat.

S ILVER-THREAD LOAVES *are airy steamed buns that may be served with any main dish in place of rice. Although some Westerners may consider these steamed breads too sweet to serve with savory dishes, the Chinese do not. In fact, sweet flavors are often paired with salty ones to satisfy the palate fully, in much the same way that yin is believed to complement yang. The "silver-thread" in the title refers to the tender strands of steamed bread encased in the individual loaves.*

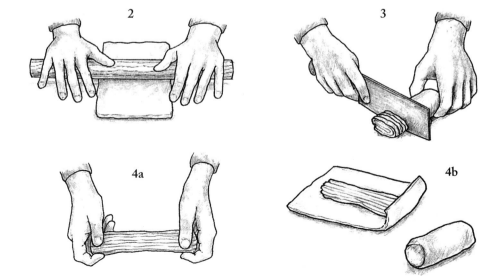

2

3

4a

4b

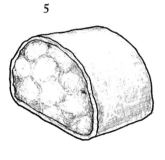

5

Golden-Thread Loaves

Jin Si Juan

6 Five-Inch-Long Loaves ⌣ Side Dish or Snack

FRYING TRANSFORMS *Silver-Thread Loaves into a totally new dish; the crisp, golden crust contrasts nicely with the fluffy lightness of the steamed interior. Serve these breads as a substitute for rice, as a snack or with a hearty soup for a filling lunch or dinner.*

1   recipe Silver-Thread Loaves (page 53)
2   cups peanut, safflower or corn oil

1. Prepare the Silver-Thread Loaves as directed, and steam as directed, but do not cut the loaves into serving slices. Leave them whole, and let them cool.

2. Heat a wok, add the oil, and heat the oil to 350 degrees F. Add 2 or 3 of the loaves, depending on the size of the wok, and deep-fry, turning constantly, until the loaves are golden brown, about 5 minutes. Remove with a handled strainer or slotted spoon, and drain on absorbent paper. Deep-fry the remaining loaves in the same manner. Cut each loaf into 5 or 6 slices. Serve immediately.

Flower Rolls

Hua Juan

15 Rolls ⌣ Side Dish or Snack

1   recipe Basic Yeast Dough (page 52)
¼   cup sesame oil

1. Prepare the Basic Yeast Dough as directed, and cut it in half. On a lightly floured surface, roll out each half to form a rectangle approximately 18 inches long and 8 inches wide. Brush the surface of the rectangles liberally with the sesame oil. Place one rectangle directly on top of the other, with both oiled surfaces facing up (**a**). Starting with one of the long edges, roll up the dough jelly-roll-style (**b**). Pinch the two ends to seal in the sesame oil. Lightly flatten the roll with the heel of your hand, and cut the roll into 15 pieces. Holding a chopstick perpendicular to one piece, firmly press the center in the vertical line (**c**). (This will cause the ends to "flower" when they are steamed.) Repeat this process for each piece. Arrange the shaped rolls about 1 inch apart on several steamer trays that have been lined with wet cheesecloth or with parchment paper punched with holes. Let the rolls rise for 15 minutes, covered.

2. Fill a wok with water level with the bottom edge of a steamer tray, and heat until boiling. Place one tray of rolls over the boiling water, cover, and steam for 15 minutes over high heat, until the rolls are light and springy. Remove, and steam the remaining rolls in the same manner. To reheat, steam for 5 minutes over high heat.

*I*N THE CITY OF TAIPEI, *food vendors pass through the alleyways day and night hawking their offerings. One man rode a bicycle with a box strapped behind his seat filled to the brim with hot steamed bread and flower rolls. Upon hearing his call, my Chinese surrogate mother would dispatch the children to buy a supply of the buns to eat with our dinner instead of rice. Flower rolls are particularly delicious with red-cooked meats and stir-fried meat and vegetable dishes.*

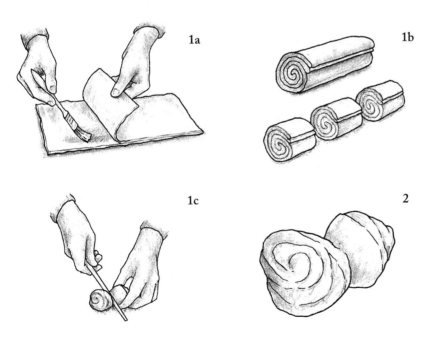

Snail Buns

Luo Si Juan

30 Buns ⌣ Side Dish or Snack

THESE DELICATELY *flavored steamed buns, which are served at many Sichuan and Hunan restaurants, are so named because they are shaped like snails. They are often deep-fried until golden brown after having been steamed. Either way, snail buns are excellent as a substitute for rice.*

1 recipe Basic Yeast Dough (page 52)
¼ cup melted lard plus ¼ cup melted butter plus ½ cup sugar, creamed to a paste
¼ cup minced cooked ham or grated carrot

1. Prepare the Basic Yeast Dough as directed, and cut it in half. On a lightly floured surface, roll out each half to form a rectangle approximately 10 by 14 inches and ⅛ inch thick. Spread the surface of one rectangle with half the lard, butter and sugar mixture. Starting with one of the long edges, roll up the rectangle jelly-roll-style. Pinch the two ends to seal the dough; lightly flatten the roll with the heel of your hand. Cut the roll crosswise into thin shreds. Separate the shreds into 15 groups, and let them rest. Repeat the process for the other rectangle.

2. Gather up each group of shreds, and lightly stretch (**a**), wrapping them Maypole-style around your index finger, third finger and thumb (**b**). Tuck the end underneath to secure. Repeat the procedure for all the shreds, and arrange the shaped buns 1 inch apart on several steamer trays that have been lined with wet cheesecloth or with parchment paper punched with holes. Sprinkle the tops with the minced ham or grated carrot, and let the buns rise for 15 minutes, covered.

3. Fill a wok with water level with the bottom edge of a steamer tray, and heat until boiling. Place one tray of buns over the boiling water, cover, and steam for 15 minutes over high heat. Remove, and steam the remaining buns in the same manner. To reheat, steam the buns for 5 minutes over high heat.

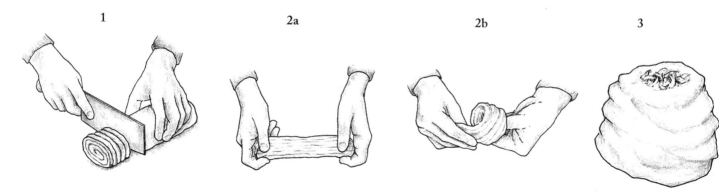

1   2a   2b   3

Barbecued Pork Buns

Cha Shao Bao

24 Buns ⌒ Snack or Side Dish

1	recipe Basic Yeast Dough (page 52)
1½	pounds Barbecued Pork (page 253)

Sauce Mixture

1½	cups water
¼	cup soy sauce
3	tablespoons oyster sauce
2	teaspoons sesame oil
½	tablespoon ketchup
2	tablespoons sugar
½	teaspoon freshly ground black pepper

Thickener

4	tablespoons water
2	tablespoons cornstarch

1. Prepare the Basic Yeast Dough as directed.

2. Cut the Barbecued Pork into ½-inch dice.

3. Heat a wok, add the *Sauce Mixture*, and heat until boiling. Add the *Thickener*, stirring constantly to prevent any lumps, and cook until the sauce is very thick. Add the diced pork, toss lightly to coat with the sauce, and remove to a platter. Refrigerate until it is cool.

4. Cut the dough in half. On a lightly floured surface, form each half into a long, snakelike roll about 1½ inches in diameter. Cut each roll into 12 pieces. With a cut edge down, use your fingers to flatten each piece into a 3-inch circle. The edges should be thinner than the center. Place a tablespoon of the

WITH THEIR FRAGRANT oyster sauce and roasted-meat filling, Barbecued Pork Buns have always been one of my favorite Cantonese snacks. They seem to be equally popular with the Chinese, since these buns are always one of the first snacks to sell out at bakeries and dim-sum parlors. In some restaurants, they are made with a baking-powder dough, but I prefer them with a yeast dough. Serve these savory buns as a snack or with soup for a light, filling meal.

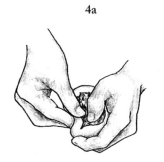
4a

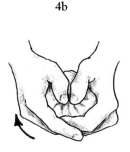
4b

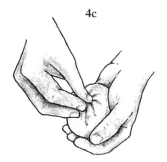
4c

5

barbecued pork mixture in the center of the dough skin. Gather the edges of the skin together (**a**), pressing to make a pleated finish (**b**). Pinch the final pleat to seal and completely enclose the filling (**c**). Place the finished buns about 1 inch apart on several steamer trays that have been lined with wet cheesecloth or with parchment paper punched with holes. Let the buns rise for 15 minutes, covered.

5. Fill a wok with water level with the bottom edge of a steamer tray, and heat until boiling. Place one tray of buns over the boiling water, cover, and steam over high heat for 15 to 20 minutes, or until the buns are puffed and springy. Remove, and steam the remaining buns in the same manner. To reheat, steam the buns for 10 minutes over high heat.

Buns With Red Bean Filling

Dou Sha Bao

24 Buns ⌢ Sweet

*W*ITH THEIR RICH, *buttery filling and airy bread wrapping, these buns are delightful with tea or for dessert.*

Red bean paste is a popular ingredient in many Chinese puddings and pastries. It may be purchased in cans at any Chinese grocery store, but homemade is far superior.

The buns are often garnished with a red stamp, improvised by dipping the square end of a chopstick into red food coloring and pressing the tip to the top of each bun before steaming.

| 1 | recipe Basic Yeast Dough (page 52) |
| 1½ | cups homemade Red Bean Paste (page 379) or 1½ cups canned red bean paste combined with 1 tablespoon vanilla extract |

1. Prepare the Basic Yeast Dough as directed, and cut the dough in half. On a lightly floured surface, form each half into a long, snakelike roll about 1½ inches in diameter. Cut each roll into 12 pieces. With a cut edge down, use your fingers to flatten each piece into a 3-inch circle. The edges should be thinner than the center. Place a heaping tablespoon of the Red Bean Paste in the center of the dough skin. Gather the edges together, pinch to seal, and roll the bun into a ball. Place the buns about 1 inch apart, joined edges down, on several steamer trays lined with wet cheesecloth or with parchment paper punched with holes. Let rise for 15 minutes, covered.

2. Fill a wok with water level with the bottom of the steamer tray, and heat until boiling. Place one tray of buns over the boiling water, cover, and steam over high heat for 15 to 20 minutes, or until the buns are puffed and springy. Remove, and steam the remaining buns in the same manner. To reheat, steam the buns for 10 minutes over high heat.

Lotus Buns

He Ye Bao

20 Buns ⌣ Side Dish or Snack

½ recipe Basic Yeast Dough (page 52)
¼ cup sesame oil

1. Prepare the Basic Yeast Dough as directed. On a lightly floured surface, form it into a long, snakelike roll about 1½ inches in diameter. Cut the roll into 20 pieces.

2. Place each piece, cut edge down, on the counter, and using a small rolling pin, roll out to a 3-inch circle (**a**). Brush the surface of the circle generously with sesame oil (**b**), and fold over to form a half-moon shape. With a sharp knife, lightly score the surface of the shaped bun with a diamond pattern, lengthwise and crosswise. Make two V-shaped indentations in the round edge of the bun with the end of a knife (**c**). Arrange the shaped buns 1 inch apart on steamer trays that have been lined with wet cheesecloth or with parchment paper punched with holes. Cover the buns with a cloth, and let rise for about 15 minutes, covered.

3. Fill a wok with water level with the bottom edge of a steamer tray, and heat until boiling. Place one steamer tray over the boiling water, cover, and steam over high heat for 10 to 15 minutes, until the buns are puffed and springy. Remove, and steam the remaining buns in the same manner. To reheat, steam the buns for 5 minutes over high heat.

*W*ITH A FEW DEFT *movements, a yeast dough can be transformed into unusual shapes, from butterflies to mock lotus leaves. Lotus buns are traditionally served with Crispy-Skin Duck (page 193), sweet bean sauce and scallion pieces. Once steamed, each bun contains a pocket into which stir-fried meats and vegetables can be stuffed. (See photograph, page 87.)*

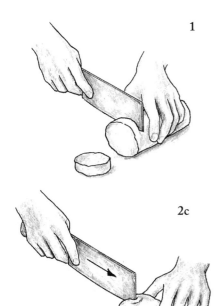

1

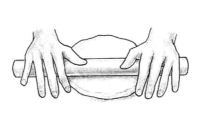

2a

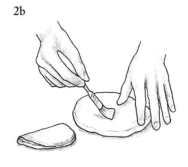

2b

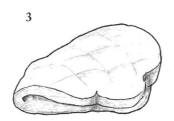

2c 3

Longevity Peach Buns

Shou Tao

24 Buns 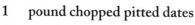 Sweet

THE RICH, SWEET DATE *filling is complemented by the steamed-bread wrapper. According to ancient Chinese thought, the peach symbolizes immortality and springtime. The God of Longevity is often pictured bearded and smiling, descending from a peach or holding a peach in one hand and a staff in the other. Accordingly, steamed buns shaped like peaches are often served stacked in mountainous piles at birthday gatherings in hopes of imparting immortality and longevity to the person whose birthday is being celebrated. Serve as a snack or as dessert.*

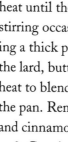

1	recipe Basic Yeast Dough (page 52)

Filling

1	pound chopped pitted dates
4	cups hot water
¼	cup lard plus ¼ cup butter, cut into tablespoon-sized pieces
½	cup sugar
1½	teaspoons freshly squeezed lemon juice
1	teaspoon vanilla extract
1	teaspoon ground cinnamon
	Red food coloring
12	pieces candied angelica (optional)

1. Prepare the Basic Yeast Dough as directed.

2. To make the *Filling*, place the dates with the hot water in a saucepan, and heat until the water is boiling. Reduce the heat to medium, and cook uncovered, stirring occasionally, for 15 to 20 minutes, or until the water has evaporated, leaving a thick paste. Cook the mixture, stirring constantly, until it is very dry. Add the lard, butter and sugar. With a wooden spoon, stir constantly over medium heat to blend the ingredients. Cook the paste until it begins to leave the sides of the pan. Remove the pan from the heat, and add the lemon juice, vanilla extract and cinnamon. Stir to combine the ingredients evenly, and set aside to cool.

3. Cut the dough in half. On a lightly floured surface, form each half into a long, snakelike roll approximately 1½ inches in diameter. Cut each roll into 12 pieces. With a cut edge down, use your fingers to flatten each piece into a 3-inch circle. The edges should be thinner and the center thicker. Place a heaping tablespoon of the date filling in the center of the dough skin (**a**). Gather the edges of the skin together at the center (**b**), pinch to seal, and roll the bun into a round

3a

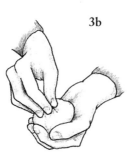

3b

3c

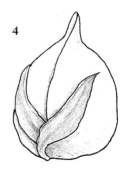

4

ball. Lightly stretch the top of the bun to a small point (**c**), and using a ball of cotton, brush some red food coloring on the bun to create a blush. Cut the angelica, if using, into leaflike shapes, and press one or two on top of each bun. Place the finished buns about 1 inch apart on several steamer trays that have been lined with wet cheesecloth or with parchment paper punched with holes. Let the buns rise for 15 minutes, covered.

4. Fill a wok with water level with the bottom edge of a steamer tray, and heat until boiling. Place one tray of buns over the water, cover, and steam for 15 to 20 minutes, or until the buns are puffed and springy. Remove, and steam the remaining buns in the same manner. To reheat, steam for 10 minutes over high heat.

Scallion Cakes

Cong You Bing

16 Pancakes 〜 Side Dish or Snack

2	cups cake flour
1	teaspoon salt
2	tablespoons corn oil
1	cup boiling water
¼	cup sesame oil
½	cup minced scallion greens
1	cup peanut, safflower or corn oil

1. Place the cake flour, the salt and the oil in a mixing bowl, and stir to blend evenly. Add the boiling water, and using a wooden spoon, mix to a rough dough. Turn the dough out onto a lightly floured surface, and knead for 5 minutes, until smooth and elastic. If the dough is very sticky, knead in ¼ cup more all-purpose flour. Cover the dough with a cloth, and let it rest for 20 minutes.

2. On a lightly floured surface, form the dough into a long, snakelike roll, and cut it into 16 pieces. Place each piece, cut edge down, on the work surface. Using a small rolling pin, roll each piece out to a 4-inch circle. Brush the surface generously with sesame oil, and sprinkle with the minced scallion greens. Starting at the edge closest to you, roll up the circle jelly-roll-style (**a**). Pinch the ends to contain the scallions and sesame oil. Lightly flatten the roll (**b**), and roll it up from one end to the other, pinching the end to seal it (**c**). Let the rolls rest for 20 minutes, covered. Turn each one so that it lies flat on the work surface, and press down with the palm of your hand. Roll out to a 4-inch circle (**d**), and place on a lightly floured tray. Stack the pancakes between lightly floured sheets of wax paper. Again, let the pancakes rest for 20 minutes.

SCALLION CAKES ARE *standard fare for a traditional Chinese breakfast with hot rice congee, but they are equally suitable for a snack or as a rice substitute. Although most northern chefs make large, thick pancakes, I prefer smaller, thinner ones that become crisp in frying. These cakes may be made in advance and reheated in a 350-degree oven for 8 to 10 minutes. Serve with any chicken, pork, beef, lamb or seafood dish.*

2a 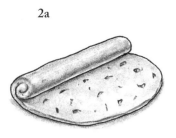 2b 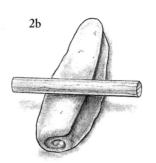 2c  2d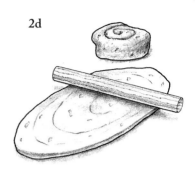

3. Preheat the oven to 200 degrees F. Heat a large frying pan, add the oil, and heat the oil to 350 degrees F. Add several of the pancakes to the oil, and fry on both sides, turning once, until they are golden brown and crisp, about 3 minutes. Remove, and drain on absorbent paper. Arrange the pancakes in a single layer on a baking sheet and keep warm in the preheated oven. Fry the remaining pancakes in the same manner. Serve immediately.

Mandarin Pancakes

Bao Bing

16 Pancakes ⌒ Side Dish

WHILE MANDARIN *Pancakes are usually associated with Peking duck and mu shu pork, they may be served with any stir-fried dish, in place of rice. They may be prepared in advance, refrigerated or frozen and reheated about 10 minutes before serving.*

2 cups all-purpose flour
1 cup boiling water
¼ cup sesame oil

1. Place the flour in a bowl. Slowly add the boiling water, mixing with a wooden spoon to form a rough dough. Let the dough cool slightly, and turn it out onto a lightly floured surface. Knead for about 5 minutes, until smooth and elastic. Cut the dough in half. Form each half into a long, snakelike roll about 1½ inches in diameter. Cut each roll into 8 pieces. Cover the dough pieces with a damp cloth to prevent them from drying out.

2. Place one piece, with a cut edge down, on the lightly floured surface. Using the palm of your hand, flatten it into a circle. Pick it up, and using your fingers, press the circle to 2 inches in diameter. Repeat the same process for another dough piece. Brush the surface of one dough circle with sesame oil, using enough oil to be generous but not so much that it runs over the edges (a). Place a circle on top, and lightly pinch the edges together to create a double circle. Repeat this process for all the dough pieces; you will have 8 double circles. Using a small rolling pin on a floured surface, roll out each double circle to 6 inches in diameter (b).

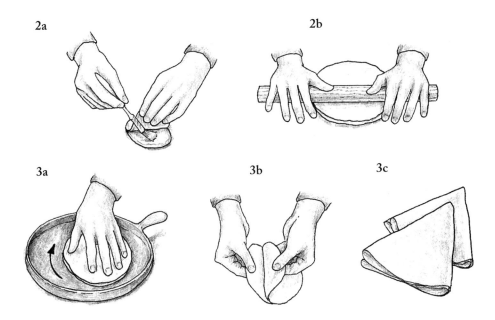

2a

2b

3a

3b

3c

3. Heat a well-seasoned 12-inch heavy skillet until very hot. (A bit of water sprinkled on the surface of the pan should evaporate immediately.) Place a double circle in the pan, and fry for about 1 minute, twirling in a circular motion with your fingertips until it puffs in the middle (**a**). Turn it over, and fry for another 30 seconds, twirling again. Remove, and let cool for a few seconds. Carefully peel the two pancakes apart (**b**), and fold each one into quarters, with the cooked side on the inside (**c**). Arrange them in a circular pattern on a plate, overlapping them slightly. Cover them with a damp cloth to keep warm and moist. Repeat for the other pancakes. Just before serving, fill a wok with water level with the bottom edge of the steamer tray. Heat until boiling and place the steamer tray over the water. Place the plate on the tray. Cover and steam the pancakes for 10 minutes over high heat. Serve immediately.

Sesame Flat Breads

Shao Bing

20 Breads ⌣ Side Dish

E VERY MORNING FOR
*the three and a half years
that I lived in Taipei, my breakfast consisted of a steaming bowl
of sweet bean milk (dou jiang),
served with a deep-fried cruller
(you tiao), which was stuffed
into a flaky sesame flat bread
(shao bing). This traditional
Chinese breakfast can be as
habit-forming as coffee.*

*In addition to being a vital
element in a Chinese breakfast,
shao bing are served with
Mongolian Barbecue and
Mongolian Fire Pot. At some
meals, these flaky breads take the
place of rice and are served with
stir-fried meat and vegetable
dishes. In that case, the shao bing
are split open, stuffed with the
stir-fried mixture and eaten
like a sandwich. (See photograph, page 176.)*

4	cups all-purpose flour
2	cups cake flour
1½	teaspoons salt
2¾	cups boiling water

Roux

¾	cup peanut, safflower or corn oil
1	cup all-purpose flour
¼	cup untoasted sesame seeds

1. Place the flours and salt in a mixing bowl. Add the boiling water, and mix with a wooden spoon to form a rough dough. Turn the dough out onto a lightly floured surface, and knead for about 5 minutes, until smooth and elastic. Cover the dough with a cloth, and let it rest for 30 minutes.

2. To prepare the **Roux**, heat a saucepan until very hot. Add the oil, and heat to 350 degrees F. Add the flour, and cook over medium heat, stirring constantly until the flour is nut-brown and very fragrant. Remove from the heat, and let cool.

3. On a lightly floured surface, roll out the dough to a rectangle that is approximately 14 inches long and 10 inches wide. Spread the roux evenly over the surface, stopping an inch away from each edge (a). Starting with one of the

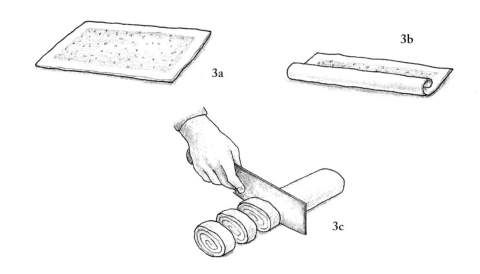

3a

3b

3c

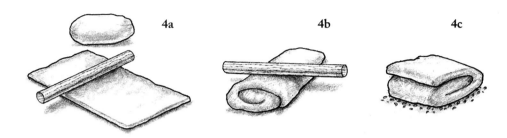

4a   4b   4c

long sides, roll up the rectangle jelly-roll-style (**b**). Pinch the ends to seal in the roux; flatten the roll lightly with the heel of your hand. Cut the roll into 20 pieces (**c**), and pinch the ends of each one to prevent the roux from coming out.

4. On a lightly floured surface, roll out one dough piece to a rectangle 6 inches by 4 inches, with the pinched ends at either end of the length (**a**). Fold the rectangle into thirds, bringing the bottom third over to the center of the length and folding the top third down in toward the center. Turn the dough clockwise a quarter turn so that the seam is vertical (**b**). (This constitutes one "turn.") Roll out once again to a 6-by-4-inch rectangle. Fold into thirds to make another turn, and turn the piece once again in a clockwise direction so that the seam is vertical. Dip the bottom (nonseam side) in the sesame seeds (**c**), and roll out to a rectangle that measures 6 inches by 4 inches. Repeat this process for the remaining dough pieces. Place the finished breads on an ungreased baking sheet, sesame side down.

5. Preheat the oven to 400 degrees F. Bake the breads for 12 minutes, or until flaky and crisp, turning once. Serve immediately. To reheat, bake in a 350-degree oven for 5 to 7 minutes, until hot and crisp.

5

Noodles

NUMBER OF YEARS AGO, I had the privilege of watching a professional Chinese chef "throw" noodles by hand. I was mesmerized as he took a bulging piece of a soft flour-and-water dough and swung it up into the air so that it formed a thick, rope-like braid. He then proceeded to wave it wildly about, stretching and wrapping the dough around itself so that it divided into two fat strands, then four thinner ones. The process continued for about 10 minutes, with the strands multiplying and dividing with each swing. At last, he held 16,000 fine, silky noodles draped over his arms. I was beside myself. And where did this wondrous scene transpire? Peking? Shandong? Hong Kong? The actual location was a Chinese restaurant kitchen in Toledo, Ohio.

What I had assumed to be a rare, ancient craft performed by a few was once a standard skill for any well-rounded northern Chinese master chef. According to Buwei Yang Chao in *How to Cook and Eat in Chinese*, "A good northern cook, or even a cooking maid, knows how to swing noodles by hand."

Unfortunately, it appears that this once popular craft is near extinction; one would be hard-pressed to find many Chinese restaurants in the United States offering hand-swung noodles. Even in Peking, where handmade noodles were once commonplace, there remain only a few small noodle stands offering the handmade variety.

Handmade noodles aside, machine-made noodles and pasta play a prominent role in the modern Chinese diet, second only to rice. In the northern regions, where wheat is grown, noodles replace rice as the main staple for everyday meals. In the other areas, a noodle dish may be a snack, a staple food or a meal in itself.

Like rice, wheat has long been a staple crop in China; records indicate that it was cultivated by Chinese farmers before 2800 B.C. Wheat, along with millet and barley, became the prime crop in the cool, arid regions of northern China because of its hardiness, its yield and its high protein content. The Chinese milled the wheat and used the resulting flour to prepare myriad steamed breads, pancakes and noodles.

Plain, Thin Noodles

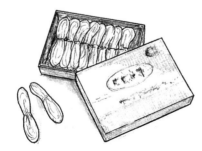

Extra-Thin Noodles, Amoy-Style

Flat Noodles

Thin, Straight Egg Noodles

The origin of noodles is still a widely disputed issue. Although noodles may seem to be a Chinese invention, some anthropological clues suggest that northern Europe might more properly be considered their source, at least for Italy. They may have been brought by a Germanic tribe as early as 405 A.D. Others maintain that noodles were definitely Asiatic; evidence suggests that they were popular in China as early as the Ming Dynasty. The commonly held belief that Marco Polo introduced the noodle to Europe after his travels to the Far East is certainly mistaken, however, since the noodle was familiar in Italy long before that.

Once the noodle concept was introduced to ancient China, it flourished; pasta has played a prominent role in the Chinese regimen for centuries. Its popularity is easily understood: it may be eaten hot or cold; it cooks quickly; it is easily prepared; and it provides an inexpensive and nutritious filler.

Equally significant is the importance of noodles in the Chinese culture; they symbolize longevity, and to consume them is considered a means of attaining long life.

Traditionally, noodles are served on birthdays in much the same way birthday cakes are presented in the West. In view of their symbolic importance, it is not surprising to find that most noodles are very long. They are made of a number of different materials —from rice, tofu (bean curd) or pea starch to flour and water—but all are long. They should be eaten with great relish and with much slurping, as most Chinese eat them, for to cut the noodles is to invite ominous repercussions. (A soup spoon and chopsticks generally are used to facilitate shoveling them into the mouth.)

While the flour-and-water variety is more popular in northern China, the Cantonese prefer a flour, egg and water noodle. Once prepared, these two doughs may be fashioned into many shapes. Hand-swung flour-and-water dough may be thrown into round, flat or triangular noodles and macaroni. These handmade noodles have a silky texture that machine-made noodles never attain. Machine-made noodles, on the other hand, although slightly less refined in texture, are available in an

Bean Curd Noodles

Fried Egg Noodles

Rice Stick Noodles

Cellophane Noodles (Bean Threads)

Thin-Egg-Noodle Clusters

amazing number of shapes, as a visit to any Chinese grocery store will prove.

Most Americans are knowledgeable about the common types of flour, egg and water noodles but frequently are unaware of the various noodles made with rice powder, mung beans (pea starch) and tofu.

Noodles made from rice powder, known as rice stick noodles or rice vermicelli (*mi fen*), are a variation on the traditional flour-and-water variety and are popular in the eastern and southern regions of China. Always sold in dried form, these thin, white noodles are widely available in 8-ounce and 16-ounce bags. The uses of rice noodles are many: once softened in warm water, they may be stir-fried with an assortment of meat, seafood or vegetables; they may be used in a broth or soup as a delicate garnish; or they may be deep-fried in very hot oil to a light, crisp mass that serves as a bed for stir-fried dishes. Rice stick noodles will keep indefinitely, wrapped, in an airtight container in a cool, dry place. The thinnest variety is recommended for stir-fried dishes and soups. For deep-frying, thin ones are suggested, but thicker noodles may also be used.

Cellophane noodles (*fen si*), also called bean threads or pea starch noodles, are made from mung beans that are first soaked, then ground to a smooth puree, mixed with water and strained to obtain a liquid. The liquid is dried in sheets and made into translucent noodles. When cooked, the noodles are transparent and have a smooth, gelatinous texture. After being softened in warm water, cellophane noodles may be used in soups, stir-fried with a savory sauce or served in cold platters or salads. They also may be deep-fried in the same manner as rice noodles to provide a crisp bed for stir-fried dishes. They absorb a considerable quantity

of the liquid in which they are cooked and, since they have no flavor of their own, assume the flavor of the dish's sauce or broth. Like rice stick noodles, cellophane noodles will keep indefinitely, wrapped, in an airtight container in a cool, dry place.

Bean curd noodles (*gan si*) are made from pressed tofu. They are made from soybeans and so are very rich in protein and low in calories. These noodles are thin and tan. After being softened in a mixture of baking soda and water and then rinsed, they are used primarily in cold dishes. They are usually sold packaged in plastic bags and, unfortunately, may only be available in sizable Chinese communities. An improvised version of bean curd noodles may be made by weighting down firm tofu until most of the water has been pressed out, leaving a compact square. The square is then cut into noodlelike shreds.

In the Far East, most neighborhoods have one or two noodle makers whose shops or stands daily provide a wealth of freshly made noodles, in addition to wonton skins and dumpling wrappers. We may not be quite as lucky in the West, but most Chinese grocery stores offer fresh plain noodles and egg noodles, as well as a generous selection of dried noodles that should fulfill the needs of any recipe. Fresh Chinese noodles are also available at some supermarkets. Alternatively, as outlined in the chart on page 69, fresh or dried Italian pasta may be substituted for the Chinese variety in a number of recipes. Cooking times for noodles vary greatly, depending on the thickness; they should be cooked until just tender but still slightly firm to the bite.

To many Americans, a Chinese noodle dish suggests a vision of chow mein served on a bed of greasy fried noodles. This

Americanized version is a far cry from the subtly seasoned and textured original. The types of noodle dishes are many and may be divided into the following categories:

Soup Noodles: Cooked noodles served in a rich broth with a garnish of seafood, meat or vegetables; or noodles simmered in a flavorful broth and topped with a mixture of seafood, meat or vegetables.

Stir-Fried Noodles: Cooked noodles tossed over heat with a garnish of meat, seafood or vegetables and cooked with a sauce. *Lo mein* dishes fall into this category.

Saucy Noodles: Cooked noodles served on a platter with a garnish of meat, seafood or vegetables and topped with a sauce or dressing. This includes both hot and cold noodle dishes.

Pan-Fried Noodles: Cooked noodles that are fried until crisp and golden, then topped with a garnish of stir-fried meat, seafood or vegetables in a sauce.

Chinese Noodles: Uses & Substitutes

Description	Chinese Name	Use	Substitute
Plain, thin noodles (flour and water)	*gan mian* *ji mian*	soup noodle	spaghettini
Extra-thin noodles, Amoy-style (flour and water)	*mian xian*	soup noodle	vermicelli
Flat noodles (flour and water)	*gan mian, bian-de* *ji mian, bian-de*	soup noodle	fettuccine or linguine
Thin, straight egg noodles (flour, egg and water)	*dan mian*	stir-fried noodle pan-fried noodle saucy noodle	spaghettini
Thin-egg-noodle clusters (flour, egg and water)	*dan mian qui*	stir-fried noodle pan-fried noodle saucy noodle	vermicelli
Fried egg noodles (flour, egg and water)	*yi mian*	stir-fried noodle	*pancit mian* *chuka soba*
Rice stick noodles/rice vermicelli (rice powder and water)	*mi fen*	stir-fried noodle soup noodle saucy noodle	no substitute
Cellophane noodles (bean threads) (pea starch and water)	*fen si*	stir-fried noodle soup noodle saucy noodle	no substitute
Bean curd noodles (tofu)	*gan si*	salads cold platters	no substitute

Cold Tossed Sichuan Noodles

Chuan Wei Ji Si Liang Mian

6 Servings ⌣ Appetizer or Main Dish

THIS TOSSED NOODLE *platter is excellent served as a meal or a starter course for a banquet. Since the climate of Sichuan and Hunan provinces is apt to be muggy and warm, cold noodle platters such as this one are extremely popular. The spicy seasonings in the sauce are intended to sensitize the palate so that the subtler flavors and the various textures may be appreciated. (See photograph, page 82.)*

1	tablespoon peanut, safflower or corn oil
½	pound thin, straight egg noodles
1	tablespoon sesame oil
2	large eggs, lightly beaten
3	cups fresh bean sprouts
1½	cups 1-inch pieces scallion greens
2	cups shredded cooked chicken meat

Peanut Dressing

½	cup chunky peanut butter
½	cup chicken broth, preferably Chinese Chicken Broth (page 345)
3	tablespoons soy sauce
3	tablespoons sesame oil
1½	tablespoons Chinese black vinegar or Worcestershire sauce
1½	teaspoons chili oil
1	tablespoon minced garlic
1	tablespoon minced gingerroot
1½	tablespoons sugar

1. Heat 2 quarts of water and the tablespoon of oil until boiling. Add the noodles, and cook until just tender. Lightly rinse the noodles under cold running water. Drain thoroughly, and toss with the sesame oil. Arrange the noodles on a large round platter or in a serving bowl.

2. Rub a nonstick frying pan or a well-seasoned wok with an oil-soaked paper towel. Heat the pan until a few drops of water sprinkled on the surface evaporate immediately. Add a quarter of the beaten eggs, and tilt the pan so that a thin pancake is formed. Cook until the pancake is lightly golden; then flip over. Cook for a few seconds, and remove. Prepare 3 more egg sheets in the same manner. Cut the egg sheets into matchstick-sized shreds. Lightly rinse the bean sprouts in cold water, and drain thoroughly.

3. Arrange the bean sprouts, the egg-sheet shreds and the scallion greens in a decorative pattern over the noodles. Place the chicken shreds on top. Pour the *Peanut Dressing* over the noodles, toss lightly, and serve.

Cold Spicy Noodles

Zha Jiang Mian

6 Servings ⌣ Main Dish or Snack

1   pound boneless center-cut pork loin

Pork Marinade

1   tablespoon soy sauce
1   tablespoon water
2   teaspoons rice wine or sake
1   teaspoon sesame oil
2   teaspoons cornstarch

1   square firm tofu, about 1 pound
2   medium-sized onions
½   cup peanut, safflower or corn oil
½   pound plain, thin noodles
1   tablespoon sesame oil
1   tablespoon minced garlic

Sauce

½   cup sweet bean sauce
5   tablespoons soy sauce
1   tablespoon rice wine or sake
2   tablespoons sugar

2   cups shredded carrot
2   cups shredded lettuce
2   cups peeled, shredded cucumber

THIS NORTHERN NOODLE *platter features some of the more prominent seasonings of the cuisine of its origin—in particular, sweet bean sauce and garlic. Both flavorings contrast beautifully with the crisp, fresh vegetable shreds and tender meat and tofu pieces. Serve it as a filling meal or as a snack.*

1. Remove any fat or gristle from the pork loin, and discard. Cut the meat into ½-inch dice. Place the pork in a bowl, add the ***Pork Marinade***, toss lightly, and let marinate for 20 minutes. Wrap the tofu in paper towels or a cotton towel and place a heavy weight, such as a skillet, on top. (This will compress the tofu and remove some water.) Unwrap, drain and dice the tofu, and dice the onions.

2. Heat 2 quarts of water and 1 tablespoon of the oil until boiling. Add the noodles, and cook until just tender. Lightly rinse the noodles under cold running water to remove the starch, and toss with the tablespoon of sesame oil. Arrange the noodles on a large platter or in a serving bowl.

3. Heat a wok, add 3½ tablespoons of the remaining oil, and heat until very

hot. Add the diced pork and stir-fry until the color changes. Remove with a handled strainer or slotted spoon, and drain. Wipe out the wok and add 2 of the remaining tablespoons of oil. Heat the oil until very hot. Add the tofu, and cook for about 1 minute, until light golden. Remove in the same manner, and drain. Wipe out the wok and add the remaining 1½ tablespoons of oil to the wok, and heat until very hot. Add the onion and garlic. Stir-fry over high heat, stirring constantly, until the onion is soft and transparent. Add the *Sauce*. Cook for a few minutes over high heat, stirring constantly until the sauce has thickened. Add the cooked pork and tofu. Stir-fry to coat the ingredients with the sauce. Spoon the mixture over a third of the noodles. Arrange the shredded carrot, lettuce and cucumber over the remaining two-thirds of the noodles in a decorative pattern next to the pork mixture. Serve at room temperature or cold. Toss lightly before portioning onto plates.

Cold Tossed Noodle Platter

Liang Ban Mian

6 Servings ⌒ Main Dish

THIS COLD NOODLE *platter defies regional classification; it is found in the cuisines of Peking, Sichuan and Hunan. It is usually served in warm weather, when the crisp textures of the cold, shredded vegetables provide a tasty respite from the heat.*

1	tablespoon peanut, safflower or corn oil
½	pound thin, straight egg noodles
1	tablespoon sesame oil
½	pound fresh bean sprouts
1½	cups cucumber, peeled, seeded and cut into julienne strips
1½	cups carrots, peeled and cut into julienne strips
½	pound medium-sized raw shrimp, shelled, deveined and cooked
¼	cup chopped dry-roasted peanuts

Cold Dressing

6	tablespoons soy sauce
3	tablespoons clear rice vinegar
2	tablespoons rice wine or sake
2	tablespoons sesame oil
1½	tablespoons sugar
1	teaspoon salt

1. Heat 2 quarts of water and the tablespoon of oil until boiling. Add the noodles, and cook until just tender. Lightly rinse the noodles under cold running water, and drain thoroughly. Toss with the sesame oil. Arrange the noodles on a large round platter, and let cool.

2. Rinse the bean sprouts, and drain thoroughly. Arrange the cucumbers and carrots in two decorative rows bordering the edge of the noodles. Place the bean sprouts in the center.

3. Cut the shrimp in half lengthwise, and arrange them, with the pink side up, in a circular row on top of the bean sprouts. Sprinkle the chopped peanuts on top. Before serving, pour the *Cold Dressing* over the noodles, and toss lightly.

Saucy Shrimp Noodles

Xia Ren Chao Mian

6 Servings ⌢ Main Dish

3	tablespoons peanut, safflower or corn oil
½	pound thin, straight egg noodles
1	tablespoon sesame oil
1½	pounds medium-sized raw shrimp, shelled

Shrimp Marinade

2	slices gingerroot, the size of a quarter, smashed with the flat side of a cleaver
2	tablespoons rice wine or sake

Seasonings

2	medium-sized onions, shredded
1	tablespoon minced garlic
1	tablespoon minced gingerroot

Sauce

2	cups chicken broth, preferably Chinese Chicken Broth (page 345)
3	tablespoons soy sauce
2	tablespoons rice wine or sake
1	tablespoon ketchup
1	teaspoon sesame oil
1	tablespoon sugar
½	teaspoon salt

Thickener

2	tablespoons water
1	tablespoon cornstarch

THIS SAUCY NOODLE *platter from the Fujian province reflects a basic characteristic of the eastern regional school—it is simple with delicate seasonings accentuating the natural flavors of the ingredients. The tart and sweet tomato sauce heightens the fresh flavor of the shrimp, which are tossed together with the noodles.*

1. Heat 2 quarts of water and 1 tablespoon of the oil until boiling. Add the noodles, and cook until just tender. Drain the noodles, add the sesame oil to them, and toss lightly. Score each shrimp along the length of the back, and remove the vein; the scoring will allow the shrimp to "butterfly" when it is cooked. Rinse all the shrimp, and drain thoroughly. Place the shrimp in a bowl. Pinch the gingerroot in the *Shrimp Marinade* repeatedly for several minutes to impart its flavor to the mixture. Add the marinade to the shrimp, toss lightly, and let marinate for 20 minutes. Discard the gingerroot.

2. Heat a wok or a pot. Add 2 cups of water, the shrimp and the marinade. Heat until boiling and cook 1 minute, or until the shrimp change color and curl. Remove them with a handled strainer or slotted spoon, and drain. Heat a wok or pan and add the remaining 2 tablespoons of oil and heat until very hot. Add the *Seasonings*, and stir-fry until the onions are soft and transparent. Add the *Sauce*, and heat until boiling. Add the cooked noodles, and toss lightly. Cook for about 1 minute, and add the *Thickener*. Cook until the sauce has thickened and the noodles are coated. Add the cooked shrimp, toss lightly to combine the ingredients, and transfer the mixture to a platter. Serve immediately.

Stir-Fried Rice Noodles With Shrimp

Xia Ren Chao Mi Fen

6 Servings ⌣ Main Dish

THIS FUJIANESE NOODLE *platter is a savory concoction of seafood and vegetables coated with seasoned sauce. The rice stick noodles not only provide a textural contrast to the shrimp and cabbage but act as a staple. The seasonings and varied garnishes make this dish suitable as a meal in itself or as a side dish at a banquet.*

1½   pounds medium-sized raw shrimp, shelled

Shrimp Marinade
2   slices gingerroot, the size of a quarter, smashed with the flat side of a cleaver
1   tablespoon rice wine or sake
1   egg white, lightly beaten, or 1 tablespoon water
1½   teaspoons cornstarch
½   teaspoon salt

1   pound rice stick noodles
6   tablespoons peanut, safflower or corn oil

Shredded Seasonings

 2 tablespoons shredded scallions

 2 teaspoons shredded gingerroot

 4 cups shredded Chinese cabbage (Napa)

Sauce

 1½ cups chicken broth, preferably Chinese Chicken Broth (page 345)

 3 tablespoons soy sauce

 2 tablespoons rice wine or sake

 1 teaspoon sesame oil

 1 teaspoon salt

 ¾ teaspoon sugar

1. Score each shrimp along the length of the back, and remove the vein; the scoring will allow the shrimp to "butterfly" when it is cooked. Rinse all the shrimp lightly, and drain thoroughly. Place the shrimp in a dishtowel, and squeeze out as much moisture as possible. Place the shrimp in a bowl. Pinch the gingerroot slices in the *Shrimp Marinade* repeatedly for several minutes to impart their flavor to the liquid. Add the marinade to the shrimp, toss lightly, and let marinate for 20 minutes. Discard the gingerroot slices. Soften the rice noodles in hot water to cover for 10 minutes. Drain them.

2. Heat a wok, add 1½ tablespoons of the oil, and heat until very hot. Add half the shrimp, and stir-fry over high heat for 1 minute, or until they change color and curl. Remove with a handled strainer or slotted spoon, and drain. Reheat the wok, add 1½ more tablespoons of oil and heat until hot. Add the rest of the shrimp, and cook in the same manner as the first batch. Remove the shrimp from the wok, drain and remove the oil. Wipe out the wok.

3. Reheat the wok, add the remaining 3 tablespoons of oil, and heat until very hot. Add the *Shredded Seasonings*, and stir-fry for about 10 seconds, until fragrant. Add the shredded cabbage, and stir-fry over high heat until it is slightly limp. (If the mixture is very dry, add a tablespoon of rice wine.) Add the *Sauce*, and heat until the mixture is boiling. Add the softened rice noodles, and cook for 1½ minutes over high heat, stirring occasionally. Add the shrimp, toss lightly, and transfer the mixture to a serving bowl. Serve immediately.

Stir-Fried Crabmeat Over Rice Noodles

Xie Rou Chao Xian Nai

6 Servings ⁓ Main Dish

THE COMBINATION OF *colors in this Cantonese platter—with its pink crabmeat and ivory-colored egg-white mixture—suggests the vibrant tones of a red and white hibiscus flower. This dish, therefore, is often classified as a fu rong (fu yung), which is the Chinese name for hibiscus.*

½   pound fresh lump crabmeat

Crabmeat Marinade
2   slices gingerroot, the size of a quarter, smashed with the flat side of a cleaver
1   tablespoon rice wine or sake
½   teaspoon salt

6   large egg whites
½   cup evaporated milk
2   teaspoons cornstarch
1   tablespoon water
1   teaspoon salt
2   cups peanut, safflower or corn oil
2   ounces rice stick noodles
¼   cup shredded scallions
2   ounces Chinese ham, sliced very thinly and cut into julienne strips, or Smithfield ham or prosciutto

1. Pick over the crabmeat, discarding any shell or cartilage that may be remaining. If the crabmeat has been frozen, squeeze out any excess water. Place in a bowl. Pinch the gingerroot slices in the *Crabmeat Marinade* repeatedly for several minutes to impart their flavor to the mixture. Discard the gingerroot. Add the marinade to the crabmeat, toss lightly, and let marinate for 20 minutes. Lightly beat the egg whites until very frothy; fold in the evaporated milk. Combine the cornstarch and water to form a smooth paste, and add it to the egg-white mixture, along with the salt. Blend until smooth.

2. Heat a wok, add the oil, and heat until nearly smoking. Add the rice noodles and deep-fry them until puffed and pale golden. This should happen almost immediately. Turn them over and deep-fry for a few seconds on the other side. Remove the noodles with a long-handled strainer or slotted spoon, and drain on absorbent paper. Transfer them to a large platter and lightly break up the noodles with your fingertips. Remove the oil from the wok, reserving 1 tablespoon.

3. Reheat the wok, add the tablespoon of oil, and when it is hot, add the crab-

meat. Stir-fry over high heat for 10 seconds, stirring constantly. Add the scallion shreds and the Chinese ham. Stir-fry for about 10 seconds over high heat; then add the egg-white mixture. Cook, stirring constantly, until the egg whites have set. Pour the mixture over the fried rice noodles, and serve immediately.

Chicken & Shrimp Noodle Platter

Ji Si Xia Ren Hui Mian

6 Servings ⌣ Main Dish

1	tablespoon peanut, safflower or corn oil
½	pound thin-egg-noodle clusters
1	tablespoon sesame oil
½	pound medium-sized raw shrimp, shelled

Shrimp Marinade

2	slices gingerroot, the size of a quarter, smashed with the flat side of a cleaver
1	tablespoon rice wine or sake
½	teaspoon salt

1	pound boneless chicken breast

Chicken Marinade

1	tablespoon soy sauce
1	tablespoon water
½	tablespoon rice wine
1	teaspoon sesame oil
1	teaspoon cornstarch

6	dried Chinese black mushrooms
9	tablespoons peanut, safflower or corn oil

Minced Seasonings

1	tablespoon minced gingerroot
1	tablespoon minced garlic

2	cups shredded Chinese cabbage (Napa)

I N THIS DISH, CHICKEN *and shrimp garnish a bed of crisp, pan-fried noodles. The pan-fried noodle cake may have inspired the invention of "chow mein," fried noodles sold in cans. In reality, however, one bears little resemblance to the other; the pan-fried noodles should be lightly crisp and golden brown on the outside and soft and tender inside. Although chow mein noodles generally are crisp, they lack the contrasting tenderness and delicacy of their pan-fried cousin.*

4   carrots, peeled and cut into matchstick-sized shreds

Sauce

3   cups chicken broth, preferably Chinese Chicken Broth (page 345)
¼   cup soy sauce
2   tablespoons rice wine or sake
1   teaspoon sesame oil
¾   teaspoon sugar
½   teaspoon freshly ground black pepper

Thickener

5   tablespoons water
3   tablespoons cornstarch

2   cups fresh bean sprouts
1   cup 1-inch pieces scallion greens

1. Heat 2 quarts of water and the 1 tablespoon of oil until boiling. Add the noodles, and cook until just tender. Drain the noodles, and toss with the sesame oil. Place the noodles in a round cake pan or a pie plate, and let cool.

2. Score each shrimp along the length of the back, and remove the vein; the scoring will allow the shrimp to "butterfly" when it is cooked. Rinse all the shrimp, and drain thoroughly. Place the shrimp in a bowl. Pinch the gingerroot slices in the *Shrimp Marinade* repeatedly for several minutes to impart their flavor to the mixture. Discard the gingerroot. Add the marinade to the shrimp, toss lightly, and let marinate for 20 minutes. Remove the skin from the chicken breasts, and discard. Cut the meat on the diagonal into thin slices about 1½ inches on each side, and place them in a bowl. Add the *Chicken Marinade*, toss lightly, and let marinate for 20 minutes. Soak the dried mushrooms in hot water to cover for 20 minutes. Remove and discard the stems, and shred the caps.

3. Preheat the oven to 350 degrees F. Heat a wok (or a cast-iron skillet), add 2 tablespoons of the oil, and heat until nearly smoking. Invert the noodle cake into the pan, and fry the noodles on both sides until golden brown, swirling the pan from time to time to move the noodles so that they cook evenly. Transfer the noodles to a deep, heatproof platter, and place in the preheated oven to keep warm and crisp.

4. Reheat the wok, add 3½ tablespoons of the remaining oil, and heat it to very hot. Add the chicken shreds, and stir-fry over high heat until they change color. Remove them with a handled strainer or slotted spoon, and drain. Reheat the wok, add 1½ tablespoons of oil and heat. Add the shrimp, and stir-fry them for 1½ minutes, until cooked. Remove in the same manner, and drain. Remove

the oil from the wok. Wipe out the wok and reheat. Add the remaining 2 tablespoons of oil, and heat it until very hot. Add the *Minced Seasonings*, and stir-fry for about 10 seconds, until fragrant. Add the mushroom shreds, and stir-fry for about 5 seconds. Add the cabbage and carrot shreds. Toss lightly over high heat until the cabbage is just limp. Add the *Sauce*. Cook until the sauce begins to boil, then add the *Thickener*, stirring constantly to prevent lumps. Add the bean sprouts, scallion greens, chicken and shrimp. Toss lightly to coat the food with sauce. Pour the mixture over the pan-fried noodles. Serve immediately.

Stir-Fried Noodles With Chicken & Leeks

Ji Chao Mian

6 Servings ⁓ Main Dish

1½   pounds boneless chicken breast, skin removed

Chicken Marinade
  1½   tablespoons soy sauce
  1½   tablespoons rice wine or sake
   1   tablespoon water
   1   teaspoon sesame oil
  1½   teaspoons cornstarch

   9   tablespoons peanut, safflower or corn oil
  ¾   pound thin, straight egg noodles
   1   teaspoon sesame oil

Minced Seasonings
   1   tablespoon minced garlic
   1   tablespoon minced gingerroot

  10   dried Chinese black mushrooms, soaked in hot water to cover for 20 minutes, stems removed and caps shredded
   3   cups leeks or Chinese chives, cut into julienne strips about 1½ inches long
   3   cups fresh bean sprouts, lightly rinsed and drained

N OODLES SYMBOLIZE *longevity, and it would be inexcusable for a Chinese birthday menu not to include a noodle dish such as this lo mein. The soft, cooked noodles are tossed in a sauce studded with shredded meat and assorted vegetables. Beef or pork may be substituted for the chicken.*

Noodle Sauce

1½   cups chicken broth, preferably Chinese Chicken Broth (page 345)
¼   cup soy sauce
2   tablespoons rice wine or sake
1   teaspoon sesame oil
1   teaspoon sugar
1   teaspoon cornstarch
¼   teaspoon freshly ground black pepper

1. Remove any fat or gristle from the chicken and cut the meat into matchstick-sized shreds, about 1½ inches long and ¼ inch thick. Place in a bowl, add the *Chicken Marinade*, toss lightly to coat, and let marinade for 20 minutes.

2. Heat 2 quarts of water and 1 tablespoon of the oil until boiling in a large pot. Add the noodles and cook until just tender, about 3 to 5 minutes. Drain in a colander. Rinse lightly under warm water, drain thoroughly in a colander, and transfer the noodles to a bowl. Toss lightly with the sesame oil and set aside.

3. Heat a wok or a skillet, add 3 tablespoons of the oil until very hot, and add half the chicken shreds. Toss lightly over high heat until the chicken pieces change color and separate, about 3 to 4 minutes. Remove with a slotted spoon and drain. Wipe out the wok, and reheat. Add 3 more tablespoons of oil, heat until very hot, and add the remaining chicken. Cook, remove, and drain. Wipe out the wok.

4. Reheat the wok, add the remaining 2 tablespoons of oil and heat until hot. Add the *Minced Seasonings* and black mushrooms, and stir-fry over high heat for 10 to 15 seconds, until fragrant. Add the leeks and stir-fry for about 1 minute, or until slightly limp. Add the bean sprouts and the *Noodle Sauce*. Stir and cook until slightly thickened. Add the cooked noodles and chicken. Toss lightly to coat and transfer to a serving platter.

Pan-Fried Noodles With Beef & Broccoli (PAGE 94)

81

82

Cold Tossed Sichuan Noodles (PAGE 70)
Celery Hearts in Mustard Sauce (PAGE 304)

Shrimp Bonnets (PAGE 114)
Pearl Balls (PAGE 37)
Four-Flavor Dumplings (PAGE 116)

83

Stir-Fried Scallops With Broccoli (PAGE 218)

Hunan-Style Smoked Chicken (PAGE 178)

Seafood Hot Pot With Noodles (PAGE 98)

Crispy-Skin Duck (PAGE 193)
Lotus Buns (PAGE 59)

Red-Cooked Tofu (PAGE 141)

Stir-Fried Chicken in Bird's Nest

Que Chao Ji Ding

6 Servings ～ Main Dish

1½ pounds boneless chicken breast

Chicken Marinade
2 tablespoons water or 1 lightly beaten egg white
1 tablespoon soy sauce
1 tablespoon rice wine or sake
1 teaspoon sesame oil
2 teaspoons cornstarch

1 cup snow peas, ends snapped and veiny strings removed
1 cup peanut, safflower or corn oil
2 ounces rice stick noodles, slightly separated

Minced Seasonings
2 tablespoons minced scallions
1½ tablespoons minced garlic
1 tablespoon minced gingerroot

2 green peppers, cored, seeded and roll-cut into bite-sized pieces
½ pound fresh button mushrooms, rinsed and quartered
1 cup water chestnuts, plunged briefly into boiling water, refreshed in cold water and cut in half crosswise
3 carrots, parboiled for 2 minutes and roll-cut into bite-sized pieces
1 cup baby corn ears, parboiled briefly and drained

Chicken Sauce
½ cup chicken broth, preferably Chinese Chicken Broth (page 345), or water
2 tablespoons soy sauce
2 tablespoons rice wine or sake
1 teaspoon sesame oil
1 tablespoon cornstarch
2 teaspoons sugar
1½ teaspoons salt

THIS COLORFUL *Cantonese platter illustrates one use of rice stick noodles. When deep-fried in hot oil, they puff up and become golden and crisp, resembling a bird's nest. In this form, they provide a delightfully crunchy bed for stir-fried dishes.*

A more complicated bird's nest is made with shredded potatoes or taro, mixed with a little cornstarch and molded in a strainer. The nest is deep-fried until crisp. Both versions form an edible garnish-staple, eliminating the need to serve rice. (See photograph, page 173.)

1. Remove the skin from the chicken, and discard. Cut the meat into 1-inch dice. Place the pieces in a bowl, add the **Chicken Marinade**, toss lightly, and let marinate for 20 minutes. Blanch the snow peas in boiling water for 5 seconds. Remove, and refresh in cold water. Drain, and reserve.

2. Heat a wok, add the oil, and heat the oil to 425 degrees F, or until nearly smoking. Drop the rice noodles into the hot oil, and deep-fry very briefly, until they are puffed and lightly golden. (This should take no longer than 5 seconds.) Turn the noodles over, and fry for a few seconds more. Remove them, and drain on absorbent paper. When they are cool, transfer the noodles to a large platter and break them up lightly with your fingertips. Drain the oil from the wok, reserving ½ cup.

3. Reheat the wok, add 3 tablespoons of the reserved oil, and heat the oil to 375 degrees F. Add half the chicken pieces, and stir-fry over high heat until the color is changed and the pieces are cooked. Remove the chicken with a handled strainer or slotted spoon, and drain. Reheat the wok and add 3 more tablespoons of the reserved oil. Heat until hot and cook the remaining chicken pieces in the same manner. Remove, drain and wipe out the wok. Add the last 2 tablespoons of the reserved oil and heat until very hot. Add the **Minced Seasonings**, and stir-fry for about 10 seconds over high heat. Add the green peppers and the mushrooms. Stir-fry, tossing constantly, for about 15 seconds; then add the water chestnuts, carrots and baby corn ears, and continue mixing until all the ingredients are heated through. Add the **Chicken Sauce**, and mix until it starts to thicken. Add the chicken and the snow peas. Toss lightly to coat with the sauce. Spoon the mixture into the center of the fried rice noodles. Serve immediately.

Li's Chop Suey

Li Gong Shi Sui

6 Servings ~ Main Dish

1   pound boneless center-cut pork loin

Pork Marinade

1   tablespoon soy sauce
2   teaspoons rice wine or sake
2   teaspoons water
1   teaspoon sesame oil

½   pound medium-sized raw shrimp, shelled

Shrimp Marinade

2   slices gingerroot, the size of a quarter, smashed with the
       flat side of a cleaver
1   tablespoon rice wine or sake
½   egg white or 2 teaspoons water
1   teaspoon cornstarch
½   teaspoon salt

2   cups peanut, safflower or corn oil
2   ounces rice stick noodles

Minced Seasonings

2   tablespoons minced scallions
2   teaspoons minced gingerroot

¼   cup dried Chinese black mushrooms, soaked in hot water to
       cover for 20 minutes, stems removed and caps cut into
       matchstick-sized shreds
¼   cup green peppers, seeded and cut into matchstick-sized shreds
½   cup carrots, cut into matchstick-sized shreds
4   cups fresh bean sprouts, lightly rinsed and drained

T HE ORIGIN OF CHOP
*suey is regarded by some
food authorities as a contro-
versial matter; Washington,
D.C., Tokyo and San Francisco
have all been named as the site of
this dish's creation. According to
my Cantonese teacher, who
managed to have the last word
on all issues, chop suey was first
prepared in the early 1900s in
Tokyo for General Li Hon
Chung. The general was so
pleased with the dish that it
was named in his honor. This
recipe offers a subtly seasoned,
authentic rendition of a greatly
abused classic.*

Sauce

¼	cup chicken broth, preferably Chinese Chicken Broth (page 345)
3	tablespoons soy sauce
1½	tablespoons rice wine or sake
1	teaspoon sesame oil
1½	teaspoons cornstarch
1	teaspoon salt
1	teaspoon sugar

1. Remove any fat or gristle from the pork loin, and discard. Cut the meat, across the grain, into slices about ¼ inch thick. (You may partially freeze the pork to facilitate slicing.) Cut the slices into matchstick-sized shreds. Place the shreds in a bowl, add the *Pork Marinade*, toss lightly, and let marinate for 20 minutes.

2. Score each shrimp along the length of the back, and remove the vein; the scoring will allow the shrimp to "butterfly" when it is cooked. Rinse all the shrimp lightly, and drain thoroughly. Place them in a dishtowel, and squeeze out as much moisture as possible. Place the shrimp in a bowl. Pinch the gingerroot slices in the *Shrimp Marinade* repeatedly for several minutes to impart their flavor to the liquid. Add the marinade to the shrimp, toss lightly, and let marinate for 20 minutes. Discard the gingerroot.

3. Heat a wok, add the oil, and heat until nearly smoking. Add the rice noodles, and deep-fry until puffed and pale golden. This should happen almost immediately. Turn them over, and deep-fry for a few seconds on the other side. Remove with a handled strainer or slotted spoon, and drain the noodles on absorbent paper. Transfer them to a large platter; break up the noodles with your fingertips, and create a depression in the center into which the stir-fried ingredients will be placed. Remove the oil from the wok, reserving 6 tablespoons.

4. Reheat the wok, add 3½ tablespoons of the reserved oil, and heat until very hot. Add the pork shreds, and stir-fry over high heat until they have changed color and are cooked. Remove the pork with a handled strainer or slotted spoon, and drain. Add 1 more tablespoon of the reserved oil, and heat until very hot. Add the shrimp, and stir-fry over high heat until they have changed color, about 1 minute. Remove the shrimp, and drain. Remove the oil from the wok. Wipe out the wok.

5. Reheat the wok, add the remaining 1½ tablespoons of oil, and heat until very hot. Add the *Minced Seasonings*, and stir-fry for about 5 seconds, until fragrant. Add the mushrooms and green pepper shreds, and stir-fry for about 10 seconds longer over high heat. Add the carrot shreds, and continue stir-frying for about 1 minute. Add the bean sprouts and the *Sauce*. Toss lightly over high heat, stirstirring constantly to prevent lumps. When the sauce has thickened, add the pork and the shrimp. Toss lightly to coat with the sauce, and pour the mixture into the depression in the fried noodles. Serve immediately.

Stir-Fried Pork With Rice Noodles

Rou Si Chao Mi Fen

6 Servings ⌒ Main Dish

1 pound boneless center-cut pork loin

Pork Marinade
2 tablespoons soy sauce
1 tablespoon rice wine or sake
1 tablespoon water
1 teaspoon sesame oil
2 teaspoons cornstarch

1 pound rice stick noodles
¼ cup peanut, safflower or corn oil

Minced Seasonings
2 tablespoons minced scallions
2 tablespoons minced garlic
1 tablespoon minced gingerroot

2 cups shredded Chinese cabbage (Napa)
1½ cups shredded carrot
2 cups 1-inch pieces scallion greens
2 cups fresh bean sprouts, lightly rinsed

Noodle Sauce
1½ cups chicken broth, preferably Chinese Chicken Broth (page 345)
4½ tablespoons soy sauce
2 tablespoons rice wine or sake
1 teaspoon sesame oil
1½ teaspoons sugar
1 teaspoon salt

1. Remove any fat or gristle from the pork loin, and discard. Cut the meat, across the grain, into slices about ¼ inch thick. (You may partially freeze the meat to facilitate slicing.) Cut the slices into matchstick-sized shreds about 1½ inches long. Place the meat shreds in a bowl, add the *Pork Marinade*, toss lightly,

W HOLE GRAINS OF rice are often ground to a fine powder and used in making very delicate noodles called mi fen—rice stick noodles or, sometimes, rice vermicelli. They are extremely versatile and may be deep-fried, served in soups or stir-fried, as in this dish. They come in dry form and will keep indefinitely stored in an airtight container. To condition them for use in soups and stir-fried dishes, soak them in warm water for 10 minutes, drain, and use as directed in the recipe. Because they are thin, they cook very quickly.

and let marinate for 20 minutes. Soak the rice stick noodles in hot water to cover for 10 minutes. Drain them.

2. Heat a wok, add 3 tablespoons of the oil, and heat the oil to very hot. Add the pork shreds, and stir-fry over high heat until the meat changes color. Remove the meat with a handled strainer or slotted spoon, and drain. Wipe out the wok and add the remaining 1 tablespoon of oil. Reheat until very hot. Add the *Minced Seasonings*, and stir-fry for about 10 seconds, until fragrant. Add the cabbage and carrot shreds, and stir-fry over high heat for about 1 minute, or until the cabbage is limp. Add the cooked meat, the scallions and the bean sprouts. Toss lightly, and add the *Noodle Sauce.* Add the rice stick noodles. Cook for about 1½ minutes over high heat. Transfer the mixture to a platter, and serve immediately.

Pan-Fried Noodles With Beef & Broccoli

Niu Rou Chao Mian

6 Servings ～ Main Dish

ALTHOUGH HARDLY AN innovative creation, this Cantonese classic is a favorite in Chinese restaurants across the globe. After tasting the crisp noodles drenched in velvety oyster sauce, the tender beef slices and broccoli spears, one can easily understand the popularity of the dish. (See photograph, page 81.)

10	tablespoons peanut, safflower or corn oil
½	pound thin-egg-noodle clusters *(thin vermicelli)*
1	teaspoon sesame oil
1½	pounds eye-of-round or top sirloin roast

Beef Marinade
2	tablespoons soy sauce
2	tablespoons water
1	tablespoon rice wine or sake
1	teaspoon sesame oil
2	teaspoons minced garlic
2	teaspoons cornstarch
1	teaspoon sugar
1	pound broccoli

Minced Seasonings
2	tablespoons minced gingerroot
2	tablespoons minced scallions

94

Sauce

3	cups chicken broth, preferably Chinese Chicken Broth (page 345)
6	tablespoons oyster sauce
¼	cup soy sauce
2	tablespoons rice wine or sake
2	teaspoons sesame oil
2	teaspoons sugar

Thickener

4	tablespoons water
3	tablespoons cornstarch

1. Heat 2 quarts of water and 1 tablespoon of the oil until boiling. Add the noodles, and cook until just tender. Drain the noodles, and toss them with the sesame oil. Place the noodles in a round cake pan or a pie plate, and let cool.

2. Remove any fat or gristle from the beef, and discard. Cut the meat, with the grain, into 2 or 3 strips about 1½ inches long. Turn and cut the meat across the grain, into slices ⅛ inch thick. (You may partially freeze the beef to facilitate slicing.) Place the meat in a bowl, add the *Beef Marinade*, toss lightly, and let marinate for 1 hour or longer. Drain the meat slices. Peel away the tough outer skin of the broccoli, and separate the florets. Roll-cut the stems into 1-inch pieces. Heat 1½ quarts salted water until boiling. Add the stem pieces, and cook for ½ minute. Add the florets, and cook for 2½ minutes, or until both stems and florets are just tender. Refresh immediately in cold water. Drain thoroughly.

3. Preheat the oven to 350 degrees F. Heat a wok or a cast-iron skillet, add 2 tablespoons of the oil, and heat until nearly smoking. Invert the noodle cake into the pan, and fry the noodles on both sides until golden brown, swirling the pan from time to time to move the noodles so that they cook evenly. Transfer the noodles to a deep, heatproof platter, and place in the preheated oven to keep warm and crisp.

4. Reheat the wok, add 3 tablespoons of the oil, and heat it to very hot. Add half the beef slices, and cook for about 1 minute, stirring constantly, until the beef changes color. Remove with a handled strainer or slotted spoon, and drain. Wipe out the wok and add 3 tablespoons oil. Add the remaining beef slices, and stir-fry in the same manner. Remove and drain. Wipe out the wok and add the remaining 1 tablespoon of oil and reheat until very hot. Add the *Minced Seasonings*, and stir-fry until fragrant, about 10 seconds. Add the *Sauce*, and heat until boiling. Add the *Thickener*, stirring constantly to prevent lumps. Add the beef and the broccoli. Toss lightly to coat with the sauce and heat through. Pour the mixture over the pan-fried noodles, and serve immediately.

Spicy Sheer Noodles (Ants on a Tree)

Ma Yi Shang Shu

6 Servings ⌢ Side Dish

THE BITS OF GROUND *pork entwined in the soft cellophane noodles are said to bear a resemblance to ants climbing a tree, giving this classic Sichuanese dish its name.*

½	pound ground pork or beef

Meat Marinade

1	teaspoon soy sauce
1	teaspoon rice wine or sake
½	teaspoon sesame oil

2	ounces cellophane noodles (bean threads)
1	tablespoon peanut, safflower or corn oil

Minced Seasonings

2	tablespoons minced scallions
1	tablespoon minced gingerroot
1	teaspoon minced garlic

1½	teaspoons chili paste

Sauce

2	cups chicken broth, preferably Chinese Chicken Broth (page 345)
2	tablespoons soy sauce
1	tablespoon rice wine or sake
1	teaspoon sesame oil
1	teaspoon salt
1	teaspoon sugar

2	tablespoons minced scallion greens

1. Place the ground meat in a bowl, add the *Meat Marinade*, toss lightly to combine, and let marinate for 20 minutes. Soften the cellophane noodles in hot water to cover for 10 minutes.

2. Heat a wok, add the oil, and heat until hot. Add the ground meat, and cook, mashing and separating it, until it changes color. Push the meat to the side of the wok, add the *Minced Seasonings*, and stir-fry for about 5 seconds, until fragrant. Add the chili paste, and stir-fry for another 5 seconds. Add the *Sauce*

and the drained cellophane noodles. Toss lightly to combine all the ingredients, and heat until boiling. Reduce the heat to low, and cook for 8 minutes, until almost all the liquid has evaporated. Transfer the mixture to a serving bowl, and sprinkle the top with the minced scallion greens. Serve immediately.

Three-Treasure Rice Noodles
San Xian Mi Fen
6 Servings ⌢ Main Dish or Side Dish

¾   pound thin rice noodles (*mi fen*)
2   tablespoons peanut, safflower or corn oil

Minced Seasonings
1½   tablespoons minced garlic
1½   tablespoons minced gingerroot

¼   pound fresh shiitake mushrooms, rinsed, drained and cut into thin julienne strips (fresh button mushrooms may be substituted)
3   cups shredded leeks or 1-inch-long scallion sections
1½   cups finely shredded carrots
1½   tablespoons rice wine or sake

Sauce
½   cup chicken broth, preferably Chinese Chicken Broth (page 345)
4½   tablespoons soy sauce
2   tablespoons rice wine or sake
2   teaspoons sesame oil
1   teaspoon salt
1   teaspoon sugar

My surrogate Chinese mother often prepared rice noodles with assorted meats and vegetables for special or everyday meals. This vegetarian version is substantial enough to be served as a main course, but lightly seasoned so that it is perfect as a staple in place of rice. Toss the noodles gently so that they remain whole.

1. Place the rice noodles in warm water to cover for about 20 minutes. Remove and drain.

2. Heat a wok or a skillet, add the oil, and heat until hot. Add the *Minced Seasonings* and stir-fry for about 10 seconds, until fragrant. Add the shredded mushrooms, leeks and carrots, and toss lightly over high heat. Add the rice wine and cook for about 1½ to 2 minutes. Add the *Sauce* and heat until boiling. Add the rice noodles and cook for a few minutes until the noodles have absorbed the liquid. Toss lightly and transfer to a platter. Serve.

Seafood Hot Pot With Noodles

San Xian Sha Guo Mian

6 Servings ⌣ Main Dish

SANDY POTS ARE covered earthenware vessels. They are well suited to slow braising, since the clay conducts and distributes heat evenly, and they may be used over direct heat or in the oven. This noodle pot, with its colorful array of seafood, is a feast for the eyes and the palate. Serve it as a meal or as one of the courses in a banquet. (See photograph, page 86.)

Oyster Marinade

2 slices gingerroot, the size of a quarter, smashed with the flat side of a cleaver

1 tablespoon rice wine or sake

2 scallions, smashed with the flat side of a cleaver

½ teaspoon salt

1 pint fresh, shucked oysters

Shrimp Marinade

2 slices gingerroot, the size of a quarter, smashed with the flat side of a cleaver

1 tablespoon rice wine or sake

½ teaspoon sesame oil

1 teaspoon salt

½ pound medium-sized raw shrimp in their shells or shelled

Scallop Marinade

2 slices gingerroot, the size of a quarter, smashed with the flat side of a cleaver

1 tablespoon rice wine or sake

½ teaspoon sesame oil

½ teaspoon salt

½ pound fresh sea scallops

Fish Marinade

2 slices gingerroot, the size of a quarter, smashed with the flat side of a cleaver

1 tablespoon rice wine or sake

½ teaspoon salt

1   pound firm-fleshed fish fillets, skin removed, diagonally cut
    into thin slices 1½ inches long and 1 inch wide

1   tablespoon peanut, safflower or corn oil
2   cups Chinese cabbage (Napa), cut into 2-inch squares

Soup Base
6   cups chicken broth, preferably Chinese Chicken Broth (page 345)
2   tablespoons rice wine or sake
1½ teaspoons salt

1   tablespoon peanut, safflower or corn oil
½   pound flat noodles
¼   cup minced leeks or scallion greens

1. Prepare the *Oyster*, *Shrimp*, *Scallop* and *Fish Marinades*, pinching the gingerroot slices in the rice wine repeatedly for several minutes to impart their flavor. Discard the gingerroot slices. Mix the seafoods with their respective marinades, and let them marinate separately for 20 minutes.

2. Heat a wok, add the oil, and heat until nearly smoking; add the cabbage pieces. Stir-fry for about 30 seconds, adding 1 tablespoon of the *Soup Base*. Add the rest of the soup base, and heat until boiling. Reduce the heat to low, partially cover, and cook for 30 minutes. Meanwhile, heat 4 quarts of water and 1 tablespoon of oil until boiling. Add the noodles and cook until just tender. Drain and rinse the noodles. Place the noodles in a sandy pot or in a Dutch oven. Pour the cabbage-broth mixture on top. Arrange the oysters, shrimp, scallops and fish on top of the cabbage, keeping each one separate from the others. Sprinkle the minced leeks over the top, and cover. Cook the casserole over high heat for 5 to 7 minutes (until the seafood is just cooked) or in a preheated 450-degree oven. Serve immediately from the pot.

Sesame Chicken With Rice Noodles in Broth

Ma You Ji Mi Fen

6 Servings ⁓ Main Dish or Snack

THIS SAVORY FUJIANESE *(Eastern regional) soup is traditionally served to a mother every day for one month following childbirth, for it is believed that the chicken and gingerroot rejuvenate the body.*

1	small roasting chicken, 3½-4 pounds
½	pound rice stick noodles
¼	cup sesame oil
6	tablespoons shredded gingerroot
1	cup rice wine or sake

Soup Base

5	cups water
2	teaspoons sugar
2	teaspoons salt

1. Remove and discard any fat from inside the cavity and around the neck of the chicken. Cut the chicken, through the bones, into bite-sized serving pieces about 2 inches square, as for Red-Cooked Chicken (page 181). Plunge the chicken pieces into boiling water for 1 minute to clean them. Rinse in cold water, and drain. Soften the rice noodles in hot water to cover for 10 minutes. Drain.

2. Heat a heavy soup pot or a 3-quart Dutch oven. Add the sesame oil, and heat until very hot. Add the gingerroot, and stir-fry over high heat for about 5 seconds, until fragrant. Add the chicken pieces, and fry in the hot oil until golden brown on both sides. Add the rice wine, and heat until boiling. Add the *Soup Base*, and heat until the liquid is boiling. Reduce the heat to low, and cook the chicken, uncovered, for 1¼ hours. Add the rice noodles, and cook for 1½ minutes, or until they are very tender. Serve immediately.

Barbecued Pork With Noodles in Broth

Cha Shao Tang Mian

6 Servings 〜 Main Dish

1 pound boneless center-cut pork loin

Pork Marinade
1½ tablespoons hoisin sauce
1 tablespoon soy sauce
1 tablespoon rice wine or sake
1 teaspoon ketchup
½ tablespoon minced garlic
2 teaspoons sugar
1 teaspoon salt

1 pound broccoli
3 tablespoons peanut, safflower or corn oil
½ pound plain, thin noodles

Minced Seasonings
2 tablespoons finely shredded scallions
1 tablespoon finely shredded gingerroot

Pork Sauce
½ cup chicken broth, preferably Chinese Chicken Broth (page 345), or water
3 tablespoons oyster sauce
2 tablespoons soy sauce
2 tablespoons rice wine or sake
1 teaspoon sesame oil
1½ teaspoons sugar
1½ teaspoons cornstarch
¾ teaspoon salt

THIS TRADITIONAL *Cantonese "soup noodle" dish may be found both in sumptuous dim-sum parlors and at small hole-in-the-wall noodle stands.*

Soup Mixture

6	cups chicken broth, preferably Chinese Chicken Broth (page 345)
1	tablespoon rice wine or sake
½	teaspoon sesame oil
1½	teaspoons salt
¼	teaspoon freshly ground black pepper

1. To prepare the barbecued pork, place the pork loin in a bowl with the *Pork Marinade*. Turn the pork to coat it with the marinade, and let marinate for at least 1 hour or overnight. Place the meat on a rack in a roasting pan. Preheat the oven to 375 degrees F. Bake the pork for 40 to 45 minutes, or until the meat is cooked. Remove, and let cool. Cut the meat into slices 1½ inches long, 1 inch wide and about ⅛ inch thick. Cut each slice in half lengthwise. Peel away the tough outer skin from the broccoli, and separate the florets. Roll-cut the stems into 1-inch pieces. Heat 1½ quarts salted water until boiling. Add the stem pieces, and cook for ½ minute. Add the florets, and cook for 2½ minutes, or until both stems and florets are just tender. Refresh immediately in cold water. Drain thoroughly.

2. Heat 2 quarts of water and 1 tablespoon of the oil until boiling. Add the noodles, and cook until barely tender. Drain them. Portion the noodles into 6 soup bowls.

3. Heat a wok, add the remaining 2 tablespoons of oil, and heat until very hot. Add the *Minced Seasonings*, and stir-fry for about 10 seconds, until fragrant. Add the *Pork Sauce*, and stir until thickened. Add the pork slices and the broccoli. Toss lightly to coat the ingredients with the sauce, and set aside.

4. Heat the *Soup Mixture* until boiling, and ladle it over the noodles in each bowl. Spoon some of the pork-broccoli mixture on top of each portion, and serve.

Pork & Vegetable Noodles in Broth

Da Lu Mian

6 Servings 〜 Main Dish

1	pound boneless center-cut pork loin

Pork Marinade

1	tablespoon soy sauce
2	teaspoons rice wine or sake
2	teaspoons water
1	teaspoon sesame oil
1	teaspoon cornstarch

18	dried lily buds
12	dried wood ears
6	dried Chinese black mushrooms
6½	tablespoons peanut, safflower or corn oil

½	pound extra-thin flour-and-water noodles (Amoy-style)

Minced Seasonings

2	tablespoons minced scallions
1	tablespoon minced garlic
2	teaspoons minced gingerroot

Pork Sauce

1	cup chicken broth, preferably Chinese Chicken Broth (page 345)
2½	tablespoons soy sauce
1	tablespoon rice wine or sake
1	teaspoon sesame oil
1	teaspoon Chinese black vinegar or Worcestershire sauce
1	teaspoon sugar
½	teaspoon freshly ground black pepper
1	tablespoon cornstarch

THE CATEGORY OF *"soup noodles"* includes those dishes in which the cooked noodles are served in a rich broth and garnished with a saucy topping of stir-fried meat and vegetables. Like many other noodle platters, this dish may be served as a meal in itself for lunch or dinner or as a hearty and filling snack. (See photograph, page 172.)

Soup Base

6	cups chicken broth, preferably **Chinese Chicken Broth (page 345)**
2	tablespoons soy sauce
2	tablespoons rice wine or sake
2	teaspoons sesame oil
1	teaspoon salt

3	tablespoons cornstarch
4	tablespoons water

1	pound fresh spinach, trimmed and cleaned
3	large eggs, lightly beaten

1. Remove any fat or gristle from the pork loin, and discard. Cut the meat, across the grain, into slices ⅛ inch thick. (You may partially freeze the pork to facilitate slicing.) Cut the slices into pieces that are approximately 1½ inches square. Place the slices in a bowl, add the *Pork Marinade*, toss lightly, and let marinate for 20 minutes. Meanwhile, soak the lily buds, wood ears and dried mushrooms separately in hot water to cover for 20 minutes. Drain. Remove and discard the mushroom stems, and cut the mushroom caps in half. Cut away and discard the hard, bitter nib on the underside of the wood ears, and cut the wood ears into bite-sized pieces, if necessary. Tie the lily buds into knots.

2. Heat 2 quarts water and 1 tablespoon of the oil until boiling. Add the noodles, and cook until just tender. Drain the noodles, and portion them into 6 soup bowls.

3. Heat a wok, add 3½ tablespoons of the oil, and heat the oil until very hot. Add the pork slices, and stir-fry over high heat until the meat changes color. Remove with a handled strainer or slotted spoon, and drain. Wipe out the wok, reheat, add the remaining 2 tablespoons of oil to the wok, and heat until very hot. Add the *Minced Seasonings*, and stir-fry for about 10 seconds, until fragrant. Add the mushrooms, wood ears and lily buds. Stir-fry for about 15 seconds over high heat, and add the *Pork Sauce*. Toss lightly until the sauce has thickened, add the pork slices, and stir to coat the pork. Remove the mixture from the wok, and set aside.

4. Place the *Soup Base* in a saucepan. Heat until boiling. In a small bowl, dissolve the cornstarch in the water. Add it to the soup base, stirring constantly to prevent lumps. Add the spinach, and remove from the heat. Slowly pour in the eggs in a thin stream. Stir the soup once or twice, and ladle the broth over the noodles. Spoon the pork mixture over the noodles, and serve immediately.

Beef With Noodles in a Pot

Niu Rou Guo Shao Mian

6 Servings ⌒ Main Dish

1   pound eye-of-round or top sirloin roast

Beef Marinade

1   tablespoon soy sauce
½   tablespoon rice wine or sake
2   teaspoons water
1   teaspoon sesame oil
2   teaspoons minced garlic
1   teaspoon cornstarch

12   dried Chinese black mushrooms
1   square firm tofu, about 1 pound
5½   tablespoons peanut, safflower or corn oil
½   pound flat noodles

Minced Seasonings

2   tablespoons minced scallions
1   tablespoon minced gingerroot

2   medium-sized tomatoes, seeded and diced
2   green peppers, cored, seeded and diced
1   tablespoon soy sauce
1   tablespoon rice wine or sake

Soup Base

6   cups chicken broth, preferably Chinese Chicken Broth (page 345)
2   tablespoons soy sauce
1   tablespoon rice wine or sake
1   teaspoon sesame oil
2   teaspoons salt
1   teaspoon sugar
¼   teaspoon freshly ground black pepper

1   pound fresh spinach, trimmed and cleaned

1. Trim any fat or gristle from the beef, and discard. Cut the meat, with the

T HIS HEARTY NOODLE *pot, with its flavorful garnish of meat and vegetables, constitutes a filling and nutritious meal.*

grain, into strips that are about 2 inches long and 2 inches thick. Cut each strip, across the grain, into slices about ⅛ inch thick. (You may partially freeze the beef to facilitate slicing.) Place the meat slices in a bowl, add the *Beef Marinade*, toss lightly, and let marinate for 20 minutes.

2. Soak the dried mushrooms in hot water to cover for 20 minutes. Drain them, and remove and discard the stems. Cut the caps in half. Cut the tofu into 1-inch cubes.

3. Heat 2 quarts of water and 1 tablespoon of the oil until boiling. Add the noodles, and cook until barely tender. Remove, drain, and place the noodles in a heatproof earthenware casserole or a Dutch oven.

4. Heat a wok, add 3½ tablespoons of the remaining oil, and heat the oil until very hot. Add the beef slices, and cookover high heat, stirring constantly, until the beef is cooked through. Remove with a handled strainer or a slotted spoon, and drain. Wipe out the wok and add the remaining 1 tablespoon of oil. Heat until very hot. Add the *Minced Seasonings*, and stir-fry for about 10 seconds, until fragrant. Add the tomatoes, green peppers, soy sauce and rice wine. Stir-fry for about 10 seconds. Add the mushrooms, and stir-fry for another 5 seconds over high heat. Add the tofu and the *Soup Base*. Heat the mixture until boiling, reduce the heat to medium, and cook, uncovered, for 8 minutes. Pour the soup mixture over the noodles. Arrange the beef slices and the spinach on top, cover, and place over high heat. Heat until the liquid is boiling and the spinach is just wilted. Remove the lid and serve.

Vegetarian Noodles in Broth
Su Cai Geng Mian
6 Servings ⌣ Side Dish or Main Dish

WESTERN VEGETARIAN cookery is often said to be somewhat bland, but Chinese vegetarian cuisine is just the opposite. Pungent seasonings, such as garlic, gingerroot and sesame oil, appear frequently, and contrasting textures are accentuated. This vegetarian noodle platter is a good example.

2	tablespoons peanut, safflower or corn oil
½	pound extra-thin flour-and-water noodles (Amoy-style)
6	dried Chinese black mushrooms
3	tablespoons dried wood ears
2	carrots, roll-cut into 1-inch pieces
1	cup straw mushrooms
¼	pound fresh snow peas, ends snapped and veiny strings removed

Minced Seasonings

1	tablespoon minced garlic
1	tablespoon minced shallots
2	teaspoons minced gingerroot

3 cups Chinese cabbage (Napa), cut in 2-inch squares

Soup Base
 6 cups liquid (water plus the dried-mushroom liquid)
 2½ tablespoons soy sauce
 2 tablespoons rice wine or sake
 1 teaspoon sesame oil
 1 teaspoon salt
 ¼ teaspoon freshly ground black pepper

Thickener
 6 tablespoons water
 ¼ cup cornstarch

 1 cup 1-inch pieces scallion greens
 1 tablespoon sesame oil

1. Heat 2 quarts water and 1 tablespoon of the oil until boiling. Add the noodles, and cook until just tender. Drain the noodles, and portion them into 6 serving bowls.

2. Soak the dried mushrooms and wood ears separately in hot water to cover for 20 minutes. Reserve the mushroom-soaking liquid, discard the stems of the mushrooms, and cut the large caps in half. Cut away and discard the hard, bitter nib on the underside of the wood ears, and cut the wood ears into bite-sized pieces, if necessary. Cook the carrot pieces for 1 minute in boiling water to cover, and refresh in cold water. Parboil the straw mushrooms and snow peas separately in boiling water to cover for 5 seconds. Remove and refresh immediately in cold water. Drain thoroughly.

3. Heat a wok, add the remaining 1 tablespoon of oil, and heat until very hot. Add the *Minced Seasonings*, and stir-fry until fragrant, about 10 seconds. Add the harder pieces of the Chinese cabbage, and stir-fry over high heat until slightly limp at the edges. Add the leafier sections, and continue stir-frying for about 20 seconds over high heat. (If the cabbage is very dry, add 1 tablespoon rice wine.) Add the *Soup Base* (including the mushroom-soaking liquid), and cook, uncovered, for 10 minutes over medium heat. Add the black mushrooms, carrot pieces, straw mushrooms and wood ears, and continue cooking for 1 minute. Add the *Thickener*, stirring constantly to prevent lumps. Add the snow peas and the scallions. Stir lightly to coat, and add the sesame oil. Toss again, and spoon the mixture over the noodles. Serve immediately.

Dumplings

THE CHINESE NEW YEAR ARRIVES in Taipei with much fanfare and ritual. Several weeks before the holiday, which usually falls in January or February, on the first month of the lunar calendar, telltale signs of its advent are clearly visible; clotheslines usually festooned with laundered pantaloons and tunics become burdened with the weight of fragrant coils of freshly made sausage. The marketplace, filled to the brim with the usual bounty of shellfish, meat and fish, offers such unusual New Year's delicacies as sweet rice cake (*nian gao*), red and white sweet rice balls and mountainous stacks of dried shark's fin, bird's nests and silver ears—prime ingredients for the New Year's banquet. The frequent boom of firecrackers exploding in the streets—set off to ward away evil spirits— becomes more pronounced as the holiday approaches, and the air fairly tingles with the electricity of expectation and excitement—for this is the most important holiday of the Chinese lunar calendar.

In Chinese homes, preparations begin at least a month in advance. Houses are cleaned from top to bottom, new clothes for the entire family are made or purchased, and the kitchen teems with activity from early morning until late at night, as many dishes are made ready for the feasting. Much of the cooking for the holiday is done in advance.

In northern China, a custom that has been observed for centuries still exists today: women friends and relatives gather before the holiday to prepare several hundred *jiao zi*, meat dumplings or Peking ravioli. The finished dumplings are arranged on trays and left to freeze in the chill winter air. During the holiday, a cauldron of water is boiled, the desired number of dumplings are cooked, and a hot, filling meal is ready in minutes. Often a silver coin is placed inside one of the dumplings, signifying good luck in the coming year for the recipient.

Some families prefer to pan-fry the dumplings (in this case, they are called *guo tie*), creating a golden brown crust that gives the ravioli the appearance of golden coins.

The Cantonese are fond of a New Year's dumpling made of sweet (glutinous) rice and a filling of powdered sesame seeds and sugar. This pastry is believed to symbolize completeness and is served to celebrate the family unit and ensure a healthy harvest and a bountiful year. In some parts of eastern China, these dumplings are eaten two weeks after the New Year, whereas in Fujian, an eastern province north of Canton, they are consumed during the Mid-Autumn Festival and are often dusted with a mixture of sesame seeds, ground peanuts and sugar.

Obviously, dumplings have a prominent place in Chinese cuisine; they are prepared in numerous variations for holidays and festivals, and they are consumed on a daily basis in several parts of China. In the north, where wheat provides the area with its wealth of noodles and steamed breads, dumplings frequently act as a staple substitute for rice, in addition to being served as a meal in themselves. The same is true in western China. In the east and the south, dumplings are considered to be a type of dim sum (*dian xin*) and are commonly served as a snack with tea or wine.

The origin of dumplings is undocumented, but it is believed that these pastries, along with other wheat products, were introduced to China from the west—most likely Persia or central Asia. They quickly were adapted to Chinese ingredients and were incorporated into the daily diet. As these snacks were adopted by various cuisines, their ingredients were altered slightly, depending on the products of that area. In the north, dumplings were filled with lamb, pork and chives. In Sichuan province, the filling included a mixture of pork, cabbage and dried shrimp. And in the eastern and southern regions, more delicate variations of the dumpling evolved (such as *hun dun* and *shao mai*), with stuffings of shrimp, bamboo shoots and black mushrooms. The methods of cooking dumplings have regional characteristics as well; in the north, they are boiled, whereas in the east, they are steamed on beds of pine needles that have been anointed with sesame oil.

By the late Sung dynasty (960 to 1279),

the ancient city of Hangzhou contained a number of food shops that prepared multitudes of dumplings for the masses. Later, in the Ch'ing dynasty (1644 to 1911), dumplings of various kinds signified the arrival of the many festivals: green dumplings with lotus root appeared during the third month of the lunar calendar. Sweet rice dumplings with sweet bean sauce were prepared for the Kitchen God Festival, celebrated on the twenty-fourth day of the twelfth lunar month. (Since these dumplings are believed to soften bones and cartilage, the initial binding of young girls' feet was performed on this day.) During the first five days of the fifth lunar month, the Dragon Boat Festival was observed, and sweet and savory dumplings wrapped in lotus leaves appeared, created as a tribute to the spirit of Chü Yuan, an ancient statesman and poet who drowned himself in the Mi-Lo River as a protest against the corruption of the government.

These snacks still exist today and are prepared as they were centuries ago—lasting tributes to traditional holiday customs.

Dumpling Skins

Jiao Zi Pi

50 Skins

2½ cups all-purpose flour plus more if necessary
1¼ cups boiling water

In Taiwan, all neigh-
borhood markets host a noodle
maker who turns out mountains
of fresh noodles, wonton skins
and dumpling skins daily. The
texture of these fresh pasta
products is positively silky in
comparison to the commercially
prepared kind. Making
dumpling skins at home is a
time-consuming process, but the
result is certainly worth the
work. If necessary, however,
store-bought dumpling skins
(goyoza) are acceptable.
Dumpling skins may be frozen if
tightly wrapped in plastic.

1. Place the flour in a mixing bowl, and add the boiling water. With a wooden spoon, mix the ingredients to a rough dough. If the dough is too hot to handle, let it cool a bit; then turn it out onto a lightly floured surface, and knead for about 5 minutes, until it is smooth and elastic. If the dough is sticky, knead in a few more tablespoons of flour. Cover the dough with a towel, and let it rest for 25 minutes.

2. Cut the dough in two, and form each half into a long, snakelike roll about 1 inch in diameter. Cut each half into 25 pieces. With a cut edge down, press each piece into a circle. Using a small rolling pin or a tortilla press that has been lightly floured, roll out each piece on a lightly floured surface to a 3-inch circle. Cover the circles with a cloth or towel to prevent them from drying out. Use as directed in the individual recipes.

Meat Dumplings

Jiao Zi

50 Dumplings ⌣ Appetizer or Main Dish

5   cups finely minced Chinese cabbage (Napa)
1   teaspoon salt
¾   pound ground pork
2   cups finely minced Chinese garlic chives or 1 cup minced
    leeks plus 1 tablespoon minced garlic

Dumpling Seasonings
2   tablespoons soy sauce
2   tablespoons sesame oil
1   tablespoon rice wine or sake
1   tablespoon minced gingerroot
1½ teaspoons minced garlic
1   tablespoon cornstarch plus more if necessary

50 Dumpling Skins, homemade (page 110) or store-bought
    dumpling skins

MEAT DUMPLINGS *typify the hearty, wholesome qualities of northern home-style cooking. Traditionally they are filled with pork and cabbage and seasoned with a generous amount of Chinese garlic chives. These versatile pastries may be boiled, steamed, pan-fried or deep-fried. Ten or fifteen of the dumplings, depending on the capacity of the diner, make a filling and nutritious meal.*

1. Place the minced cabbage in a large mixing bowl, add the salt, toss lightly to mix evenly, and let sit for 30 minutes to remove the water from the cabbage, so the filling will not soak through the dumpling skins. Take a handful of the minced cabbage and squeeze out as much water as possible. Place the squeezed cabbage in a mixing bowl. Squeeze out the water from the rest of the cabbage and discard the water. Add the ground pork, minced chives and the *Dumpling Seasonings*, and stir vigorously in one direction to combine the ingredients evenly. If the mixture seems loose, add another tablespoon of cornstarch.

2. Place a heaping teaspoon of filling in the center of each Dumpling Skin and fold the skin over to make a half-moon shape. Spread a little water along the edge of the skin. Use the thumb and index finger of one hand to form small

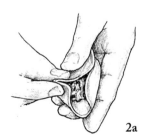

2a

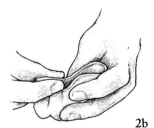

2b

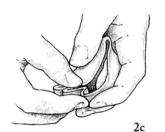

2c

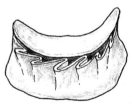

2d

pleats along the outside edge of the skin (**a**); with the other hand, press the two opposite edges of the skin together to seal (**b**). The inside edge of the dumpling should curve in a semicircular fashion to conform to the shape of the pleated edge (**c**). Place the sealed dumplings (**d**) on a baking sheet that has been lightly dusted with cornstarch.

3. In a large wok or pot, bring about 3 quarts of water to a boil. Add half the dumplings, stirring immediately to prevent them from sticking together, and heat until the water begins to boil. Add ½ cup cold water and continue cooking over high heat until the water boils. Add another ½ cup of cold water and cook until the water boils again. Remove and drain. Cook the remaining dumplings in the same manner. (This is the traditional method of cooking dumplings; for a simpler method, boil them for about 8 minutes, uncovered, over high heat.) Serve the boiled dumplings with one of the following *Dipping Sauces:*

Dipping Sauce I

| ½ | cup soy sauce |
| 3 | tablespoons Chinese black vinegar or Worcestershire sauce |

Dipping Sauce II

½	cup soy sauce
2	tablespoons Chinese black vinegar or Worcestershire sauce
1	tablespoon chili oil (for homemade chili oil, see page 16)

Variation

Add 1 tablespoon shredded gingerroot or minced garlic to either of the above sauces.

Pan-Fried Meat Dumplings
Guo Tie

25 Dumplings ⌢ Main Dish or Snack

3½   tablespoons peanut, safflower or corn oil
½   recipe Meat Dumplings (page 111), prepared as directed through step 2
1   cup boiling water

Heat a large wok or a well-seasoned skillet until very hot. Add 3 tablespoons of the oil, and heat until very hot. Arrange the dumplings, pleated side up, to line the bottom of the pan. They should be packed closely together in a circular pattern. Fry the dumplings over medium-high heat until their bottoms are a deep golden brown. Add the boiling water to the pan, and cover. Reduce the heat to low, and cook for about 10 minutes. Uncover, and pour out the water. Place the pan containing the dumplings over medium-high heat. Drizzle the remaining ½ tablespoon of oil around the dumplings, and fry until the bottoms are again crisp, about 2 minutes. Use a spatula to loosen any dumplings that seem to be sticking to the bottom. Invert the dumplings directly onto a platter. Serve with either of the *Dipping Sauces* on the previous page.

L ITERALLY TRANSLATED, *guo tie* means "pot stickers," *and anyone who has not used a well-seasoned pan to cook these dumplings will understand the appropriateness of this title; the dumplings often refuse to dislodge themselves from the pan. In their perfect form, the fried dumplings have a crusty, golden surface that enhances their flavor.*

Shrimp Bonnets

Xia Jiao

30 Dumplings ⌣ Appetizer, Main Dish or Snack

SHRIMP BONNETS *(commonly called har gow on Cantonese menus) are a common and popular sight in any Cantonese dim-sum parlor. With their delicate filling of chopped shrimp and water chestnuts and their translucent skins, these dumplings make a fine, light appetizer. The texture of their skin is a result of the blending of two starch flours—wheat starch and tapioca starch. Wheat starch is the powder remaining from flour once the gluten has been removed, and tapioca starch is a product of the cassava root, or manioc plant, which is native to the West Indies. Since the shrimp is so lean, a bit of pork fat is usually added to the filling to help hold it together. (See photograph, page 83.)*

1	pound medium-sized raw shrimp, shelled
½	cup water chestnuts
1	ounce pork fat, finely chopped to a paste (optional)

Dumpling Seasonings

1	tablespoon rice wine or sake
2	teaspoons soy sauce
2	teaspoons sesame oil
1	egg white
2	teaspoons minced scallions
1½	teaspoons minced gingerroot
2	tablespoons cornstarch
1	teaspoon salt
½	teaspoon sugar
¼	teaspoon freshly ground white pepper

Homemade Dumpling Dough (recipe follows) or 30 store-bought dumpling skins

Homemade Dumpling Dough

1¼	cups wheat starch
½	cup tapioca starch
1	cup boiling water
2	teaspoons peanut, safflower or corn oil

Soy sauce

1. Devein the shrimp, rinse lightly, and drain thoroughly. Place the shrimp in a dishtowel, and squeeze out as much excess moisture as possible. Cut the shrimp into ¼-inch dice. Plunge the water chestnuts into boiling water for a few seconds to remove the tinny flavor. Refresh in cold water, and mince them. Place the shrimp, water chestnuts, pork fat, if using, and the *Dumpling Seasonings* in a mixing bowl. Stir the ingredients in one direction to combine evenly. Refrigerate for 20 minutes.

2. If making the *Homemade Dumpling Dough*, place the wheat starch and tapioca starch in a mixing bowl, and combine well. Add the boiling water,

stirring constantly to prevent lumps. Add the oil, and mix to a rough dough. Turn the dough out onto a counter, and knead lightly for about 2 minutes, until smooth. Cut the dough in half, and form each half into a long, snakelike roll about 1 inch in diameter. Cut each roll into 15 pieces. Cover the pieces with a damp cloth.

3. Lightly grease a cleaver, and place a piece of the dough, cut edge down, on the counter. Place the cleaver blade parallel to the counter, flat on the dough. Press down on the blade, and turn it clockwise so that the dough is pressed out to form a thin circle about 2½ inches in diameter. Repeat the process for the remaining dough pieces. Alternatively, you may use a tortilla press: Place a square of plastic wrap in the press, or lightly brush it with oil; place a section of dough, cut edge down, in the press, and press out to a thin circle. (A ravioli rolling pin may also be used.)

4. Shrimp Bonnets are formed in the same way as Meat Dumplings, page 111: Place a heaping teaspoon of the filling in the center of one circle, and fold the skin over to make a half-moon shape. Use the thumb and index finger of one hand to form small pleats on the outer edge of the dumpling skin; with the other hand, press the two opposite edges of the skin together to seal. The inside edge of the dumpling skin should curve in a semicircular fashion to conform to the shape of the pleated edge. Make the remaining dumplings in the same manner. Place the sealed dumplings about ¼ inch apart in 2 steamer trays that have been lined with wet cheesecloth or with parchment paper punched with holes.

5. Fill a wok with water level with the bottom edge of a steamer tray, and heat until boiling. Stack the steamer trays in the wok, and cover. Steam for 12 minutes over high heat, reversing the trays after 6 minutes. Serve with soy sauce.

Four-Flavor Dumplings

Se Fang Shao Mai

50 Dumplings ～ Main Dish, Snack or Appetizer

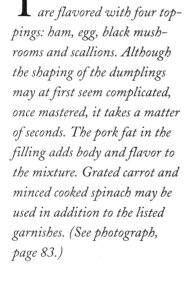

THESE SAVORY DUMPLINGS are flavored with four toppings: ham, egg, black mushrooms and scallions. Although the shaping of the dumplings may at first seem complicated, once mastered, it takes a matter of seconds. The pork fat in the filling adds body and flavor to the mixture. Grated carrot and minced cooked spinach may be used in addition to the listed garnishes. (See photograph, page 83.)

1	pound medium-sized raw shrimp, shelled
½	cup water chestnuts
1	ounce pork fat, finely chopped to a paste (optional)

Dumpling Seasonings

½	egg white
1	tablespoon rice wine or sake
2	teaspoons soy sauce, preferably light
2	teaspoons sesame oil
2	teaspoons minced scallions
1½	teaspoons minced gingerroot
2	tablespoons cornstarch
1	teaspoon sugar
½	teaspoon salt
¼	teaspoon freshly ground white pepper

50	Dumpling Skins (page 110) or Shao Mai Skins (page 119) or store-bought dumpling skins

Dumpling Garnishes

½	cup minced cooked ham
½	cup minced hard-boiled egg
½	cup minced dried Chinese black mushrooms (about 7-8 whole), soaked in hot water to cover for 20 minutes, stems removed and caps minced
½	cup minced scallion greens

Soy sauce

1. Devein the shrimp, rinse lightly, and drain thoroughly. Place the shrimp in a dishtowel, and squeeze out as much moisture as possible. Mince the shrimp to a coarse paste. Plunge the water chestnuts into boiling water for a few seconds to remove the tinny flavor. Refresh them in cold water, and chop coarsely. Place the shrimp, water chestnuts, pork fat, if using, and *Dumpling Seasonings* in a mixing bowl. Stir vigorously in one direction to combine evenly. Refrigerate the filling for 20 minutes.

2. Place a teaspoon of filling in the center of a Dumpling Skin. Dip a finger in cold water, and dot four points equidistant from one another at the centers and at points midway around the edge of the skin. Gather together the opposite edges of the skin (**a**), and press to seal them at these four points (**b**). The dumpling should look something like a four-leaf clover, with round openings replacing the "leaves." Further enlarge the openings with a chopstick, and fill each opening with a different minced *Dumpling Garnish*—ham, egg, mushroom and scallion (**c**). Make the remaining dumplings in the same manner. Arrange the finished dumplings (**d**) about ¼ inch apart in 2 steamer trays that have been lined with wet cheesecloth or with parchment paper punched with holes.

3. Fill a wok with water level with the bottom edge of a steamer tray, and heat until boiling. Stack the steamer trays in the wok, cover, and steam for 15 minutes over high heat, reversing the trays once. Serve with soy sauce. To reheat, steam for 5 minutes over high heat.

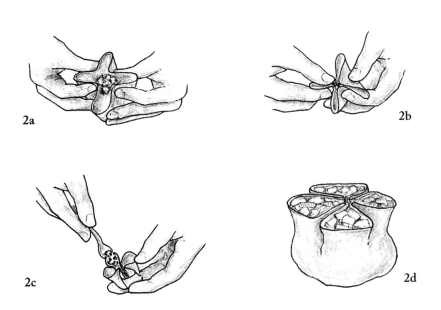

2a

2b

2c

2d

Phoenix-Eye Dumplings

Feng Yan Shao Mai

50 Dumplings 〜 Main Dish, Snack or Appetizer

THE FILLING MIXTURE *for these dumplings is a combination of ground pork, shrimp, black mushrooms and shredded carrot.*

The phoenix, a symbol of beauty and peace, has long been revered by the Chinese. A number of dishes are said to have been inspired by this mythical bird and so bear its name. Such is the case with this dumpling, which is said to resemble the eye of a phoenix.

¼	pound medium-sized raw shrimp, shelled
4	dried Chinese black mushrooms
½	cup water chestnuts
¾	pound ground pork
¼	cup shredded raw carrot

Dumpling Seasonings

2	teaspoons soy sauce
2	teaspoons sesame oil
1	teaspoon rice wine or sake
2	tablespoons minced scallions
2	teaspoons minced gingerroot
2	tablespoons cornstarch
¼	teaspoon freshly ground black pepper

50 Dumpling Skins (page 110) or Shao Mai Skins (page 119) or store-bought dumpling skins

Soy sauce

1. Devein the shrimp, rinse lightly, and drain thoroughly. Place the shrimp in a dishtowel, and squeeze out as much excess moisture as possible. Mince the shrimp to a coarse paste. Soak the dried mushrooms in hot water to cover for 20 minutes. Remove and discard the stems, and mince the caps. Plunge the water chestnuts into boiling water for a few seconds to remove the tinny flavor. Refresh them in cold water, and chop coarsely. Place the shrimp paste, mushrooms, water chestnuts, ground pork, shredded carrot and *Dumpling Seasonings* in a mixing bowl. Stir vigorously in one direction to combine the ingredients evenly.

2. Place a teaspoon of filling in the center of one Dumpling Skin. Gather the opposite edges together (**a**), and pinch at the midpoint of each edge to join the two sides at the center (**b**). (Use a dab of water as an adhesive.) Place your index

2a

2b

2c

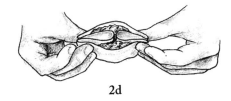

2d

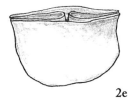

2e

fingers in the holes at each end of the dumpling, and draw the opposite edges together again from each side (**c**), pinching at the midpoints (**d**). Make the remaining dumplings in the same manner. Arrange the shaped dumplings (**e**) ¼ inch apart on 2 steamer trays that have been lined with wet cheesecloth or with parchment paper punched with holes.

3. Fill a wok with water level with the bottom edge of a steamer tray, and heat until boiling. Stack the steamer trays in the wok, cover, and steam for 15 minutes over high heat, reversing the trays after 8 minutes. Serve with soy sauce. To reheat, steam for 5 minutes over high heat.

Shao Mai Skins or Wonton Wrappers

Shao Mai Pi, Yun Dun Pi

50 Skins

1⅓	cups all-purpose flour
1	teaspoon salt
1	large egg, lightly beaten
¼	cup cold water

1. Place the flour and salt in a mixing bowl, and combine. Add the egg and water. Using a wooden spoon, blend the mixture into a rough dough. Turn the dough out onto a lightly floured surface, and knead for about 5 minutes, until smooth and elastic. If it is sticky, knead in a few tablespoons of flour. Cover the dough with a cloth or towel, and let it rest for 25 minutes.

2. Cut the dough in half. Using a small rolling pin or a pasta machine, roll out each half to a rectangle (about ¹⁄₁₆ inch thick). Using a ruler, cut a 3-inch square for a Wonton Wrapper and use that square as a guide for making the rest of the wrappers, or cut 3-inch circles for the Shao Mai Skins. Cover the wrappers or skins with a cloth or towel to prevent them from drying out. Use as directed in the individual recipes.

T HIS VERSATILE EGG *dough may be used to make egg noodles and Cantonese spring roll skins, as well as wonton wrappers and shao mai skins. The wrappers or skins, lightly floured or dusted with cornstarch, may be frozen if wrapped securely in plastic.*

Shao Mai

Shao Mai

30 Dumplings ～ Main Dish, Snack or Appetizer

SOME PURISTS CONSIDER the addition of seafood to the traditional, all-meat shao mai filling an act just short of sacrilege, but I believe the shrimp adds additional depth and contrast in flavor. Shrimp, prawns or crabmeat may be substituted for the carrot garnish to create a more exotic dumpling.

¼ pound medium-sized raw shrimp, shelled
½ cup water chestnuts
1 pound ground pork

Shao Mai Seasonings
1 egg white
1 tablespoon rice wine or sake
2 teaspoons soy sauce
2 teaspoons sesame oil
1 tablespoon minced scallions
2 teaspoons minced gingerroot
2 tablespoons cornstarch
1 teaspoon salt
½ teaspoon sugar
¼ teaspoon freshly ground black pepper

30 Shao Mai Skins (page 119) or Dumpling Skins (page 110) or store-bought dumpling skins
½ cup shredded carrot

1. Devein the shrimp, rinse lightly, and drain thoroughly. Place the shrimp in a dishtowel, and squeeze out as much moisture as possible. Mince the shrimp to a coarse paste. Plunge the water chestnuts into boiling water for a few seconds to remove the tinny flavor. Refresh them in cold water, and chop coarsely. Place the shrimp, water chestnuts, ground pork and the *Shao Mai Seasonings* in a mixing bowl, and stir vigorously in one direction to combine the ingredients evenly.

2. Place a heaping tablespoon of filling in the center of one Shao Mai Skin (a). Gather up the edges of the skin around the filling. Holding the shao mai between your thumb and index finger, lightly squeeze it to form a "waist"; at the

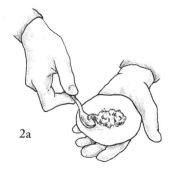

2a

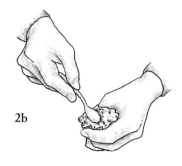

2b

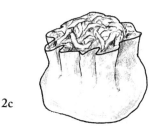

2c

same time, push up the filling from the bottom with the other hand, creating a flat bottom. Smooth the surface of the filling with the flat of a knife or spoon dipped in water (**b**). Sprinkle the surface with the shredded carrot. Make the remaining dumplings in the same manner. Arrange the shaped shao mai (**c**) about ¼ inch apart in 2 steamer trays that have been lined with wet cheesecloth or with parchment paper punched with holes.

3. Fill a wok with water level with the bottom edge of a steamer tray, and heat until boiling. Stack the steamer trays in the wok, cover, and steam the dumplings for 15 minutes over high heat, reversing the trays after 8 minutes. To reheat, steam for 5 minutes over high heat.

Wontons in Broth

Yun Dun Tang

6 Servings ⌣ Main Dish or Snack

¼	pound medium-sized raw shrimp, shelled
¼	cup water chestnuts
½	pound ground pork

Wonton Seasonings

2	teaspoons soy sauce
2	teaspoons rice wine or sake
1½	teaspoons sesame oil
1	teaspoon minced gingerroot
1½	tablespoons cornstarch
½	teaspoon salt
¼	teaspoon freshly ground black pepper

30	Wonton Wrappers (page 119) or store-bought wrappers

Broth

6	cups chicken broth, preferably Chinese Chicken Broth (page 345)
3	tablespoons soy sauce
1	tablespoon rice wine or sake
1	teaspoon sesame oil
1	teaspoon salt

1	pound fresh spinach, trimmed and cleaned
2	tablespoons minced scallion greens

L ITERALLY TRANSLATED, *yun dun* means "swallowing a cloud," which is very appropriate considering the appearance of the finished dish: delicate wontons suspended in clear chicken broth amidst fresh green spinach, evoking (perhaps with a little imagination) clouds floating in the sky. Imagery aside, the dish is pleasing as a light lunch or dinner or as a filling snack.

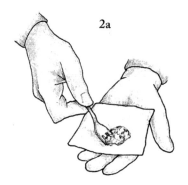

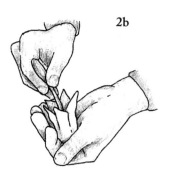

1. Devein the shrimp, rinse lightly, and drain thoroughly. Place the shrimp in a dishtowel, and squeeze out as much moisture as possible. Mince the shrimp to a coarse paste. Plunge the water chestnuts into boiling water for a few seconds to remove the tinny flavor. Refresh them in cold water, and chop coarsely. Place the shrimp, water chestnuts, ground pork and *Wonton Seasonings* in a mixing bowl. Stir vigorously in one direction to combine the ingredients evenly.

2. Using a fork (or spoon), place a scant teaspoon of the filling in the center of one Wonton Wrapper (**a**). Gather the edges of the skin together around the filling, and squeeze to form a "waist" (**b**). Gradually remove the fork. Squeeze the waist completely to enclose the filling. Place the finished wontons (**c**) on a tray that has been dusted with cornstarch or flour.

3. Heat 4 quarts of water until boiling. Add the wontons, and cover. Cook for 5 to 6 minutes, or until the wontons have risen to the surface. Using a handled strainer or a colander, remove the wontons. Portion them into 6 serving bowls.

4. Place the *Broth* in a pot, and heat until boiling. Add the spinach, and cook briefly, just until it is barely wilted. Pour the hot soup over the wontons in the bowls. Sprinkle the top with the scallion greens, and serve immediately.

Fried Wontons

Zha Yun Dun

30 Wontons ⁓ Appetizer or Main Dish

¼   pound medium-sized raw shrimp, shelled
½   cup water chestnuts
½   pound ground pork

Wonton Seasonings
1½   tablespoons soy sauce
2   teaspoons rice wine or sake
1½   teaspoons sesame oil
2   teaspoons minced scallions
1½   teaspoons minced gingerroot
1½   tablespoons cornstarch
½   teaspoon salt
¼   teaspoon freshly ground black pepper

30   Wonton Wrappers (page 119) or store-bought wrappers
3   cups peanut, safflower or corn oil

Sweet & Sour Dipping Sauce
¼   cup water
3   tablespoons ketchup
1   tablespoon clear rice vinegar
1   teaspoon soy sauce
½   teaspoon sesame oil
3   tablespoons sugar
2   teaspoons cornstarch
1   teaspoon salt

THE VERSATILITY OF *wontons is apparent, since these savory pastries may be deep-fried, steamed or boiled in a broth. Whatever the cooking method, they are appropriately served as a snack or as a light meal. I often serve fried wontons as an hors d'oeuvre with drinks. Their crisp, dry texture is excellent with wine or beer.*

1. Devein the shrimp, rinse lightly, and drain thoroughly. Pat the shrimp dry with paper towels, and chop coarsely. Plunge the water chestnuts into boiling water for a few seconds to remove the tinny flavor. Refresh them in cold water, and chop coarsely. Place the shrimp, water chestnuts, ground pork and *Wonton Seasonings* in a mixing bowl, and stir vigorously in one direction to combine the ingredients evenly.

2a

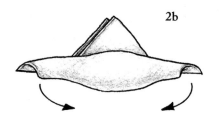

2b

2c

2. Place a scant teaspoon of the filling in the center of one Wonton Wrapper. Fold the wrapper over to form a triangle (**a**). Working from the longest straight edge, fold in the wrapper to a point three-quarters of the length from the opposite edge. Dip a finger in some water, and dab the ends of the triangle; press the two ends together, and pinch to seal (**b**). Make the remaining wontons in the same manner. Place the finished wontons (**c**) on a tray that has been dusted with cornstarch or flour.

3. Heat a wok, add the oil, and heat the oil to 350 degrees F. Add a batch of wontons, and deep-fry for 3 to 4 minutes, until the skins are golden brown and crisp and the filling is cooked. Remove with a handled strainer or slotted spoon, and drain on absorbent paper. Reheat the oil, and deep-fry the remaining wontons in the same manner. Serve with *Sweet & Sour Dipping Sauce*. (To prepare the dipping sauce, stir together the ingredients in a saucepan, and heat until boiling and thickened, stirring constantly.)

Curry Turnovers

Jia Li Jiao

35 Turnovers ⌣ Appetizer or Main Dish

½   pound ground pork or beef

Meat Marinade
- 1   teaspoon soy sauce
- 1   teaspoon rice wine or sake
- ½   teaspoon sesame oil

- ¼   cup peanut, safflower or corn oil
- ¾   cup minced onion
- 1   tablespoon curry powder

Filling Sauce
- ½   cup chicken broth, preferably Chinese Chicken Broth (page 345)
- 2   teaspoons sugar
- 1   teaspoon salt

Thickener
- 2   tablespoons water
- 1   tablespoon cornstarch

Turnover Dough
- 2   cups all-purpose flour
- 1   teaspoon salt
- ⅔   cup shortening or lard
- ⅓   cup ice water

Egg Wash
- 1   large egg, lightly beaten
- 1   tablespoon water
- ½   teaspoon salt

*I*N THE TRADITIONAL *recipe for this snack, two doughs—one that is very "short," or tender, made of lard and flour, and another that is less so—are combined and folded together in a manner similar to that used in making puff pastry. Since I find this process slightly tedious, I have adapted the recipe to create a much simpler dough. Although traditionally the turnovers are deep-fried, I prefer to bake them. Either cooking method may be used. They freeze beautifully. Freeze them uncooked and bake them while still frozen.*

1. Place the ground meat in a bowl, add the *Meat Marinade*, and toss lightly.

2. Heat a wok, add 2 tablespoons of the oil, and heat until hot. Add the ground meat, and cook over high heat, stirring constantly to break up the meat, until it changes color. Remove the meat, and drain.

3. Heat a wok, add the remaining 2 tablespoons of oil, and heat until very

6a
6b
6c
6d

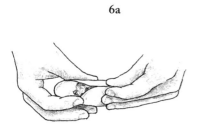
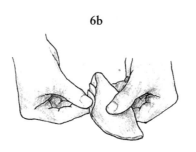
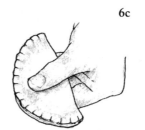
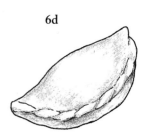

hot. Add the minced onion, and stir-fry until soft and transparent. Add the curry powder, and stir-fry for about 15 seconds, until very fragrant. Add the *Filling Sauce*, and heat until boiling. Slowly add the *Thickener*, stirring constantly, and cook until thick. Add the cooked meat, toss lightly to coat with the sauce, and transfer the mixture to a platter. Refrigerate until cool.

4. To make the *Turnover Dough*, combine the flour and salt in a bowl. Cut the shortening into the flour until the mixture is the consistency of cornmeal. Add the water, and mix lightly until the dough is smooth and homogeneous. (Do not overwork the dough.) Divide the dough in two, wrap each piece in plastic wrap, and refrigerate for 20 minutes.

5. Preheat the oven to 400 degrees F. On a lightly floured surface, roll out half the dough to a large rectangle about ⅛ inch thick. Using a round 3-inch cookie cutter, cut out circles. Gather the scraps together into a ball, and chill. Roll out the other half of the dough, and cut more circles. Gather up the scraps, and combine with the scraps from the first half. Roll out, and cut more circles. Repeat until all the dough is used.

6. Place a teaspoon of the curry filling in the center of one dough circle, and fold it over to make a half-moon shape. Pinch the two edges together to seal and enclose the filling (**a**). Seal the edge tightly by scalloping by hand (**b**) into a decorative pattern (**c**) or crimping with a fork. Place the finished turnovers (**d**) on 2 baking sheets, and brush with the *Egg Wash*. Bake for 20 minutes in the preheated oven. Cool the turnovers, and serve.

Savory Baked Turnovers

Jiu Cai Su Bing

35 Turnovers ～ Appetizer or Main Dish

¾   pound boneless center-cut pork loin

Pork Marinade
- 2   teaspoons soy sauce
- 1½   teaspoons rice wine
- ½   teaspoon sesame oil

⅓   pound medium-sized raw shrimp, shelled

Shrimp Marinade
- 1   teaspoon rice wine or sake
- 1   slice gingerroot, the size of a quarter, smashed with the flat side of a cleaver
- ½   teaspoon salt

4½   tablespoons peanut, safflower or corn oil
6   dried Chinese black mushrooms, soaked in hot water to cover for 20 minutes, stems removed and caps cut into ¼-inch dice
½   cup minced scallions or leeks

Filling Sauce
- 2   tablespoons soy sauce
- 2   tablespoons chicken broth, preferably Chinese Chicken Broth (page 345)
- 1   tablespoon rice wine or sake
- 2   teaspoons sesame oil
- ½   tablespoon cornstarch
- ½   teaspoon salt
- ½   teaspoon sugar

Turnover Dough
- 2   cups all-purpose flour
- 1   teaspoon salt
- ⅓   cup butter plus ⅓ cup lard
- ⅓   cup ice water

THE SOFT FILLING OF pork, shrimp and black mushrooms contrasts with the crisp skin. Customarily, lard is used in Chinese pastry because it provides a flaky texture and a rich taste. Westerners may feel more comfortable using vegetable shortening, margarine or half butter and half lard. I am partial to the last combination, since the butter provides a pleasing flavor and the lard the proper texture.

Egg Wash

1 large egg, lightly beaten
1 tablespoon water
1 teaspoon salt

1. Remove any fat or gristle from the pork, and discard. Cut the meat into ¼-inch dice. Place the pork in a mixing bowl, add the *Pork Marinade*, toss lightly, and let marinate for 20 minutes. Devein the shrimp, rinse lightly, and drain thoroughly. Pat dry with paper towels, and cut into ¼-inch dice. Place the shrimp in a bowl, add the *Shrimp Marinade*, toss lightly, and let marinate for 20 minutes. Discard the gingerroot.

2. Heat a wok, add 2 tablespoons of the oil, and heat until very hot. Add the diced pork, and stir-fry until the color changes, about 1½ minutes. Remove, and drain. Add another 2 tablespoons of oil, and heat until very hot. Add the diced shrimp, and stir-fry until the color changes, about 1 minute. Remove, and drain. Reheat the wok, add the remaining ½ tablespoon of oil, and heat until very hot. Add the mushrooms, and stir-fry for about 5 seconds, until fragrant. Add the minced scallions, and stir-fry for another 10 seconds. Add the *Filling Sauce*, and cook, stirring constantly over high heat, until thick. Add the pork and shrimp, toss lightly to coat with the sauce, and remove. Transfer the mixture to a platter, and refrigerate until cool.

3. To make the *Turnover Dough*, combine the flour and salt in a bowl. Cut the butter and lard into the flour until the mixture is the consistency of corn-meal. Add the ice water, and mix lightly until the dough is smooth and homogeneous. (Do not overwork the dough.) Divide the dough in two, wrap each piece in plastic wrap, and refrigerate for 20 minutes.

4. Preheat the oven to 400 degrees F. On a lightly floured surface, roll out half the dough to a large rectangle about ⅙ inch thick. Using a round 3-inch cookie cutter, cut out circles. Gather the scraps together into a ball, and chill. Roll out the other half of the dough, and cut out more circles. Gather up the scraps, and combine with the scraps from the first half. Roll out, and cut more circles. Repeat until all the dough is used. (You should have 35 turnovers.)

5. These turnovers are formed in the same manner as Curry Turnovers, page 125: Place a teaspoon of the filling in the center of one dough circle, and fold it over to make a half-moon shape. Pinch the two edges together to seal and enclose the filling. Seal the edge tightly by scalloping by hand into a decorative pattern or crimping with a fork. Place the finished turnovers on 2 baking sheets, and brush with the *Egg Wash*. Bake for 20 minutes in the preheated oven. Cool the turnovers, and serve.

Flaky Chinese Turnip Cakes
Luo Bo Si Bing
24 Cakes ⁓ Appetizer or Snack

2½ cups finely shredded daikon radish (Chinese turnip)
1 teaspoon salt
1 cup peanut, safflower or corn oil
½ pound Chinese pork sausage, cut into ¼-inch dice (for homemade, see page 275)

Filling Seasoning
2 teaspoons rice wine or sake
2 teaspoons sesame oil
½ teaspoon salt
¼ teaspoon freshly ground black pepper

Dough
2 cups all-purpose flour
1 cup cake flour
1 teaspoon salt
⅓ cup butter plus ⅓ cup lard
⅓ cup ice water

T URNIP CAKES ARE
*frequently served as a
Chinese New Year's snack; their
fried golden exteriors are said to
resemble golden coins. They were
so popular in my household in
Taipei that we made and served
them year-round. I have simpli-
fied the skin by substituting a
simple dough for the more complicated one normally used. The
slightly sweet daikon radish is
studded with bits of Chinese
sausage and encased in a flaky
crust. They make terrific hors
d'oeuvres.*

1. Place the shredded daikon in a bowl, add the salt, toss lightly, and let sit for 20 minutes. Squeeze out any water that has accumulated, and set the shredded turnip aside.

2. Heat a wok, add ½ tablespoon of the oil, and heat until very hot. Add the diced sausage, and stir-fry over low heat, stirring constantly for about 2 minutes, until the sausage is golden and most of the fat has been rendered. Remove the sausage with a handled strainer or slotted spoon, and drain.

3. Remove all but 2 tablespoons of fat from the wok, and heat until hot. Add the shredded daikon, and stir-fry over high heat until tender, about 2 minutes. Add the sausage and the *Filling Seasoning*. Toss lightly over high heat for about 30 seconds. Transfer the filling to a platter, and refrigerate until cool.

4. To make the *Dough*, combine the flours and salt in a mixing bowl. Add the butter and lard, and cut it into the flour until the mixture is the consistency of cornmeal. Add the water, and mix lightly until the dough is smooth and homogeneous. (Do not overwork the dough.) Wrap the dough in plastic wrap, and refrigerate for 20 minutes.

5. Roll out the dough to a rectangle about ⅙ inch thick. Using a round 4-inch

cookie cutter, cut out circles. Gather the scraps together into a ball, and chill for 15 minutes. Roll out the dough again, and cut out more circles, making 24 in all.

6. Place a tablespoon of the filling in the center of one dough circle. Gather up the edges of the circle, and pinch to seal, enclosing the filling and forming a ball. Lightly flatten each cake into a round approximately 2½ inches wide.

7. Heat a large skillet, and add the remaining oil. Heat the oil to 375 degrees F. Spacing the turnip cakes in the pan, fry over medium heat on both sides until crisp and golden brown, about 5 minutes per side. Remove with a handled strainer or slotted spoon, and drain on absorbent paper. Reheat the oil, and fry the remaining cakes in the same manner. Arrange on a platter, and serve.

Fried Shrimp & Sweet Potato Turnovers

Xia Ren Yu Jiao

24 Turnovers ⁓ Appetizer or Snack

I N THE ORIGINAL RECIPE *for these turnovers, taro, a starch root vegetable, is used as the base of the dough. Since this vegetable is available only on a seasonal basis in sizable Chinese communities, I often substitute sweet potato, mashing it to a paste and shaping it into a dough. The texture of the crust is sweeter than fried potato, crisp outside and soft and tender within.*

¾	pound boneless center-cut pork loin

Pork Marinade

2	teaspoons soy sauce
1½	teaspoons rice wine or sake
½	teaspoon sesame oil
¼	pound medium-sized raw shrimp, shelled

Shrimp Marinade

1	teaspoon rice wine or sake
1	slice gingerroot, the size of a quarter, smashed with the flat side of a cleaver
½	teaspoon salt
3	cups peanut, safflower or corn oil
6	dried Chinese black mushrooms, soaked in hot water to cover for 20 minutes, stems removed and caps cut into ¼-inch dice

Filling Sauce

2	tablespoons soy sauce
2	tablespoons chicken broth, preferably Chinese Chicken Broth (page 345)
1	tablespoon rice wine or sake
1	teaspoon sesame oil
½	tablespoon cornstarch
½	teaspoon salt
½	teaspoon sugar

Turnover Dough

1	pound sweet potato or taro, cooked and mashed to a smooth puree
¼	cup shortening or lard, at room temperature
1	cup cornstarch plus more if needed
1½	teaspoons salt

1. Remove any fat or gristle from the pork loin, and discard. Cut the meat into ¼-inch dice. Place the pork in a mixing bowl, add the *Pork Marinade*, toss lightly, and let the pork marinate for 20 minutes. Devein the shrimp, rinse lightly, and drain thoroughly. Pat dry with paper towels, and cut into ¼-inch dice. Place the shrimp in a bowl, add the *Shrimp Marinade*, pinching the ginger slices in the rice wine to impart their flavor. Toss lightly, and let the shrimp marinate for 20 minutes. Discard the gingerroot.

2. Heat a wok, add 2 tablespoons of the oil, and heat until very hot. Add the diced pork, and stir-fry until the color changes, about 1½ minutes. Remove, and drain. Add another 2 tablespoons of oil to the pan, and heat until very hot. Add the diced shrimp, and stir-fry until the color changes, about 1 minute. Remove, and drain. Reheat the pan, add ½ tablespoon of oil, and heat until very hot. Add the black mushrooms, and stir-fry until fragrant, about 5 seconds. Add the *Filling Sauce*, and cook, stirring constantly over high heat, until thick. Add the pork and shrimp, toss lightly to coat with the sauce, and remove. Refrigerate this mixture until it is cool. Clean the wok.

3. To make the *Turnover Dough*, place the pureed sweet potato in a bowl, add the shortening, and mix until smooth. Refrigerate this mixture for 1 hour, covered, in the bowl. Add the cornstarch and salt, and mix to form a smooth dough. (If the dough is too sticky, add more cornstarch.) Form the dough into a long, snakelike roll about 1¼ inches in diameter, and cut it into 24 pieces. Sprinkle them with a little cornstarch.

4. These turnovers are formed in the same manner as Curry Turnovers, page 125: Using your fingers, flatten one dough piece into a 2½-inch circle, and place a heaping teaspoon of the filling in the center. Fold the skin over to make a half-moon shape; pinch the edges together to seal. (Handle the skins lightly, and

sprinkle with cornstarch if sticky.) Crimp the edge decoratively, and place the turnover on a baking sheet that has been lightly dusted with cornstarch. Make the remaining turnovers in the same way.

5. Reheat the wok, add the remaining oil, and heat the oil to 375 degrees F. Add 6 or 7 of the turnovers to the wok. Deep-fry over high heat until they are golden brown and crisp. Remove with a handled strainer or slotted spoon, and drain on absorbent paper. Reheat the oil, and deep-fry the remaining turnovers in the same manner. Serve hot. To reheat, bake in a 350-degree oven until crisp and piping hot.

Sweet-Rice Shao Mai

Nuo Mi Shao Mai

36 Shao Mai ⌣ Snack

*S*HAO MAI, OR OPEN-
*faced dumplings are a
well-known Cantonese dim
sum, characterized by their
unique shape. Though the more
popular version has a filling of
pork, water chestnuts and
shrimp, the addition of sweet rice
creates a flavorful, more substantial pastry. Serve these steamed
dumplings with soup as a filling
lunch or supper.*

1	cup sweet (glutinous) rice
2	tablespoons peanut, safflower or corn oil

Shao Mai Garnishes

10	dried Chinese black mushrooms, soaked in hot water to cover for 20 minutes, stems removed and caps diced (½ cup minced)
1½	cups diced cooked pork loin
½	cup diced medium-sized cooked shrimp
¼	cup minced scallion greens

Shao Mai Sauce

3	tablespoons soy sauce
2	tablespoons rice wine or sake
2	tablespoons chicken broth, preferably Chinese Chicken Broth (page 345)
1	teaspoon sesame oil
1	teaspoon sugar
¼	teaspoon freshly ground black pepper
36	Dumpling Skins (page 110), Shao Mai Skins (page 119) or store-bought dumpling skins

1. Using your fingers as a rake, rinse the rice in cold running water until the water runs clear. Place the rice in cold water to cover, and let soak for 1 hour. Drain, and place in a saucepan with 1 cup water. Place the saucepan over high

heat, and heat until the liquid boils. Turn the heat to low, cover, and cook for 20 minutes. Turn off the heat, and let sit for 10 minutes. Uncover, and let cool to room temperature.

2. Heat a wok, add the oil, and heat until very hot. Add the diced mushrooms, and stir-fry for about 15 seconds over high heat. Then add the remaining *Shao Mai Garnishes*. Toss lightly, and add the cooked rice. Toss the mixture repeatedly over the heat to mix the ingredients evenly. Add the *Shao Mai Sauce*, and mix. Roughly divide the rice mixture into 36 portions.

3. Line 2 steamer trays with cheesecloth that has been moistened with water or with parchment paper that has been punched with holes. Place a portion of the rice mixture in the center of each Dumpling Skin. Gather up the edges of the skin around the filling. Holding the dumpling between your thumb and index finger, lightly squeeze it to form a "waist"; at the same time, push up the filling from the bottom with the other hand, creating a flat bottom. Smooth the surface of the filling with the underside of a spoon dipped in water. (See the recipe for Shao Mai on page 120 for step-by-step illustrations.) Arrange the shao mai in the steamer trays about ¼ inch apart.

4. Fill a wok with water level with the bottom of the steamer tray or trays, and heat until boiling. Stack the steamer trays in the wok, cover, and steam the dumplings for 15 minutes over high heat, reversing the trays after 8 minutes. Serve with soy sauce.

Egg Dumplings

Dan Jiao

6 Servings ～ Appetizer, Main Dish or Side Dish

DUMPLINGS OF ALL types are a popular New Year's delicacy. In some cases, as in this dish, they are said to resemble golden coins, and serving them conveys the wish of continuing prosperity. So delectable are egg dumplings that they have become a main dish enjoyed throughout the year. The finished dumplings have a hearty ground-meat filling pungent with ginger, and the egg skin is tender. With its vivid spinach garnish, this platter may be served with rice as a sumptuous main-dish meal.

Egg Mixture
5	large eggs
½	teaspoon salt
½	teaspoon freshly ground white pepper

1	teaspoon dried shrimp, soaked in hot water for 1 hour (optional)
1	pound ground pork or beef

Meat Seasonings
1	tablespoon soy sauce
2	teaspoons rice wine or sake
2	teaspoons sesame oil
2	teaspoons minced scallions
1	teaspoon minced gingerroot
1	tablespoon cornstarch
½	teaspoon salt

1½	tablespoons peanut, safflower or corn oil
1	pound fresh spinach, trimmed and cleaned

Spinach Seasonings
1	tablespoon chicken broth, preferably Chinese Chicken Broth (page 345)
1	tablespoon rice wine or sake
½	teaspoon salt
1	teaspoon minced garlic

Dumpling Sauce
1	cup chicken broth, preferably Chinese Chicken Broth (page 345)
2	teaspoons soy sauce
1	teaspoon cornstarch
½	teaspoon sugar
½	teaspoon salt
¼	teaspoon freshly ground white pepper

1	teaspoon sesame oil

1. Beat the *Egg Mixture* until frothy. Drain the dried shrimp, if using, and mince finely. Chop the ground meat for a few minutes until fluffy, and place it in a large bowl with the dried shrimp and the *Meat Seasonings*. Stir vigorously in one direction, and throw the mixture lightly against the inside of the bowl to combine evenly.

2. Heat a wok or a nonstick frying pan, and add ½ tablespoon of the oil. Heat the oil, swirling it around in the pan, and add a heaping tablespoon of the egg mixture. Tilt the pan so that a thin 3-inch pancake is formed. Place a heaping teaspoon of the ground-meat mixture on one half of the pancake, and fold over the other half to form a half-moon shape and to seal in the meat. Press down along the edge of the circle with the spatula. Remove the dumpling. Make the remaining dumplings in the same manner.

3. Reheat the wok, add the remaining 1 tablespoon of oil, and heat the oil until nearly smoking. Add the spinach, and stir-fry over high heat for about 5 seconds. Add the *Spinach Seasonings*, and continue stir-frying until the spinach is just limp. Arrange the spinach around the outer edge of a platter.

4. Reheat the wok, add the *Dumpling Sauce*, and add the dumplings. Cook over high heat until the sauce begins to boil. Reduce the heat to medium, and continue cooking for 3 minutes. Add the sesame oil, toss lightly to mix, and transfer the mixture to the center of the platter. Serve immediately.

Soybeans & Tofu

TAIPEI IS A CITY TEEMING WITH the smells of good food. The morning is heralded by the penetrating odor of deep-fried Chinese crullers and roasted sesame-seed rolls. At midmorning, the smells of ripe, sweet melons, pineapples, mangoes and other subtropical fruits perfume the air as the fruit vendor wheels his cart, bulging with the ripe offerings of the season, through the streets. Lunchtime is marked by the aroma of red-cooked beef noodles or pan-fried noodle cakes garnished with assorted meats and vegetables. And at dinnertime, the smell of garlic frying in hot oil permeates the atmosphere. This was my favorite part of the day. As the sun slowly descended and a slight breeze enveloped the city in a balmy coolness, I would roam the alleyways of our neighborhood, moving from one kitchen window to the next, inhaling the assorted aromas and trying to guess the menu for that evening's dinner. I became intimate with my neighbors' palates: those in the house to my left had a passion for hot, spicy dishes, while those to my right favored blander foods.

As evening fell after dinner, the luscious scents of crispy onion crepes and pan-fried stuffed buns mingled with the other snacks offered at that time of day—steamed sweet corn, deep-fried sesame balls with red bean paste and steamed peanuts. Also present throughout the day in this panorama of fragrances was a putrid smell that defied classification. What was that baffling, pungent odor, present in every part of the city? After a bit of research, I soon traced the source and discovered that it was stinky bean curd (*chou dou fu*), or tofu, a favorite snack of the Chinese.

Vendors of this "unsavory" (at least to my unsophisticated palate) delicacy ran rampant all over the city with their portable deep-fryers. My Chinese surrogate sister and brothers, who were all great fans of the stuff, used to race outside, armed with empty bowls and chopsticks, at the sound of the stinky-bean-curd man's call. (The smell usu-

Soybeans & Tofu

Bean Milk Sheets

ally preceded him by two blocks, giving everyone plenty of notice.) What makes this food so fragrant is that it is actually "turned bean curd," which is made by fermenting fresh tofu squares in a brine with assorted spices and a pickled vegetable. The resulting squares are deep-fried in hot oil until golden and eaten with soy sauce, vinegar, mashed garlic or chili paste.

Stinky bean curd and fresh bean curd are just two of the many products derived from the soybean—a legume that has been prominent in the Chinese diet for centuries. It is believed that soybeans were first cultivated in China and, along with wheat and millet, were a staple food for the ancient Chinese. The durability of the plant endeared it to the farmers. Bean stew was a common dish during the Han dynasty (206 B.C. to 220 A.D.), and soybean milk and bean curd were also prominent in the Han diet.

Considering the many uses of this versatile legume, it is not difficult to understand why the soybean is so revered by the Chinese. It is used in making not only soy sauce but also other notable seasonings, such as sweet bean sauce or paste, hoisin sauce and hot bean paste. Its by-products include soybean milk and its many derivatives. When ground, the soybean produces oil and flour. The fresh, green beans are cooked and served with soy sauce and sesame oil, and dried beans are fried and eaten as a snack or soaked for sprouting.

The nutritious properties of the soybean further explain why it is so popular with the health-conscious Chinese. A serving of soybeans provides more protein than the minimum dietary requirement. In addition, soybeans are a major source of lecithin, a vital substance that aids digestion and the absorption of fats. Tofu has a higher protein value than the soybean in its raw state because during its manufacture, the tofu coagulates with most of the bean's protein, leaving much of the carbohydrates behind with the water. It is also more easily digested.

黃豆與豆腐類

Bean Curd Sheets

Bean Curd Sticks

Bean Curd Noodles

137

The actual process of making tofu is relatively simple. Dried soybeans, after being soaked, are ground to a puree, mixed with water and strained to form **soybean milk**. The bean milk is heated and used to make a number of by-products. Thin layers of skin from the milk are dried, forming **bean milk sheets** (*fu pi*), or rolled and deep-fried, creating **bean curd sticks** (*fu zu*). For cooking, they are usually softened and braised in a rich soy-sauce mixture. Then a coagulant is added to the heated milk, and the mixture is poured into a square mold. To make **bean curd sheets** (*bai ye*), a small amount of the bean curd mixture is added and pressed to create a flat sheet. Dried bean curd sheets are softened before cooking, used to wrap foods, and deep-fried or braised, depending on the dish. These sheets are sometimes shredded, making **bean curd noodles** (*gan si*). Many of these foods are braised with other ingredients so they acquire the flavors of the foods they are cooked with.

When the pureed soybean mixture itself has been properly pressed, the squares of tofu are removed. Although most Asian markets in North America offer a choice of soft or firm tofu, in Asia there are usually at least three types of tofu available. The difference in the varieties is the result of the size of the weight used and the length of pressing time. **Soft** or **silken tofu** is generally used for cold dishes and delicate soups; it has a loose, fragile consistency. **Firm tofu** is deep-fried, used in soups and in some stir-fried dishes. **Extra-firm tofu** (*dou fu gan*) is more appropriate for stir-fried dishes and stewing in a *lu*, a soy-based braising mixture. Since North American tofu contains a great deal of liquid, it is advisable to press it with a weight to remove the excess water.

Tofu is also fermented in rice wine and spices to make a popular seasoning (*dou fu ru*) with a slightly cheeselike flavor and pickled in a brine to make the infamous stinky bean curd.

Today, the popularity of the soybean and its many derivatives is unsurpassed. According to E.N. Anderson, Jr., and Marja L. Anderson in *Food in Chinese Culture*, edited by K.C. Chang, "A huge bowl of rice, a good mass of bean curd and a dish of cabbages—fresh in season, otherwise pickled—is the classic fare of the everyday south Chinese world." As most nutritionists will agree, the soybean and its many by-products are the foods of the future.

Cold Tossed Tofu & Celery Shreds

Liang Ban Gan Si

6 Servings ⁓ Appetizer or Side Dish

2½	squares extra-firm tofu, about 2½ pounds
2	cups celery, cut into matchstick-sized shreds
1	cup carrot, cut into matchstick-sized shreds

Dressing

2½	tablespoons sesame oil
1½	teaspoons salt

1. Lightly rinse the tofu, and drain it. Wrap the tofu in paper towels or a cotton towel and place a heavy weight, such as a skillet, on top. Let stand for 30 minutes to press out the excess liquid. Unwrap the tofu. Holding a cleaver parallel to the cutting surface, slice the tofu in half through the thickness. Cut the tofu into thin slices, and cut the slices into matchstick-sized shreds.

2. Heat 2 quarts of water until boiling, and blanch the tofu shreds for 15 seconds. Remove, and drain. Reheat the water until boiling, and blanch the celery and carrot shreds for 5 seconds. Remove, and refresh immediately in cold water. Drain thoroughly, and pat dry.

3. Arrange the shredded tofu, carrot and celery in a large serving bowl. Add the *Dressing*, toss lightly to coat the shreds, and serve.

THIS FLAVORFUL COLD salad is a familiar sight in any Sichuanese restaurant, where it is served with other small dishes to nibble on while browsing over the menu and awaiting the arrival of the meal. Although this dish is ideally suited for warm-weather eating, the contrasting textures of tofu and celery, bathed in the fragrant sesame oil, make it popular whatever the season. Bean curd noodles (gan si) are usually used in this dish, but slivers of tofu suit the purpose admirably.

凉拌干絲

Northern-Style Tofu

Guo Ta Dou Fu

6 Servings 〜 Side Dish

NORTHERN-STYLE TOFU,
*or tofu brain, as it was
originally titled, is said to have
been a favorite of Dowager
Empress Tzu-Hsi in the 19th
century. After you sample this
dish, the reason for its popularity
becomes evident: the simmered
tofu squares, seasoned with
sesame oil and chicken broth,
melt in your mouth.*

3	squares firm tofu, about 3 pounds
½	cup peanut, safflower or corn oil
1½	cups cornstarch
3	large eggs, lightly beaten
1	tablespoon minced gingerroot

Tofu-Cooking Liquid

2	cups chicken broth, preferably Chinese Chicken Broth (page 345)
2	tablespoons rice wine or sake
2	teaspoons salt
½	teaspoon sugar

2	teaspoons sesame oil
2	tablespoons minced scallion greens

1. Rinse the tofu lightly, and drain thoroughly. Trim off any hard edges. Wrap the tofu in paper towels or a cotton towel and place a heavy weight, such as a skillet, on top. Let stand for 30 minutes to press out the excess liquid. Unwrap the tofu. Holding a cleaver parallel to the cutting surface, slice each tofu square in half through the thickness; then cut each piece in half to form 1½-inch squares ½ inch thick.

2. Heat a wok, add the oil, and heat the oil to 350 degrees F. Dredge each piece of tofu in the cornstarch, and then dip in the beaten eggs to coat. Place a batch of tofu in the wok, and fry over medium heat until golden brown on both sides, about 3½ to 4 minutes per side. Remove with a handled strainer or slotted spoon, and drain the tofu. Reheat the oil, and fry the remaining tofu in several batches. Remove the oil from the wok, reserving 1 tablespoon.

3. Reheat the wok, add the tablespoon of oil, and heat until very hot. Add the minced gingerroot, and stir-fry until fragrant, about 5 seconds. Add the *Tofu-Cooking Liquid*, and heat until boiling. Add the fried tofu, and pierce the pieces of tofu with a fork so that they will absorb the cooking liquid. Cook the tofu, uncovered, for about 20 minutes over medium heat, or until all the liquid is absorbed. Dribble the sesame oil over the tofu, toss lightly to coat, and transfer the tofu to a platter. Sprinkle the minced scallions on top, and serve.

Red-Cooked Tofu

Hong Shao Dou Fu

6 Servings ⌢ Main Dish or Side Dish

3	squares firm tofu, about 3 pounds
½	pound boneless center-cut pork loin

Pork Marinade

2	teaspoons soy sauce
½	tablespoon rice wine or sake
½	teaspoon sesame oil
1	teaspoon cornstarch

10	dried Chinese black mushrooms
½	cup peanut, safflower or corn oil
3	tablespoons scallions, cut into 1-inch lengths

Braising Liquid

2	cups chicken broth, preferably Chinese Chicken Broth (page 345)
3	tablespoons soy sauce
1	tablespoon rice wine or sake
1	teaspoon sesame oil
¾	teaspoon sugar
½	teaspoon salt
¼	teaspoon freshly ground black pepper

2	carrots, parboiled for 2½ minutes and roll-cut into 1-inch pieces

Thickener

1½	tablespoons water
1½	teaspoons cornstarch

1	cup snow peas, ends snapped and veiny strings removed

TOFU IS IDEALLY SUITED *for red-cooking, or cooking slowly in a soy-based liquid, because it absorbs the rich braising liquid. The assorted vegetables in this dish provide color and additional flavor. Serve this dish with a generous portion of steamed rice and a steamed vegetable. (See photograph, page 88.)*

1. Rinse the tofu lightly, and drain thoroughly. Trim off any hard edges. Wrap the tofu in paper towels or a cotton towel and place a heavy weight, such as a skillet, on top. Let stand for 30 minutes to press out the excess liquid. Unwrap the tofu. Holding a cleaver parallel to the cutting surface, slice the tofu squares in half through the thickness; then cut each piece in half to form 1½-inch squares ½ inch thick. Remove and discard any fat or gristle from the pork loin.

Cut the meat into slices about ¼ inch thick, 1½ inches long and 1 inch wide, and place them in a bowl. Add the *Pork Marinade*, toss lightly, and let marinate for 20 minutes. Soak the dried mushrooms in hot water to cover for 20 minutes. Remove and discard the stems, and cut the caps in half.

2. Heat a wok, add the oil, and heat the oil to 375 degrees F. Add enough tofu pieces to fill the pan; fry on both sides over high heat, until golden brown. Remove with a handled strainer or slotted spoon, drain, reheat the oil, and fry the remaining tofu in the same manner. Remove the oil from the wok, reserving 3 tablespoons.

3. Reheat the wok, add the 3 tablespoons of oil, and heat until very hot. Add the meat slices, and stir-fry until they change color. Add the scallions and the mushrooms. Stir-fry over high heat for about 10 seconds, until fragrant. Add the *Braising Liquid*, and heat until boiling. Add the cooked tofu; when the liquid begins to boil, reduce the heat to medium, and cook, uncovered, for 5 minutes. Add the carrots, and cook for about 30 seconds to heat them through. With the liquid boiling, add the *Thickener*, stirring constantly to prevent lumps. Add the snow peas, toss lightly to coat with the sauce, and transfer the mixture to a platter. Serve immediately.

Braised Tofu With Black Mushrooms in Oyster Sauce

Dong Gu Pa Dou Fu

6 Servings ⌢ Main Dish

3	squares firm tofu, about 3 pounds
10	dried Chinese black mushrooms
1	cup peanut, safflower or corn oil
3	tablespoons scallions, cut into 1-inch lengths

Braising Liquid

2	cups chicken broth, preferably Chinese Chicken Broth (page 345)
½	cup mushroom-soaking liquid
3	tablespoons soy sauce
1½	tablespoons oyster sauce
1	tablespoon rice wine or sake
1	teaspoon sugar

Thickener

1	tablespoon water
1	teaspoon cornstarch

1½	teaspoons sesame oil

THIS SICHUANESE DISH *was a favorite of my Chinese surrogate grandfather. His discerning palate was highly respected in our household. The smoky flavor of the black mushrooms mingles harmoniously with the rich oyster sauce and provides a fine contrast to the flavor of the tofu. Ideally, the more expensive, thicker Chinese black mushrooms should be used for this dish.*

1. Rinse the tofu lightly, and drain thoroughly. Trim off any hard edges. Wrap the tofu in paper towels or a cotton towel and place a heavy weight, such as a skillet, on top. Let stand for 30 minutes to press out the excess liquid. Unwrap the tofu. Holding a cleaver parallel to the cutting surface, slice each square in half through the thickness; then cut each piece diagonally in half to form triangles. Soak the dried mushrooms in hot water to cover for 20 minutes. Remove and discard the stems, and cut the caps in half. Retain ½ cup of the soaking liquid for the braising liquid.

2. Heat a wok, add the oil, and heat the oil to 375 degrees F. Add a batch of tofu, and deep-fry in the hot oil until golden brown. Remove with a handled strainer or slotted spoon, and drain. Reheat the oil, and deep-fry the remaining tofu in the same manner in several batches. Remove the oil from the wok, reserving 1 tablespoon.

3. Reheat the wok, add the tablespoon of oil, and heat until very hot. Add the scallions and black mushrooms, and stir-fry until fragrant, about 10 seconds.

Add the *Braising Liquid*, and bring to a boil. Add the tofu, and heat until the liquid boils again. Reduce the heat to medium, and cook for 7 minutes, or until the liquid has reduced by half. Add the *Thickener*, stirring constantly. Add the sesame oil, toss lightly, and transfer the mixture to a platter. Serve immediately.

Ma Po Tofu

Ma Po Dou Fu

6 Servings ⌒ Side Dish

THIS POPULAR SICHUANESE *dish is said to be named after a Mrs. Chen, whose complexion was marred by prominent pockmarks. (Ma means pox.) Soft tofu is traditionally used in this dish, as it provides the palate with creamy relief from the numbing chili paste and Sichuan peppercorns.*

3	squares soft tofu, about 3 pounds
½	pound ground pork or beef

Meat Marinade

1	tablespoon soy sauce
½	tablespoon rice wine or sake
1	teaspoon sesame oil

2	tablespoons peanut, safflower or corn oil

Minced Seasonings

2	tablespoons minced scallions
1	tablespoon minced garlic
1	tablespoon minced gingerroot

1½	teaspoons chili paste

Braising Liquid

2	cups chicken broth, preferably Chinese Chicken Broth (page 345)
3	tablespoons soy sauce
1	tablespoon rice wine or sake
½	teaspoon salt

Thickener

1½	tablespoons water
1½	teaspoons cornstarch

3	tablespoons minced scallion greens
1	teaspoon Sichuan peppercorns, toasted until fragrant and pulverized

1. Rinse the tofu lightly, and drain thoroughly. Cut away any hard edges. Wrap the tofu in paper towels or a cotton towel and place a heavy weight, such as a skillet, on top. Let stand for 30 minutes to press out the excess liquid. Unwrap and cut the tofu into ½-inch dice. Place the ground meat in a bowl, add the *Meat Marinade*, toss lightly, and let sit briefly.

2. Heat a wok, add the oil, and heat until hot. Add the meat, and cook until it changes color, mashing and separating the clumps of meat. Remove the meat with a handled strainer or slotted spoon, and heat the oil until any liquid from the meat has evaporated. Add the *Minced Seasonings*, and stir-fry for about 10 seconds, until fragrant. Add the chili paste, and stir-fry for another 5 seconds. Add the *Braising Liquid*, heat until boiling, and add the tofu and meat. Return the mixture to a boil, reduce the heat to medium, and cook for about 5 minutes, uncovered, until the sauce has reduced by one-fourth. With the mixture boiling, add the *Thickener*, stirring constantly to prevent lumps. Transfer the mixture to a serving bowl or a platter. Sprinkle the top with the minced scallions and the Sichuan peppercorn powder.

Stuffed Tofu

Niang Dou Fu

6 Servings ⌣ Main Dish or Side Dish

3	squares extra-firm tofu, about 3 pounds
1	teaspoon dried shrimp (optional)
1	pound ground pork

Pork Seasonings

1	tablespoon soy sauce
2	teaspoons rice wine or sake
1½	teaspoons sesame oil
1½	tablespoons minced scallions
1½	tablespoons minced gingerroot
1	teaspoon salt
¼	teaspoon freshly ground black pepper

3	tablespoons cornstarch
3	tablespoons peanut, safflower or corn oil

B RAISED FOODS ARE *usually considered hearty fare, but this Cantonese platter seems to belie that description. The seasoned pork provides a delicious contrast to the creamy tofu.*

Tofu-Braising Liquid

2 cups chicken broth, preferably Chinese Chicken Broth (page 345)
2 tablespoons soy sauce
1 tablespoon rice wine or sake
1 teaspoon salt

Thickener

1 tablespoon water
1 teaspoon cornstarch

2 tablespoons minced scallion greens

1. Rinse the tofu lightly, and drain thoroughly. Trim off any hard edges. Wrap the tofu in paper towels or a cotton towel and place a heavy weight, such as a skillet, on top. Let stand for 30 minutes to press out the excess liquid. Unwrap the tofu. Cut the tofu squares diagonally in half to form triangles. Cut each triangle in half again so that each square has been cut into 4 triangles. Soften the dried shrimp, if using, in hot water to cover for 1 hour. Drain, and mince. Lightly chop the ground pork until fluffy, and place it in a mixing bowl. Add the minced shrimp and the *Pork Seasonings*. Stir vigorously in one direction, and lightly throw the mixture against the inside of the bowl to combine evenly.

2. Using a knife and a spoon, scoop out a pocket in the longest side of one tofu triangle. Be careful not to pierce the side. Dust the pocket with cornstarch, and generously stuff with the ground-pork mixture. Use the underside of a spoon dipped in water to smooth the surface. Repeat for the remaining tofu triangles.

3. Heat a wok, add the oil, and heat the oil until very hot. Place a batch of the stuffed tofu triangles in the pan, meat side down, and fry briefly over high heat until the meat is golden brown. Remove with a handled strainer or slotted spoon, reheat the oil, and fry the remaining tofu triangles in the same manner, and remove. Add the *Tofu-Braising Liquid*, and heat until boiling. Add the stuffed tofu, meat side down, and heat until the liquid is boiling. Reduce the heat to medium-low, cover, and cook for 10 minutes. Uncover, raise the heat to high, and remove the tofu triangles from the wok, arranging them on a platter. Add the *Thickener* to the cooking liquid, stirring constantly to prevent lumps. Pour the thickened liquid over the stuffed tofu, sprinkle the minced scallion greens on top, and serve.

Eight-Treasure Stir-Fried Vegetables With Meat

Ba Bao La Jiang

6 Servings ～ Main Dish

1½   squares firm tofu, about 1½ pounds
½   pound boneless center-cut pork loin

Pork Marinade
2   teaspoons soy sauce
1   teaspoon rice wine or sake
½   teaspoon sesame oil
½   teaspoon cornstarch

¼   cup peanut, safflower or corn oil
1½   teaspoons chili paste

Sauce
¼   cup soy sauce
3   tablespoons sweet bean sauce
3   tablespoons water
2   tablespoons sugar

¾   cup carrot, parboiled for 2½ minutes and cut into ½-inch dice
¾   cup English (gourmet seedless) cucumber or small pickling
     cucumbers, cut into ½-inch dice, plunged into boiling water
     for 10 seconds and refreshed in cold water
¾   cup water chestnuts, plunged briefly into boiling water, refreshed
     in cold water and cut into ½-inch dice
¾   cup green peas (If fresh, cook for 5 minutes in boiling water, and
     refresh in cold water. If frozen, defrost, and set aside.)
¾   cup roasted, unsalted peanuts

To MOST, THE CUISINE *of Sichuan province brings to mind fiery seasonings and the ever-present chili pepper. Foreigners will not be disappointed when they taste the spicy sauce of this stir-fried platter featuring tofu, marinated lean pork, carrots, cucumber, water chestnuts, peas and roasted peanuts. Traditionally, dried shrimp are the eighth treasure, but I have omitted them in this adapted version, leaving only seven treasures. An extra vegetable may be added in place of the missing shrimp.*

1. Rinse the tofu lightly, and drain. Cut away any hard edges, wrap the tofu in paper towels or a cotton towel and place a heavy weight, such as a skillet, on top. Let stand for 30 minutes to press out the excess liquid. Unwrap and cut the tofu into ½-inch dice. Remove any fat or gristle from the pork loin. Cut the meat into ½-inch dice. Place the meat in a bowl, add the *Pork Marinade*, toss lightly, and let marinate for 20 minutes.

2. Heat a wok, add 2 tablespoons of the oil, and heat until very hot. Add the pork, and stir-fry over high heat until the meat changes color and is cooked. Remove, and drain. Remove the oil from the wok.

3. Reheat the wok, add the remaining 2 tablespoons of oil, and heat until very hot. Add the chili paste, and stir-fry over high heat for 5 seconds, until fragrant. Add the *Sauce*, and stir-fry over high heat until the sauce starts to boil. Add the tofu, carrots, cucumbers, water chestnuts and green peas. Toss lightly over high heat for a minute, until the ingredients are heated through. Add the peanuts and cooked meat, and stir to coat with the sauce. Transfer to a platter, and serve immediately.

Meatball & Soybean Casserole

Huang Dou Rou Wan

6 Servings ⌣ Main Dish

B EAN STEWS HAVE BEEN *a vital part of the Chinese diet since ancient times. In modern China, their popularity continues, and these dishes are considered hearty, filling fare. This casserole is a fine example of such a dish. Soybeans are sold in any well-stocked Asian market or health-food store.*

4	cups dried soybeans
12	cups water
1	pound ground pork

Pork Seasonings

1	tablespoon soy sauce
2	teaspoons rice wine or sake
1½	teaspoons sesame oil
1	large egg, lightly beaten
1	tablespoon minced scallions
2	teaspoons minced gingerroot
1½	tablespoons cornstarch
2	cups peanut, safflower or corn oil

Braising Mixture

6	cups chicken broth, preferably Chinese Chicken Broth (page 345)
6	tablespoons soy sauce
¼	cup rice wine or sake
2	scallions, smashed with the flat side of a cleaver
2	slices gingerroot, the size of a quarter, smashed with the flat side of a cleaver
1	tablespoon sugar
1	teaspoon salt
1	whole star anise

1. Rinse the soybeans, and drain. Place the soybeans in a bowl with the 12 cups of water to cover, and let them soak for 8 hours or overnight. Discard any beans that have risen to the surface. Drain thoroughly, and pat dry on a towel. Lightly chop the ground pork until fluffy. Place the meat in a mixing bowl with the *Pork Seasonings*. Stir the meat in one direction, and throw it lightly against the inside of the bowl to combine the ingredients evenly. Shape the meat into 15 meatballs.

2. Heat a wok, add the oil, and heat the oil to 375 degrees F. Add the soybeans, and deep-fry until golden brown, stirring constantly. Remove with a handled strainer or slotted spoon, and drain. Reheat the oil to 375 degrees, and add half the meatballs. Deep-fry the meatballs briefly in the hot oil until golden brown. Remove with a handled strainer or slotted spoon, and drain. Reheat the oil, and deep-fry the remaining meatballs in the same manner.

3. Place the soybeans and the *Braising Mixture* in a heavy pot or Dutch oven. Bring the liquid to a boil, reduce the heat, cover, and simmer for 20 minutes over low heat. Add the meatballs, partially cover, and simmer for 45 minutes, or until almost all the liquid has evaporated. Serve immediately.

Sweet & Sour Fish Slices

Tang Cu Fu Pi Yu Juan

6 Servings 〜 Main Dish

IN THIS DISH, THE FAMILIAR *classic of sweet and sour is given a new twist with the use of bean milk sheets, which not only provide a crisp coating for the fish slices but also eliminate the mess of a batter. Bean milk sheets are thin skins made from soybean milk. They are found fresh or dried in most Asian markets. If they are unavailable, or if you prefer, simply coat the fish pieces with cornstarch.*

1½   pounds firm-fleshed fish fillets, such as haddock, sea bass or cod

Fish Marinade
- 1   tablespoon rice wine or sake
- 1   egg white or 1 tablespoon water
- 1   teaspoon minced gingerroot
- 2   tablespoons cornstarch
- 1   teaspoon salt

10   dried bean milk sheets

Paste
- ¾   cup water
- 6   tablespoons all-purpose flour

2   cups peanut, safflower or corn oil

Minced Seasonings
- 1   tablespoon minced scallions
- 2   teaspoons minced garlic

Sweet & Sour Sauce
- ½   cup water
- 6   tablespoons ketchup
- ¼   cup clear rice vinegar
- 2   teaspoons soy sauce
- 1   teaspoon sesame oil
- 6   tablespoons sugar
- 2   teaspoons cornstarch
- 1   teaspoon salt

1. Remove the skins from the fish fillets, if necessary, and discard. Lightly rinse the fillets, and drain thoroughly. Holding the knife at a 45-degree angle, cut the fillets into slices that are ½ inch thick, 2 inches long and 1 inch wide. Place the slices in a bowl, add the *Fish Marinade*, toss lightly, and let the fish marinate for 20 minutes. Soften the bean milk sheets in hot water for 5 minutes.

Lightly squeeze out as much water as possible. Pat dry with towels. Cut the bean milk sheets into 4-inch squares. Stir the *Paste* until smooth.

2. Lay out one bean milk sheet, and spread the paste generously over the surface. Place a fish slice in the center, and gather up the edges, bringing in the sides and folding them over and over so the fish slice is completely enclosed in a rectangular package. Press the ends to seal. Repeat for the remaining fish slices.

3. Heat a wok, add the oil, and heat the oil to 375 degrees F. Add a few of the fish rolls, and deep-fry for 3 to 4 minutes, until the fish is cooked and the rolls are lightly golden. Remove with a handled strainer or slotted spoon, and drain. Reheat the oil, and deep-fry the remaining fish rolls in the same manner. Reheat the oil to 425 degrees. Add all the fish rolls and deep-fry briefly, stirring constantly, until they are golden brown and crisp. Drain the fish rolls on absorbent paper. Remove the oil from the wok, reserving 1 tablespoon.

4. Reheat the wok, add the tablespoon of oil, and heat until very hot. Add the *Minced Seasonings*, and stir-fry for about 5 seconds, until fragrant. Add the *Sweet & Sour Sauce*, and cook until thick, stirring constantly to prevent lumps. Add the fish rolls, toss lightly to coat with the sauce, and transfer to a platter. Serve immediately.

Buddha's Delight

Luo Han Su Cai

6 Servings ⌢ Main Dish or Side Dish

1	teaspoon baking soda
2	ounces bean curd sticks
14	fried wheat-gluten balls (step 3, page 341)
10	dried wood ears
8	dried Chinese black mushrooms
2	cups peanut, safflower or corn oil

Minced Seasonings

2	tablespoons minced scallions
2	tablespoons minced gingerroot

½	pound Chinese cabbage (Napa), cut into 2-inch squares
½	cup thinly sliced carrots

THIS WELL-KNOWN vegetarian dish, a stir-fry of myriad vegetables coated in sauce, is one of the most popular of its kind among the Chinese. The ingredients vary from one region to the next. Whatever the mix, this dish is an enticing combination of textures and flavors. Fried wheat-gluten balls are available frozen in Asian markets. Instructions for making fried wheat-gluten balls at home appear on page 341, in the recipe for Mock Sweet & Sour Pork.

Braising Liquid
2	cups mushroom-soaking liquid
4½	tablespoons soy sauce
2	tablespoons rice wine or sake
2	teaspoons sesame oil
2	teaspoons sugar
¼	teaspoon freshly ground black pepper
¼	cup canned bamboo shoots, plunged briefly into boiling water, refreshed in cold water and cut into thin slices about 1½ inches square
2	teaspoons Chinese black vinegar or Worcestershire sauce

Thickener
1	tablespoon water
1	teaspoon cornstarch

1. Dissolve the baking soda in 6 cups hot water, and place the bean curd sticks in the water. Let soak for 1 hour. Rinse in cold water to remove the baking soda; squeeze out the water. Cut the sticks into pieces 1½ inches long. Parboil the fried Wheat-Gluten balls for 1 minute, and rinse in cold water. Drain thoroughly, and squeeze out any excess water. Soak the wood ears and dried mushrooms separately in hot water to cover for 20 minutes. Drain the wood ears, and cut away the hard, bitter nib on the underside, if necessary. Cut the wood ears into pieces about 1 inch square. Drain the mushrooms, retaining 2 cups of the soaking liquid for the braising liquid. Remove and discard the stems; cut the caps into quarters.

2. Heat a wok, add the oil, and heat the oil to 375 degrees F. Add half the bean curd sticks, and deep-fry, stirring constantly, until the sticks are golden brown. Remove with a handled strainer or slotted spoon, and drain. Press the sticks to squeeze out as much oil as possible. Deep-fry the remaining bean curd sticks, drain and press out the oil. Remove the oil from the wok, reserving 3 tablespoons.

3. Reheat the wok, add the 3 tablespoons of oil, and heat until very hot. Add the *Minced Seasonings*, and stir-fry for about 5 seconds, until fragrant. Add the wood ears and mushrooms, and stir-fry for another 5 seconds over high heat. Add the cabbage and the carrots. Toss lightly, adding a tablespoon of rice wine if the mixture is very dry. Cook over high heat until the cabbage is slightly limp. Add the fried gluten balls, the bean curd sticks and the *Braising Liquid*. Stir the mixture, heat until the liquid boils, reduce the heat to medium-low, and cover. Cook for 12 to 15 minutes, or until the liquid has almost completely evaporated. Add the bamboo shoots, Chinese black vinegar and *Thickener*, stirring constantly to prevent lumps. Transfer the mixture to a platter, and serve immediately.

Sweet Soybean Milk

Dou Jiang

8 Cups ⌣ Snack or Breakfast

2	cups dried soybeans
8	cups water
1	cup sugar plus more, if desired

1. Rinse the soybeans in a bowl of water, and discard any beans that rise to the surface. Place in a bowl with cold water to cover, and let soak for 12 hours or overnight. Drain the soybeans.

2. In a blender or a food processor fitted with the steel blade, puree the soybeans to a smooth paste in two or three batches, adding some of the 8 cups of water to each batch as it is blended. Line a colander with fine cheesecloth, and pour the soybean mixture into the colander, adding the remainder of the water. Strain the mixture through the cheesecloth; the mixture should now resemble milk. Discard the soybean sediment. Pour the strained mixture into a saucepan, and place the pan over medium heat. Add the sugar (if the mixture is not sweet enough, add more sugar to taste), and stir constantly until the liquid is hot and the sugar is dissolved.

FOR MOST AMERICANS, *breakfast is not complete without a cup of coffee, whereas for many Chinese, a steaming bowl of sweet soybean milk, accompanied by a Sesame Flat Bread (shao bing, page 64) and a fried cruller (you tiao), is obligatory. A savory rendition of this dish is prepared by substituting Chinese black vinegar, chili oil, soy sauce, sesame oil and minced scallions for the sugar. Both versions are filling, flavorful and nutritious. Although it is typically served in the morning, the soothing, sweet milk can be drunk throughout the day.*

Eggs

IN THE CHINESE CULTURE, the birth of a child is an occasion attended by age-old customs. Tradition dictates that the mother must rest for one month, confined to the house, to recuperate from the intense rigors of childbirth. During this period, friends and relatives send such varied gifts as eggs pickled in fermented wine rice, a condiment made by steeping sweet rice until it becomes a "wine" (the wine is believed to "fire up" the body), chicken soup with gingerroot or sesame oil and, in more recent times, milk powder. All of these foods are considered beneficial in restoring the body to its original state. If the baby is a boy, at the end of the month a custom called *man yue* ("a full month") is observed: scarlet eggs are sent to relatives and friends announcing the joyous event and thanking the deities for their generosity.

Eggs, both in their natural color and dyed red, frequently are used by the Chinese on festivals and notable occasions as offerings to the supernatural powers. To the Chinese, the egg—with its yolk and white—symbolizes yin and yang, the two opposing forces of the universe.

Eggs are simmered in a fragrant tea-based solution and served during the New Year's holiday. Tea eggs are believed to "roll in," or impart, good luck for the coming year. On the occasion of the Dragon Boat Festival, celebrated on the fifth day of the fifth month of the lunar calendar, people in Hunan province eat salty duck eggs. This holiday marks the beginning of warm weather, and the preserved eggs keep beautifully in the heat.

Archaeological evidence supports the belief that eggs were extremely popular among rich and poor alike even before the Han dynasty (206 B.C. to 220 A.D.). During the T'ang dynasty (618 to 907), eggs with mutton and pork were cooked in hot sulfur springs and fed to invalids. Equally favored were duck, goose, quail and peacock eggs. Turtle eggs were treasured as a delicacy for special occasions.

Since eggs are extremely perishable, preservation techniques were devised to prevent them from spoiling. Chicken eggs were smoked, red-cooked (slow-cooked in a soy-based liquid), or braised in a soy-sauce-based liquid and simmered in a strong tea-flavored brew. Duck eggs, which were enjoyed in both sweet and savory dishes, were also packed in lime and ash and pickled in a salty brine. The resulting "pickles" were served as a garnish to rice or congee.

These preserving practices still exist today, and the methods used are almost exactly the same as those of ancient times. "Thousand-year-old" eggs are made by submerging duck eggs in a mixture of lime, pine ash and salt, then coating them with mud and rolling them in straw. The eggs are then left to ferment for 50 days. The minerals seep through the shell, changing the color, flavor and texture of the eggs. Since the dried mud coating suggests an ancient origin and encourages the belief that the eggs may have been buried in the ground for a period, they acquired the somewhat exaggerated

English name. Although many Westerners do not care for their rich, unctuous flavor and texture, thousand-year-old eggs are considered a delicacy by the Chinese and are particularly favored in cold appetizers.

Similarly, salty duck eggs are an avidly consumed variety of preserved eggs and are enjoyed in both sweet and savory dishes. To achieve the salty product, duck eggs are immersed in a saline marinade for 30 days. Like thousand-year-old eggs, these acquire a unique texture and flavor in the fermentation process; the shells take on a bluish tinge, the whites become intensely opaque, and the yolks turn deep orange. A salty duck egg with rice congee is the traditional breakfast of many southern Chinese, but salty duck eggs are enjoyed by Chinese the world over, and they are sold in any well-stocked Chinese grocery store in the United States.

The reasons for the popularity of chicken eggs are obvious. In addition to their nutritional value (they contain all the essential amino acids and are an important source of protein), eggs are extremely versatile: they may be stir-fried, steamed, deep-fried, poached or fried to form egg sheets and are added to innumerable soups, savory concoctions, sweet pastries and cakes. Egg yolks are used in batters and meat fillings for color and flavor; and the whites, combined with cornstarch, are added to seafood and chicken marinades to give fluffiness and firmness or to soups to form silken threads. Furthermore, eggs are economical, filling and easy to digest.

蛋類

Tea Eggs

Cha Ye Dan

20 Eggs ⌒ Appetizer or Snack

*I*N TAIPEI, TEA EGG *vendors wheeling carts of bubbling cauldrons brimming with eggs are often seen in parks and in the parking lots of museums, beaches and other recreational areas. The eggs make an excellent portable snack. At home, we often cooked a potload of eggs to be served as a salty pickle with rice and other simple main dishes at our family meals. They reheat beautifully, and the flavor is equally good whether they are hot or cold.*

20	large eggs

Tea-Cooking Mixture

10	cups water
½	cup loose black tea leaves
¼	cup rice wine or sake
2	tablespoons soy sauce
6	slices gingerroot, the size of a quarter, smashed with the flat side of a cleaver
1½	tablespoons salt
3	whole star anise
2	cinnamon sticks

1. Place the eggs in a saucepan with cold water to cover. Bring to a boil, reduce the heat to low, and let the eggs simmer for 10 minutes, until they are hard-boiled. Refresh them in cold water. Drain the eggs, and lightly tap the shells on a hard surface to crack them. Do not remove the shells.

2. Place the *Tea-Cooking Mixture* in a heavy pot, and heat until boiling. Reduce the heat to low, and let simmer for 20 minutes, uncovered. Add the cooked eggs, and continue simmering for 45 minutes. Turn off the heat, and let the eggs sit in the tea mixture until they are cool. Remove, shell, and serve the eggs warm or chilled, cut into wedges.

Steamed Shrimp Rolls
Ru Yi Xia Juan

6 Servings ～ Appetizer, Main Dish or Side Dish

1   pound medium-sized raw shrimp, shelled

Shrimp Seasonings
½   tablespoon rice wine or sake
½   teaspoon sesame oil
1   teaspoon minced gingerroot
1   teaspoon salt
½   teaspoon freshly ground white pepper

½   egg white, beaten until frothy
1   tablespoon cornstarch

Egg Sheets
3   large eggs, lightly beaten
½   tablespoon water
1   teaspoon salt
½   teaspoon cornstarch

Egg Paste
½   large egg
2   tablespoons cornstarch

6   sheets nori (dried seaweed, also called purple laver)

Shrimp-Roll Sauce
⅓   cup chicken broth, preferably Chinese Chicken Broth (page 345)
2   teaspoons rice wine or sake
½   teaspoon sesame oil
½   teaspoon cornstarch

R U YI MEANS HAPPI-NESS, *and since the shape of these steamed shrimp rolls is reminiscent of the Chinese scepter of happiness, we find the word in the title. Once steamed, the sliced rolls may be used as a garnish in Mongolian Fire Pot and other soups, as well as in stir-fried vegetable dishes. Or they may be deep-fried and served with a dipping sauce. In this dish, thin, tender egg crepes are wrapped around a firm mousseline of shrimp.*

1. Devein the shrimp, rinse lightly, and drain thoroughly. Place the shrimp in a dishtowel, and squeeze out as much moisture as possible. Smash the shrimp with the flat edge of a cleaver, and chop to a fine paste—or use a food processor fitted with the steel blade. Place the shrimp paste in a large bowl; add the *Shrimp Seasonings*. Stir vigorously in one direction and lightly throw the mixture against the side of the bowl to combine evenly. Add the beaten egg white, and

mix until the paste is slightly stiff. Then add the cornstarch, and continue mixing until the mixture is evenly combined. It should be stiff and slightly sticky, not loose.

2. Lightly beat the ingredients for the *Egg Sheets* until slightly frothy. Wipe the surface of a well-seasoned wok or a nonstick 10-inch frying pan with an oil-soaked paper towel. Heat the wok until a little water sprinkled onto the surface evaporates immediately. Remove from the heat, add one-sixth of the egg mixture, and tilt the wok to form a thin, circular pancake. Place the wok back over the heat, and cook until set. Flip the egg sheet, and cook until lightly golden. Remove the egg sheet, and set aside to cool. Trim to a square. Make 5 more egg sheets in the same manner.

3. Lay an egg sheet on a flat surface (**a**), and spread some of the *Egg Paste* over the sheet. Place a nori sheet on top of the egg sheet. Spread one-sixth of the shrimp mixture on the nori sheet, using the underside of a spoon dipped in water to smooth the surface. Starting at the edge nearest you, roll up the egg sheet as shown (**b**), rolling tightly as you go along. Make the remaining rolls in the same manner. Place the finished rolls, seam side down, on a lightly oiled heatproof plate. Put the plate in a steamer tray.

4. Fill a wok with water level with the bottom edge of the steamer tray, and heat until boiling. Place the steamer tray over the boiling water, cover, and steam for 12 minutes over high heat. Cut each roll into 1-inch pieces (**a**), and arrange the slices (**b**) on a platter.

5. Remove the water from the wok, and reheat the wok. Add the *Shrimp -Roll Sauce*, and heat until boiling and slightly thick, stirring constantly. Pour the sauce over the shrimp-roll slices, and serve immediately.

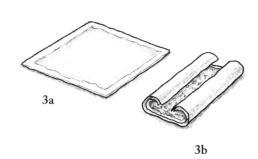

3a

3b

4a

4b

Stir-Fried Eggs With Crab

Fu Rong Xie Rou

6 Servings ⌒ Main Dish or Side Dish

½ pound fresh lump crabmeat

Crabmeat Marinade
2 slices gingerroot, the size of a quarter, smashed with the flat side of a cleaver
2 teaspoons rice wine or sake

¼ cup peanut, safflower or corn oil

Crab Sauce
1 teaspoon sesame oil
½ teaspoon salt

Minced Seasonings
1 tablespoon minced scallions
2 teaspoons minced gingerroot

Egg Mixture
6 large eggs
1 teaspoon salt
¼ teaspoon freshly ground white pepper

1 tablespoon minced scallion greens

ALTHOUGH THE TERM *fu rong was originally reserved for dishes with egg whites and crabmeat or shrimp, this category was later broadened to include whole-egg dishes with a garnish of pork, chicken and beef. Any of these may be used in place of crabmeat in this dish. Most Chinese prefer that eggs be undercooked and creamy. Americans may prefer to lengthen the cooking time, producing a slightly drier version. For a complete meal, serve with a stir-fried or steamed green vegetable.*

1. Pick over the crabmeat, and remove any shell or cartilage. Shred the crabmeat, and place it in a bowl. Pinch the gingerroot slices in the *Crabmeat Marinade* repeatedly for several minutes to impart their flavor. Discard the gingerroot, and add the marinade to the crabmeat. Toss lightly, and let marinate for 20 minutes.

2. Heat a wok, add 1 tablespoon of the oil, and heat until hot. Add the crabmeat and the *Crab Sauce*. Toss lightly over high heat until the mixture is dry, about 2 minutes, and remove to a plate. Reheat the wok. Add the remaining 3 tablespoons of oil; heat until very hot. Add the *Minced Seasonings*, and stir-fry until fragrant, about 10 seconds. Lightly whisk the *Egg Mixture* until frothy, and add the crabmeat. Stir-fry over medium heat until the eggs are just set. Transfer to a platter, sprinkle with the minced scallion greens, and serve immediately.

Spicy Egg Omelet

Yu Xiang Hong Dan

6 Servings ⁓ Main Dish or Side Dish

THE FAMOUS SICHUANESE *sauce in this dish was originally developed for fish dishes. It is also a superb complement to shrimp, chicken, pork, eggplant and eggs, as in this recipe. The fluffy omelet is an excellent foil for the spicy stir-fried topping. Serve with a steamed or stir-fried vegetable and rice for a filling meal.*

8	large eggs
1	teaspoon salt
10	small dried wood ears, soaked in hot water to cover for 20 minutes
12	water chestnuts, plunged briefly into boiling water and refreshed in cold water
½	pound boneless center-cut pork loin

Pork Marinade

1	tablespoon soy sauce
½	tablespoon rice wine or sake
1	teaspoon sesame oil
1	teaspoon water
1	teaspoon cornstarch

7	tablespoons peanut, safflower or corn oil

Minced Seasonings

1	tablespoon minced scallions
1	tablespoon minced garlic
1	tablespoon minced gingerroot

1½	teaspoons chili paste

Spicy Sauce

¼	cup chicken broth, preferably Chinese Chicken Broth (page 345)
1½	tablespoons soy sauce
1	tablespoon rice wine or sake
1½	teaspoons Chinese black vinegar or Worcestershire sauce
1	teaspoon sesame oil
2	teaspoons sugar
2	teaspoons cornstarch

2	tablespoons minced scallion greens

1. Lightly beat the eggs until frothy, and add the salt. Drain the wood ears. Cut away and discard the hard, bitter nib on the underside of the wood ears, and

cut the wood ears into shreds. Cut the water chestnuts into thin slices. Remove and discard any fat or gristle from the pork loin. Cut the meat into thin slices. Shred the slices into matchstick-sized shreds. Place the shreds in a bowl, add the *Pork Marinade*, toss lightly, and let marinate for 20 minutes.

2. Heat a wok, add 3 tablespoons of the oil, and heat the oil until very hot. Add the eggs, cover, and reduce the heat to low. Cook for about 5 minutes, until the eggs are set and the bottom is lightly golden. Uncover, and turn the omelet over. Cook until golden, and remove to a heatproof platter. Keep the omelet warm while preparing the sauce.

3. Reheat the wok, add 2 more tablespoons of oil, and heat until very hot. Add the shredded pork loin, and stir-fry over high heat, stirring constantly, until the meat changes color. Remove, and drain. Reheat the pan, and add the remaining 2 tablespoons of oil. Heat the oil until very hot, and add the *Minced Seasonings*. Stir-fry for about 10 seconds, until fragrant, and add the chili paste. Stir-fry for 5 seconds, and add the water chestnuts and wood ears. Cook until the ingredients are heated through, and add the *Spicy Sauce*. Cook the sauce over high heat, stirring constantly, until thickened. Add the pork loin, toss lightly to coat with the sauce, and pour the mixture over the omelet. Sprinkle the top with the minced scallions, and serve immediately.

Poultry

WHEN I WAS A CHILD, Christmas and the New Year heralded a time of gift giving from my parents' friends, relatives and business associates. There was always the latest Japanese electronic equipment or expensive stemware mail-ordered from glossy catalogues. If it had been a very good year, our subscription to the Fruit-of-the-Month Club would be renewed—each month, a huge box bursting with a different kind of ripe, fragrant fruit would be joyfully received in our household.

Years later, I was delighted to relive the same ritual with my surrogate family in Taiwan on the occasion of the Chinese New Year in late January or early February. According to custom, food gifts are exchanged at this time of the year. These usually included fat links of freshly made Chinese sausage, huge bags of dried Chinese black mushrooms, dried, salted ducks and gift boxes bursting with expensive American canned goods.

Two weeks before the holiday, one room of the house would be emptied completely in anticipation of the influx of gifts. As the New Year approached, we would watch the once vacant space become packed with mountains of edible delicacies.

It also was not unusual to find two or three cackling chickens roaming around our backyard, compliments of one of my Chinese father's grateful customers. Obahsan, our family's stalwart old maid, would fatten them up with corn and rice for a few days before slaughtering them with her trusty cleaver. No part of the bird would be wasted. The feathers would be plucked, gathered up in a bag and shipped off to her relatives in the country. The blood would be drained, mixed with rice and cooked into a solid cake to be administered to my Chinese brother, who suffered from anemia. (Chicken blood contains iron and vitamins and is often served shredded in soups.) The chicken itself would be cooked whole in a soy-sauce braising liquid or a soup, or it would be cut up and used in several dishes.

Chicken, duck, goose, pigeon and all types of fowl are of greatest importance to the Chinese, both symbolically and dietetically. According to ancient Chinese thought, fowl were considered more noble than four-footed animals, and the meat was considered far healthier for the body. In Chinese ritual, fowl has been used as a sacrificial offering throughout the ages—probably because of its auspicious symbolic significance. The rooster, or cock, is the tenth symbolic animal of the Twelve Terrestrial Branches, corresponding to the zodiac sign Capricorn, and is thought to personify the warm, vital component of yang, the positive element of universal life. The ancient Chinese credited the cock with supernatural powers and considered the crowing of roosters at sunrise responsible for driving away the nocturnal ghosts. Cocks shaped from white sugar frequently are eaten by the bride and bridegroom at wedding ceremonies as a protection against harmful astrological powers.

The pigeon is a symbol of longevity, and in a custom dating back to the Han dynasty

(206 B.C. to 220 A.D.), a jade scepter, or "pigeon staff," often is presented to elderly persons as a token of long life.

The duck is the emblem of felicity and happiness, with special respect accorded to the Mandarin duck, which represents conjugal fidelity. It is said that once two ducks of this species are paired and then separated, they will pine away and die. The ancient T'ang pharmacologists recommended duck soup as a suitable means for reconciling differences between an estranged couple.

Fowl in general played a significant role in ancient Chinese pharmacology: numerous digestive aids were prepared from the fowl gizzards. Medicines made from chicken were believed to regulate the menstrual cycle and were given to women undergoing menopause. Essences made from black-bone chicken, a species believed to have particularly healthful properties, were said to aid sufferers of consumption and feebleness. According to a Chinese friend from Peking, a popular treatment in healing broken bones was to place a freshly killed, pounded chicken on the break for three days to a week. And the eating of dove and pigeon eggs was believed to prevent smallpox.

The ancient Chinese consumed fowl in many forms—braised chicken, casseroled duck, wild duck stew, fried flesh of the crane, roasted wild goose and wild duck stew are some of the dishes recorded from the menus of the great Han feasts. All types of fowl were available to both the common people and the upper classes, and the raising of chickens was encouraged by the government as a household hobby.

Today, as in ancient times, fowl is favored fare; chicken and duck are staples of the modern Chinese diet and are admired for their delicate flavor and versatility. Both are steamed, braised, deep-fried, stir-fried, simmered in soy-sauce-based liquid, stuffed, baked and boiled in soups. And regional specialties abound: northern chefs are masters of Peking duck and Shandong braised chicken; Easterners excel in making drunken chicken and saltwater duck. In western China, the Hunanese are experts at minced squab in bamboo cups, duck breast soup and smoked chicken, while the Sichuanese prefer crispy-skin duck, steamed duck in seasoned rice powder and spicy stir-fried chicken with peanuts. The Cantonese offer poultry dishes ranging from roasted duck, steamed chicken with scallions and roasted quail to fried goose with plum sauce.

Pigeons, too, serve the Chinese in gastronomic and other notable ways. An ancient Chinese practice still observed in parts of China today is the attachment of wooden pipes or whistles to the feet of domestic pigeons. As a flock of these birds circles in the sky, it creates harmonious melodies for its earthly audience below.

家禽類

Lemon Chicken Wings

Ning Meng Feng Chi

6 Servings ⌣ Appetizer or Main Dish

LEMON CHICKEN IS A
*popular Cantonese main
dish of boned, fried chicken
lightly glazed with a tart,
lemony sauce. Chicken wings,
marinated and deep-fried to a
golden crispness, are equally
delicious when coated with the
sauce. Serve the wings as an hors
d'oeuvre with drinks or as a
main dish with rice. Lemon
Chicken Wings reheat beautifully
in a 375-degree oven.*

18	chicken wings

Marinade

2	tablespoons soy sauce
1½	tablespoons rice wine or sake
½	teaspoon salt
¼	teaspoon freshly ground black pepper
4	scallions, smashed with the flat side of a cleaver
3	slices gingerroot, the size of a quarter, smashed with the flat side of a cleaver
2	cloves garlic, smashed with the flat side of a cleaver
2	egg yolks, lightly beaten
1½	cups cornstarch
3	cups peanut, safflower or corn oil

Lemon Sauce

6	tablespoons chicken broth, preferably Chinese Chicken Broth (page 345)
2	tablespoons freshly squeezed lemon juice
1	teaspoon sesame oil
1	tablespoon sugar
1	teaspoon salt
1	teaspoon cornstarch

Soy sauce or plum sauce and hot mustard

1. Rinse the chicken wings, and drain thoroughly. Cut each wing in two at the "elbow," and place in a bowl. Add the *Marinade*, toss lightly, and let marinate for at least 1 hour, or overnight in the refrigerator. Discard the gingerroot, scallions and garlic, and add the egg yolks to the wings. Toss lightly to coat with the yolks. Dredge each wing in the cornstarch, pressing lightly to make sure the cornstarch adheres.

2. Heat a wok, add the oil, and heat the oil to 375 degrees F. Add half the wings, and deep-fry over high heat for about 5 minutes, stirring constantly. Remove the chicken wings with a handled strainer or slotted spoon. Drain on

absorbent paper. Reheat the oil, and deep-fry the remaining wings in the same manner. Reheat the oil to 425 degrees. Add all the wings, and deep-fry a second time, until crisp and golden brown. Drain the wings, and remove the oil from the wok.

3. Reheat the wok, add the *Lemon Sauce*, and heat, stirring constantly, until thick. Add the fried wings, toss them in the sauce, and transfer to a platter. Serve immediately with soy sauce, or plum sauce and hot mustard.

Cantonese-Style Chicken Wings

Guang Shi Ji Yi

6 Servings ⁓ Appetizer or Main Dish

24	chicken wings, preferably "drumettes" only

Chicken Marinade

2½	tablespoons soy sauce
1½	tablespoons rice wine or sake
1	teaspoon sesame oil
1½	tablespoons minced garlic
1½	tablespoons minced gingerroot
1	teaspoon sugar
1	large egg, lightly beaten
1	cup cornstarch
3-4	cups peanut, safflower or corn oil

Soy sauce or plum sauce and hot mustard

MY FATHER IS ESPECIALLY *fond of the deep-fried chicken wing appetizers served in most Chinese restaurants. Here is my rendition of this regional classic. The crisp wings are infused with the flavor of garlic, ginger and sesame oil. For extra-crispness, reheat the cooked wings in the oven before serving.*

1. If using the whole wings, cut each one at both joints, separating the drumettes and wing tips. Set aside the wing tips. (You may use these in the recipe, marinating and cooking as directed, or you may discard them.) Using a sharp knife or a cleaver, cut through the skin, meat and tendons at the larger tip of each drumette, cutting all the way around the bone. With the tip of your knife, scrape and push the meat and skin toward the opposite end of the bone. Using your hands and the tip of the knife, push the meat and the skin inside out so that it is bunched up at the end of the bone. Prepare all the drumettes in the same manner, and place them in a bowl.

2. Add the *Chicken Marinade* to the drumettes. Toss lightly to coat and cover with plastic wrap. Let marinate for at least 1 hour at room temperature or, if possible, overnight in the refrigerator. Add the egg and toss lightly to coat. Dredge the drumettes in the cornstarch, coating thoroughly. Lightly press the cornstarch to make it adhere to the chicken. Arrange the drumettes on a tray and let air-dry for 1 hour, turning once.

3. Heat a wok, add the oil, and heat to 375 degrees F. Add 7 or 8 of the drumettes and deep-fry, turning carefully, until golden brown and crisp, about 5 to 6 minutes. Remove and drain for about 1 minute in a handled strainer or slotted spoon. Drain on absorbent paper until cool. Reheat the oil and deep-fry the remaining drumettes in batches. Drain and serve with soy sauce, or plum sauce and hot mustard. To reheat, bake 10 to 15 minutes in a preheated 400-degree oven.

Deep-Fried Chicken Packages
Cai Bao Ji
6 Servings ⁓ Appetizer or Main Dish

ALTHOUGH THIS DISH *requires a bit of preparation, it is certainly worth the effort. The boned chicken pieces, marinated in oyster sauce, are encased in the tender cabbage leaves and a crisp batter coating. I usually double-fry this dish, cooking the packages in 375-degree oil early in the day, and giving them a last-minute final frying in a hotter oil. In this way, most of the preparation can be done in advance.*

1½   pounds boneless chicken breast

Chicken Marinade
- 3 tablespoons oyster sauce
- 2 tablespoons soy sauce
- 1 tablespoon rice wine or sake
- 1 teaspoon sesame oil
- 2 tablespoons minced scallions
- 1 tablespoon minced gingerroot
- 1 tablespoon minced garlic
- 2 tablespoons cornstarch
- 2 teaspoons sugar

18-24   whole cabbage leaves

Batter
- 1 cup all-purpose flour
- 1 teaspoon salt
- 1 cup ice water
- 1 large egg, lightly beaten

3   cups peanut, safflower or corn oil

1. Remove the skin and any fat from the chicken, and cut the meat into ¾-inch cubes. Place the cubes in a bowl, add the *Chicken Marinade*, toss lightly, and let marinate for at least 1 hour, or overnight in the refrigerator.

2. Holding a knife parallel to the cutting surface, trim the stem of each cabbage leaf so that it is the same thickness as the leaf itself. Blanch the leaves, a few at a time, in boiling water for 1 minute. Remove them with a slotted spoon and immediately place in cold water. Drain, and pat dry with towels. Whisk the *Batter* until smooth.

3. Place a tablespoon of the chicken in the middle of a cabbage leaf. Fold in the end nearest you, fold in the two sides, and fold over the far edge to enclose the chicken in a square package. Repeat for the remaining chicken and cabbage leaves.

4. Heat a wok, add the oil, and heat the oil to 375 degrees F. Dip one-third of the cabbage packages in the batter, making sure that they are completely coated, and place in the hot oil. Deep-fry, turning constantly, for about 5 minutes; remove with a handled strainer or slotted spoon, and drain on absorbent paper. Deep-fry the remaining packages in the same manner, reheating the oil between batches. Reheat the oil to 400 to 425 degrees. Add all the packages, and deep-fry until golden brown and crisp. Remove, and drain on absorbent paper; cut each package crosswise in half, and arrange the packages on a platter. Serve immediately.

Chicken Noodle Salad With Chili-Oil Dressing

La You Liang Ban Mian

6 servings ⁓ Appetizer, Main Dish or Side Dish

S ICHUAN PROVINCE, IN
*southwestern China, is
known for its spicy home-style
fare. This fragrant noodle platter
admirably demonstrates the
salad-style delights of this
particular cuisine. Serve with a
main dish as a flavorful staple,
or as a light meal for lunch or
dinner. This salad is also perfect
warm-weather fare for a picnic.*

Chili-Oil Dressing

¼	cup peanut, safflower or corn oil
¼	cup sesame oil
12	slices gingerroot, the size of a quarter, smashed with the flat side of a cleaver
12	scallions, smashed with the flat side of a cleaver
6	dried red chili peppers, cut into ¼-inch sections, seeds removed
5-6	tablespoons Chinese black vinegar or Worcestershire sauce
¼	cup soy sauce
3	tablespoons rice wine or sake
3	tablespoons sugar

½	pound thin, straight egg noodles, such as *dan mian* or spaghettini
1	teaspoon sesame oil
2	cups carrots, peeled and cut into julienne strips
2	cups cucumber, peeled, seeded and cut into julienne strips
2	cups fresh bean sprouts, rinsed lightly and drained
1	cup scallion greens, cut into 1-inch lengths
2	cups cooked chicken, cut into julienne strips

1. To prepare the **Chili-Oil Dressing**, heat the oils in a wok or a saucepan with a lid until nearly smoking. Add the smashed gingerroot, scallions and chili pepper pieces. Cover and remove from the heat. Let cool, covered, until the oil has reached room temperature. Strain the oil, discarding the seasonings. Mix the seasoned oil with the black vinegar, soy sauce, rice wine and sugar, stirring to dissolve the sugar. Set aside.

2. In a large pot, bring 2 quarts of water to a boil. Add the noodles and cook until just tender. (Do not overcook.) Drain in a colander. Lightly rinse the noodles under cold running water. Drain thoroughly and toss with the sesame oil.

3. Arrange the noodles in the bottom of a deep, round dish. Arrange the carrots, cucumbers, bean sprouts and scallions in concentric circles over the noodles, and place the chicken pieces in the center. Just before serving, pour the dressing over the salad, toss lightly, if desired, to combine the ingredients and coat them. Serve at room temperature or cold.

Stir-Fried Squid With Hot Red Peppers (PAGE 225)

Five-Treasure Vegetable Platter (PAGE 317)

Red-Cooked Squab (PAGE 191)

Pork & Vegetable Noodles in Broth (PAGE 103)

Stir-Fried Chicken in Bird's Nest (PAGE 89)

Two Winters (PAGE 333)

Sweet & Sour Fish With Pine Nuts (PAGE 238)

175

Mongolian Barbecue (PAGE 292)
Sesame Flat Breads (PAGE 64)

Pang Pang Chicken

Bang Bang Ji

6 Servings ⁓ Main Dish

1 whole frying chicken, cut into pieces, or chicken parts, about 3½ pounds

Chicken-Cooking Liquid

10 cups water

⅓ cup rice wine or sake

3 slices gingerroot, the size of a quarter, smashed with the flat side of a cleaver

Peanut Dressing

6 tablespoons smooth peanut butter

4-6 tablespoons reserved Chicken-Cooking Liquid

3½ tablespoons soy sauce

3 tablespoons Chinese black vinegar or Worcestershire sauce

2 tablespoons rice wine or sake

1½ tablespoons sesame oil

1½ teaspoons hot chili paste or to taste

1½ tablespoons minced garlic

1½ tablespoons minced fresh gingerroot

2½ tablespoons sugar

3 English (gourmet seedless) cucumbers or 6 small pickling cucumbers

1 teaspoon salt

2 ounces cellophane noodles (bean threads)

1 teaspoon sesame oil

1 tablespoon minced scallion greens

THIS SICHUANESE COLD *platter offers a sampling of some notable characteristics of the western regional style: the crisp, fresh cucumber slices are a delightful contrast to the smooth cellophane noodles, and the peanut-butter base of the sauce adds a sumptuous richness. Roasted sesame paste, which is sold in Asian markets, may be substituted for the peanut butter.*

1. Rinse the chicken, drain thoroughly, and remove any fat from the cavity and neck. Place the chicken, breast side down, in a soup pot, add the *Chicken-Cooking Liquid,* and heat until boiling. Reduce the heat to medium and simmer 1 hour. Remove the chicken, let it cool, and discard the skin. Cut or shred the chicken by hand into matchstick-sized pieces. Retain 4 to 6 tablespoons of the cooking liquid for the dressing. Combine the ingredients for the *Peanut Dressing* by hand or in a food processor. Transfer to a serving bowl.

2. Slice the cucumbers lengthwise. Cut each half crosswise into thirds; cut

each piece lengthwise into thin slices that are 2 inches long and 1 inch wide. Place the slices in a bowl, add the salt, toss lightly, and let sit for 20 minutes. Pour off any water that has accumulated. Drain the cucumbers on paper towels.

3. Soften the cellophane noodles for 10 minutes in hot water to cover. Drain thoroughly and toss in the sesame oil. Arrange them on a large platter, making a slight indentation in the center. Arrange the cucumber slices on top. Place the cooked chicken shreds in the middle and sprinkle the minced scallion greens on top. Serve with the dressing on the side.

Hunan-Style Smoked Chicken

Hu Nan Xun Ji

6 Servings ⌢ Appetizer or Main Dish

I N CHINESE CUISINE, *smoking is a process used for flavoring foods rather than cooking them; the food is first steamed or boiled until just done; then it is suspended over the smoking mixture, which includes black tea, brown sugar, anise seed and sometimes flour or rice. Heat is applied, and the fragrant fumes color and flavor the food. Chicken is particularly suited to this process because the smoky flavor accentuates the sweetness of the meat. (See photograph, page 85.)*

1   whole roasting chicken, 4-5 pounds

Chicken Marinade
3   tablespoons rice wine or sake
3   scallions, smashed with the flat side of a cleaver
3   slices gingerroot, the size of a quarter, smashed with the flat side of a cleaver
1   tablespoon Sichuan peppercorns
2   teaspoons salt

Smoking Mixture
¼   cup loose black tea leaves
2   tablespoons brown sugar
2   tablespoons anise seed

2   teaspoons sesame oil

1. Rinse the chicken lightly, drain thoroughly, and remove any fat from the cavity and neck. Rub the *Chicken Marinade* inside the cavity and all over the skin. Place the chicken, with the marinade, breast side down in a bowl, and let marinate for at least 4 hours, or overnight in the refrigerator. Transfer the chicken and the marinade to a heatproof bowl, and place the bowl in a steamer tray. Cover the steamer tray. (Alternatively, if you do not have a steamer large enough to hold the chicken, you may tightly wrap the chicken in heavy-duty aluminum foil and bake for 1 hour in a preheated 400-degree oven, discard the marinade, then smoke the chicken as directed in steps 3 and 4.)

OULTRY

2. Fill a wok with water level with the bottom edge of the steamer tray, and heat until boiling. Place the steamer tray over the boiling water, and steam for 1 hour over high heat. Remove the chicken, and let it cool. Discard the marinade.

3. Line the inside of a wok or a deep pot with several layers of heavy-duty aluminum foil. Place the *Smoking Mixture* in the wok, and stir to combine the ingredients. Place a steaming rack or a smoking rack or two crisscrossed chopsticks over the smoking mixture. Place the steamed chicken, breast side down, on the rack. Line the inside of the wok lid or the deep pot lid with several layers of heavy-duty aluminum foil, and cover the pan securely with the lid.

4. Place the pan over high heat, and smoke the chicken for 12 minutes. (Start timing when the smell of smoke becomes very pronounced.) Turn off the heat, and let the chicken sit, covered, for 10 minutes; then remove it, and brush the outside of the chicken with the sesame oil. Cut the chicken, through the bones, into bite-sized pieces, as for Red-Cooked Chicken (page 181). Discard the seasonings. Arrange the chicken on a platter, and serve.

Sweet & Sour Glazed Chicken Livers

Sao Zhu Feng Gan

6 Servings ⌒ Appetizer or Main Dish

In Chinese cuisine, liver, whether from the pig, cow, duck or chicken, is treated with a versatility rarely found in other cuisines. It is deep-fried, stir-fried, pan-fried, simmered in a soy-based marinade and used as a garnish in soups. In this Cantonese platter, the crisp, deep-fried livers are coated in a light sweet-and-sour glaze. It is suitable as an hors d'oeuvre or a main dish served with rice.

2	pounds chicken livers

Liver Marinade

2	tablespoons rice wine or sake
1½	tablespoons soy sauce
1½	teaspoons minced garlic
4	scallions, smashed with the flat side of a cleaver
3	slices gingerroot, the size of a quarter, smashed with the flat side of a cleaver

3	cups peanut, safflower or corn oil

Liver Sauce

¼	cup ketchup
¼	cup water
2	teaspoons soy sauce
2	teaspoons Chinese black vinegar or Worcestershire sauce
1	teaspoon sesame oil
1½	tablespoons sugar
½	teaspoon salt

1. Rinse the chicken livers lightly, and drain thoroughly. Separate the livers at the natural division, and remove and discard any fat. Place the livers in a bowl, add the *Liver Marinade*, toss lightly, and let marinate for 20 minutes. Discard the scallions and gingerroot. Drain the livers.

2. Heat a wok, add the oil, and heat the oil to 375 degrees F. Add half the livers, covering the oil with the wok lid to prevent the oil from splashing. Uncover, and deep-fry the livers for about 4 minutes, stirring occasionally, until golden brown. Remove with a handled strainer or slotted spoon. Drain the livers. Reheat the oil and deep-fry the remaining livers. Remove the oil from the wok. Wipe out the wok.

3. Reheat the wok, add the *Liver Sauce*, and heat until boiling, stirring constantly over high heat. Add the livers and cook, stirring constantly over high heat, until the liquid has reduced to a thick glaze. Serve immediately.

Red-Cooked Chicken

Hong Shao Ji

6 Servings ⌣ Main Dish

Red-Cooking Liquid

6	cups water
1½	cups soy sauce
½	cup rice wine or sake
⅓	cup sugar
2	pieces dried tangerine or orange peel, or fresh, about 2 inches long
1	cinnamon stick or piece of Chinese cinnamon bark, if available
1	whole star anise
½	teaspoon fennel seeds
1	whole roasting chicken, 4-5 pounds
1	tablespoon sesame oil

1. Place the *Red-Cooking Liquid* in a heavy pot or a Dutch oven, and heat until boiling. Reduce the heat to low, and let the liquid simmer, uncovered, for 30 minutes.

2. Rinse the chicken lightly, drain, and remove any fat from the cavity and neck. Place the chicken, breast side down, in the red-cooking liquid, and cook for 1¼ hours, turning the chicken two or three times during the cooking. Turn off the heat, and let the chicken sit in the liquid for 15 minutes; then remove it. Brush the surface of the chicken with the sesame oil. Cut the chicken, through the bones, into bite-sized serving pieces as shown (discarding the backbone), and arrange them on a platter. Spoon a little of the cooking liquid over the chicken, and serve.

RED-COOKING, OR SLOW cooking in a soy-sauce-based liquid, is extremely popular all over China, since the preparation is simple and the flavor is complementary to rice. The cooking liquid (lu) may be used repeatedly to braise not only chicken but pork, lamb, beef, liver, tofu and hard-boiled eggs as well. In fact, the flavor intensifies and improves with each use. Half the ingredients (except the spices) should be replenished with every other reuse. By the fifth use, the spices should be replaced.

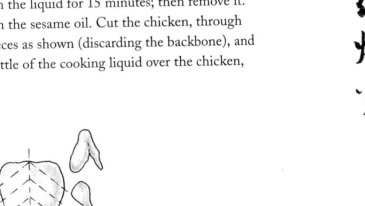

Red-Cooked Eight-Treasure Chicken

Nuo Mi Ji

6 Servings 〜 Main Dish

EIGHT-TREASURE CHICKEN *is a sumptuous dish inspired by the equally notable eastern classic of eight-treasure duckling. In both these dishes, the sticky rice provides a superb foil for the red-cooked sauce and a delicate filler for the garnishes of sausage and black mushrooms.*

Although a bit more time and effort are involved, the chicken may be boned before being stuffed, which simplifies cutting and eating the cooked chicken.

1	whole roasting chicken, 4½-5 pounds
1½	tablespoons soy sauce
¾	cup sweet (glutinous) rice, rinsed thoroughly and soaked in cold water to cover for 1 hour
2	tablespoons peanut, safflower or corn oil

Stuffing Ingredients

½	cup diced carrot
½	cup diced Chinese pork sausage, fried in oil until golden brown (for homemade, see page 275)
½	cup water chestnuts, plunged briefly into boiling water, refreshed in cold water and diced
½	cup fresh peas or thawed frozen peas
⅓	cup dried Chinese black mushrooms, soaked in hot water to cover for 20 minutes, stems removed and caps diced

Stuffing Sauce

1½	cups water or chicken broth, preferably Chinese Chicken Broth (page 345)
1	tablespoon soy sauce
1	tablespoon rice wine or sake
1	teaspoon sesame oil

Chicken-Braising Liquid

3½	cups water
¼	cup soy sauce
2	tablespoons rice wine or sake
1	tablespoon sugar
3	scallions, smashed with the flat side of a cleaver
3	slices gingerroot, the size of a quarter, smashed with the flat side of a cleaver
1	whole star anise
2	cups peanut, safflower or corn oil

Thickener
- 1½   **tablespoons water**
- 1   **teaspoon cornstarch**

1. Remove the fat pockets from the cavity of the chicken, and discard. Rinse the chicken, drain it thoroughly, and rub the soy sauce inside the cavity and all over the skin. Let the chicken sit for 15 minutes. Drain the rice.

2. Heat a wok, add the oil, and heat until very hot. Add the *Stuffing Ingredients*, and stir-fry over high heat, stirring constantly, for 1 minute. Add the rice and the *Stuffing Sauce*. Heat until the liquid boils, stirring constantly; then reduce the heat to medium and cook until the liquid is almost evaporated, stirring occasionally. Remove the stuffing, and let cool to room temperature. Clean the wok. Drain any liquid in the chicken into a heavy pot or Dutch oven. Add the *Chicken-Braising Liquid* to the pot. Stuff the cavity of the chicken with the cooled stuffing, and sew up the opening with twine.

3. Reheat the wok, add the 2 cups of oil, and heat to 400 degrees F. Preheat the oven to 350 degrees F. Carefully lower the chicken into the oil, breast side down, and ladle the hot oil over the chicken. Deep-fry it for several minutes until golden brown. Remove, and drain.

4. Place the chicken, breast side up, in the heavy pot or Dutch oven. Cover, and cook for 1½ hours, until the chicken is cooked and golden brown. Remove the chicken, remove the twine, and spoon the stuffing into a serving bowl. Carve the chicken meat into slices, or cut the chicken, through the bones, into bite-sized serving pieces, as for Red-Cooked Chicken (page 181). Arrange the chicken on a platter. Skim off any fat from the braising liquid, and strain out the seasonings. Heat the liquid until boiling, and add the *Thickener*, stirring constantly. Pour over the chicken, and serve immediately with the stuffing.

Salt-Baked Chicken

Yan Jiu Ji

6 Servings ～ Main Dish

*B*OTH FRENCH AND *Chinese chefs are fond of cooking chicken in salt because, like clay, it acts as an excellent conductor of heat, sealing in the natural juices and producing remarkably tender and moist meat without any salty flavor. Generally, the chicken is packed directly in the salt; however, I have adapted the recipe slightly by first wrapping it in parchment paper or an oven-roasting bag. This prevents the juices from leaking into the salt; thus the salt may be used again and again.*

1   whole roasting chicken, 4-5 pounds

Chicken Marinade

2   tablespoons rice wine or sake
1   tablespoon salt
3   scallions, smashed with the flat side of a cleaver
3   slices gingerroot, the size of a quarter, smashed with the flat side of a cleaver
1   whole star anise, smashed with the flat side of a cleaver
1   tablespoon Sichuan peppercorns

1   30-inch square parchment paper or a large oven-roasting bag
4   pounds rock salt or kosher salt
3   whole star anise, smashed with the flat side of a cleaver
1   tablespoon Sichuan peppercorns

Dipping Sauce

¼   cup chicken broth, preferably Chinese Chicken Broth (page 345)
1   teaspoon sesame oil
1   tablespoon shredded scallions
1   tablespoon finely shredded gingerroot
1   teaspoon salt

1. Lightly rinse the chicken and remove any fat from the cavity and neck. Drain the chicken thoroughly, and place it in a bowl. Add the *Chicken Marinade,* and rub it inside the cavity and all over the skin. Let the chicken marinate, breast side down, for at least 2 hours, or overnight, in the refrigerator. Remove from the marinade, and wrap the chicken in the parchment paper or place in the oven-roasting bag, breast side down.

2. Preheat the oven to 450 degrees F. Heat a wok or a heavy skillet, and add the rock salt, star anise and Sichuan peppercorns. Stir-fry over high heat, stirring constantly, until the salt begins to pop and is very hot. Spoon about one-third of the salt mixture into a 4-quart Dutch oven or casserole, shaping a well in the center of the salt. Place the chicken, breast side down, in the well, and cover with the remaining salt. Cover the pot, and place it in the preheated oven.

3. Bake the chicken for 1 hour; then remove it from the oven and let it sit in

the covered pot for 10 minutes before cutting. Cut the chicken, through the bones, into bite-sized pieces, as for Red-Cooked Chicken (page 181), and arrange on a platter. Discard the seasonings. Pour the *Dipping Sauce* into a saucepan, and heat until boiling. Pour the heated sauce over the chicken, and serve.

Steamed Chicken With Scallions

Cong Yu Ji

6 Servings ⌒ Main Dish

| 1 | whole roasting chicken, 4-5 pounds |

Chicken Marinade

2	tablespoons rice wine or sake
1	tablespoon soy sauce
1	tablespoon salt
3	scallions, smashed with the flat side of a cleaver
3	slices gingerroot, the size of a quarter, smashed with the flat side of a cleaver

⅓	cup finely shredded scallions
¼	cup finely shredded gingerroot
3	tablespoons sesame oil

Thickener

| 1 | tablespoon water |
| 1 | teaspoon cornstarch |

1. Lightly rinse the chicken, and drain thoroughly. Remove any fat from the cavity and neck. Place the chicken in a bowl, add the *Chicken Marinade*, and rub the marinade inside the cavity and all over the skin. Let the chicken marinate, breast side down, for at least 1 hour. Place the chicken, breast side up, in a heat-proof bowl or on a plate, and place in a steamer tray. (Alternatively, if you do not have a steamer large enough to hold the chicken, you may balance the chicken on an empty tuna can in a wok containing boiling water and cover with a domed lid or with a double layer of heavy-duty aluminum foil.)

2. Fill a wok with water level with the bottom edge of the steamer tray, and

CANTONESE CHEFS ARE renowned for their mastery in cooking chicken, preferring to accentuate the flavor rather than disguise it. Such is the case with this dish; the pungent seasonings of gingerroot and scallions highlight the taste of the chicken. The technique in this recipe is also used in cooking fish.

heat until boiling. Place the steamer tray containing the chicken over the boiling water, cover, and steam for 1 hour over high heat, adding more boiling water if necessary. Remove the chicken; drain off the liquid, and set it aside; let the chicken cool slightly. Cut the chicken, through the bones, into bite-sized pieces, as for Red-Cooked Chicken (page 181), and arrange them on a platter. Sprinkle the shredded scallions and gingerroot over the chicken.

3. Remove the water from the wok, and reheat the wok. Add the sesame oil, and heat until smoking. Slowly pour the sesame oil over the chicken. Heat the reserved chicken-cooking liquid, and skim off any fat. Slowly add the *Thickener*, stirring constantly to prevent lumps. Pour the thickened liquid over the chicken, and serve immediately.

Stir-Fried Chicken With Cashews

Yao Guo Ji

6 Servings ⁓ Main Dish

SICHUANESE CUISINE IS *known for its hot and spicy seasonings, and Sichuanese chefs employ a technique that further intensifies the pungent flavorings: they toss the assorted spices in oil over very high heat, which enlivens the flavors and infuses the oil with the seasonings. The technique is used not only in this dish but in many other Sichuanese stir-fried platters as well.*

1½	pounds boneless chicken breast

Chicken Marinade

2½	tablespoons rice wine or sake
2	tablespoons soy sauce
2	tablespoons water
1	teaspoon sesame oil
1	tablespoon cornstarch

1½	cups water chestnuts
1	tablespoon sesame oil
1	pound fresh spinach, trimmed and cleaned

Spinach Seasonings

1	tablespoon rice wine or sake
2	teaspoons minced garlic
1	teaspoon salt

1	cup peanut, safflower or corn oil

Chicken Seasonings

   3   tablespoons minced scallions

2½   tablespoons minced garlic

   2   tablespoons minced gingerroot

   2   teaspoons chili paste

Chicken Sauce

  ½   cup chicken broth, preferably Chinese Chicken Broth (page 345)

3½   tablespoons soy sauce

2½   tablespoons rice wine or sake

2½   teaspoons Chinese black vinegar or Worcestershire sauce

   1   teaspoon sesame oil

   2   tablespoons sugar

   2   teaspoons cornstarch

1½   cups raw cashews, toasted in a 350-degree oven until golden

1. Remove the skin and any fat from the chicken, and cut the meat into 1-inch cubes. Place the cubes in a bowl, add the *Chicken Marinade*, toss lightly, and let marinate for at least 20 minutes. Plunge the water chestnuts into boiling water for a few seconds to remove the tinny flavor. Refresh them in cold water, and slice thinly.

2. Heat a wok, add the sesame oil, and heat until nearly smoking. Add the spinach and the *Spinach Seasonings*. Stir-fry, turning constantly over high heat, until the spinach is barely limp. Arrange the spinach around the outer edge of a platter.

3. Reheat the wok, add the oil, and heat the oil to 375 degrees F. Add half the chicken pieces, and stir-fry over high heat, turning constantly until the meat changes color. Remove with a handled strainer or slotted spoon, and drain. Reheat the oil. Cook the remaining chicken in the same manner. Remove the oil from the wok, reserving 2 tablespoons. Wipe out the wok.

4. Reheat the wok, add the 2 tablespoons of oil, and heat until very hot. Add the *Chicken Seasonings*, and stir-fry for about 5 seconds. Add the chili paste, and stir-fry for another 5 seconds, until fragrant. Add the sliced water chestnuts, and stir-fry for about 15 seconds, until heated through. Add the *Chicken Sauce*, and heat, stirring constantly, until thick. Add the cooked chicken and the cashews. Toss lightly to coat with the sauce. Transfer the chicken to the center of the platter, and serve.

Tangerine-Peel Chicken

Chen Pi Ji

6 Servings ⌣ Main Dish

I N THE FOLLOWING SPICY *Sichuanese platter, the dried tangerine peel adds another dimension of flavor to the hot, tart sauce. Dried tangerine peel and dried orange peel are available in most Chinese grocery stores; however, fresh peel, blanched to remove any bitterness, may be substituted.*

2   pounds boneless chicken breast

Chicken Marinade

2   tablespoons soy sauce
2   tablespoons rice wine or sake
1   tablespoon water
1½   teaspoons sesame oil
1   teaspoon minced gingerroot
1½   tablespoons cornstarch

½   cup peanut, safflower or corn oil
2   tablespoons dried chili peppers, cut into ½-inch pieces, seeds removed
6   strips dried tangerine or orange peel, about 2 inches long, softened in hot water for 20 minutes and shredded (fresh peel may be substituted)

Chicken Sauce

¼   cup chicken broth, preferably Chinese Chicken Broth (page 345), or water
3   tablespoons soy sauce
2   tablespoons rice wine or sake
1   tablespoon clear rice vinegar
1½   teaspoons sesame oil
2   teaspoons sugar
1½   teaspoons cornstarch
¼   teaspoon freshly ground black pepper

1. Remove the skin and any fat from the chicken, and cut the meat into 1-inch cubes. Place the cubes in a bowl, add the *Chicken Marinade*, toss lightly, and let marinate for at least 20 minutes.

2. Heat a wok, add 3 tablespoons of the oil, and heat the oil until very hot. Add half the chicken, and cook, stirring constantly, over high heat until the meat changes color. Remove with a handled strainer or slotted spoon, and drain. Reheat the wok, add 3 more tablespoons of oil and heat until hot. Add the remaining chicken, cook, remove and drain. Wipe out the wok.

3. Reheat the wok, add the remaining 2 tablespoons of oil, and heat until very hot. Add the dried pepper pieces and the tangerine peel shreds; stir-fry for about 15 seconds over high heat, stirring constantly, until the peppers turn black. Add the *Chicken Sauce*, and cook, stirring constantly, until the sauce is thick. Add the chicken, toss lightly to coat the pieces, and transfer the mixture to a platter. Serve immediately.

Chicken Wings in Oyster Sauce

Hao Yu Bao Feng Chi

6 Servings 〜 Main Dish

18   chicken wings

Marinade
1½   tablespoons soy sauce
1   tablespoon rice wine or sake
1   teaspoon sesame oil

1   pound broccoli
1   cup peanut, safflower or corn oil

Braising Sauce
1   cup chicken broth, preferably Chinese Chicken Broth (page 345)
3   tablespoons oyster sauce
3   tablespoons rice wine or sake
1½   tablespoons soy sauce
1½   teaspoons sugar

Seasonings
12   1-inch pieces scallion, white part only
12   paper-thin slices gingerroot

Thickener
1   tablespoon water
1   teaspoon cornstarch

2   teaspoons minced garlic

THE THRIFTY CHINESE *savor every part of the chicken's anatomy, and wings are no exception; they are braised, deep-fried, boiled and used in soups. In this dish, they are simmered to a succulent tenderness in rich oyster sauce.*

Broccoli Sauce

2 tablespoons chicken broth, preferably Chinese Chicken Broth (page 345)

1 tablespoon rice wine or sake

¾ teaspoon salt

1. Cut each chicken wing in two at the "elbow." Place the wings in a bowl, add the *Marinade*, toss lightly, and let marinate for 20 minutes. Peel away the tough outer skin from the broccoli, and separate the florets. Roll-cut the stems into 1-inch pieces. Heat 1½ quarts salted water until boiling. Add the stem pieces, and cook for 30 seconds. Add the florets, and cook for 2½ minutes, or until both stems and florets are just tender. Refresh immediately in cold water. Drain thoroughly.

2. Heat a wok, and add the oil. Heat the oil to 375 degrees F. Drain the wings, and add the marinade to the *Braising Sauce*. Add a batch of the wings to the oil, and fry over high heat until golden brown. Remove with a handled strainer or slotted spoon, and drain. Reheat the oil, and fry the remaining wings in the same manner. Remove the oil from the wok, reserving 2 tablespoons. Wipe out the wok. Reheat the wok, add 1 tablespoon of the oil, and heat until very hot. Add the *Seasonings*, and stir-fry over high heat for about 10 seconds, until fragrant. Add the braising sauce and the chicken wings. Heat until the liquid is boiling, reduce the heat to medium, partially cover, and cook for 45 minutes, until the wings are very tender. With the liquid boiling, add the *Thickener*, stirring constantly to prevent lumps. Remove to a bowl, and keep warm. Wipe out the wok.

3. Reheat the wok, add the remaining 1 tablespoon of oil, and heat until very hot. Add the minced garlic, and stir-fry until fragrant, about 5 seconds. Add the broccoli, and stir-fry until heated through, about 10 seconds. Add the *Broccoli Sauce*, and stir-fry for about 10 more seconds over high heat. Arrange the broccoli around the outer edge of a platter. Place the chicken wings in the center, cover with the sauce, and serve.

Red-Cooked Squab

Hong Shao Ge Zi

6 Servings ⌢ Main Dish

6   squabs, about 1 pound each, or 3 Rock Cornish game hens

Seasonings

3   whole cloves
2   strips dried tangerine or orange peel, about 2 inches long (fresh peel may be substituted)
1   tablespoon Sichuan peppercorns
1   whole star anise
1   cinnamon stick

Red-Cooking Liquid

6   cups water
1½   cups soy sauce
½   cup rice wine or sake
¼   cup rock sugar, chopped coarsely (granulated sugar may be substituted)

1. Rinse the squabs, and drain them thoroughly.

2. Place the *Seasonings* in a square of cheesecloth, gather up the edges, and tie securely to make a spice bag. Place the seasonings and the *Red-Cooking Liquid* in a large pot, and heat until boiling. Reduce the heat to low, and simmer, uncovered, for 45 minutes. Add the squabs, and heat until boiling. Reduce the heat to low, and simmer the squabs for about 35 minutes, turning them several times. Remove the squabs, and cut each one, through the bones, into serving-sized pieces. Spoon a little of the cooking liquid over the squabs, and serve.

GAME BIRDS, SUCH AS *squab, are especially popular with the Cantonese, and the chefs from Canton use a great deal of imagination in preparing them. Perhaps one of the simplest and tastiest cooking methods is simmering in a soy-sauce-based marinade, as in this recipe. The spicy cooking liquid is equally suitable for cooking other poultry and meats, and the flavor of the liquid increases with each use. Rock sugar is available in Asian markets. (See photograph, page 171.)*

Steamed Duck With Oranges

Ju Zhi Men Ya

6 Servings ⁓ Main Dish

LIKE THE FRENCH, THE *Chinese are partial to the combination of oranges and duck. In this platter, the duck is first deep-fried in hot oil to give it a golden brown color. Then the whole bird is steamed with oranges and other seasonings, resulting in a superb mingling of flavors. This dish is an excellent companion to rice.*

1	whole duck, 5½-6 pounds
2	tablespoons soy sauce

Duck Sauce

½	cup chicken broth, preferably Chinese Chicken Broth (page 345), or water
1½	tablespoons ketchup
1	tablespoon rice wine or sake
1	tablespoon sugar
1	teaspoon salt
¼	teaspoon freshly ground black pepper

3	cups peanut, safflower or corn oil
1	cup shredded onions
2	teaspoons minced garlic
2	navel oranges, peeled and sectioned

Thickener

1½	tablespoons water
2	teaspoons cornstarch

1. Rinse the duck, drain, and remove any fat from the cavity and neck. Using a heavy cleaver, cut the duck, through the bones, into bite-sized serving pieces, as for Red-Cooked Chicken (page 181). Place the pieces in a bowl, add the soy sauce, and toss lightly to coat. Let sit for 15 minutes. Drain the pieces, and add the soy sauce to the *Duck Sauce*.

2. Heat a wok, add the oil, and heat the oil to 400 degrees F. Add a portion of the duck pieces, covering the oil with the wok lid to prevent the oil from splashing. Uncover, and deep-fry the duck pieces for about 2 minutes, until golden brown. Remove with a handled strainer or slotted spoon, and drain. Reheat the oil, and deep-fry the remaining duck in the same manner. Remove the oil from the wok, reserving 2 tablespoons. Wipe out the wok.

3. Reheat the wok, add the 2 tablespoons of oil, and heat until hot. Add the shredded onions, and stir-fry over high heat, stirring constantly until the onions are soft and transparent. Add the minced garlic, and stir-fry for about 5 seconds, until fragrant. Add the orange sections, and stir-fry for another 5 seconds. Add

the duck sauce, and heat until boiling. Add the *Thickener*, stirring constantly to prevent lumps. Arrange the duck pieces in a heatproof 2-quart soufflé dish or bowl. Pour the thickened sauce on top. Place in a steamer tray. Wipe out the wok.

4. Fill the wok with water level with the bottom edge of the steamer tray, and heat until boiling. Place the steamer tray over the boiling water, cover, and steam for 1 hour over high heat, replenishing the boiling water when necessary. (Alternatively, if you do not have a steamer large enough to hold the dish, you may cover the dish tightly with a double layer of heavy-duty aluminum foil and bake for 1 hour in a preheated 400-degree oven.) Remove and arrange the duck pieces on a platter. Skim the fat off the sauce, and pour the sauce over the duck pieces. Serve immediately.

Crispy-Skin Duck

Xiang Su Ya

6 Servings ⌒ Main Dish

1	whole duck, 5½-6 pounds

Duck Marinade

1	tablespoon rice wine or sake
6	slices gingerroot, the size of a quarter, smashed with the flat side of a cleaver
5	scallions, smashed with the flat side of a cleaver
2	tablespoons salt
2	teaspoons Sichuan peppercorns
1	whole star anise, smashed with the flat side of a cleaver
2	tablespoons soy sauce
1	cup cornstarch
3	cups peanut, safflower or corn oil

1. Rinse the duck, drain, and remove any fat from the cavity and neck. Rub the *Duck Marinade* inside the cavity and all over the skin. Place the duck, breast side down, in a bowl with the marinade, and let marinate for at least 1 hour. Transfer the duck and the marinade to a heatproof plate or bowl; arrange the duck breast side up. Place the plate or bowl in a steamer tray.

2. Fill a wok with water level with the bottom edge of the steamer tray, and heat until boiling. Place the steamer tray over the boiling water, cover, and steam

THE EXTRAORDINARY contrast of textures in Crispy-Skin Duck may be one reason for the popularity of this Sichuanese dish. The combination of cooking methods accounts for the result: the steaming gently cooks the meat, leaving it juicy and tender, while the deep-frying further seals in the juices and crisps the skin. Serve the duck plain or with steamed Lotus Buns (page 59) and sweet bean sauce or hoisin sauce.(See photograph, page 87.)

the duck for 2 hours over high heat, replenishing the boiling water when necessary. (Alternatively, if you do not have a steamer large enough to hold the plate, you may cover the plate with a double layer of heavy-duty aluminum foil and bake for 1½ hours in a preheated 400-degree oven.) Remove the duck, discard the marinade, and let the duck cool. Rub the soy sauce all over the outside of the duck, and then dredge the duck in the cornstarch; press lightly to make the cornstarch adhere to the skin. Let the duck air-dry for 15 minutes. Remove the water from the wok.

3. Reheat the wok, add the oil, and heat the oil to 425 degrees F. Slowly lower the duck into the hot oil, and deep-fry it on both sides, ladling the oil over the top, until the skin is crisp and golden brown, about 3 to 4 minutes per side. Remove the duck, and drain. Cut it, through the bones, into bite-sized pieces, as for Red-Cooked Chicken (page 181), and arrange the duck pieces on a platter.

Cantonese-Style Roasted Duck

Yue Shi Kao Ya

6 Servings ⌣ Main Dish

THOUGH ROASTED DUCK is considered by most to be an exclusive specialty of northern China, Cantonese chefs prepare a variation that rivals even Peking duck in flavor—the famous Cantonese-style roasted duck. The two do have their similarities: The skin of both is basted with a syrup so that it will be crisp and golden, and both ducks are served with Mandarin Pancakes (page 62) and either sweet bean sauce or hoisin sauce.

1	whole duck, 5½-6 pounds

Duck Marinade

4	scallions, smashed with the flat side of a cleaver
4	slices gingerroot, the size of a quarter, smashed with the flat side of a cleaver
1	tablespoon rice wine or sake
1½	teaspoons salt
1½	teaspoons five-spice powder
½	teaspoon freshly ground black pepper

Coating Mixture

2	cups boiling water
¼	cup honey
3	tablespoons rice wine or sake
1	tablespoon clear rice vinegar

1. Rinse the duck, drain, and remove the fat from the cavity and neck. Pinch the scallions and the gingerroot in the **Duck Marinade** repeatedly for several

minutes to impart their flavor. Rub the marinade inside the cavity and all over the skin. Let the duck marinate for at least 2 hours, or overnight in the refrigerator. Discard the scallions and gingerroot.

2. Bring about 4 quarts of water to a boil. Wrap a length of twine around each wing. Grab the ends of the twine in one hand, and use them to suspend the duck over the water. Ladle the boiling water over the duck for 1 minute. (This will clean it and open the pores of the skin.) Drain thoroughly.

3. Place the *Coating Mixture* in a large pan, and heat until boiling. Hold the duck over the boiling mixture in the same manner as above, and baste the duck for several minutes. Hang the duck in a cool, dry place or in front of a fan. Place a pan underneath the duck to catch the drippings. Do not touch the duck, or the cooked skin will have spots. Let the duck air-dry for 4 hours, or overnight if possible.

4. Preheat the oven to 375 degrees F. Place the duck, breast side up, on a rack in a roasting pan, and roast for 2½ hours, turning several times. Let the duck cool briefly, and cut it, through the bones, into bite-sized pieces, as for Red-Cooked Chicken (page 181). Arrange the pieces on a platter, and serve.

Stir-Fried Minced Squab

Chao Ge Song

6 Servings ⁓ Main Dish

In this dish, mixed *meat and water chestnuts are drenched in a fragrant sauce and poured over crisp-fried noodles. Then the noodles and meat are rolled up in a lettuce leaf. The dish is a fine example of the best in Chinese cuisine: the pungency of the fresh gingerroot, the crispness of the lettuce and the crunchiness of the fried noodles provide a superb combination of flavors and textures. If squab is unavailable, Rock Cornish game hen or dark chicken may be substituted.*

1	head leafy or Boston lettuce
2	cups peanut, safflower or corn oil
1	ounce rice stick noodles
2	1-pound squabs
1	pound boneless center-cut pork loin

Meat Seasonings

3	tablespoons water
1½	tablespoons soy sauce
1	tablespoon rice wine or sake
1½	teaspoons sesame oil

Minced Seasonings

2	tablespoons minced scallions
1	tablespoon minced gingerroot

5	dried Chinese black mushrooms, soaked in hot water to cover for 20 minutes, stems removed and caps coarsely chopped
1½	cups water chestnuts, plunged briefly into boiling water, refreshed in cold water and coarsely chopped

Meat Sauce

¼	cup water
2½	tablespoons soy sauce
1	tablespoon rice wine or sake
1½	teaspoons sesame oil
1	teaspoon sugar
1	teaspoon cornstarch
1	teaspoon salt

1. Rinse the lettuce, and separate the leaves. Drain thoroughly, and lightly pound each leaf with the flat side of a cleaver. Arrange the flattened leaves on a platter, and set aside.

2. Heat a wok, add the oil, and heat the oil to 425 degrees F, or until nearly smoking. Add the rice noodles, and deep-fry for about 5 seconds, until puffed and pale golden. Turn over immediately, and cook for a few seconds on the other

side. Remove with a handled strainer or slotted spoon, and drain on absorbent paper. Arrange the noodles on a platter, and lightly break them up with your fingers. Remove the oil from the wok, reserving 7 tablespoons.

3. Remove the skin from the squabs, and remove the meat from the bones. Mince the meat. Remove any fat and gristle from the pork loin, and discard; mince the meat. Place the minced meats in a bowl, add the *Meat Seasonings*, toss lightly, and let marinate for 20 minutes.

4. Reheat the wok, add 4 tablespoons of the reserved oil, and heat until hot. Add the minced meats, and stir-fry over high heat, mashing and separating the pieces, until the color changes. Remove, and drain. Wipe out the wok. Reheat the wok, add the remaining 3 tablespoons of oil, and heat until very hot. Add the *Minced Seasonings*, and stir-fry over high heat, turning constantly, until fragrant, about 10 seconds. Add the mushrooms, and stir-fry for another 5 seconds, turning constantly. Add the water chestnuts, and stir-fry for about 15 seconds, until heated through. Add the *Meat Sauce*, and stir-fry, stirring constantly until thick. Add the cooked meats, toss lightly in the sauce, and spoon the mixture over the fried rice noodles. To serve, place some of the stir-fried meat and fried rice noodles in the lettuce leaf, roll up, and eat.

Beggar's Chicken

Fu Gui Ji

6 Servings ⌒ Main Dish

ACCORDING TO CHINESE legend, this dish originated many years ago in China when a beggar had "borrowed" a chicken from a local farmer and was roasting it on a spit for his dinner. Suddenly, he heard the thunder of approaching horses. To protect his meal, he wrapped the chicken in a lotus leaf and buried it in mud near a fire. Once the unwelcome visitors had come and gone, he unearthed the wrapped chicken and smashed open the casing, which had dried to clay. The chicken had cooked to a glorious tenderness, basting in its own juices. I find that a bread dough works well in place of the baker's clay in the traditional recipe. The dough casing is usually not eaten, but it absorbs the juices of the chicken, so I like to nibble on it. Similarly, a clay cooker, sealed with a flour-and-water paste to make it airtight, would be ideal in place of the dough.

1 whole roasting chicken, 4-4½ pounds

Chicken Marinade
3 tablespoons rice wine or sake
2 tablespoons soy sauce

2 whole star anise, smashed with the flat side of a cleaver
3 scallions, ends trimmed and smashed with the flat side of a cleaver

Dough
4 cups all-purpose flour
1 teaspoon salt
1 tablespoon peanut, safflower or corn oil
1¼ cups warm water

10-12 dried Chinese black mushrooms, soaked in hot water to cover for 20 minutes
3 tablespoons peanut, safflower or corn oil

Filling
½ pound boneless center-cut pork loin (fat removed), cut into matchstick-sized shreds
1 tablespoon soy sauce
1 tablespoon rice wine or sake
1 teaspoon sesame oil

¼ cup Tientsin preserved vegetables, rinsed and drained (optional)
3 tablespoons minced scallions, white part only
2 tablespoons minced garlic
½ cup matchstick-sized shreds canned bamboo shoots, blanched in boiling water for 15 seconds, refreshed in cold water, and drained
2 tablespoons rice wine or sake
1 tablespoon soy sauce
1 teaspoon sugar or to taste
1 large egg, lightly beaten

1. Rinse the chicken and remove any fat deposits from the neck and cavity. Pat dry and place in a bowl. Add the *Chicken Marinade*, and rub over the surface of the chicken and inside the cavity. Stuff the star anise and the scallions inside the cavity, cover the chicken with plastic wrap, and let stand in the refrigerator overnight.

2. To prepare the *Dough*, place the flour and salt in the mixing bowl. Add the oil and water, and mix to a rough dough. (Add a little more water if the dough feels dry and a little flour if it feels too wet.) Transfer the dough to a lightly floured surface, and knead until smooth and elastic. Wrap in plastic wrap and chill for 30 minutes.

3. Drain the mushrooms, cut off the stems and discard, and cut the caps into matchstick-sized shreds. Heat a wok until hot. Add 2 tablespoons of the oil, and heat until very hot. Add the *Filling*, and stir-fry until the meat has changed color and separated. Remove the cooked meat with a handled strainer or slotted spoon, and drain. Wipe out the wok. Reheat the wok, add the remaining 1 tablespoon oil, heat until hot, and add the black mushrooms, preserved vegetables, if using, minced scallions and minced garlic. Stir-fry for 15 seconds, until fragrant, and add the bamboo shoots. Stir-fry for another 15 seconds. Add the cooked pork, rice wine, soy sauce and sugar. Stir-fry briefly, and remove. Spread the mixture out on a tray to cool.

4. Preheat the oven to 350 degrees F. Stuff the filling into the cavity of the chicken. On a lightly floured surface, roll out the dough to a large rectangle about ½ inch thick. The edges should be slightly thinner than the center. Place the chicken, breast side down, in the center of the dough. Fold in the edges from the sides and the ends to enclose the chicken like a package. You may use extra dough to make a decoration on top. Brush the surface of the dough with the beaten egg and place the chicken, breast side up, on a sturdy baking sheet.

5. Bake for 1 hour, pouring off any excess fat if necessary. Reduce the oven temperature to 250 degrees, and bake another hour. The casing should be golden brown. Remove, and cool slightly. To serve, cut through the dough lengthwise and then crosswise to expose the chicken, which should be very tender. Remove the dough casing, and cut the chicken into serving pieces. Serve, along with some of the filling.

Fish & Seafood

THE MAGNIFICENT SCENIC BEAUTY of Hong Kong is legendary. The breathtaking panoramic skyline has inspired numerous writers to produce stunning prose, and the mystique of this Far Eastern city is such that Hong Kong is a frequent backdrop for sizzling spy thrillers and torrid romances. So it was with a great deal of excitement that I prepared for my first visit to this famed colony, poring over guidebooks by the score at the public library.

"Rugged peaks studded with skyscrapers and surrounded by azure waters" was what one travel author had written about the stunning aerial view of Hong Kong. Sadly, on the day my plane landed, the entire area was shrouded in a muggy fog so thick the runway was barely perceptible, even as the wheels of the plane touched down. The view from the taxi window as we sped into the city was hardly more enlightening. That night, I felt quite let down as I crawled into my bunk at the hostel, but I vowed that I would rise at dawn to view the magnificent vistas of the city.

Bright sunlight awakened me the next morning, and joyfully, I ran to the window. The view that greeted me from our 15-story high rise located in the inner recesses of Hong Kong was not at all what I expected. Instead of "rugged peaks" and "azure waters," I glimpsed endless tenement rooftops brimming with all types of seafood drying in the blistering sun. Later, on a jaunt through the neighborhood, I passed row after row of shop fronts displaying dried fish maw, shark's fin and bird's nest, with signs proclaiming WHOLESALE PURVEYORS OF DRIED SEA PRODUCTS. The air fairly reeked of the sea and its products.

The sea dominates the atmosphere of Hong Kong: it surrounds the island in varying shades of azure and aquamarine, it provides a portion of the population with its livelihood, and it furnishes an inexhaustible supply of food products. Seafood is plentiful and readily available at a very reasonable price here, and one immediately senses its importance to the Chinese. It figures prominently in the diets of all Chinese and is consumed in all forms; though fresh seafood is readily available, dried seafood is eaten frequently and preferred by some as a flavorful and nutritious garnish to rice.

Because China abounds in rivers, lakes, streams, canals and ponds (not to mention the fact that a large portion of the country borders the sea), numerous freshwater and saltwater fish, shellfish, crustaceans and mollusks are available and have enjoyed prominence throughout Chinese history.

The ancient Chinese were the first to employ nets, weirs, rods and lines in fishing. The legendary Emperor Fu Hsi, who ruled China from 2953 B.C. to 2838 B.C., is credited with teaching his people how to weave nets, in addition to showing them how to utilize the many food products of the sea. Later, fishing became an enjoyable and lucrative pastime, and during the T'ang dynasty (618 to 907), fish farming became extremely popular.

Fish and "sea savories," as shellfish were called, became mainstays of the ancient

Chinese diet. Clams, mussels, shrimps and oysters were particularly relished by the officials of the Imperial Court; the finest specimens were sent off to the Imperial kitchens before the rest of the daily catch reached the marketplace. Red-bellied trout and striped mullet were both highly prized, and flatfish such as sole and halibut were also very popular.

Fish relishes, too, were very much in demand. The fermented pastes contained fish, notably carp and mullet, with the addition of rice, salt and occasionally milk products. Some of the relishes were extremely sophisticated, with special emphasis placed on aesthetics; one was composed of paper-thin slices of pink fish flesh arranged like the petals of a blooming hibiscus.

Fish is highly regarded by the Chinese not only as a source of food. Owing to its plentiful numbers and the speed with which it reproduces, the fish is a symbol of regeneration, and since it is a creature seemingly content with its environment, it signifies harmony. Fish frequently swim in pairs and are therefore emblematic of the joys of union. Accordingly, a pair of fish is customarily given as a betrothal gift to a future bride. Also, by tradition, fish are served at the end of a banquet; a whole fish is displayed on the banquet table at the New Year to represent bounty, wealth and abundance. Fish were often presented as offerings in ancient ceremonial worship, and certain species were prized for their beauty.

Certain seafoods signified events in the ancient culinary calendar: the appearance of crab claws in the marketplace heralded the Mid-Autumn Festival (the fifteenth day of the eighth lunar month), whole crabs and clams bespoke the arrival of winter, and in Suzhou, a city renowned for its culinary refinement, sea scallops were eaten to mark the arrival of summer.

The popularity of these foods has not diminished. All types of fish and shellfish are notably evident in the modern Chinese diet. In their fresh state, they are seasoned with light, delicate flavorings—such as gingerroot, scallions and rice wine—to highlight their natural, sweet tastes. (The Chinese believe that freshwater fish is sweeter and more refined than saltwater species.) The cooking methods used are generally characterized by extremely high temperatures and brief cooking times, as in stir-frying, steaming and deep-frying. These same foods in dried form play a prominent role in Chinese cuisine as flavorings in soups, stir-fried dishes, braised stews and fillings or stuffings.

The accompanying Seafood Glossary offers some background information, starting with the most commonly served foods of this category.

SEAFOOD GLOSSARY

~

Fish

Freshness is a trait particularly stressed by the Chinese where fish is concerned. Fish are often purchased live and then stored in large tanks until they are ready to be cooked. When purchasing a whole fish, the following guidelines should be used in determining the freshness: (1) The flesh should be firm, springing back when pressed. (2) The eyes should be clear, well rounded and not sunken. (3) The gills should be bright red. (4) The fish should have a mild, fresh odor, especially in the gills.

Although the Chinese do prepare and serve fillets and steaks, the majority of their dishes call for a whole fish with head and tail intact. It is believed that in this form, the natural juices are retained with less chance of the flesh drying out. The tongue and cheeks of certain fish are greatly relished. Some of the most notable varieties of freshwater fish used by the Chinese are carp, buffalo, bream, trout and grouper. Of the saltwater fish, sea bass, sole, turbot, porgy, butterfish, whitefish, flounder and shark are widely used. Shad, millet and perch, all extremely popular, defy classification, since they migrate seasonally from the ocean into the rivers. Eel and turtle are favored as well.

Shrimp

Unlike the fairly limited selection of shrimp found in most American markets, numerous sizes are available in the Far East. They are most often stir-fried, deep-fried, boiled or minced to a paste. In Hunan, miniature shrimp the size of rice grains are collected from mountain streams and cooked with squash in a soup. Miniature shrimp are also used in a fermented paste prepared in southern China. This paste is used as a pungent flavoring and is an extremely rich form of calcium and protein. These same shrimp are dried and used as a seasoning in fillings, soups and vegetable dishes.

Prawns

Although something of an expensive delicacy, prawns are used extensively in Chinese cooking. Like shrimp, they may be stir-fried, deep-fried or boiled. Prawns are also extremely tasty when braised and served cold with assorted dipping sauces.

Crab

As with fish and other seafoods, freshwater crabs are preferred by the Chinese to the saltwater variety because the flavor is considered more delicate. Several kinds of crab are found in the many fresh waters of China, as well as in the China Sea. Crabs are customarily steamed, stir-fried or deep-fried.

Lobster

Lobster—or sea dragon, as it is commonly called in the Far East—is rarely consumed in areas other than southernmost China. Even here, it is enjoyed only by a select few because of its exorbitant price. The spiny lobster, native to the Far East, does not have large claws; the bulk of its meat is in the tail, and the texture is coarser than that of the American East Coast lobster. Lobster should always be purchased live and cooked as soon as possible. The Chinese serve this seafood steamed, stir-fried or sliced cold in salads.

Scallops

Scallops are greatly admired for their sweet, delicate flavor and unique texture. Fresh scallops are available exclusively in the coastal regions, where they are stir-fried and poached. Dried scallops, a delicacy popular throughout China, are used as a flavoring in soups, braised stews and vegetable dishes.

Clams

Clams are generally enjoyed by the Chinese living in coastal areas. Some of the more exotic varieties favored by the Chinese are not available in American markets, but cherrystones, littlenecks and razor clams are consumed regularly. Simplicity is stressed when cooking clams. Steamed or boiled clams with a dipping sauce are commonly served with wine. Clams are also stir-fried, stuffed and simmered.

Oysters

Contrary to the popular Western belief that oysters are an aphrodisiac, the Chinese feel that the opposite is true, so this shellfish is rarely eaten in the nocturnal hours. Oysters are often served as a snack with wine and are stir-fried, deep-fried and used in soups and omelets. Dried oysters are used in stuffings, soups and stir-fried dishes. In southern China, oysters and seasonings are reduced to a thick, pungent sauce (oyster sauce) and used as a flavoring in vegetable, meat and seafood dishes.

Squid

Squid has been a popular food in China since ancient times. It is enjoyed both fresh and dried. Dried squid is soaked in hot water and, like the fresh variety, scored into decorative shapes and used in stir-fried dishes, or parboiled and served with a dipping sauce. In the Far East, strips of dried squid are sold by street vendors with grills as a snack that is eaten like beef jerky. Squid meat has an unusually high protein content, and it is available not only fresh and dried but frozen, canned and salted as well. Cuttlefish, a cousin to squid, with short tentacles and a thick body, is also very popular, particularly with the southern Chinese.

How to Clean Squid

1. Pull the head and body apart. Cut off the tentacles just below the eyes, reserving the tentacles and body sac.

2. Remove and discard the transparent quill from the inside of the body sac.

3. Gently pull the back flaps from the body sac, and reserve them. Peel off and discard the purple membrane covering the body sac and the back flaps.

4. Slice the squid body lengthwise, and use as directed.

Shark's Fin

Shark's fin is, as the name implies, the fin of the shark. It is one of the costliest and most delicious Chinese delicacies. In some Chinese grocery stores, the entire fin, with the cartilage and gelatinous needles, is avail-able. But the dried gelatinous needles, often slightly preconditioned, are most widely sold. A lengthy soaking period and precooking time are necessary to rid this food of its fishy flavor, for it is relished merely for its texture. Shark's fin may be added to soups, braised with meats or used in savory pastries. It is also extremely nutritious.

Bird's Nest

Bird's nest has been used by the Chinese since the beginning of the Ming dynasty (1368 to 1644). This delicacy is made from a combination of seaweed and the saliva of a swallow that inhabits the Malay Archipelago. The gathering of the nests is a perilous procedure, which accounts for the formidable expense of this food. There are two types of bird's nest: the more precious are white nests, made entirely from the saliva; black nests are those dotted with feathers and bits of seaweed. White nests are gathered once a year, while black nests are gathered twice. Both varieties are highly nutritious and are reputed to possess powers of restoring youth. Once this dried delicacy has been soaked in water, it is used as a garnish in sweet and savory soups. Like shark's fin, it is admired for its texture.

Shrimp With Two Dipping Sauces
Xia Er Chi

6 Servings ⌒ Appetizer or Main Dish

2 pounds medium-sized raw shrimp, shelled

Shrimp Marinade
3 tablespoons rice wine or sake
4 scallions, smashed with the flat side of a cleaver
4 slices gingerroot, the size of a quarter, smashed with the flat side of a cleaver
1 teaspoon salt

Mustard Dipping Sauce
2½ tablespoons mustard powder
¼ cup hot water
2 tablespoons rice wine or sake
2 teaspoons soy sauce
1 teaspoon sesame oil
1 teaspoon salt
½ teaspoon sugar
1 tablespoon minced fresh cilantro

Spicy Sweet & Sour Dipping Sauce
½ cup ketchup
Scant 2 tablespoons clear rice vinegar
1½ teaspoons soy sauce
1 teaspoon hot chili paste
1 teaspoon minced gingerroot
1½ tablespoons sugar
½ teaspoon salt

In China, shrimp is relished for its simple, sweet flavor. In fact, many prefer shrimp to be steamed and served unadorned with a dipping sauce on the side. In this country, since most shrimp are fresh-frozen, I generally boil them in a seasoned marinade with water. I like to offer a choice of two sauces—one mustard-based and one hot sweet-and-sour mixture. The contrasting flavors are excellent.

1. Holding the cleaver or a sharp knife parallel to the cutting surface, score each shrimp along the back; the scoring will allow the shrimp to "butterfly" when cooked. Remove the vein and rinse thoroughly. Place the shrimp in a bowl, and add the *Shrimp Marinade*. Toss lightly to coat and let marinate for at least 30 minutes, or longer if possible.

2. While the shrimp are marinating, prepare the dipping sauces. To make the

Mustard Dipping Sauce, mix the mustard powder with the hot water to form a smooth paste. Add the remaining ingredients, blending until smooth. Transfer the sauce to a serving dish. To make the *Spicy Sweet & Sour Dipping Sauce*, combine the ingredients and blend until evenly mixed. Transfer the sauce to a serving dish.

3. In a wok or a heavy saucepan, bring 2 quarts of water to a boil. Add the shrimp and marinade and cook for about 3 minutes, or until the shrimp curl and change color. Remove with a handled strainer or a slotted spoon, discarding the liquid and seasonings, and arrange on a serving platter. Serve at room temperature or cold, with the two dipping sauces.

Hundred-Corner Shrimp Balls

Bai Jiao Xia Qiu

6 Servings ⌒ Appetizer

THESE PUFFS ARE SO *named because of their light coating of bread cubes. Serve them as finger food with drinks accompanied by Sichuan-peppercorn salt for dipping.*

1	pound medium-sized raw shrimp, shelled
½	cup water chestnuts, plunged briefly into boiling water, refreshed in cold water and coarsely chopped

Shrimp Seasonings

1	egg white
1	tablespoon rice wine or sake
1	teaspoon sesame oil
1	teaspoon minced scallions
1	teaspoon minced gingerroot
1	teaspoon salt
3	tablespoons cornstarch
12	slices thin sandwich bread, crusts removed
4	cups peanut, safflower or corn oil

1. Devein the shrimp, rinse lightly, and drain thoroughly. Place the shrimp in a dishtowel, and squeeze out as much moisture as possible. Mince the shrimp to a smooth paste using a blender or a food processor fitted with the steel blade, or by hand with two cleavers. Place the shrimp paste in a mixing bowl, and add the water chestnuts and the *Shrimp Seasonings*. Stir to combine, and add the cornstarch. Stir vigorously in one direction, and lightly throw the mixture against the inside of the bowl to combine evenly.

2. Cut the bread into ¼-inch cubes. Spread the cubes out on a baking sheet,

and let them dry for 2 hours, turning occasionally.

3. Dip your hands in water to prevent the shrimp paste from sticking. Shape the paste into balls ¾ inch in diameter. Roll the shrimp balls in the bread cubes, pressing lightly to make sure that the cubes adhere firmly.

4. Heat a wok, add the oil, and heat the oil to 350 degrees F. Add a third of the shrimp balls, and deep-fry, turning constantly over high heat, for about 4 minutes, or until the shrimp paste is cooked and the balls are golden. Remove with a handled strainer or slotted spoon, and drain on absorbent paper. Reheat the oil, and deep-fry the remaining shrimp balls in the same manner, reheating the oil between batches. Arrange the shrimp balls on a platter; serve immediately.

Crispy-Fried Shrimp With Garlic

Yan Su Xia

6 Servings ⌣ Main Dish or Appetizer

2   pounds medium-sized raw shrimp, in their shells, or shelled

Shrimp Marinade

2   slices gingerroot, the size of a quarter, smashed with the flat side of a cleaver

2   tablespoons rice wine or sake

2½   tablespoons cornstarch

2   cups peanut, safflower or corn oil

Shrimp Seasonings

3   tablespoons minced garlic

2½   teaspoons salt

1. Cut away the legs and antennae of the shrimp, if remaining. Devein the shrimp using a needle or a toothpick, and rinse the shrimp thoroughly. Pat them dry, and place them in a mixing bowl. Pinch the gingerroot slices in the *Shrimp Marinade* repeatedly for several minutes to impart the flavor; add the marinade to the bowl. Toss the shrimp lightly, and let them marinate for 20 minutes. Discard the gingerroot. Add the cornstarch to the shrimp, and toss lightly.

2. Heat a wok, add the oil, and heat the oil to 425 degrees F. Add the shrimp in batches, and deep-fry over high heat for about 2½ minutes, turning constantly

T HIS APPARENTLY SIMPLE *eastern dish is actually an unusual mélange of texture and flavor. The shrimp are superb, deep-fried to a crisp, golden color and lightly seasoned with salt and minced garlic. While they are traditionally cooked and served with shells on, you may prefer them shelled.*

until golden brown and crisp. Remove with a handled strainer or slotted spoon, and drain. Remove the oil from the wok.

3. Reheat the wok until very hot. Add the fried shrimp and the *Shrimp Seasonings*. Toss lightly over high heat for about 20 seconds, until fragrant. Transfer the mixture to a platter, and serve immediately.

Crispy Squid

Su Zha You Yu

6 Servings ⌣ Appetizer

1   pound squid, cleaned (page 203), with tentacles

Marinade
2   tablespoons rice wine or sake
1½   tablespoons minced gingerroot
1   tablespoon minced scallions
½   teaspoon salt

½   cup cornstarch
2   cups peanut, safflower or corn oil

THERE IS NO BETTER *appetizer than crisp, fried squid rings. The cornstarch gives the squid a delightfully light coating. Serve this dish plain, with soy sauce, with Spicy Sweet & Sour Dipping Sauce (page 205) or with Sichuan-pepper-corn salt (page 18).*

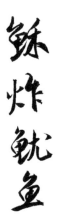

1. Cut the squid body into rings, leaving the tentacles in one piece. Place in a bowl with the *Marinade*. Toss lightly to coat, and cover with plastic wrap. Let marinate in the refrigerator for 1 hour, or longer if possible. Remove, and spread the cornstarch on a plate. Dredge the pieces of squid in the cornstarch to coat and press lightly to adhere the cornstarch to the surface. Arrange the coated squid on a baking sheet and let them air-dry for 30 minutes, turning once.

2. Heat a wok, add the oil to the pan, and heat to 375 degrees F. Add a batch of the squid pieces and deep-fry, turning constantly, until golden brown and crisp. Remove with a handled strainer or slotted spoon, and drain. Transfer to paper towels and drain further. Strain the oil between batches by running a fine-meshed strainer through it; reheat it before frying the next batch. Transfer the fried squid to a serving platter, and serve.

Spicy Squid Flowers

Hong You You Hua

6 Servings ～ Appetizer or Main Dish

1½ pounds cleaned squid, page 203 (2 pounds uncleaned)

Squid Marinade
2 slices gingerroot, the size of a quarter, smashed with the flat side of a cleaver
2 tablespoons rice wine or sake
1 teaspoon salt

3 English (gourmet seedless) cucumbers or 6 small pickling cucumbers
1½ teaspoons salt
1½ teaspoons sesame oil

Squid Dressing
¼ cup soy sauce
1 tablespoon clear rice vinegar
2 teaspoons chili oil or chili paste
1½ tablespoons sesame oil
1 tablespoon minced scallions
2 teaspoons minced gingerroot
1 tablespoon sugar

SQUID IS A SEAFOOD *frequently overlooked by many Americans, but it is popular with the Chinese. Chefs use their cleavers to score the meat into myriad shapes. Once blanched, the pieces are transformed into delicate designs.*

1. Cut the tentacles from the squid and place them in a bowl. Make a lengthwise cut in the body sac of a squid to open it up and form a flat piece. Rinse lightly, and drain. Holding the cleaver at a 45-degree angle to the squid, on the inside surface (not the skin side), make deep scores at ⅛-inch intervals lengthwise across the body sac. (The scores should be deep, but be careful not to cut through to the other side.) Turn the squid, and make scores at ⅛-inch intervals perpendicular to the first scores, to create a diamond pattern. Repeat for all the body sacs. Score the back flaps in the same manner. Cut the squid into 1-inch squares, and add the pieces to the bowl.

2. Pinch the gingerroot slices in the *Squid Marinade* repeatedly for several minutes to impart their flavor. Add the marinade to the squid, toss lightly, and let marinate for 20 minutes. Discard the gingerroot. Cut the cucumbers in half lengthwise. Remove any seeds, and cut each half crosswise into 2-inch pieces. Cut each piece lengthwise into paper-thin slices, and place them in a mixing

bowl. Add the salt, toss lightly, and let sit for 20 minutes. Drain the cucumbers, pat dry, toss with the sesame oil, and arrange in a mound on a platter.

2. Heat 3 quarts of water until boiling. Add the squid pieces, and cook for about 1 minute, until the pieces "blossom" into flowers and change color. Drain thoroughly, and arrange on top of the cucumbers. Just before serving, pour the *Squid Dressing* on top and toss lightly.

Drunken Clams

Xian Xian

6 Servings ⌒ Appetizer or Main Dish

Although some Chinese insist that the clams found in the Far East are more tender and sweet than those found in the United States, I must admit partiality to those found in New England. Littleneck and soft-shelled clams are both excellent in this dish. The term "drunken" refers to the potent cooking marinade, which is made with generous quantities of rice wine.

4	pounds steamers or littleneck clams
½	teaspoon salt

Clam Marinade

½	cup clam-cooking liquid
1½	cups Shaohsing or another good-quality rice wine or sake
¾	cup chicken broth, preferably Chinese Chicken Broth (page 345)
1	teaspoon salt
10	slices gingerroot, the size of a quarter, smashed with the flat side of a cleaver
8	cloves garlic, smashed with the flat side of a cleaver
8	scallions, smashed with the flat side of a cleaver

1. Rinse the clams thoroughly in cold running water to remove any sand; place them in cold water to cover for 30 minutes. Drain them; place 1 cup water and the salt in a large pot. Heat until boiling, and add the clams. Cover, and reduce the heat to low. Cook, shaking the pot occasionally, until the clams just open. Remove the pot from the heat, and transfer the clams, still in their shells, to a bowl, reserving ½ cup of the clam-cooking liquid. Add the reserved clam-cooking liquid to the *Clam Marinade*, and add the marinade to the bowl. Toss lightly to coat the clams with the marinade; refrigerate for at least 3 hours, turning the clams from time to time.

2. Serve cold. To eat, remove the "shirt" from the neck, dip the clam in the marinade, and eat.

Savory Seafood Custard

Ha Li Zheng Dan

6 Servings ⌣ Main Dish or Side Dish

1	pound cherrystone clams
½	teaspoon salt

Custard Mixture

6	large eggs
2	tablespoons rice wine or sake
1	teaspoon minced gingerroot
1	teaspoon salt

1. Rinse the clams thoroughly in cold running water to remove any sand. Place them in cold water to cover for 30 minutes; drain. Put 1 cup of water in a large pot, and add the salt. Heat until boiling, and add the clams. Cover, and cook until the clams have just opened, shaking the pot occasionally to distribute the heat evenly.

2. Remove the clams with a handled strainer or slotted spoon, reserving the liquid, and place the clams in a 1½-quart soufflé dish or a heatproof bowl. Add 1 cup of the clam-cooking liquid to the *Custard Mixture* while beating vigorously. Pour the custard mixture into the soufflé dish, straining it as it is added. Place the dish in a steamer tray.

3. Fill a wok with water level with the bottom edge of the steamer tray, and heat until boiling. Place the steamer tray over the boiling water, cover, and steam over high heat for 12 to 15 minutes, until the custard is set. Serve immediately.

S O OUTSTANDING ARE *the flavor and texture of this dish that to my mind, it ranks with the likes of chicken velvet and shark's fin soup. The tender, savory custard provides the perfect foil for the seafood. Oysters, shrimp or crabmeat may be substituted for the clams, each creating a subtle variation in flavor. Serve with a vegetable and rice for a sumptuous meal.*

Scallops in Oyster Sauce

Hao You Xian Bei

6 Servings ⌒ Main Dish

THE FRAGRANT SEASONINGS of scallion and gingerroot accentuate the sweet flavor of fresh scallops. Add a light coating of oyster sauce.

2   pounds fresh sea scallops

Scallop Marinade
2   slices gingerroot, the size of a quarter, smashed with the flat side of a cleaver
2   tablespoons rice wine or sake
½   teaspoon salt

Shredded Seasonings
3   tablespoons finely shredded gingerroot
3   tablespoons finely shredded scallions

2   tablespoons rice wine or sake

Oyster Sauce
¼   cup water
3   tablespoons oyster sauce
2   tablespoons soy sauce
2   tablespoons rice wine or sake
1½   teaspoons sesame oil
2   teaspoons sugar

1. Rinse the scallops lightly, and drain thoroughly. Holding the knife blade parallel to the cutting surface, slice each scallop in half through the thickness. Place the scallops in a bowl. Pinch the gingerroot in the *Scallop Marinade* repeatedly for several minutes to impart their flavor. Add the scallop marinade to the scallops, toss lightly, and let marinate for 20 minutes. Discard the gingerroot slices. Place the *Shredded Seasonings* in ice water to cover for 20 minutes. Drain the shredded seasonings, and place them on a platter.

2. Heat a wok, add 4 cups of water and the rice wine, and heat until boiling. Add the scallops, and poach for about 30 seconds, until barely cooked. Remove the scallops with a slotted spoon, and arrange them over the shredded seasonings. Remove the liquid from the wok.

3. Reheat the wok, add the *Oyster Sauce*, and heat until boiling. Cook for about 1 minute, until slightly thickened. Pour the sauce over the scallops, toss lightly, and serve.

Three-Flavor Lobster Slices

San Wei Long Xia

6 Servings ～ Appetizer or Main Dish

5   fresh or frozen lobster tails, about 5-6 ounces each, or 1½ pounds cooked lobster meat

Lobster Seasonings

2   tablespoons freshly squeezed lemon juice

1   teaspoon salt

6   dried vermicelli sheets or 2 ounces cellophane noodles (bean threads)

Vermicelli Seasonings

1   teaspoon sesame oil

½   teaspoon salt

Sesame Sauce

½   cup sesame paste or smooth peanut butter

¼   cup chicken broth, preferably Chinese Chicken Broth (page 345), or water

3   tablespoons soy sauce

2   tablespoons sesame oil

2   teaspoons Chinese black vinegar or Worcestershire sauce

1   teaspoon chili oil or chili paste

1   tablespoon minced gingerroot

1   tablespoon minced scallions

1   tablespoon minced garlic

1   tablespoon sugar

Peppercorn Sauce

¼   cup soy sauce

1½   tablespoons Chinese black vinegar or Worcestershire sauce

1½   tablespoons sesame oil

2   tablespoons minced scallions

2   tablespoons minced gingerroot

1   tablespoon Sichuan peppercorns, roasted for 5 minutes and pulverized

1   tablespoon sugar

½   teaspoon salt

ALTHOUGH SICHUANESE cuisine is renowned for its fiery seasonings and spicy flavors, several dishes from this area are more subtle and delicate. Such is the case with this cold salad platter, a specialty frequently served at the opening of a Chinese banquet. The softened noodles form a base for the lobster meat, which is arranged on top, and the diners can choose from one of three dipping sauces.

Dried vermicelli sheets, which are available at most Chinese markets, are made from the starch of mung beans. They have no flavor and are used as a base for a number of Chinese cold platters. Cellophane noodles may be substituted.

Ginger Sauce

¼ cup clear rice vinegar
2 tablespoons finely shredded gingerroot
¾ teaspoon salt
½ teaspoon sugar

1. If the lobster tails are still uncooked and in the shell, cut the shell down the back with a pair of kitchen shears. Fill a pan with 3 quarts of water, and add the *Lobster Seasonings*. Heat until boiling, add the lobster tails, and cook for 5 minutes (begin timing after the water boils again). Remove the tails, let them cool, and remove the meat from the shells. (If the lobster meat is already cooked, omit this step.) Holding the knife at a 45-degree angle to the meat, cut it crosswise into paper-thin slices.

2. Soften the vermicelli sheets in hot water to cover for 10 minutes. Drain; cut the vermicelli sheets into strips 1 inch wide or the cellophane noodles into 3-inch lengths. Cook the vermicelli sheets or the noodles for 1 minute in boiling water. Refresh immediately in cold water. Drain thoroughly, and mix with the *Vermicelli Seasonings*. Place the vermicelli sheets or noodles on a platter, and arrange the lobster slices overlapping in a circular pattern on top.

3. Make the *Sesame Sauce*, *Peppercorn Sauce* and *Ginger Sauce*, and serve cold in separate small bowls. Serve the lobster slices with the three dipping sauces.

Fried Oysters

Zha Sheng Hao

6 Servings ⌒ Appetizer

2 pints freshly shucked oysters

Oyster Marinade

2 slices gingerroot, the size of a quarter, smashed with the flat side of a cleaver

2 scallions, smashed with the flat side of a cleaver

1 tablespoon rice wine or sake

12 10-inch bamboo skewers

Dipping Sauce

¼ cup water

1 tablespoon ketchup

1 tablespoon soy sauce

2 teaspoons Chinese black vinegar or Worcestershire sauce

1 teaspoon sesame oil

1 tablespoon minced garlic

2 teaspoons minced gingerroot

1 tablespoon sugar

1½ teaspoons cornstarch

Oyster Coating

1 cup cornstarch

1 teaspoon salt

¼ teaspoon freshly ground black pepper

2 large eggs, lightly beaten

4 cups bread crumbs

4 cups peanut, safflower or corn oil

F RESH OYSTERS ARE *greatly relished in the province of Fujian. There, the plumpest and freshest are dipped in batter and deep-fried until golden brown. Equally popular is a coating of bread crumbs, which, to my mind, tends to be lighter than the flour-egg batter.*

1. Carefully rinse the oysters in a colander to remove any bits of shell. Drain thoroughly, and place the oysters in a bowl. Pinch the gingerroot and the scallions in the *Oyster Marinade* repeatedly for several minutes to impart their flavors. Add the oyster marinade to the oysters, toss lightly, and let marinate for 20 minutes. Discard the gingerroot and scallions. Soak the skewers in water to cover for 1 hour. Heat the *Dipping Sauce* until thick, and transfer to a serving bowl.

2. Heat 2 quarts of water until boiling, and add the oysters. Blanch the oysters for 10 seconds, until the edges just begin to curl. Drain thoroughly. Carefully thread the oysters onto the skewers, distributing them evenly among the skewers.

3. Dredge the oysters in the *Oyster Coating*, making certain that they are completely covered. Dip the oysters in the beaten eggs, and then dredge in the bread crumbs, once again making certain that all sides are covered. Lightly press the oysters to make sure the bread crumbs adhere.

4. Heat a wok, add the oil, and heat the oil to 375 degrees F. Add half the oysters, and deep-fry for about 5 minutes, until they are golden brown and crisp. Remove, and drain on absorbent paper. Reheat the oil, and deep-fry the remaining oysters in the same manner. Arrange the oysters on a platter, and serve immediately with the dipping sauce.

Black Mushrooms Stuffed With Shrimp

Xia Ren Niang Dong Gu

6 Servings ⌣ Appetizer or Main Dish

THE RICH, SMOKY *flavor of dried Chinese black mushrooms contrasts with the sweet flavor of the minced shrimp filling. If possible, thick black mushroom caps should be used, as they are superior in flavor to the small, thin ones and more attractive.*

24   medium-sized dried Chinese black mushrooms

Mushroom Seasonings
2   tablespoons mushroom-soaking liquid
1   tablespoon soy sauce
1   tablespoon rice wine or sake
1   teaspoon sesame oil
½   teaspoon sugar
2   scallions, smashed with the flat side of a cleaver
2   slices gingerroot, the size of a quarter, smashed with the flat side of a cleaver

Shrimp Sauce
     Mushroom-steaming liquid
½   cup chicken broth, preferably Chinese Chicken Broth (page 345)
2   teaspoons rice wine or sake
1½   teaspoons cornstarch
½   teaspoon salt

¾ pound medium-sized raw shrimp, shelled

Shrimp Seasonings

1½ teaspoons rice wine or sake
1 teaspoon sesame oil
½ egg white
½ teaspoon minced gingerroot
1½ tablespoons cornstarch
¾ teaspoon salt

2 tablespoons cornstarch
1 tablespoon peanut, safflower or corn oil
1 teaspoon minced garlic
1 pound fresh spinach, trimmed and cleaned

Spinach Seasonings

1 tablespoon chicken broth, preferably Chinese Chicken Broth
(page 345)
2 teaspoons rice wine or sake
½ teaspoon sesame oil
½ teaspoon salt

1. Rinse the dried mushrooms, and soak them in hot water to cover for 20 minutes. Reserve 2 tablespoons of the soaking liquid. Remove and discard the mushroom stems; place the caps in a heatproof bowl. Add the *Mushroom Seasonings*, toss lightly, and place the bowl in a steamer tray. Fill a wok with water level with the bottom edge of the steamer tray. Place the steamer tray over the water, cover, and steam the mushroom caps for 15 minutes over high heat. Let the mushrooms cool, drain off the liquid in the bowl, and add it to the *Shrimp Sauce*, discarding the scallions and gingerroot. Set the shrimp sauce aside.

2. Devein the shrimp, rinse lightly, and drain thoroughly. Place the shrimp in a dishtowel, and squeeze out as much moisture as possible. Mince the shrimp to a paste using a blender or a food processor fitted with the steel blade, or by hand with two cleavers. Place the shrimp paste in a mixing bowl, and add the *Shrimp Seasonings*. Stir vigorously in one direction, and lightly throw the mixture against the inside of the bowl to combine evenly.

3. Sprinkle the inside of a mushroom cap with a little bit of cornstarch, and spoon the shrimp mixture generously into the cap. Smooth the surface with the underside of a spoon dipped in water. Stuff the remaining caps in the same manner, and place them on a lightly greased heatproof plate. Put the plate in a steamer tray. Following the procedure described in step 1, steam for 7 minutes over high heat.

4. Heat a wok, add the 1 tablespoon of oil, and heat until nearly smoking. Add the minced garlic, and stir-fry over high heat for 5 seconds. Add the spinach, toss lightly, and add the *Spinach Seasonings*. Toss briefly over high heat until the spinach is slightly wilted. Arrange the spinach around the outer edge of a platter. Place the steamed mushroom caps in the center of the platter.

5. Reheat the wok, add the shrimp sauce, and stir until the sauce thickens. Pour the sauce over the mushrooms, and serve immediately.

Stir-Fried Scallops With Broccoli

Bi Lu Xian Bei

6 Servings ⌒ Main Dish

THIS STIR-FRIED PLATTER *illustrates the seasonings and crisp textures that give Cantonese cuisine its great reputation. High heat and a short cooking time are essential to the success of this dish. (See photograph, page 84.)*

| 2 | pounds fresh sea scallops |

Scallop Marinade
2	slices gingerroot, the size of a quarter, smashed with the flat side of a cleaver
2	scallions, smashed with the flat side of a cleaver
2	tablespoons rice wine or sake
½	teaspoon salt

| 1 | pound broccoli |
| 2 | tablespoons peanut, safflower or corn oil |

Scallop Seasonings
1½	tablespoons shredded scallions
1	tablespoon finely shredded gingerroot
2	teaspoons finely sliced garlic

Scallop Sauce
½	cup chicken broth, preferably Chinese Chicken Broth (page 345)
2	tablespoons rice wine or sake
1½	teaspoons sesame oil
1	teaspoon salt
½	teaspoon sugar
¼	teaspoon freshly ground white pepper
1½	teaspoons cornstarch

1. Rinse the scallops lightly, and drain. Holding the knife blade parallel to the cutting surface, slice each scallop in half through its thickness. Place the scallops in a mixing bowl. Pinch the gingerroot and the scallions in the *Scallop Marinade* repeatedly for several minutes to impart their flavors. Add the marinade to the scallops, toss lightly, and let marinate for 20 minutes. Discard the scallions and gingerroot.

2. Peel the tough outer skin from the broccoli, and separate the florets. Roll-cut the stems into 1-inch pieces. Heat 1½ quarts of salted water until boiling. Add the stem pieces, and cook for 30 seconds. Add the florets, and cook for 2½ minutes, or until both stems and florets are just tender. Refresh immediately in cold water. Drain thoroughly.

3. Heat 2 quarts of water until boiling. Add the scallops, and cook them for 30 seconds, until they change color. Drain thoroughly.

4. Heat a wok, add the oil, and heat until very hot. Add the *Scallop Seasonings*, and stir-fry for about 10 seconds over high heat. Add the *Scallop Sauce*, and cook, stirring constantly, until it thickens. Add the broccoli and scallops. Toss lightly to coat with the sauce, and transfer the mixture to a platter. Serve immediately.

Stir-Fried Shrimp With Cucumbers & Pine Nuts

Song Zi Xia Ren

6 Servings ⁀ Main Dish

THIS DISH REFLECTS *three basic characteristics of eastern regional cooking: it is exquisite in appearance, rich in flavor and sweet in taste. Tiny river shrimp are traditionally used in the recipe, but even frozen saltwater shrimp are delicious when prepared in this manner.*

1½   pounds medium-sized raw shrimp, shelled

Shrimp Marinade

2   slices gingerroot, the size of a quarter, smashed with the flat side of a cleaver

1   tablespoon rice wine or sake

1   teaspoon sesame oil

1   teaspoon salt

3   English (gourmet seedless) cucumbers or 6 small pickling cucumbers

2   cups peanut, safflower or corn oil

2   ounces rice stick noodles

Minced Seasonings

1   tablespoon minced scallions

2   teaspoons minced gingerroot

Shrimp Sauce

2½   tablespoons chicken broth, preferably Chinese Chicken Broth (page 345)

1½   tablespoons rice wine or sake

2   teaspoons soy sauce

1   teaspoon sesame oil

¾   teaspoon sugar

¾   teaspoon salt

2   cups pine nuts, toasted in a 325-degree oven until golden

1. Score each shrimp along the length of the back, and remove the vein; the scoring will allow the shrimp to "butterfly" when cooked. Rinse all the shrimp, and drain thoroughly. Place the shrimp in a dishtowel, and squeeze out as much moisture as possible. Place the shrimp in a bowl. Pinch the gingerroot slices in the **Shrimp Marinade** repeatedly for several minutes to impart the flavor. Add

the marinade to the shrimp, toss lightly, and let marinate for 20 minutes. Discard the gingerroot slices. Trim the ends off the cucumbers, and discard. Cut the cucumbers in half lengthwise, remove any seeds, and cut each half lengthwise into thirds. Roll-cut the lengths into 1-inch pieces.

2. Heat a wok, add the oil, and heat the oil to 425 degrees F, or until nearly smoking. Drop the rice stick noodles into the hot oil, and deep-fry very briefly until they are puffed and lightly golden. (This should take no longer than 5 seconds.) Turn the noodles over, and fry for a few seconds more. Remove them with a handled strainer or slotted spoon, and drain on absorbent paper. Transfer the noodles to a platter, and break them up lightly with your fingertips; make a slight depression in the center. Remove the oil from the wok, reserving 5 tablespoons.

3. Reheat the wok, add 1½ tablespoons of the oil, and heat until very hot. Drain the shrimp, and add half of them to the hot oil. Stir-fry over high heat for about 1 minute, or until the shrimp change color. Remove with a handled strainer or slotted spoon, and drain. Wipe out the wok, add 1½ tablespoons more oil and reheat the oil until very hot. Stir-fry the remaining shrimp in the same manner. Remove the oil from the wok, and wipe out the wok.

4. Reheat the wok, add the remaining 2 tablespoons of oil, and heat until very hot. Add the *Minced Seasonings*, and stir-fry for about 10 seconds, until fragrant. Add the cucumber pieces, and stir-fry over high heat for about 30 seconds, until the cucumbers are heated through. Add the *Shrimp Sauce* and the shrimp. Toss lightly over high heat for about 20 seconds; then add the pine nuts. Toss lightly to combine the mixture, and spoon it over the fried noodles. Serve immediately.

Spicy Shrimp With Hot Chili Peppers

La Wei Xia

6 Servings ⌣ Main Dish

THE SAUCE IN THIS classic Sichuanese specialty lends itself beautifully to either shrimp or chicken, as well as to scallops, pork or squid. I like to serve this dish with plenty of steamed rice or buns to soak up the flavorful juices. For a meal-in-one dish, increase the sauce by half and add ½ pound of cooked asparagus, broccoli or snow peas just before removing the food from the pan.

1½ pounds medium-sized raw shrimp, shelled

Shrimp Marinade

2 slices gingerroot, the size of a quarter, smashed with the flat side of a cleaver
2 tablespoons rice wine or sake
1 teaspoon sesame oil
1 tablespoon cornstarch
½ teaspoon salt

6 small, dried hot chili peppers or 1 teaspoon crushed hot red peppers
5 tablespoons peanut, safflower or corn oil

Minced Seasonings

2 tablespoons minced scallions, white part only
1½ tablespoons minced gingerroot
1 tablespoon minced garlic

2 cups thinly sliced water chestnuts, blanched in boiling water for 10 seconds, refreshed in cold water and drained

Spicy Sauce

¾ cup chicken broth, preferably Chinese Chicken Broth (page 345)
3¾ tablespoons soy sauce
3 tablespoons rice wine or sake
1½ teaspoons sesame oil
1½ tablespoons Chinese black vinegar or Worcestershire sauce
3 tablespoons sugar
2 teaspoons cornstarch

1. Score each shrimp along the length of the back and remove the vein; the scoring will allow the shrimp to "butterfly" when cooked. Rinse all the shrimp and drain thoroughly. Place the shrimp in a dishtowel and squeeze out as much

moisture as possible. Place the shrimp in a bowl. Pinch the gingerroot slices in the **Shrimp Marinade** repeatedly for several minutes to impart their flavor. Add the marinade to the shrimp, toss lightly, and let marinate for 20 minutes. Discard the gingerroot slices. Slice the peppers lengthwise, and scrape out the seeds with the tip of a knife, then cut into ¼-inch sections.

2. Heat a wok, add 1½ tablespoons of the oil, and heat until hot. Add half the shrimp and stir-fry over high heat until the shrimp change color. Remove with a handled strainer or a slotted spoon, and drain. Reheat the pan, add 1½ more tablespoons of the oil and heat until hot. Add the remaining shrimp and stir-fry in the same manner. Remove, and drain. Wipe out the wok.

3. Reheat the wok, add the remaining 2 tablespoons of oil and heat until very hot. Add the **Minced Seasonings** and dried hot peppers and stir-fry for about 15 seconds, until the peppers turn black. Add the sliced water chestnuts and stir-fry for about 1 minute, until heated through. Add the **Spicy Sauce** and cook, stirring constantly to prevent lumps, until thickened. Add the cooked shrimp and toss lightly to coat. Transfer to a serving platter, and serve immediately.

Spicy Prawns in Tomato Sauce

Gan Shao Ming Xia

6 Servings ⌒ Main Dish

SERVE THIS SPICY *Sichuanese dish with rice and a stir-fried green vegetable for a simple yet superb meal.*

| 2 | pounds large raw prawns or shrimp, shelled |

Prawn Marinade

2	slices gingerroot, the size of a quarter, smashed with the flat side of a cleaver
1½	tablespoons rice wine or sake
½	teaspoon salt

| 2 | tablespoons peanut, safflower or corn oil |

Minced Seasonings

2	tablespoons minced scallions
1½	tablespoons minced garlic
1	tablespoon minced gingerroot

| 1½ | teaspoons chili paste |

Prawn Sauce

6	tablespoons water
5	tablespoons ketchup
2	tablespoons rice wine or sake
1½	tablespoons sugar
1½	teaspoons cornstarch
1	teaspoon salt

1. Devein the prawns, using a needle or a toothpick. Rinse lightly, drain thoroughly, and pat dry. Holding a cleaver or chef's knife parallel to the cutting board, score the prawns along the back so they will "butterfly" when cooked. Pinch the gingerroot slices in the *Prawn Marinade* repeatedly for several minutes to impart their flavor. Place the prawns in a mixing bowl, add the marinade, toss lightly, and let marinate for 20 minutes. Drain the prawns, and discard the gingerroot.

2. Heat the wok, add the 2 tablespoons of oil, and heat until very hot. Add the *Minced Seasonings*, and stir-fry for about 10 seconds, until fragrant. Add the

chili paste, and stir-fry for about 5 seconds over high heat. Add the prawns and cook about 1 minute, then add the *Prawn Sauce*, and stir until it begins to thicken. Toss lightly, and transfer the mixture to a platter. Serve immediately.

Stir-Fried Squid With Hot Red Peppers

Gong Bao You Yu Juan

6 Servings ⌣ Main Dish

1½   pounds cleaned squid, page 203 (2 pounds uncleaned)

Squid Marinade

   3   slices gingerroot, the size of a quarter, smashed with the flat side of a cleaver
   2   tablespoons rice wine or sake
   1   teaspoon salt
   1   teaspoon cornstarch

   10   dried chili peppers
   3   tablespoons peanut, safflower or corn oil
   2   teaspoons minced garlic

Squid Sauce

   ¼   cup soy sauce
   ¼   cup chicken broth, preferably Chinese Chicken Broth (page 345), or water
   2   tablespoons rice wine or sake
   1   tablespoon Chinese black vinegar or Worcestershire sauce
   1½   teaspoons sesame oil
   2   tablespoons sugar
   1   teaspoon cornstarch

W ITH ITS MILD TASTE *and tender texture, squid is delicious when stir-fried. Scored and flash-cooked, the squid forms "flower" shapes. Though the Chinese use dried squid in this recipe, I prefer the fresh variety; the spicy sauce highlights the sweet flavor of the fresh meat. (See photograph, page 169.)*

1. Cut the tentacles from the squid and place them in a bowl. Make a lengthwise cut in a body sac of the squid to open it up and form a flat piece. Rinse lightly, and drain. Holding the cleaver at a 45-degree angle to the squid, on the inside surface (not the skin side), make deep scores at ⅙-inch intervals lengthwise across the body sac. (The scores should be deep, but be careful not to cut through to the other side.) Turn the squid, and make scores at ⅙-inch intervals

perpendicular to the first scores, to create a diamond pattern. Repeat for all the body sacs. Score the back flaps in the same manner. Cut the squid into 1-inch squares, and add the pieces to the bowl. Pinch the gingerroot slices in the *Squid Marinade* repeatedly for several minutes to impart their flavor. Add the marinade to the squid, toss lightly, and let marinate for 20 minutes. Discard the gingerroot. Cut the dried chili peppers into 1-inch pieces, and shake out the seeds.

2. Heat 3 quarts of water until boiling, add the squid pieces, and cook for about 1 minute, until they change color and "blossom" into flowers. Drain thoroughly.

3. Heat a wok, add the oil, and heat until very hot. Add the chili peppers, and stir-fry over high heat for about 30 seconds, until they turn black. Add the minced garlic, and stir-fry for about 10 seconds. Add the *Squid Sauce*, and stir-fry until it begins to thicken. Add the cooked squid pieces, toss lightly to coat with the sauce, and transfer the mixture to a platter. Serve immediately.

Scallion-Oil Fillets

Cong You Yu Pian

6 Servings ⁓ Main Dish

SCALLION OIL IS HELD IN *high regard by a number of eastern Chinese chefs. My chef-teacher substituted this fragrant oil for sesame oil in a number of recipes. It plays up the fresh flavor of the fried fillets.*

2 pounds firm-fleshed, skinned fish fillets, such as haddock, cod or pickerel

Fish Marinade
2 slices gingerroot, the size of a quarter, smashed with the flat side of a cleaver
1 tablespoon rice wine or sake
1 teaspoon salt

Scallion Oil
2 tablespoons peanut, safflower or corn oil
2 tablespoons sesame oil
½ cup shredded scallions

½ cup cornstarch
1 cup peanut, safflower or corn oil

Fish Sauce

½	cup chicken broth, preferably Chinese Chicken Broth (page 345)
2	tablespoons rice wine or sake
1	teaspoon salt
¼	teaspoon freshly ground white pepper

Thickener

1	tablespoon water
1	teaspoon cornstarch

1. Rinse the fillets lightly, drain thoroughly, and place in a mixing bowl. Pinch the gingerroot in the *Fish Marinade* repeatedly for several minutes to impart their flavor. Add the marinade to the fillets, toss lightly, and let marinate for 20 minutes. Discard the gingerroot slices.

2. To make the *Scallion Oil,* heat the oils in a wok until nearly smoking. Add the scallions, and turn off the heat. Cover, and let stand for 20 minutes. Strain the oil, and discard the scallions.

3. Dredge the fillets in the cornstarch, pressing lightly to be sure the cornstarch adheres. Heat a wok, add the 1 cup of oil, and heat the oil to 400 degrees F. Add a batch of the fillets, and fry on both sides over high heat for about 5 minutes, until the fish is golden brown and flaky. Remove with a handled strainer or slotted spoon, and drain. Reheat the oil. Fry the remaining fillets in the same manner. Arrange the fish on a platter. Remove the oil from the wok.

4. Reheat the wok, add the *Fish Sauce*, and heat until boiling. Add the *Thickener*, stirring constantly to prevent lumps. Slowly pour the thickened sauce over the fish fillets. Sprinkle 2 tablespoons of the scallion oil on top, and serve immediately.

Steamed Fish Fillets in Black Bean Sauce

Dou Shi Zheng Yu

6 Servings ⌢ Main Dish

FEW SEASONINGS
*complement the flavor of
fresh fish as well as fermented
black beans. Though the beans
may be salty and strong-tasting
on their own, combined in a
sauce with the rice wine, sugar
and chicken broth, they highlight
the flavor of the fish fillets.*

1½ pounds firm-fleshed, skinned fish fillets, such as flounder, sole, pickerel or lake trout

Fish Marinade
2 slices gingerroot, the size of a quarter, smashed with the flat side of a cleaver
1 tablespoon rice wine or sake
1 teaspoon salt

2 tablespoons peanut, safflower or corn oil

Minced Seasonings
1 tablespoon fermented black beans, rinsed, drained and minced
1 tablespoon minced scallions
2 teaspoons minced garlic

Fish Sauce
¼ cup chicken broth, preferably Chinese Chicken Broth (page 345)
1 tablespoon soy sauce
1 tablespoon rice wine or sake
½ teaspoon sugar
¼ teaspoon freshly ground black pepper

1. Rinse the fillets lightly, and pat them dry. Place the fillets in a mixing bowl. Pinch the gingerroot slices in the *Fish Marinade* repeatedly for several minutes to impart their flavor. Add the marinade to the fish fillets, toss lightly, and let marinate for 20 minutes. Discard the gingerroot, and arrange the fillets in a heatproof pie plate or quiche pan.

2. Heat a wok, add the oil, and heat until very hot. Add the *Minced Seasonings*, stir-fry for about 10 seconds until fragrant, and add the *Fish Sauce*. Heat the mixture until boiling, and cook for about 2 minutes, stirring constantly. Pour the sauce over the fish fillets. Place the pie plate or quiche pan in a steamer tray.

3. Fill a wok with water level with the bottom edge of the steamer tray, and

heat until boiling. Place the steamer tray over the boiling water, cover, and steam the fish for 10 minutes over high heat, or until it flakes when prodded with a chopstick or a fork. Serve immediately.

Steamed Fish With Ham & Mushroom Slices

Huo Tui Dong Gu Zheng Yu

6 Servings ⌣ Main Dish

1   whole firm-fleshed fish, such as flounder, red snapper, pickerel or lake trout, about 3½ pounds

Fish Marinade
2   slices gingerroot, the size of a quarter, smashed with the flat side of a cleaver
1   tablespoon rice wine or sake
2   teaspoons salt

8   dried Chinese black mushrooms
5   paper-thin slices (about 2 ounces) Chinese ham, Smithfield ham or prosciutto
1   tablespoon soy sauce

Fish Seasonings
2   tablespoons shredded scallions
2   tablespoons shredded gingerroot

2   tablespoons sesame oil

THE SAVORY RICHNESS of Chinese ham and black mushrooms provides a superb contrast to fresh fish. Topped with shreds of fresh scallion and gingerroot, this dish is pleasing to both the eye and the palate.

1. Direct the fishmonger to clean the fish through the gills, if possible, leaving the belly intact. Scale the fish, rinse thoroughly, and drain. Holding the knife at a 45-degree angle to the fish, make deep scores crosswise along the length of the fish, an inch apart, from the dorsal fin to the tail. Pinch the gingerroot slices in the *Fish Marinade* repeatedly for several minutes to impart their flavors. Rub the marinade all over the outside of the fish and into the scores. Let the fish marinate for 30 minutes. Discard the gingerroot. Soak the dried mushrooms in hot water to cover for 20 minutes. Remove and discard the stems, and cut the caps in half. Cut the ham into pieces 2 inches long.

2. Arrange the fish on a heatproof platter, scored side up, and stuff a ham slice and a mushroom half into each of the scores. Sprinkle the soy sauce over the fish, and place the platter in a steamer tray.

3. Fill a wok with water level with the bottom edge of the steamer tray, and heat until boiling. Place the steamer tray with the fish over the boiling water, cover, and steam for 15 to 17 minutes over high heat, or until the fish flakes when prodded with a chopstick or a fork. Remove the platter, and sprinkle the *Fish Seasonings* over the fish. (Alternatively, if you do not have a steamer large enough to hold the platter, you may bake the fish on the platter, tightly wrapped in a double layer of heavy-duty aluminum foil, in a 475-degree oven for 15 to 17 minutes. Check to see if it is done and bake 5 minutes longer, if necessary.) Remove the water from the wok.

4. Reheat the wok, add the sesame oil, and heat until nearly smoking. Pour the sesame oil over the fish. Serve immediately.

Poached West Lake Fish

Xi Hu Cu Yu

6 Servings ⌣ Main Dish

TANGZHOU, A PICTUR-esque *city in eastern China, is famous for its refined cuisine and exquisite scenery—particularly majestic West Lake. A specialty of this region is West Lake Fish: a whole poached fish, freshly caught from the lake, doused with a spicy hot-and-sour sauce. One restaurant in Hangzhou has a large sign that reads: IF YOU WANT GOOD FISH, EAT WEST LAKE FISH. One can well understand this message after tasting the dish.*

| 1 | whole firm-fleshed fish, such as sea bass, pickerel or lake trout, about 3½ pounds |

Fish Marinade
2	slices gingerroot, the size of a quarter, smashed with the flat side of a cleaver
2	scallions, smashed with the flat side of a cleaver
1	tablespoon rice wine or sake
1	teaspoon salt
1	tablespoon peanut, safflower or corn oil

Fish-Poaching Liquid
| 5 | quarts boiling water |
| 3 | tablespoons rice wine or sake |

Fish Seasonings

¼	cup finely shredded gingerroot
¼	cup finely shredded scallions
1	fresh red chili pepper, seeds removed and shredded finely
½	teaspoon freshly ground white pepper

Fish Sauce

1½	cups fish-poaching liquid
2½	tablespoons soy sauce
1½	tablespoons Chinese black vinegar or Worcestershire sauce
2½	tablespoons sugar
1	teaspoon salt

Thickener

3	tablespoons water
1	tablespoon cornstarch

1. Direct the fishmonger to clean the fish through the gills, if possible, leaving the belly intact. Scale the fish, rinse thoroughly, and drain. Holding the knife at a 45-degree angle to the fish, make deep scores crosswise along the length of the fish, an inch apart, from the dorsal fin to the tail. Turn the fish over, and repeat on the other side. Pinch the gingerroot slices and the scallions in the *Fish Marinade* repeatedly for several minutes to impart their flavors. Rub the marinade all over the outside of the fish and into the scores. Let the fish marinate for 30 minutes. Discard the gingerroot and scallions.

2. Heat a large wok, add the oil, and heat until hot. Add the *Fish-Poaching Liquid*, and heat until boiling. Slowly lower the fish into the poaching liquid, and heat until boiling. Turn off the heat, cover, and let the fish sit for 20 minutes, or until the fish flakes when prodded with a chopstick or a fork. If the fish is not done, turn the heat to low and cook for 5 minutes. Using slotted utensils, carefully lift the fish, and transfer it to a platter. Reserve 1½ cups of the fish-poaching liquid for the sauce. Sprinkle the *Fish Seasonings* over the fish. Remove the poaching liquid from the wok.

3. Reheat the wok, add the *Fish Sauce*, and heat it until boiling. Slowly add the *Thickener*, stirring constantly to prevent lumps. Pour the thickened sauce over the fish, and serve immediately.

Stir-Fried Fish Rolls With Broccoli

Sheng Chao Yu Qiu

6 Servings ⁓ Main Dish

I WAS FIRST SERVED THIS *memorable dish in a restaurant in Canton at a banquet in celebration of my husband's birthday. Dusted with cornstarch and fried, the fish slices resemble "rolls"—hence the name. With their smoky black-mushroom-and-Chinese-ham filling, they make up an elegant platter befitting any special occasion.*

1½	pounds firm-fleshed fish fillets, such as haddock, cod, sea bass, pickerel or lake trout

Fish Marinade

2	slices gingerroot, the size of a quarter, smashed with the flat side of a cleaver
1	tablespoon rice wine or sake
1	teaspoon salt
1	egg white, lightly beaten
5	dried Chinese black mushrooms, soaked in hot water to cover for 20 minutes
4	paper-thin slices (about 2 ounces) Chinese ham, Smithfield ham or prosciutto
1	pound broccoli
3	tablespoons cornstarch
2	cups peanut, safflower or corn oil

Minced Seasonings

1	tablespoon minced scallions
2	teaspoons minced gingerroot

Fish Sauce

¼	cup chicken broth, preferably Chinese Chicken Broth (page 345)
1	tablespoon rice wine or sake
1	teaspoon sesame oil
1	teaspoon salt
1	teaspoon cornstarch
½	teaspoon sugar

1. Rinse the fillets lightly, and drain thoroughly. Pat them dry, and remove the skin. Holding the blade of a cleaver or a chef's knife at a 45-degree angle to the cutting surface, cut the fillets into slices about 1½ inches long, 1 inch wide and ⅛ inch thick. Place the slices in a bowl. Pinch the gingerroot slices in the *Fish*

Marinade repeatedly for several minutes to impart their flavor. Add the marinade and the egg white to the fish slices. Toss lightly, and let marinate for 20 minutes. Drain the mushrooms. Remove and discard the stems. Cut the caps into matchstick-sized shreds about 1 inch long. Cut the Chinese ham into shreds the same size. Peel away the tough outer skin from the broccoli, and separate the florets. Roll-cut the stems into 1-inch pieces.

2. Heat 1½ quarts of salted water until boiling. Add the stem pieces, and cook for ½ minute. Add the florets, and cook for 2½ minutes, or until both stems and florets are just tender. Refresh immediately in cold water. Drain thoroughly.

3. Arrange the fish slices on a flat surface. Generously sprinkle the top of a fish slice with cornstarch. Place a strip of ham and a strip of mushroom crosswise at one end of the fish slice, and roll it up so that they are completely enclosed. Lightly squeeze each roll to secure it so that it won't open while cooking. (You may piece together a fish slice using any little bits, using cornstarch as an adhesive.) Make the remaining rolls in the same manner.

4. Heat a wok, add the oil, and heat the oil to 375 degrees F. Add a batch of the fish rolls, and fry for about 2 minutes over high heat, carefully stirring all the while, until the rolls are cooked. Remove with a handled strainer or slotted spoon, and drain. Reheat the oil, and fry the remaining rolls in the same manner, reheating the oil between batches. Remove the oil from the wok, reserving 2 tablespoons. Wipe out the wok.

5. Reheat the wok, add the 2 tablespoons of oil, and heat until very hot. Add the *Minced Seasonings*, and stir-fry over high heat for about 10 seconds, until fragrant. Add the broccoli, and toss lightly over high heat for 15 seconds. Add the *Fish Sauce*. Stir slowly until the sauce has thickened. Add the fish rolls, and toss lightly and carefully to coat with the sauce. Transfer the mixture to a platter, and serve immediately.

Sichuanese Braised Fish in Spicy Sauce

Dou Ban Jian Yu

6 Servings ⌒ Main Dish

IN CHINESE CUISINE, *gingerroot, scallions, rice wine and vinegar are invariably used in the preparation of fish. It is believed that these ingredients remove any undesirable fishy flavors. In this dish, chili paste is added to these standard seasonings.*

1 whole firm-fleshed fish, such as sea bass, haddock, carp, pickerel or lake trout, about 3½ pounds

Fish Marinade

2 slices gingerroot, the size of a quarter, smashed with the flat side of a cleaver
1 tablespoon rice wine or sake
½ teaspoon salt

2 cups peanut, safflower or corn oil

Minced Seasonings

2 tablespoons minced scallions
1½ tablespoons minced gingerroot
1½ tablespoons minced garlic

1½ teaspoons chili paste
10 dried wood ears, soaked in hot water to cover for 20 minutes, drained and shredded

Fish-Braising Sauce

2 cups chicken broth, preferably Chinese Chicken Broth (page 345)
1½ tablespoons soy sauce
1 tablespoon rice wine or sake
1 tablespoon Chinese black vinegar or Worcestershire sauce
½ tablespoon sugar
½ teaspoon salt

Thickener

2 tablespoons water
1 tablespoon cornstarch

1 teaspoon sesame oil
2 tablespoons minced scallion greens

1. Direct the fishmonger to clean the fish through the gills, if possible, leaving the belly intact. Scale the fish, rinse thoroughly, and drain. Holding the knife at a 45-degree angle to the fish, make deep scores crosswise along the length of the fish, an inch apart, from the dorsal fin to the tail. Pinch the gingerroot slices in the *Fish Marinade* repeatedly for several minutes to impart their flavor. Rub the marinade all over the outside of the fish and into the scores. Let the fish marinate for 30 minutes. Discard the gingerroot, and drain the fish.

2. Heat a wok, add the oil, and heat the oil to 400 degrees F. Slowly lower the fish into the hot oil, and deep-fry over high heat for 5 minutes, constantly ladling the oil over the fish, until golden. Remove, and drain. Remove the oil from the wok, reserving 2 tablespoons. Wipe out the wok.

3. Reheat the wok, add the 2 tablespoons of oil, and heat until very hot. Add the *Minced Seasonings*, and stir-fry for 10 seconds, until fragrant. Add the chili paste, and stir-fry for another 5 seconds. Add the wood ears, toss lightly, and add the *Fish-Braising Sauce;* heat until boiling. Slowly lower the fish into the sauce, scored side up, and heat until the liquid is boiling. Cover, reduce the heat to medium, and cook for about 12 minutes, or until the meat flakes when prodded with a chopstick or a fork. Using slotted utensils, transfer the fish to a platter. Heat the sauce until boiling, and slowly add the *Thickener*, stirring constantly to prevent lumps. When the sauce has thickened, add the sesame oil, toss lightly, and pour the sauce over the fish. Sprinkle the minced scallion greens over the fish, and serve immediately.

Red-Cooked Yellow Fish

Hong Shao Huang Yu

6 Servings ⌒ Main Dish

ALTHOUGH RED-COOKING, *or slow cooking in a soy-based liquid, is frequently used for preparing tough cuts of meat, admirable results occur when the method is used to braise a whole fish. The pungent seasonings of scallions, ginger-root and garlic with the soy sauce transform any fish into a delectable platter that is excellent served with rice.*

1   whole firm-fleshed fish, such as sea bass, haddock, pickerel or lake trout, about 3½ pounds

Fish Marinade

2   slices gingerroot, the size of a quarter, smashed with the flat side of a cleaver
1   tablespoon rice wine or sake
2   tablespoons soy sauce

Fish-Braising Liquid

4   cups chicken broth, preferably Chinese Chicken Broth (page 345), or water
¼   cup soy sauce
2   tablespoons rice wine or sake
1   teaspoon sesame oil
2   teaspoons sugar

½   pound boneless center-cut pork loin

Pork Marinade

1   tablespoon soy sauce
½   tablespoon rice wine or sake
½   tablespoon water
1   teaspoon sesame oil
1   teaspoon cornstarch

2   cups peanut, safflower or corn oil

Fish Seasonings

6   dried Chinese black mushrooms, soaked in hot water to cover for 20 minutes, drained, stems removed and caps shredded
2   tablespoons minced scallions
1   tablespoon minced garlic

Thickener
- 2 tablespoons water
- 1 tablespoon cornstarch

½ cup canned bamboo shoots, blanched briefly in boiling water and cut into matchstick-sized shreds
2 tablespoons finely shredded gingerroot

1. Direct the fishmonger to clean the fish through the gills, if possible, leaving the belly intact. Scale the fish, rinse thoroughly, and drain. Holding the knife at a 45-degree angle to the fish, make deep scores crosswise along the length of the fish, an inch apart, from the dorsal fin to the tail. Pinch the gingerroot slices in the *Fish Marinade* repeatedly for several minutes to impart the flavor. Rub the marinade all over the outside of the fish and into the scores. Let the fish marinate for 30 minutes. Discard the gingerroot, and drain the fish, adding the fish marinade to the *Fish-Braising Liquid*.

2. Remove any fat or gristle from the pork loin, and discard. Cut the pork, across the grain, into slices ⅛ inch thick. (You may partially freeze the meat to facilitate slicing.) Cut the slices into matchstick-sized shreds. Place the pork shreds in a bowl, add the *Pork Marinade*, toss lightly, and let marinate for 20 minutes.

3. Heat a wok, add the oil, and heat the oil to 400 degrees F. Slowly lower the fish into the pan, and deep-fry the fish for 5 minutes over high heat, constantly ladling the oil over it. Remove, and drain. Remove the oil from the pan, reserving 4 tablespoons.

4. Reheat the wok, add 3 tablespoons of the reserved oil, and heat until very hot. Add the pork, stir-fry over high heat until the shreds turn color, remove, and drain. Wipe out the wok. Add the remaining 1 tablespoon of oil, heat until very hot, add the *Fish Seasonings*, and stir-fry for about 10 seconds, until fragrant. Add the pork shreds and the fish-braising liquid, and heat until boiling. Add the fish, scored side up, and heat until the liquid boils. Reduce the heat to medium, cover, and cook for 12 to 15 minutes, or until the fish flakes when prodded with a chopstick or a fork. Using slotted utensils, carefully lift the fish, and transfer it to a platter. Heat the sauce until boiling, and add the *Thickener*, stirring constantly to prevent lumps. When the sauce has thickened, add the bamboo shoots. Toss lightly, and pour the sauce over the fish. Sprinkle the shredded gingerroot over the fish, and serve immediately.

Sweet & Sour Fish With Pine Nuts

Song Zi Chuan Yu

6 Servings ⌢ Main Dish

SWEET & SOUR FISH *is a dish found in all regional cuisines, but it is the addition of buttery pine nuts that distinguishes this eastern version from all others. (See photograph, page 175.)*

1	whole firm-fleshed fish, such as sea bass, pickerel or lake trout, about 3½ pounds

Fish Marinade

2	scallions, smashed with the flat side of a cleaver
2	slices gingerroot, the size of a quarter, smashed with the flat side of a cleaver
1	tablespoon rice wine or sake
¾	teaspoon salt
1	egg yolk
1	cup cornstarch
4	cups peanut, safflower or corn oil

Fish Seasonings

½	cup shredded onions
½	cup shredded green peppers
1	tablespoon minced garlic

Fish Sauce

½	cup water
5	tablespoons ketchup
5	tablespoons clear rice vinegar
2	teaspoons soy sauce
½	teaspoon sesame oil
5	tablespoons sugar
1½	teaspoons cornstarch
½	teaspoon salt
1	ounce pine nuts, toasted in a 325-degree oven until golden (about ½ cup)

1. Direct the fishmonger to clean the fish through the gills, if possible, leaving the belly intact. Scale the fish, rinse thoroughly, and drain. Holding the knife at a

45-degree angle to the fish, make deep scores crosswise along the length of the fish, an inch apart, from the dorsal fin to the tail. Turn the fish over, and repeat. Pinch the scallions and gingerroot slices in the *Fish Marinade* for several minutes to impart their flavors. Rub the marinade over the outside of the fish and into the scores. Let marinate for 20 minutes. Discard the gingerroot and scallions.

2. Rub the egg yolk over the fish, and coat the fish with the cornstarch, making certain that the scores are also coated.

3. Heat a wok, add the oil, and heat to 425 degrees F. Holding the fish curled in a semicircular shape so that the scores are open, slowly lower the fish into the hot oil. Deep-fry over high heat for about 10 minutes, or until the meat is flaky and the outside is crisp and golden brown. (Ladle hot oil over the fish as it is frying.) Remove the fish, drain, and arrange on a platter. Remove the oil from the wok, reserving 2 tablespoons. Wipe out the wok.

4. Reheat the wok, add the 2 tablespoons of oil, and heat until very hot. Add the *Fish Seasonings*, and stir-fry for about 1 minute over high heat, until the onion shreds are soft and transparent. Add the *Fish Sauce*, and cook, stirring occasionally, until the sauce has thickened. Pour the sauce over the fish, and sprinkle the pine nuts on top. Serve immediately.

Lobster Cantonese

Yue Shi Chao Long Xia

6 Servings ⁓ Main Dish

4	live lobsters, 1½-2 pounds each
½	pound ground pork

Pork Marinade

2	teaspoons soy sauce
1	teaspoon rice wine or sake
1	teaspoon water
½	teaspoon sesame oil
2	tablespoons peanut, safflower or corn oil

Minced Seasonings

2	tablespoons fermented black beans, rinsed, drained and minced
1	tablespoon minced garlic
1	tablespoon minced scallions
2	teaspoons minced gingerroot

A NEW ENGLAND PURIST at heart, I had always maintained that the only way to serve lobster was boiled with drawn butter; any other method was desecration of the highest order. My point of view changed radically, however, one evening many years ago when I was served this famous Cantonese dish. Large chunks of lobster meat, which are scrambled with eggs, are generously coated with a garlicky black bean sauce.

粤
式
燜
龍
蝦

Lobster Sauce

1	cup chicken broth, preferably Chinese Chicken Broth (page 345)
2½	tablespoons soy sauce
2	tablespoons rice wine or sake
1	teaspoon sesame oil
1	teaspoon sugar
¼	teaspoon freshly ground black pepper

Thickener

1	tablespoon water
1½	teaspoons cornstarch
2	large eggs, lightly beaten
1	tablespoon minced scallion greens

1. Using a sharp cleaver or a large chef's knife, cut through the undershell of the lobster lengthwise, cutting through the head and back toward the tail, splitting the lobster in two. Remove the sand sac from the head, and remove the intestinal tract. Cut off and discard the tip of the head with the eyes and the antennae. Cut off and discard the legs. Cut the body, through the shell, into pieces about 2 inches square. (Those wary of cutting up a live lobster may blanch it for 2 to 3 minutes in boiling water before cutting.)

2. Chop the ground pork until fluffy, place it in a mixing bowl, add the *Pork Marinade*, and toss lightly.

3. Heat a wok, add the oil, and heat until very hot. Add the *Minced Seasonings*, and stir-fry for about 10 seconds, until fragrant. Add the ground pork, and stir-fry, mashing and stirring the meat to separate, for about a minute, or until the color changes. Add the lobster pieces, and stir-fry for about 1 minute over high heat. Add the *Lobster Sauce*, and heat until boiling. Cover, and cook for about 3 minutes over high heat. Uncover, and slowly add the *Thickener*, stirring constantly to prevent lumps. When the sauce has thickened, turn off the heat, and slowly add the beaten eggs in a thin stream around the side of the wok. Stir once or twice, and transfer the mixture to a platter. Sprinkle the minced scallion greens on top, and serve immediately.

Steamed Crabs With Ginger Dipping Sauce

Qing Zheng Pang Zie

6 Servings ⌣ Main Dish

6   medium-sized live blue crabs, approximately 5-7 ounces each, preferably females

Crab Marinade

3   tablespoons rice wine or sake

4   scallions, smashed with the flat side of a cleaver

4   slices gingerroot, the size of a quarter, smashed with the flat side of a cleaver

Ginger Dipping Sauce

½   cup light soy sauce

2½   tablespoons clear rice vinegar

1   tablespoon sesame oil

½   tablespoon finely shredded gingerroot

1   tablespoon sugar

1. Plunge the crabs in boiling water to cover for about 1 minute; remove and rinse them in cold water. Twist off and discard the apron. Remove the upper shell from each crab, and reserve the roe that may be attached to it. Remove and discard the spongy gill tissue from inside the crab. Rinse the bodies, and drain well. Cut off the last two hairy joints of the legs on each side of the body, and separate the crab claws from the main body. Using the blunt edge of a cleaver, tap the claws so that the shells crack. (This will facilitate removal of the meat later.) Place the prepared crabs on a heatproof plate or plates. Pinch the scallions and gingerroot in the *Crab Marinade* repeatedly for several minutes to impart their flavor. Pour the marinade over the crab pieces and let marinate for 20 to 30 minutes. Place the crab, still on the plates, in a steamer tray or trays, stacking the steaming trays one on top of the other if necessary, and cover.

2. Prepare the *Ginger Dipping Sauce* by combining the ingredients, stirring until the sugar dissolves. Transfer the sauce to individual serving bowls.

3. Fill a wok with water level with the bottom edge of the steamer tray, and heat until boiling. Place the steamer over the boiling water, and steam the crabs for 5 to 8 minutes, reversing the order of the steamer trays once. Remove the crabs and discard the seasonings. Serve the steamed crabs with the dipping sauce.

IN CHINA, THE ARRIVAL *of fresh river crabs in the marketplace is cause for celebration. Many Chinese believe that the only way to eat this delicacy is steamed and served simply with a dipping sauce of vinegar and shredded ginger, as in this recipe. In this country, fresh blue or stone crab claws are best for this dish; ideally they should be alive and kicking until they are ready to be cooked. To identify a female crab, look on the underside; the tail should be an oval shape.*

Chinese Cabbage With Crabmeat

Xie Rou Bai Cai

6 Servings ⌢ Main Dish or Side Dish

I N EASTERN CHINA, *where this dish originated, vegetables like baby hearts of cabbage are paired with foods like crabmeat or shrimp to bring out their natural sweetness. Baby cabbage hearts are suggested, but bok choy, asparagus and snow peas work equally well. Serve this dish as a light main dish with rice or as an elegant vegetable side dish.*

10-12	baby hearts of cabbage, about 2 pounds, or bok choy
1	tablespoon safflower or corn oil

Minced Seasonings

2	tablespoons minced scallions
1	tablespoon minced gingerroot
8	ounces fresh lump crabmeat, picked over to remove any cartilage or shell
2	tablespoons rice wine or sake

Sauce

⅓	cup chicken broth, preferably Chinese Chicken Broth (page 345)
1	teaspoon sesame oil
1	teaspoon cornstarch
¾	teaspoon salt

1. Remove any wilted outer leaves from the hearts of baby cabbage. Trim off the remaining leaf tips, leaving about 1 inch on the end. If the cabbage hearts are large, cut them in half lengthwise. If using bok choy, cut away the ends of the leaves and roll-cut the stalks into 1½-inch lengths, about 1 inch thick. Heat 2 quarts of water until boiling, add the cabbage, and cook for 10 to 12 minutes, or until just tender. Drain and plunge immediately into cold water. Drain thoroughly.

2. Heat a wok until very hot. Add the oil and heat until hot. Add the *Minced Seasonings* and stir-fry for about 10 seconds, until fragrant. Add the crabmeat and continue stir-frying over very high heat for about 1 minute. Add the rice wine and cook for 10 seconds, tossing over high heat. Add the *Sauce* and heat, stirring constantly, until it begins to thicken. Add the cabbage hearts and toss lightly to coat. Transfer to a serving platter and serve immediately.

Crab in Sweet & Sour Sauce

Cu Liu Xie Rou

6 Servings ⌢ Main Dish

6   medium-sized live blue crabs, about 5 ounces each

Crab Marinade
3   slices gingerroot, the size of a quarter, smashed with the flat side of a cleaver
2   tablespoons rice wine or sake

1   cup cornstarch
1   cup peanut, safflower or corn oil

Minced Seasonings
2   tablespoons minced scallions
1   tablespoon minced garlic

Crab Sauce
6   tablespoons water
5   tablespoons ketchup
¼   cup clear rice vinegar
1   teaspoon soy sauce
½   teaspoon sesame oil
5   tablespoons sugar
2   teaspoons cornstarch
¾   teaspoon salt

FRESH CRABMEAT *provides a perfect foil for piquant sweet-and-sour sauce. Soft-shell and blue crab are ideally suited to this tasty Cantonese dish, as are Dungeness and Alaskan king crab legs.*

1. Plunge the crabs into boiling water for about 1 minute; remove and rinse them in cold water. Twist off and discard the apron. Remove the upper shell from each crab, and reserve the roe that may be attached to it. Remove and discard the spongy gill tissue from inside the crab. Rinse the bodies, and drain well. Cut off the last two hairy joints of the legs on each side of the body. Cut each crab into 4 to 6 pieces, cutting so that a portion of the body is attached to one or two legs. Place the crab pieces and any roe in a mixing bowl. Pinch the gingerroot slices in the *Crab Marinade* repeatedly for several minutes to impart the flavor, and add the crab marinade to the bowl. Toss lightly, and let the crab marinate for 20 minutes. Discard the gingerroot. Add the cornstarch, and toss lightly to coat the crab.

2. Heat a wok or a frying pan, add the oil, and heat the oil to 400 degrees F.

Add half the crab pieces, and deep-fry for about 4 minutes over high heat, until golden brown and crisp. (The roe should be cooked only briefly, about 1 minute.) Remove and drain the pieces. Reheat the oil, and deep-fry the remaining crab in the same manner. Remove the oil from the wok, reserving 2 tablespoons. Wipe out the wok.

3. Reheat the wok, add the 2 tablespoons of oil, and heat until very hot. Add the *Minced Seasonings*, and stir-fry for about 10 seconds over high heat, until fragrant. Add the *Crab Sauce*, and stir-fry until it begins to thicken. Add the fried crab pieces and the roe, and toss lightly to coat with the sauce. Transfer the mixture to a platter, and serve immediately.

Crab in Sweet Bean Sauce

Jing Jiang Xie Rou

6 Servings ⌣ Main Dish

SWEET BEAN SAUCE AND *additional seasonings— green pepper, scallions and garlic—combine with the crab for a flavor that is unusually tasty and excellent with white rice.*

6	medium-sized live blue crabs, about 5 ounces each

Crab Marinade

3	slices gingerroot, the size of a quarter, smashed with the flat side of a cleaver
2	tablespoons rice wine or sake
1	cup cornstarch
1	cup peanut, safflower or corn oil

Minced Seasonings

1	tablespoon minced scallions
1	tablespoon minced garlic
2	green peppers, cored, seeded and roll-cut into 1-inch pieces

Crab Sauce

¼	cup water
1½	tablespoons sweet bean sauce
1½	tablespoons soy sauce
1	tablespoon rice wine or sake
1	tablespoon sugar

1. Plunge the crabs into boiling water for about 1 minute; remove and rinse

them in cold water. Twist off and discard the apron. Remove the upper shell of the crab, and reserve the roe that may be attached to it. Remove and discard the spongy gill tissue from inside the crab. Rinse the bodies, and drain well. Cut off the last two hairy joints of the legs on each side of the body. Cut each crab into 4 to 6 pieces, cutting so that a portion of the body is attached to one or two legs. Place the crab pieces and any roe in a mixing bowl. Pinch the gingerroot slices in the *Crab Marinade* repeatedly for several minutes to impart the flavor, and add the marinade to the crab pieces. Toss lightly, and let the crab marinate for 20 minutes. Discard the gingerroot. Add the cornstarch, and toss lightly to coat the pieces of crab.

2. Heat a wok, add the oil, and heat to 400 degrees F. Add a batch of the crab pieces, and fry for about 4 minutes over high heat, until golden brown and crisp. (The roe should be cooked only briefly, about 1 minute.) Remove and drain the pieces. Reheat the oil, and fry the remaining crab in the same manner. Remove the oil from the wok, reserving 2 tablespoons. Wipe out the wok.

3. Reheat the wok, add the 2 tablespoons of oil, and heat until very hot. Add the *Minced Seasonings*, and stir-fry for about 10 seconds over high heat. Add the green peppers, and stir-fry for another 10 seconds. Add the *Crab Sauce*, and cook until the sauce begins to thicken after boiling. Add the crab pieces and the roe, and toss lightly to coat with the sauce. Transfer the mixture to a platter, and serve immediately.

Flash-Cooked Crab With Ginger & Scallions

Cong Bao Pang Xie

6 Servings ⌒ Main Dish

THIS DISH ILLUSTRATES *the simple refinement of classic Cantonese cooking. Fresh crab pieces are tossed with smashed ginger, scallions and rice wine over a scorching-hot fire until the crab is just cooked. The sweetness of the crab is underscored nicely by the basic Chinese seasonings. Only the freshest crab should be used in this dish. Serve it with rice and a vegetable for a satisfying meal.*

6	medium-sized live blue crabs, approximately 5-7 ounces each, preferably females

Crab Marinade

4	scallions, smashed with the flat side of a cleaver
4	slices gingerroot, the size of a quarter, smashed with the flat side of a cleaver
3	tablespoons rice wine or sake
1	tablespoon peanut, safflower or corn oil
4	scallions, ends trimmed, cut into 1-inch lengths
3	slices gingerroot, the size of a quarter, shredded finely
2½	tablespoons rice wine or sake
1	teaspoon salt

1. Plunge the crabs into boiling water for about 1 minute; remove and rinse them in cold water. Twist off and discard the apron. Remove the upper shell from each crab, and reserve the roe that may be attached to it. Remove and discard the spongy gill tissue from inside the crab. Rinse the bodies, and drain well. Cut off the last two hairy joints of the legs on each side of the body, and separate the crab claws. Using the blunt edge of a cleaver, tap the claws so that the shells crack. (This will facilitate removal of the meat later.) Cut the bodies of the crab into quarters, portioning each piece with one or two legs.

2. Pinch the scallions and gingerroot repeatedly in the *Crab Marinade* for several minutes to impart their flavor. Pour the marinade over the crab pieces, and let marinate for 20 to 30 minutes. Drain the crabs, discarding the seasonings.

3. Heat a wok or a skillet until very hot. Add the oil and heat until nearly smoking. Add the scallions and shredded ginger and stir-fry about 10 seconds, until fragrant. Add the crabs and stir-fry over high heat, tossing them. Add the rice wine and salt, cover and cook the crabs for 5 to 7 minutes. Uncover and cook briefly, for about 1 minute, then transfer to a serving platter. Serve immediately.

Braised Chicken With Shark's Fin

Yu Chi Shao Ji

6 Servings ⁓ Main Dish

1	whole roasting chicken, about 4½ pounds

Chicken Marinade

2	tablespoons soy sauce
1	tablespoon rice wine or sake
2	scallions, smashed with the flat side of a cleaver
2	slices gingerroot, the size of a quarter, smashed with the flat side of a cleaver

Chicken-Braising Mixture

4	cups chicken broth, preferably Chinese Chicken Broth (page 345)
3	tablespoons soy sauce
1½	tablespoons rice wine or sake
1	teaspoon sugar

2	cups peanut, safflower or corn oil
2	ounces shark's fin needles
¼	cup rice wine or sake
4	scallions, smashed with the flat side of a cleaver
4	slices gingerroot, the size of a quarter, smashed with the flat side of a cleaver

Chicken Seasonings

4	dried Chinese black mushrooms, soaked in hot water to cover for 20 minutes, stems removed and caps shredded
¼	cup finely shredded Chinese ham, Smithfield ham or prosciutto
2	tablespoons finely shredded scallions
1	tablespoon finely shredded gingerroot

Thickener

3	tablespoons water
1½	tablespoons cornstarch

1½	teaspoons Chinese black vinegar or Worcestershire sauce

D**RIED SHARK'S FIN IS** *available in Chinese grocery stores in two forms: the whole fin or as gelatinous needles. This eastern dish, which uses the needles, is a delightful departure from the usual Cantonese rendition of shark's fin. Serve with a stir-fried or steamed vegetable and rice as the final dish at a special banquet. For the uninitiated, shark's fin may seem strange. It is one of the most highly relished Chinese foods, yet it is mainly prized for its smooth and gelatinous texture. Its innately fishy flavor disappears when it is cooked with chicken bones and ginger, leaving a delicate and refined flavor.*

½ cup canned bamboo shoots, plunged briefly into boiling water, refreshed in cold water and cut into matchstick-sized shreds

1. Remove and discard any fat from the cavity and neck of the chicken. Rinse the chicken lightly, and place it in a bowl. Rub the **Chicken Marinade** all over the chicken and inside the cavity. Let marinate for 1 hour. Drain the chicken, discard the scallions and gingerroot, and add the liquid to the **Chicken-Braising Mixture**.

2. Heat a wok, add the oil, and heat the oil to 400 degrees F. Slowly lower the chicken into the hot oil, and deep-fry on both sides, over high heat, until golden brown. (Ladle hot oil over the chicken as it is frying.) Remove, and drain. Remove the oil from the wok.

3. Place the chicken and the braising mixture in a heavy casserole or a Dutch oven. Heat the mixture until boiling. Reduce the heat to low, cover, and cook for 45 minutes.

4. Meanwhile, place the shark's fin needles in a pan with cold water to cover. Add 2 tablespoons of the rice wine, 2 scallions and 2 slices of the gingerroot. Heat the mixture until just below the boiling point, turn the heat to low, and let simmer for ½ hour. Remove the pan from the heat, and let cool to room temperature. Rinse the shark's fin needles, discarding the gingerroot and scallion. Repeat the procedure in its entirety, using the remaining 2 tablespoons of rice wine, the remaining 2 scallions and the remaining 2 slices of gingeroot. Let cool to room temperature. Discard the liquid, scallions and gingerroot, and rinse the shark's fin needles lightly.

5. Add the shark's fin needles to the chicken, along with the **Chicken Seasonings**. Continue cooking, covered, for 30 minutes. Remove the chicken, let it cool slightly, and cut it, through the bones, into bite-sized serving pieces, as for Red-Cooked Chicken (page 181). Arrange the pieces on a platter.

6. Heat the braising mixture until boiling, and slowly add the **Thickener**, stirring constantly to prevent lumps. Add the black vinegar and the shredded bamboo shoots. Toss lightly, and pour the mixture over the chicken pieces. Serve immediately.

Fluffy Eggs & Shrimp (Shrimp Fu Rung)

Fu Rong Xia

6 Servings ⁓ Main Dish

¾   pound medium-sized raw shrimp, shelled

Shrimp Marinade
1   tablespoon rice wine or sake
1   tablespoon minced gingerroot

Egg Mixture
6   large eggs, lightly beaten
1½   teaspoons sesame oil
2   tablespoons minced scallions
1   teaspoon salt
¼   teaspoon freshly ground black pepper

2   tablespoons peanut, safflower or corn oil
1   tablespoon minced scallion greens

1. Score each shrimp along the back so that it will "butterfly" when cooked. Remove the vein, rinse and drain thoroughly. Place the shrimp in a dishtowel, and squeeze out as much water as possible or blot dry on paper towels. Place the shrimp in a bowl. Add the *Shrimp Marinade*, toss lightly, and let stand for 30 minutes. Beat the *Egg Mixture* lightly.

2. Heat a wok or a skillet, and add 1 tablespoon of the oil. Heat until very hot. Drain the shrimp, and add to the pan. Stir-fry for several minutes over high heat until they change color. Remove, and drain. Wipe out the wok.

3. Reheat the wok, and add the remaining tablespoon of oil. Heat until hot, and add the egg mixture and the cooked shrimp. Stir-fry over medium heat until the eggs are just set and soft-cooked. Transfer the mixture to a serving platter, and sprinkle the scallion greens on top. Serve immediately.

Years ago, Cantonese master chefs created a number of "fu rung" dishes, named for the hibiscus flower with its pink petals and green leaves. In this dish, a fluffy omelet seasoned with ginger and scallions is garnished with shrimp. Serve with plenty of steamed rice and a steamed vegetable.

Pork

THE CHINESE PORK BUTCHER IN our small neighborhood market in Taipei was a jovial fellow given to regaling his favorite customers with witty anecdotes, but when it came time to do business, his mood immediately turned sober; he took his meat very seriously. Every morning at six, he would arrive at his humble stand with two massive sides of freshly slaughtered pig slung over his Vespa scooter. His first order of business was to hang the carcasses from the racks positioned on the side of his concession.

After scrubbing down the counter and rinsing off his cleaver and knife, he would begin to cut up the meat. Working methodically and with the confidence of a man who knows his business, he would divide the pig into loin, shoulder, leg, belly and feet. The innards—liver, intestines and kidney—would be cleaned and hung up for sale. The next 20 minutes would be devoted to arranging the cuts of meat to display their finest features; the importance of this procedure was evident as he painstakingly positioned each piece of meat until he was satisfied with its appearance. Although he was one of many butchers selling pork in the marketplace, his meat always stood out for its high quality and attractive arrangement. No meat would be sold until the daily routine had been completed.

The pig—or "long-nosed general," as it is sometimes affectionately called—was among the first animals domesticated in China. Raising pigs appears to have been a widespread practice; excavations of an ancient Chinese village dating back to 2000 B.C. have uncovered evidence of pig remains in most dwellings.

Whereas beef is the most popular meat in the Western diet, pork has assumed this role for the Chinese. So prominent is pork, in fact, that the Chinese word for meat can also be used to mean pork. During the T'ang dynasty (618 to 907), pork was prepared in a number of ways: a tart, rich porridge of pig, chicken, goat, deer and seasonings was very popular. Wild boar and dried and pickled pork were savory companions to rice. Overconsumption of pork and meat was frowned upon, however, by the T'ang pharmacologists.

Marco Polo attested to the fondness for pork among the southern Chinese during the Sung dynasty (960 to 1279). After observing the volume of this meat sold daily in the market of Hangzhou, he recorded, "Each day each shop hangs sides of pork—not less than ten sides. In two holidays of wintertime, each shop sells tens of sides daily." The popularity of pork was not restricted to the gentry; the lower classes also ate much pork and particularly savored the lung, kidneys, liver and heart.

The pig has served a crucial role of religious significance as a sacrificial offering. Meat and fish historically have been the main ingredients of feast and ritual dishes, but the presentation of a whole pig was an honor reserved for the most revered deities. A roast pig was offered annually in the celebration of Ching-ming, the Festival of the Dead.

The symbolic significance of the pig is equally notable. It is the last animal of the Twelve Terrestrial Branches, corresponding to the astrological sign of Pisces. The wild boar symbolizes the wealth of the forest.

The popularity of the pig continues to the present day. The reasons are obvious: the meat is highly versatile and reasonably priced, and the subtle flavor complements many ingredients. The pig is easily raised on little feed—often scraps—and in turn produces a meat rich in vitamins and minerals.

The Chinese allow no waste. Every part of the pig's anatomy is utilized. The meat may be stir-fried, deep-fried, steamed, braised, red-cooked (slow-cooked in a soy-based liquid), white-cooked (slow-cooked in a clear liquid), ground and used in fillings and sausages or dried and salted, producing a popular garnish for rice. The feet are red-cooked, stewed, braised, chilled in aspic, pickled in vinegar or cooked in soups. The kidney and liver are stir-fried, simmered, deep-fried or cooked in soups. Pig's ear, a celebrated Chinese delicacy, is cooked, shredded and served cold with a spicy dressing. Even the brain is cooked—deep-fried in a batter, fritter-style.

Perhaps one of the simplest yet most classic pork recipes is Tung-po pork, a braised meat dish invented by the celebrated Chinese poet Su Tung-po. He immortalized the dish in a poem titled "Eating Pork":

Huang Chou produces good pork
Which is cheap as dirt
The rich spurn and won't eat it.
The poor know not how to cook it.
Keep the fire low,
Use very little water,
Give it plenty of water to get tender
I take a bowl of pork first thing in the
    morning
I like it this way—mind your own
    business!

猪
肉
類

Standard American Cuts of Pork and Their Appropriate Chinese Cooking Methods

Section	Cut of Meat	Suitable Cooking Method
Shoulder	blade, Boston roast, pork butt, Boston butt	red-cook (braise in a soy-based liquid), simmer, braise, grind for filling and sausage
	picnic shoulder	red-cook, simmer, braise, white-cook (braise in a clear liquid), grind for filling and sausage, preserve by salting and drying
Loin	chops, roasts, tenderloin	stir-fry, deep-fry, braise, steam, barbecue, grind for filling and sausage
	ribs	deep-fry, steam, braise, simmer, cook in soups, barbecue
	fatback	add to filling for flavor and body, render to a cooking oil
Belly	fresh bacon	red-cook, braise, simmer, steam, deep-fry, roast, preserve by salting and drying
Leg	fresh ham	stir-fry, steam, braise, red-cook, simmer, deep-fry, grind for filling
	center roast, sirloin	simmer, red-cook, steam, white-cook, grind for filling, cure to make Chinese ham
	shank	red-cook, steam, white-cook, preserve by salting and drying
Feet	hocks and trotters	red-cook, braise, simmer, white-cook, cook in soups

Barbecued Pork Loin

Cha Shao Rou

6 Servings ⌣ Appetizer or Main Dish

2	pounds boneless center-cut pork loin

Pork Marinade

2	tablespoons hoisin sauce
2	tablespoons soy sauce
1½	tablespoons rice wine or sake
1	tablespoon ketchup
1½	tablespoons minced garlic
2½	tablespoons sugar
1	teaspoon salt

1. Remove most of the fat and all the gristle from the pork loin, and discard. Cut the meat, with the grain, into strips about 3 inches thick. Place the meat in a mixing bowl. Add the *Pork Marinade*, toss lightly, and let marinate for 4 hours, or overnight in the refrigerator, turning occasionally.

2. Preheat the oven to 375 degrees F. Arrange the meat strips on a rack in a roasting pan, and bake for 45 minutes, or until the inside is cooked and the outside is brown. Let cool slightly, slice, and serve.

BARBECUED PORK LOIN IS *extremely versatile: it may be sliced and served by itself as an appetizer, stir-fried in meat and vegetable platters or used in a stuffing for steamed Lotus Buns (page 59).*

Glazed Pork Slices

Jin Quian Rou

6 Servings ⁓ Appetizer or Main Dish

GLAZED WITH A LIGHT *coating of sweet bean sauce and baked until golden brown, these succulent pork slices are said to resemble golden coins. The salt pork slices provide flavor and moisture to the lean meat pieces. Serve these tender slices stuffed into steamed Lotus Buns (page 59) or between slices of bread.*

2	pounds boneless center-cut pork loin or tenderloin

Pork Marinade

3	tablespoons soy sauce
2	tablespoons rice wine or sake
1½	tablespoons sweet bean sauce or hoisin sauce
1	teaspoon sesame oil
1	tablespoon sugar
½	teaspoon five-spice powder
3	slices gingerroot, the size of a quarter, smashed with the flat side of a cleaver
3	scallions, smashed with the flat side of a cleaver
2	cloves garlic, smashed with the flat side of a cleaver

12	10-inch bamboo skewers
1	pound salt pork

1. Remove any fat or gristle from the pork loin, and discard. Cut the meat, across the grain, into slices ⅙ inch thick. (You may partially freeze the pork to facilitate cutting.) Cut each slice lengthwise into thirds. Place the slices in a bowl, add the *Pork Marinade*, toss lightly, and let marinate for at least 3 hours, or as long as overnight. Soak the bamboo skewers in water to cover for 1 hour. Blanch the salt pork in boiling water for 1 minute; rinse it in cold water. Remove the rind, and cut the salt pork into slices about ¼ inch thick. Cut the slices into pieces the same size as the pork; reserve the marinade.

2. Preheat the oven to 375 degrees F. Thread the skewers with alternating slices of pork loin and salt pork. Place the skewers in a roasting pan, and baste with the reserved marinade. Bake the pork slices for about 20 minutes, turning and basting occasionally. Remove the pork slices from the skewers, and arrange on a platter. Discard the salt pork slices. Serve.

Steamed Spareribs in Black Bean Sauce

Shi Zhi Pai Gu

6 Servings ⌢ Main Dish or Appetizer

   3   pounds spareribs

Sparerib Marinade
3	tablespoons soy sauce
2	tablespoons rice wine or sake
1	teaspoon sesame oil
1	tablespoon minced garlic

Sparerib Sauce
6	tablespoons soy sauce
6	tablespoons chicken broth, preferably Chinese Chicken Broth (page 345), or water
2	tablespoons rice wine or sake
1½	tablespoons sugar
1	teaspoon cornstarch

   2   cups peanut, safflower or corn oil

Minced Seasonings
2	tablespoons fermented black beans, rinsed, drained and coarsely chopped
2	tablespoons minced scallions
1	tablespoon minced gingerroot
1	tablespoon minced dried chili peppers
1	tablespoon minced scallion greens

I N THE TRADITIONAL version of this dish, the spareribs are first deep-fried, then braised in the black bean sauce. I prefer to steam the spareribs instead of braising them, giving the dish a subtler, more refined flavor. Either method will provide an exquisitely savory concoction that is the perfect foil for white rice.

   1. Direct the butcher to cut the slab of spareribs crosswise into thirds so that they measure 1½ to 2 inches in length. Separate the ribs, cutting between the bones. Place the pieces in a bowl, add the *Sparerib Marinade*, toss lightly, and let marinate for at least 3 hours, or overnight in the refrigerator. Drain the spareribs, and add the marinade to the *Sparerib Sauce*.

   2. Heat a wok, add the oil, and heat the oil to 425 degrees F. Add a third of the spareribs, and deep-fry over high heat for about 3 minutes, stirring

constantly until the ribs are golden. Remove with a handled strainer or slotted spoon, and drain. Reheat the oil. Deep-fry the remaining spareribs in the same manner, reheating the oil between batches. Remove the oil from the wok, reserving 2 tablespoons. Wipe out the wok.

3. Reheat the wok, add the 2 tablespoons of oil, and heat until very hot. Add the *Minced Seasonings*, and stir-fry for about 10 seconds, until fragrant. Add the sparerib sauce, and heat until boiling. Cook for about 1 minute, until the sauce has thickened, and add the spareribs. Toss lightly to coat with the sauce, and transfer to a heatproof bowl or a pie plate. Sprinkle the minced chili peppers over the spareribs. Place the bowl in a steamer tray, and cover. Clean and dry the wok.

4. Fill the wok with water level with the bottom edge of the steamer tray, and heat until boiling. Place the steamer tray over the boiling water, and steam, covered, for 45 minutes over high heat, adding additional water, if necessary. Sprinkle the minced scallion greens over the spareribs, and serve immediately.

Home-Style Spareribs

Jia Chang Pai Gu

6 Servings ⁓ Main Dish or Appetizer

I WAS FIRST SERVED THIS *dish at an excellent eastern restaurant in Taipei, and the wrapping and baking of the spareribs in aluminum foil intrigued me. The head chef, when questioned, admitted that he had adapted the dish from the classic version, which called for a paper wrapping. He assured me, however, that the flavor of the adapted version remained true to that of the traditional recipe.*

3	pounds country-style spareribs

Sparerib Marinade

2	tablespoons rice wine or sake
1½	tablespoons soy sauce
1	teaspoon salt
6	scallions, smashed with the flat side of a cleaver
6	slices gingerroot, the size of a quarter, smashed with the flat side of a cleaver

Braising Mixture

3	cups chicken broth, preferably Chinese Chicken Broth (page 345), or water
3	tablespoons soy sauce
2	tablespoons rice wine or sake
1½	tablespoons sugar
2	cinnamon sticks
1	whole star anise
2	cups peanut, safflower or corn oil

Minced Seasonings
     2   tablespoons minced scallions
     1   tablespoon minced gingerroot

1. Direct the butcher to cut the slab of spareribs into shorter pieces so that they measure 1½ to 2 inches in length. Separate the ribs, cutting between the bones. Place the pieces in a bowl, add the *Sparerib Marinade*, toss lightly, and let marinate for at least 3 hours, or overnight in the refrigerator. Discard the scallions and gingerroot, drain the ribs, and add the marinade to the *Braising Mixture*. Cut the aluminum foil into 6-inch squares, one for each sparerib piece.

2. Heat a wok, add the oil, and heat the oil to 425 degrees F. Add a third of the spareribs, and deep-fry over high heat for about 3 minutes, stirring constantly until the ribs are golden. Remove with a handled strainer or slotted spoon, and drain. Reheat the oil. Deep-fry the remaining spareribs in the same manner, reheating the oil between batches. Remove the oil from the wok, reserving 1 tablespoon. Wipe out the wok.

3. Reheat the wok, add the tablespoon of oil, and heat until very hot. Add the *Minced Seasonings*, and stir-fry for about 10 seconds, until fragrant. Add the braising mixture, and heat until boiling. Add the spareribs. Heat the mixture until boiling, reduce the heat to medium, partially cover, and cook for 30 minutes, tossing occasionally. Uncover, turn up the heat, and cook the sauce to a syrupy glaze, stirring constantly. Discard the cinnamon sticks and star anise.

4. Preheat the oven to 450 degrees. Wrap each sparerib piece in a square of aluminum foil, and place the wrapped pieces on a baking sheet. Bake for 10 minutes. Transfer the ribs to a platter, and serve immediately.

Saucy Spareribs in Squash

Nan Gua Pai Gu

6 Servings ⌣ Main Dish

In Sichuan province, where this dish originated, pork is one of the most popular meats. When marinated in a pungent mixture of bean or hoisin sauce seasoned with garlic and ginger and steamed until tender, the ribs become succulent and a superb complement to the sweet squash.

3 pounds country-style spareribs

Sparerib Marinade
¼ cup sweet bean or hoisin sauce
3 tablespoons soy sauce
2 tablespoons rice wine or sake
2 teaspoons hot chili paste or crushed red peppers
1 teaspoon sesame oil
1 tablespoon sugar
1 teaspoon five-spice powder (optional)

2 acorn or 1 butternut squash, about 4 pounds
2 tablespoons minced scallion greens

Steamed or boiled rice

1. Direct the butcher to cut the spareribs into shorter pieces so that they measure about 2 to 2½ inches in length. Separate the ribs, cutting between the bones. Trim off any excess fat, and place the ribs in a bowl. Add the *Sparerib Marinade*. Toss lightly to coat the ribs, and cover with plastic wrap. Let marinate for 3 hours in the refrigerator or overnight. Cut the squash in half, and using a spoon, scoop out the seeds, slightly enlarging the cavity. Arrange the squash halves, cut surface up, in a steamer that has been lined with blanched cabbage leaves or parchment paper. Cover.

2. Fill a wok with water level with the bottom edge of the steamer tray, and heat until boiling. Place the steamer tray containing the squash over the boiling water, and steam for 30 minutes. Spoon the spareribs into the cavities of the squash. (If there are any remaining spareribs, spoon into a heatproof bowl and place in another steamer tray.) Steam the spareribs and the squash for 35 minutes, or until done. (Alternatively, you may bake this dish: Preheat the oven to 350 degrees F. Bake the squash in a covered ovenproof dish for 45 minutes, add the spareribs, and cook for another 35 minutes.)

3. Remove, and sprinkle the tops of the spareribs with the minced scallion greens. Serve with steamed or boiled rice. Spoon out the ribs, and scoop out the squash meat.

Pork Slices With Garlic Sauce

Suan Ni Bai Rou

6 Servings ⌣ Main Dish

1½ pounds fresh ham or boneless center-cut pork loin, with a thin border of fat

White-Cooking Liquid

2 quarts water

3 tablespoons rice wine or sake

3 slices gingerroot, the size of a quarter, smashed with the flat side of a cleaver

3 scallions, smashed with the flat side of a cleaver

Garlic Sauce

3 tablespoons soy sauce

2 tablespoons white-cooking liquid

2 teaspoons sesame oil

2 teaspoons chili oil or chili paste

1 tablespoon minced garlic, chopped into a smooth paste

1½ teaspoons sugar

Fresh cilantro sprigs for garnish

1. Rinse the ham, and drain. Place the *White-Cooking Liquid* in a pot. Add the meat, and heat the mixture until boiling. Reduce the heat to low, and simmer, uncovered, for 1 hour, turning the meat from time to time. Remove the meat, and let it cool to room temperature. Add the 2 tablespoons of the white-cooking liquid to the *Garlic Sauce*.

2. Cut the meat, across the grain, into paper-thin slices. If possible, there should be a border of fat on each slice. Blanch each slice in boiling water for about 2 minutes, or until cooked through, and arrange the meat slices in an overlapping circular pattern on the plate. Before serving, pour the garlic sauce on top. Garnish with sprigs of cilantro, and serve.

T HERE ARE MANY *parallels in French and Chinese cooking methods. One example is white-cooking, used in this recipe. This process is almost identical to the French practice of cuire à blanc, or simmering in a clear liquid. The cooked meat maintains its original color and provides an attractive contrast to the dark, pungent sauce. The meat is traditionally sliced for serving with a border of fat, lending a richness that most Chinese savor.*

Spicy Hot & Sour Stir-Fried Pork

Yu Xiang Rou Si

6 Servings ⌢ Main Dish

THE SAUCE IN THIS DISH *is found in a number of Sichuanese platters, and it is equally delicious with eggplant, beef or eggs. This classic version illustrates well the sensual qualities of Sichuan cuisine: the fiery seasonings sensitize the palate to the textures of the wood ears and water chestnuts.*

1½	pounds boneless center-cut pork loin

Pork Marinade

2	tablespoons water
1½	tablespoons soy sauce
1½	tablespoons rice wine or sake
1	teaspoon sesame oil
1	tablespoon cornstarch

10	dried wood ears, soaked in hot water to cover for 20 minutes
½	cup peanut, safflower or corn oil

Minced Seasonings

3	tablespoons minced scallions
2	tablespoons minced gingerroot
2	tablespoons minced garlic

2	teaspoons chili paste
2	cups water chestnuts, plunged briefly into boiling water and refreshed in cold water, sliced

Pork Sauce

¼	cup soy sauce
¼	cup water
2	tablespoons rice wine or sake
2	teaspoons Chinese black vinegar or Worcestershire sauce
1	teaspoon sesame oil
1	tablespoon sugar
2	teaspoons cornstarch
¼	teaspoon freshly ground black pepper

1. Remove any fat or gristle from the pork loin, and discard. Cut the meat, across the grain, into slices ⅛ inch thick. (You may partially freeze the pork to facilitate cutting.) Cut the slices into matchstick-sized shreds. Place the shreds

in a bowl, add the *Pork Marinade*, toss lightly, and let marinate for 30 minutes. Cut away and discard the hard, bitter nib from the wood ears, and shred the wood ears.

2. Heat a wok, add 3 tablespoons of the oil, and heat until very hot. Add half the pork shreds, and stir-fry over high heat, stirring constantly, until the shreds change color. Remove with a handled strainer or slotted spoon, and drain. Wipe out the wok, add 3 more tablespoons of oil, and stir-fry the remaining shreds in the same manner. Remove the oil from the wok, and wipe out the wok.

3. Reheat the wok, add the remaining 2 tablespoons of oil, and heat until very hot. Add the *Minced Seasonings*, and stir-fry for about 10 seconds, until fragrant. Add the chili paste, stir-fry for about 5 seconds, and add the water chestnuts and the wood ears. Toss lightly over high heat for 20 seconds, and add the *Pork Sauce*. Stir-fry until the sauce thickens, add the pork shreds, toss lightly to coat with the sauce, and transfer the mixture to a platter. Serve immediately.

Chinese-Style Pork Steak
Zhong Shi Zhu Pai
6 Servings 〜 Main Dish

2 pounds boneless center-cut pork loin

Pork Marinade
1 tablespoon soy sauce
1 tablespoon rice wine or sake
1 tablespoon water
1 teaspoon sesame oil
2 teaspoons minced garlic
2 teaspoons cornstarch

2 medium-sized onions
½ cup peanut, safflower or corn oil

Pork Sauce
6 tablespoons chicken broth, preferably Chinese Chicken Broth (page 345), or water
3 tablespoons soy sauce
3 tablespoons ketchup
1½ tablespoons Chinese black vinegar or Worcestershire sauce
1½ tablespoons sugar

ALTHOUGH THIS DISH might not be considered a classic Chinese platter, its flavor has made it a contemporary favorite of many Chinese. The tart, oniony sauce provides an excellent contrast to snowy grains of steamed rice.

| 1 | teaspoon cornstarch |
| ½ | teaspoon freshly ground black pepper |

Steamed or boiled rice

1. Remove any fat or gristle from the pork loin, and discard. Cut the meat, across the grain, into slices ¼ inch thick. (You may partially freeze the pork to facilitate cutting.) Using the blunt edge of the cleaver, lightly pound the pork slices in a diamond pattern, to tenderize the meat. Cut the slices lengthwise in half, and place them in a bowl. Add the *Pork Marinade*, toss lightly, and let marinate for at least 3 hours, or overnight in the refrigerator. Peel the onions, and shred them lengthwise.

2. Heat a wok, add 3 tablespoons of the oil, and heat until very hot. Add half the pork slices, and fry on both sides until golden. Remove with a handled strainer or slotted spoon, and drain. Wipe out the wok, reheat, add 3 more tablespoons of oil and heat until very hot. Add the remaining pork slices, and fry in the same manner. Remove and drain. Wipe out the wok.

3. Reheat the wok, add the remaining 2 tablespoons of oil, and heat until very hot. Add the shredded onions, and stir-fry over high heat, stirring constantly until soft and transparent. Add the *Pork Sauce*, and toss lightly until the sauce has thickened a bit. Add the cooked pork slices, toss lightly to coat with the sauce, and transfer the mixture to a platter. Serve immediately over rice.

Shredded Pork With Sweet Bean Sauce

Jing Jiang Rou Si

6 Servings ⌒ Main Dish

2	pounds boneless center-cut pork loin

Pork Marinade

3	tablespoons water
2	tablespoons soy sauce
1	tablespoon rice wine or sake
1	teaspoon sesame oil
1	teaspoon cornstarch

½	cup peanut, safflower or corn oil
2	cups finely shredded scallions or leeks, placed in cold water to cover

Pork Sauce

5	tablespoons water
2	tablespoons soy sauce
1½	tablespoons sweet bean sauce
1½	tablespoons rice wine or sake
1½	tablespoons sugar

THIS FLAVORFUL STIR-*fried platter illustrates the subtle seasoning that makes northern Chinese cuisine so popular. The saucy richness of the sweet bean sauce contrasts beautifully with the shredded scallions. Serve with steamed Mandarin Pancakes (page 62).*

1. Remove any fat or gristle from the pork loin, and discard. Cut the meat, across the grain, into slices ⅛ inch thick. (You may partially freeze the pork to facilitate cutting.) Cut the slices into matchstick-sized shreds. Place the shreds in a bowl, add the *Pork Marinade*, toss lightly, and let marinate for 20 minutes.

2. Heat a wok, add the oil, and heat the oil to 400 degrees F. Add half the pork shreds, and stir-fry over high heat, turning constantly until the shreds change color. Remove with a handled strainer or slotted spoon, and drain. Reheat the oil, and stir-fry the remaining pork in the same manner. Remove and drain.

3. Drain the scallion shreds, and arrange them in a mound on a platter. Heat the wok, and add the *Pork Sauce*. Stir-fry the sauce over high heat until it thickens. Add the cooked pork shreds, toss lightly, and place over the scallions on the platter. Toss lightly before serving with Mandarin Pancakes.

Stir-Fried Vegetables & Pork With Egg Cap

He Cai Dai Mao

6 Servings 〜 Main Dish

THIS DISH TYPIFIES *the mild flavors and seasonings often used in the north. Since wheat is a major staple crop in northern China, meat and vegetable dishes there are commonly served with steamed bread or pancakes, instead of rice. This dish is the closest thing to mu shu pork in the repertory of classic dishes: pork and vegetables are wrapped in a steamed Mandarin pancake (page 62) that has been slathered in pungent bean sauce.*

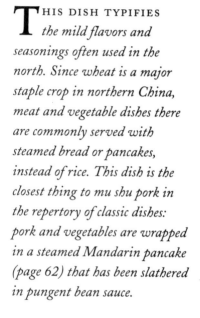

1   pound boneless center-cut pork loin

Pork Marinade

1   tablespoon soy sauce
1   tablespoon rice wine or sake
1   tablespoon water
1   teaspoon sesame oil
2   teaspoons cornstarch

6-8   dried Chinese black mushrooms, soaked in hot water to cover for 20 minutes
1   ounce cellophane noodles (bean threads)
3   large eggs, lightly beaten
6½   tablespoons peanut, safflower or corn oil
1   cup shredded Chinese cabbage (Napa)
1   cup shredded leeks or scallion greens
3   cups fresh bean sprouts, lightly rinsed

Pork Sauce

¼   cup chicken broth, preferably Chinese Chicken Broth (page 345), or water
3   tablespoons soy sauce
2   tablespoons rice wine or sake
1½   teaspoons cornstarch
½   teaspoon sugar
½   teaspoon salt
¼   teaspoon freshly ground black pepper

Scallion brushes for garnish

1. Remove any fat or gristle from the pork loin, and discard. Cut the meat, across the grain, into slices ⅛ inch thick. (You may partially freeze the pork to facilitate cutting.) Cut the slices into matchstick-sized shreds. Place them in a bowl, add the *Pork Marinade*, toss lightly, and let marinate for 20 minutes. Drain

mushrooms, cut off the stems and discard and cut the caps into shreds. Soften the cellophane noodles in hot water to cover for 10 minutes; drain, then cut into 6-inch lengths.

2. Rub the surface of a well-seasoned wok or an omelet pan with an oil-soaked cloth or paper towel, and heat until a few drops of water sprinkled on the surface evaporate immediately. Add the beaten eggs, and tilt the pan so that the eggs form a thin pancake about 8 inches in diameter. Cook the pancake (egg cap) over medium heat until golden and set. Flip it over, and cook briefly on the other side. Remove, and set aside.

3. Heat a wok, add 3½ tablespoons of the oil, and heat until very hot. Add the pork shreds, and stir-fry until they change color, about 1 minute. Remove, and drain. Wipe out the wok.

4. Reheat the wok, add the remaining 3 tablespoons of oil, and heat until very hot. Add the black mushrooms, and stir-fry for about 10 seconds, until fragrant. Add the cabbage and the leeks. Toss lightly over high heat for 1 minute. Add the softened cellophane noodles, the cooked pork and the bean sprouts, and cook for 1 minute. Add the *Pork Sauce*, and stir-fry over high heat until the sauce is thick. Transfer the mixture to a platter. Place the egg cap on top, completely covering the stir-fried mixture. Serve with scallions, sweet bean sauce and Mandarin Pancakes. Each person spreads some sweet bean sauce on a Mandarin Pancake with a scallion, puts some of the stir-fried mixture on top, rolls up the pancake and eats.

Sweet & Sour Pork

Gu Lu Rou

6 Servings 〜 Main Dish

ALTHOUGH SWEET AND *sour pork often seems a cliché in Chinese cuisine, any collection of classical pork recipes would be incomplete without it. This version is deliciously light and refined—a contrast to the ersatz renditions one often finds in American Cantonese eateries.*

Pickled Carrots

2	cups carrots, roll-cut into 1-inch pieces
3	tablespoons clear rice vinegar
3	tablespoons sugar
3	slices gingerroot, the size of a quarter, smashed with the flat side of a cleaver

2	pounds boneless center-cut pork loin

Pork Marinade

2	tablespoons rice wine or sake
1½	tablespoons soy sauce
1	teaspoon sesame oil

2	green peppers, cored and seeded
2	egg yolks
2	cups cornstarch
2	cups peanut, safflower or corn oil
1½	tablespoons minced garlic
2	cups pickled carrots, drained
1	cup pineapple chunks, drained

Sweet & Sour Sauce

⅔	cup water
¼	cup ketchup
3	tablespoons vinegar
2	teaspoons soy sauce
½	teaspoon sesame oil
3	tablespoons sugar
2	teaspoons cornstarch
1	teaspoon salt

1. To make the *Pickled Carrots*, place the carrot pieces in a bowl, and add the remaining ingredients. Toss lightly, and marinate for 12 hours (or overnight) in the refrigerator. Toss the carrots occasionally, if possible.

2. Remove any fat or gristle from the pork loin, and discard. Cut the meat into 1-inch cubes. Place the cubes in a bowl, add the *Pork Marinade*, toss lightly, and let marinate for at least 1 hour. Roll-cut the green peppers into 1-inch pieces. Add the egg yolks to the pork cubes, and stir to coat. Dredge the pork cubes in cornstarch, lightly squeezing each piece to make sure the cornstarch adheres. Place the cubes on a tray to air-dry for 1 hour.

3. Heat a wok, add the oil, and heat the oil to 400 degrees F. Add a third of the pork cubes, and deep-fry over high heat for about 3 minutes, stirring constantly, until the meat is cooked and golden. Remove with a handled strainer or slotted spoon, and drain. Reheat the oil. Fry the remaining pork in the same manner, reheating the oil between batches. Remove and drain. Strain the oil to remove bits of cooked cornstarch. Reheat the oil to 425 degrees. Add all the pork cubes, and deep-fry for about 1 minute, turning constantly, until the cubes are crisp and golden brown. Remove, and drain thoroughly. Remove the oil from the wok, reserving 2 tablespoons. Wipe out the wok.

4. Reheat the wok, add the 2 tablespoons of oil, and heat until very hot. Add the garlic and green peppers. Stir-fry for about 1 minute over high heat. Add the pickled carrots and the pineapple. Stir-fry for another minute, and add the *Sweet & Sour Sauce*. Heat the mixture, stirring constantly, until it begins to thicken. Add the fried pork cubes, and toss lightly to coat with the sauce. Transfer the mixture to a platter, and serve immediately.

Cashew-Coated Pork Slices

Yao Guo Rou Pian

6 Servings ⌣ Main Dish or Appetizer

A TRADITIONAL CHINESE banquet begins with a period of drinking and toasting, and at this time, several dishes are usually served. These dishes are often deep-fried, because their dry, crisp texture is complementary to wine. Cashew-Coated Pork Slices is a good example of this category.

1½   pounds boneless center-cut pork loin

Pork Marinade
2   tablespoons soy sauce
2   tablespoons rice wine or sake
2   tablespoons minced scallions
2   teaspoons minced gingerroot
1½   teaspoons sugar
1   teaspoon salt
½   teaspoon five-spice powder

1½   cups cornstarch
3   large eggs, lightly beaten
4   cups raw cashews, coarsely chopped
2   cups peanut, safflower or corn oil

1. Remove any fat or gristle from the pork loin, and discard. Cut the meat, across the grain, into slices ⅛ inch thick. (You may partially freeze the pork to facilitate cutting.) Cut the slices into pieces that are approximately 2 inches square. Place the slices in a mixing bowl, and add the *Pork Marinade*. Toss lightly, and let marinate for at least 3 hours, or overnight in the refrigerator.

2. Dredge each pork slice in the cornstarch, dip in the beaten eggs, drain, and coat with the chopped cashews. Lightly press the meat slices so that the cashews adhere to them. Arrange the meat slices on a tray, and let them air-dry for 20 minutes.

3. Heat a wok, add the oil, and heat the oil to 375 degrees F. Add a third of the pork slices, and fry over high heat for about 2½ minutes, turning constantly, until the meat is cooked and golden brown. Remove with a handled strainer or slotted spoon, and drain on absorbent paper. Reheat the oil. Fry the remaining slices in the same manner, reheating the oil between batches. Remove and drain. Arrange the slices on a platter, and serve immediately.

Pork Meatballs With Spinach

Dong Po Xiu Qiu

6 Servings ⌒ Main Dish

¾	pound ground pork or beef

Meat Seasonings

6-8	dried Chinese black mushrooms, soaked in hot water to cover for 20 minutes, stems removed and caps chopped
2	teaspoons dried shrimp, soaked for 1 hour in hot water, drained and minced (optional)
2	teaspoons minced gingerroot
1½	tablespoons soy sauce
1½	teaspoons sesame oil
1	tablespoon cornstarch
½	teaspoon salt

4	large eggs, lightly beaten
1	tablespoon peanut, safflower or corn oil
1	pound fresh spinach, trimmed and cleaned

Spinach Seasonings

1	teaspoon sesame oil
1	teaspoon minced garlic
½	teaspoon salt

Egg-Ball Sauce

½	cup chicken broth, preferably Chinese Chicken Broth (page 345)
1	tablespoon rice wine or sake
1	teaspoon cornstarch
1	teaspoon salt
¼	teaspoon freshly ground white pepper

A CCORDING TO AN ancient Chinese custom, a maiden of marrying age would throw an embroidered ball of silk or a bouquet (xiu qiu) to a group of her suitors. The young man fortunate enough to catch the missile would then become her husband. This dish—steamed meatballs covered with shreds of egg pancake and surrounded by a ring of spinach—is said to bear some resemblance to her bouquet.

1. Lightly chop the meat until fluffy, and place it in a mixing bowl. Add the *Meat Seasonings*, and stir vigorously in one direction to combine evenly. Lightly throw the meat against the inside of the bowl for 1 minute. Form the mixture into 1-inch meatballs.

2. Wipe the surface of a well-seasoned wok or a nonstick skillet with an oil-soaked paper towel. Heat the pan until hot. Add a third of the beaten eggs, and tilt the pan so that the eggs form a thin pancake. Cook over medium heat until

the egg sheet is firm. Flip it over, and cook for 5 seconds. Remove, cook, and cut into thin shreds. Make two more egg sheets in the same manner, and shred them. Roll the meatballs in the egg shreds, making sure they are completely coated.

3. Lightly coat a heatproof plate with oil. Arrange the meatballs on the plate about ½ inch apart. Sprinkle any remaining egg shreds over the meatballs. Place the plate in a steamer tray.

4. Fill a wok with water level with the bottom edge of the steamer tray, and heat until boiling. Place the steamer tray over the boiling water, cover, and steam for 20 minutes over high heat. Remove the steamer and the water from the wok.

5. Reheat the wok, add the tablespoon of oil, and heat until nearly smoking. Add the spinach and the *Spinach Seasonings*. Toss lightly over high heat until the spinach begins to wilt slightly. Arrange the spinach around the outer edge of a platter, and place the steamed-egg meatballs in the center.

6. Reheat the wok, add the *Egg-Ball Sauce*, and heat, stirring constantly, until slightly thick. Pour the sauce over the egg balls, and serve immediately.

Lion's Head

Shi Zi Tou

6 Servings ⁓ Main Dish

2	pounds Chinese cabbage (Napa)
¼	cup peanut, safflower or corn oil
1	tablespoon rice wine or sake
4	cups chicken broth, preferably Chinese Chicken Broth (page 345), or water
1½	pounds ground pork butt or picnic shoulder

Pork Seasonings

1	tablespoon rice wine or sake
2	teaspoons sesame oil
1	tablespoon minced scallions
1	teaspoon minced gingerroot
1½	tablespoons cornstarch
1½	teaspoons salt

Meatball Coating

1½	tablespoons soy sauce
1	tablespoon water
1	tablespoon cornstarch

Broth Seasonings

1	tablespoon soy sauce
¾	teaspoon salt

THIS FAMOUS EASTERN *dish was once reserved for banquets because of the quantity of meat called for in the recipe. In recent times, however, it has joined the ranks of the family-style platters, and it is now regularly served at home. The large meatballs are said to look like a lion's head, and the cabbage, slightly browned and wilted at the edges, suggests a lion's mane.*

1. Rinse the cabbage, and drain thoroughly. Remove and set aside 4 of the big outer leaves. Cut the remaining leaves into 2-inch squares, and discard the core.

2. Heat a wok, add 1 tablespoon of the oil, and heat until nearly smoking. Add the harder sections of cabbage, and stir-fry for about 1 minute over high heat, stirring constantly. Add the leafier sections, and sprinkle the rice wine over the cabbage. Stir-fry for another minute, and add the chicken broth. Cook the mixture for about 10 minutes over high heat; then transfer it to a heavy 3-quart casserole or a Dutch oven.

3. Lightly chop the ground pork until fluffy, and place it in a mixing bowl. Add the *Pork Seasonings*, and stir vigorously in one direction for about 5 minutes. Lightly throw the meat against the inside of the bowl to combine evenly. Divide the meat into 4 portions, and form each into an oval meatball.

4. Reheat the wok, add the remaining 3 tablespoons of oil, and heat until very hot. Dip the meatballs in the ***Meatball Coating***, and slide them into the pan. Pan-fry the meatballs over high heat until brown. Remove them with a slotted spoon, and drain. Arrange the meatballs on the cabbage in the casserole, and cover with the 4 reserved cabbage leaves. Cover the casserole.

5. Preheat the oven to 400 degrees F. Bake the casserole for 1 hour. Add the ***Broth Seasonings***, stir, and bake for 10 more minutes. Serve immediately.

Double-Cooked Pork Slices

Hui Guo Rou

6 Servings ⌢ Main Dish

2	pounds boneless pork butt or fresh ham
3	squares firm tofu, about 2 pounds
3	green peppers, cored and seeded
2	leeks, cleaned
1	cup peanut, safflower or corn oil
1	tablespoon minced garlic
1½	teaspoons chili paste

Pork Sauce

¼	cup soy sauce
¼	cup water
3	tablespoons rice wine or sake
2	tablespoons sweet bean sauce
2	tablespoons sugar

1. Rinse the meat, and place it in a pot with water to cover. Heat until the water is boiling, reduce the heat to low, and cook for 1½ hours, turning the meat occasionally. Remove the meat from the pot, and let it cool to room temperature. Cut the meat, across the grain, into slices ⅛ inch thick. Cut the slices into 2-inch squares. Cut the tofu squares into slices that are 1½ inches long and 1 inch wide. Roll-cut the green peppers into 1-inch pieces. Slice the leeks lengthwise in half, and cut them into 1-inch pieces.

2. Heat a wok, add the oil, and heat the oil to 400 degrees F. Drain any water that may have collected around the tofu slices, and fry them in batches over high heat until golden brown, about 2 minutes. Remove with a handled strainer or slotted spoon, and drain. Reheat the oil between batches.

3. Heat the oil to 425 degrees F. Add the pork slices, and fry, stirring constantly over high heat, for 2 minutes. Add the green peppers and leeks. Fry over high heat for 1 minute. Remove all the food, and drain. Remove the oil from the wok, reserving 1 tablespoon. Wipe out the wok.

4. Reheat the wok, add the tablespoon of oil, and heat until very hot. Add the minced garlic, and stir-fry over high heat for 10 seconds, until fragrant. Add the chili paste, and stir-fry for 5 seconds. Add the *Pork Sauce*. Toss lightly until the sauce begins to boil and thicken. Add the pork, green peppers, leeks and tofu. Toss to coat with the sauce, transfer to a platter, and serve immediately.

To my mind, this dish ranks as one of the best that Sichuanese cuisine has to offer. The marriage of flavorings among the pork loin, green peppers and tofu slices, all glazed with the sweet and spicy sauce, is superb. Fresh green garlic is traditionally used in the Far East, but I find that a combination of leeks and garlic makes an excellent substitute. The pork is twice-cooked: first to cook the meat, then to give it a crisp, golden brown finish, which contrasts with the crunchy peppers and tender tofu.

Tung-Po Pork

Dong Po Rou

6 Servings ⌣ Main Dish

Su Tung-po, the
famed poet, statesman and
gourmet of the Sung dynasty,
was admired for his many
talents. He is credited with
inventing this savory dish. The
combination of slow-simmering
and steaming reduces the sauce to
a lustrous glaze and transforms
the meat to a buttery tenderness.
To allow the casserole to cook in
its own juices, a flour-and-
water paste is used to seal the pot
shut, ensuring a concentration of
flavors.

3½-4	pounds fresh belly pork or 4½ pounds pork picnic shoulder
¼	cup rock sugar, lightly pounded to a coarse powder (rock sugar is available in Asian markets; granulated sugar may be substituted)

Braising Sauce

½	cup soy sauce
⅓	cup rice wine or sake
5	slices gingerroot, the size of a quarter, smashed with the flat side of a cleaver
4	scallions, smashed with the flat side of a cleaver

Sealing Paste

3	tablespoons water
6	tablespoons all-purpose flour

1. Heat 2 quarts of water until boiling. Place the meat in the water, and blanch it for 2 minutes. Rinse the meat in cold water, and drain thoroughly.

2. Place the meat, skin side down, in a heavy casserole or a Dutch oven. Sprinkle the rock sugar on top. Pour the *Braising Sauce* over the meat, and rub the sugar and sauce into the meat. Put the lid securely on the pot, and mix the *Sealing Paste* until smooth. Spread the sealing paste around the rim of the lid, making sure that there are no openings between the lid and the casserole. Place the pot over medium heat, and cook for 10 minutes. Reduce the heat to low, and simmer for 2 hours. Remove the pan from the heat, and let it sit for 10 minutes. Cut away the hardened sealing paste, and discard. Skim most of the fat from the braising sauce, and discard.

3. Transfer the pork, skin side up, to a heatproof bowl, and pour the braising sauce on top. Place the bowl in a steamer tray.

4. Fill a wok with water level with the bottom edge of the steamer tray, and heat until boiling. Place the steamer tray over the boiling water, cover, and steam for 1½ hours over high heat. (Alternatively, if you do not have a steamer large enough to hold the bowl, you may cover the bowl with a double layer of heavy-duty aluminum foil and bake in a preheated 475-degree oven for 1¼ hours.) Remove the pork, and cut, across the grain, into slices ½ inch thick. Skim off any fat remaining on the braising sauce, discard the scallions and gingerroot, and pour the sauce over the pork. Serve immediately.

Chinese Pork Sausage

La Chang

6 Servings ⌒ Appetizer

1½   pounds pork fat
2   pounds ground pork picnic shoulder, pork loin or fresh ham

Sausage Seasonings
¾   cup Gaoling wine or Scotch
¼   cup honey
1½   tablespoons salt
1   teaspoon five-spice powder

10   feet sausage casing (available at a specialty butcher)

1. Chop the pork fat, and place it in a mixing bowl along with the ground pork and the *Sausage Seasonings*. Stir vigorously in one direction, and lightly throw the mixture against the inside of the bowl. Let the meat marinate overnight in the refrigerator.

2. Rinse the sausage casing, and carefully attach it to the end of a funnel. Tie the other end of the casing. Push the ground-meat mixture into the funnel, and squeeze the casing to distribute the meat evenly throughout. The sausage should be loosely packed. Once all the meat has been stuffed in the casing, tie off the funnel end. Tie the casing at 4-inch intervals, and prick the sausage all over with a pin. Refrigerate it at least overnight, but preferably 2 or 3 days, before cooking.

3. Pan-fry the sausage in a little bit of oil, or steam it for 10 minutes over high heat. Slice and serve, or use as directed in individual recipes.

S AUSAGE IS A SPECIALTY *made once a year by many Chinese families before the New Year's Festival. At this time, a pig is slaughtered in preparation for the holiday. The air is cool enough to permit hanging the sausages outside to dry. The following recipe is Cantonese, accounting for the addition of honey and the resulting sweet flavor. Traditionally, a very strong wine is used to provide extra flavor and to help preserve the meat. You may serve the sausage as an hors d'oeuvre, steamed and cut into thin slices, or use in other dishes as directed in the individual recipes.*

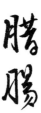

Beef & Lamb

ONE CHILLY MARCH EVENING several years ago, three friends and I had the pleasure of dining at the Barbecue Chi Restaurant in Peking. After a frantic half-hour taxi ride—weaving in and out of a sea of cyclists silhouetted in the dusk and accompanied by the majestic strains of "The Hearts of the Yunnan People Are Turned to Chairman Mao" blaring from the radio—we arrived at our destination. The restaurant is situated in the northern sector of the city on South Lake, which provides a cool sanctuary for diners during the summer months when the unrelenting heat forces a number of the city's restaurants to close.

The Barbecue Chi (barbecue meats) Restaurant has maintained an outstanding reputation for more than a century. The specialty of the house is Mongolian Barbecue, a dish made with paper-thin slices of only the most tender beef and lamb dipped in a sauce of rice wine, ginger-flavored water, shrimp oil, soy sauce and other seasonings of the diner's choice, then grilled over a charcoal brazier. The fuel used is limited to cypress and willow, as these woods are believed to provide the most fragrant smoke. Once cooked to a turn with Mongolian chopsticks some two feet long, the meat slices are stuffed into a hot, flaky sesame roll (*shao ping*), sprinkled with shredded scallions and eaten immediately.

According to Kenneth Lo, an eminent authority on Chinese cuisine, barbecued meats were first introduced in Peking toward the end of the Ming dynasty (1368 to 1644). The emperor at that time liked to cater to the culinary tastes of the many dignitaries and princes visiting the Imperial Palace, and his Mongolian guests were keen on beef and lamb.

For most ancient Chinese, however, the cow was a beast of burden rather than a source of food. "Do not eat the cow, for it is a hardworking and sympathetic beast," states an early proverb. Oxen were work animals, and rulers generally prohibited their slaughter except as a sacrifice to honor particularly revered officials or ancestors.

The ox or bull is the second symbolic animal of the Twelve Terrestrial Branches, corresponding to the astrological sign Taurus, and is emblematic of spring and agriculture. Each year on the fifth of February, a ceremony called Meeting of the Spring is conducted, with the cow playing the leading role. A huge clay image of a cow, along with numerous smaller ones, is carried to a designated field. While the field is plowed, the huge cow is beaten with sticks, representing the arrival of spring. The observers then disperse, carrying the smaller images and bits of soil to their own fields. The soil is then sprinkled over their own land in hopes of cultivating a good crop.

The cow's ritual importance notwithstanding, beef was consumed on occasion in ancient China. During the Han dynasty (206 B.C. to 220 A.D.), stews were made with beef and turnip, a combination still popular today, or beef and sonchus, a wild grass. Beef flank was apparently a feast dish; meatballs made of beef, pork, mutton and rice were generally reserved for the elderly, as was beef marinated in good wine. Salt-cured beef was served with rice or millet, stir-fried or cooked in soups. Beef was also pounded, mixed with salt, millet and yeast and fermented to a relish. Though during the T'ang dynasty (618 to 907) and Sung dynasty (960 to 1279) beef was not a favorite food, beef tea was a popular beverage that supposedly possessed strengthening powers. Similarly, beef bone marrow was recommended for blood disorders and fatigue.

The number of beef dishes in modern Chinese cuisine has been on the increase in recent years—perhaps because of Western influences—but chicken, pork and fish are still far more prominent. All parts of the animal are used, and many cooking methods are employed. Although there are beef dishes in most of the regional cuisines, the largest number is found in the northern and western schools. The reasons are obvious: the greatest concentrations of Moslems are in these areas (beef and lamb figure prominently in the Moslem diet because pork is prohibited), and oxen are used in the western provinces to haul salt from the mines. In Hunan province, braised beef and beef tendons are favorite dishes. The tendons, which have a slightly gelatinous, resilient texture, are extremely nutritious and are said to prolong life. Smoked beef is frequently served with wine, and tangerine-peel beef is a well-loved garnish for rice. (Dairy products have never played a substantial role in the Chinese diet, but in some areas of northern China and in Yunnan province, milk products such as cheese, fried milk and yogurt are commonly consumed.)

Like beef, lamb and mutton are favored by the present-day Moslems, and these meats were sometimes eaten by the ancient Chinese. During the Han dynasty, boiled or roasted mutton was an important offering and was served during the Chinese New Year, the Summer Festival and other important holidays. Lamb flank, shoulder and stomach were used in Han feast dishes, whereas lamb with assorted seasonings over noodles was a popular snack. Believed to have beneficial properties, lamb was suggested fare for the infirm.

During the Sung dynasty, cooking with lamb and kid became widespread among all classes. Milk-steamed lamb and lamb's head are examples of the unusual delicacies of this period. In the ancient city of Kaifeng, large shops specializing in roast lamb flourished.

With the takeover of China by the Mongolian rulers in the Yüan dynasty (1271 to 1368), mutton became a regular item on the Imperial menu. According to existing records, an average of four or five sheep were slaughtered daily, and huge vats for boiling whole sheep were installed in the Imperial kitchens. Whole lamb was also prepared in a manner similar to roast suckling pig; the unskinned animal was put in a pit lined with red-hot stones, covered with willow branches and sealed with mud. Lamb and mutton were present in a variety of forms in Mongolian dishes: wontons were made with a dough of bean paste and a filling of minced lamb and dried tangerine

牛羊肉類

peel, boiled and served in lamb broth; and Mongolian meat cakes consisted of almost every edible portion of sheep, stewed, minced and mixed with yams, cheese and eggs. Mongolian fire pot, barbecued or scorched lamb, lamb shish kebab and thrice-cooked lamb became popular in Peking restaurants. Lamb is believed to have a warming effect on the body, so these dishes were especially popular in cold weather. Even mutton wine, with an alcohol level of more than 9 percent, was brewed by the Mongols. Today, the major consumption of lamb still occurs in northern China, but the meat is eaten on occasion in the southern and western regions, particularly during the winter months when hearty lamb stews are

common fare. The Chinese rarely draw a distinction between lamb, mutton or goat, as the same Chinese word is used for all three. The lamb represents filial piety because the young animals habitually assume a kneeling position, suggesting respect, while nursing. The sheep is the eighth symbolic animal of the Twelve Terrestrial Branches, corresponding to Scorpio on the zodiac.

Whatever the method of preparation, including those outlined in the following recipes, it seems safe to conclude that one's culinary odds will be much higher than those given by the poet Yüan Mei when he wrote, "There are seventy-two ways of cooking lamb. Of these, only eighteen or nineteen are palatable."

Standard American Cuts of Beef
and Their Appropriate Chinese Cooking Methods

Section	Cut of Meat	Suitable Cooking Method
Chuck (blade, arm half and shoulder)	chuck roasts, chuck steaks	braise, simmer, stir-fry, deep-fry, steam, grind for filling
Foreshank, Brisket	foreshank, brisket	braise, simmer, grind for filling
Rib	rib roasts	stir-fry, steam, smoke
Plate ("white abdomen")	Yankee pot roast, short ribs, spareribs	braise, simmer, barbecue, cook in soups
Loin, Hip	loin roasts, loin steaks, sirloin steaks, sirloin roasts, tenderloin	stir-fry, deep-fry, steam, smoke
Flank	flank steak, London broil	stir-fry, deep-fry, steam, smoke
Round	rump roast, bottom round, shank, sirloin tip, eye-of-round, top round	simmer, braise, stir-fry, deep-fry, smoke
Oxtail	oxtail	braise, simmer, cook in soups
Variety Meats	tongue, liver, tripe	stir-fry, braise, simmer, deep-fry, cook in soups

Standard American Cuts of Lamb
and Their Appropriate Chinese Cooking Methods

Section	Cut of Meat	Suitable Cooking Method
Neck	neck meat	braise, simmer, roast, grind for filling
Shoulder, Foreshank, Hindshank	blade chop, arm chop, shoulder roasts, foreshank, hindshank	braise, simmer, roast, grind for filling, barbecue
Breast	riblets, roasts, spareribs	steam, braise, simmer, grind for filling, cook in soups
Rib	rib chops, rib roast, crown roast	stir-fry, steam, deep-fry, roast, barbecue
Loin and Sirloin, Flank	loin chops, loin roasts, sirloin chops and roasts	stir-fry, deep-fry, roast
Leg	whole leg, sirloin half, center leg, shank half	stir-fry, steam, roast, barbecue

Sliced Beef in Hot Sauce

Ma La Niu Rou

6 Servings ⌒ Main Dish or Appetizer

THE SICHUAN PEPPER-corns in this dish contribute a numbingly spicy flavor. The crisp cucumber slices and the smooth vermicelli sheets bathed in the peppery sauce combine with the beef to create an unforgettable dish. Cellophane noodles (bean threads) may be used in place of the vermicelli sheets.

1	pound top sirloin roast or eye-of-round roast
5	dried vermicelli sheets or 2 ounces cellophane noodles

Vermicelli Seasonings

½	teaspoon salt
¾	teaspoon sesame oil

2	English (gourmet seedless) cucumbers or 6 small pickling cucumbers
2	teaspoons salt
1	tablespoon Sichuan peppercorns

Beef Seasonings

¼	cup soy sauce
1	tablespoon Chinese black vinegar or Worcestershire sauce
2	tablespoons sesame oil
2	tablespoons minced scallions
2	tablespoons minced gingerroot
2	teaspoons sugar
½	teaspoon salt

1	bunch fresh cilantro, rinsed and drained

1. Rinse the beef, and place it in a pot with 4 cups of cold water. Heat until boiling, reduce the heat to low, and simmer the beef, uncovered, for about 1 hour, until tender. Remove the beef from the pot, and let it cool. Cut the beef, across the grain, into slices ⅛ inch thick. (You may partially freeze the beef to facilitate cutting.) Cut the slices into pieces 1½ inches long and 1 inch wide.

2. Soften the vermicelli sheets in hot water to cover for 10 minutes. Drain the sheets, and cut them into strips 1 inch wide, or the cellophane noodles into 3-inch lengths. Cook the vermicelli strips or the noodles in boiling water for 1 minute. Refresh them in cold water, drain thoroughly, and place in a bowl. Add the *Vermicelli Seasonings*, toss lightly, and arrange on a platter.

3. Cut the cucumbers in half lengthwise, and remove any seeds. Cut each half crosswise into 1½-inch pieces, and cut each piece lengthwise into paper-thin slices. Place the cucumber slices in a bowl, add the salt, toss lightly, and let sit for

20 minutes. Drain the cucumbers, rinse off the salt with cold water, and pat the slices dry. Arrange the slices on top of the vermicelli strips. Arrange the beef slices in the center of the cucumber strips.

4. Heat a wok, add the Sichuan peppercorns, and stir-fry for 5 minutes over medium heat, stirring constantly, until the peppercorns are fragrant and golden brown. Pulverize the peppercorns in a blender or a food processor fitted with the steel blade. Add the Sichuan peppercorn powder to the *Beef Seasonings*. Just before serving, pour the mixture over the beef, and arrange the cilantro around the edge of the platter. Toss lightly, and serve.

Braised Soy-Sauce Beef

Hong Shao Niu Rou

6 Servings ~ Main Dish or Appetizer

2   pounds boneless stewing beef, such as chuck or shin
¼   cup peanut, safflower or corn oil

Braising Mixture
1   cup water
¼   cup rice wine or sake
¼   cup soy sauce
1   tablespoon sugar
3   scallions, smashed with the flat side of a cleaver
3   slices gingerroot, the size of a quarter, smashed with the flat side of a cleaver
1   whole star anise

1. Remove any fat or gristle from the beef, and discard. Cut the meat into 1-inch cubes.

2. Heat a 3-quart casserole or a Dutch oven, add the oil, and heat until very hot. Add half the meat cubes, and fry over high heat until golden brown on all sides. Remove the meat. Reheat the oil, and fry the remaining beef cubes in the same manner.

3. Remove the oil from the casserole, and add the beef and the *Braising Mixture*. Heat the liquid until boiling. Reduce the heat to low, and simmer, covered, for 1½ hours, or until the meat is tender; stir occasionally. The sauce should be reduced to about ½ cup. If not, turn the heat to high, and reduce the sauce, stirring constantly. Remove the star anise, scallions and gingerroot. Transfer the beef and sauce to a bowl, and serve hot or cold.

I N THIS SIMPLE BRAISED *dish, the slow-cooking process heightens the licorice flavor of the star anise and the mellow richness of the soy sauce. Serve it hot with rice or cold over shredded lettuce.*

Stir-Fried Beef With Scallions

Cong Bao Niu Rou

6 Servings ⌣ Main Dish

THE SUBTLE SEASONING *of northern cooking is apparent in this stir–fried platter, with its light glaze of soy sauce and sugar and its scallion garnish. This home–style dish is delicious whether it is served with Mandarin Pancakes (page 62) or with rice.*

2   pounds beef sirloin or tenderloin

Beef Marinade
- ¼   cup soy sauce
- 2   tablespoons rice wine or sake
- 2   tablespoons minced garlic
- 2   tablespoons cornstarch
- 1   tablespoon sugar

- ½   cup peanut, safflower or corn oil
- 4   cups shredded scallion greens or leeks

Beef Sauce
- 6   tablespoons soy sauce
- 1½   tablespoons sugar

- 1½   teaspoons sesame oil

1. Remove any fat or gristle from the beef, and discard. Cut the meat, across the grain, into slices about ⅛ inch thick. (You may partially freeze the beef to facilitate cutting.) Cut each slice into pieces about 1½ inches long and 1 inch wide. Place the pieces in a bowl, add the *Beef Marinade*, toss lightly, and let marinate for at least 1 hour. Drain the meat.

2. Heat a wok, add 3 tablespoons of the oil, and heat the oil until very hot. Add half the beef, and stir-fry over high heat, stirring constantly, until the pieces change color, about 1½ minutes. Remove with a handled strainer or slotted spoon, and drain. Wipe out the wok, reheat, add 3 more tablespoons of the oil and reheat. Add the remaining beef, and cook in the same manner. Remove and drain. Wipe out the wok.

3. Reheat the wok, add the remaining 2 tablespoons of oil, and heat until very hot. Add the shredded scallions, and stir-fry for about 1 minute over high heat. Add the cooked beef pieces and the *Beef Sauce*. Toss lightly to coat the meat and scallions with the sauce. Add the sesame oil, toss lightly, and transfer the mixture to a platter. Serve immediately.

Stir-Fried Beef With Green Peppers

Qing Jiao Niu Rou Si

6 Servings ⌣ Main Dish

2 pounds flank steak, eye-of-round roast or sirloin roast

Beef Marinade

2 tablespoons soy sauce
2 tablespoons water
1 tablespoon rice wine or sake
1 teaspoon sesame oil
2 teaspoons cornstarch

6 medium-sized green peppers, cored and seeded
½ cup peanut, safflower or corn oil

Minced Seasonings

2 tablespoons minced scallions
2 tablespoons minced garlic
2 tablespoons fermented black beans, rinsed, drained and coarsely chopped
1 tablespoon minced gingerroot

Beef Sauce

⅓ cup chicken broth, preferably Chinese Chicken Broth (page 345)
2 tablespoons rice wine or sake
1 tablespoon soy sauce
2 teaspoons sesame oil
1 tablespoon cornstarch
2 teaspoons sugar

THE LEANNESS OF FLANK *steak makes it a particularly good cut of beef for stir-frying, but eye-of-round or top sirloin also does nicely. When the meat has been shredded and marinated, it assumes a tenderness comparable to sirloin or tenderloin. This is an excellent version of a well-known Cantonese dish.*

1. Remove any fat or gristle from the beef, and discard. Cut the meat, across the grain, into slices about ⅛ inch thick. (You may partially freeze the meat to facilitate cutting.) Cut each slice into matchstick-sized shreds, and place them in a bowl. Add the *Beef Marinade*, toss lightly, and let marinate for 30 minutes. Cut the green peppers into matchstick-sized shreds. Drain the beef.

2. Heat a wok, add 3 tablespoons of the oil, and heat the oil until very hot. Add half of the meat shreds, and stir-fry, stirring constantly, over high heat for

about 2 minutes, until the pieces change color. Remove with a handled strainer or slotted spoon, and drain. Wipe out the wok and add 3 more tablespoons of the oil. Reheat the oil, and stir-fry the remaining beef in the same manner. Remove from the wok and drain. Wipe out the wok.

3. Reheat the wok, add the remaining 2 tablespoons of oil, and heat until very hot. Add the *Minced Seasonings*, and stir-fry over high heat for about 10 seconds, until fragrant. Add the green pepper shreds, and stir-fry for about 1 minute over high heat. Add the *Beef Sauce*, and toss lightly until the sauce begins to thicken. Add the cooked beef pieces, and toss lightly to coat with the sauce. Transfer the mixture to a platter, and serve immediately.

Stir-Fried Beef With Snow Peas in Oyster Sauce

Hao You Niu Rau

6 Servings ～ Main Dish

v. Good

WHILE THIS DISH HAS *become something of a classic in Cantonese–American restaurants across the country, it remains a venerable delicacy when prepared properly. Tender slices of meat are tossed with snow peas in a garlicky oyster sauce. Substitute chicken, pork, or turkey for the beef.*

1½	pounds flank steak or London broil

Beef Marinade

2	tablespoons soy sauce
1	tablespoon rice wine or sake
1	teaspoon sesame oil
1	tablespoon minced garlic
1	teaspoon cornstarch
½	cup peanut, safflower or corn oil

Minced Seasonings

3	tablespoons minced scallions, white part only
1	tablespoon minced gingerroot
½	tablespoon minced garlic
1¼	pounds fresh snow peas, ends snapped and veiny strings removed

Sauce

¾	cup chicken broth, preferably Chinese Chicken Broth (page 345)
¼	cup oyster sauce
1	teaspoon soy sauce
1⅓	tablespoons cornstarch
2	teaspoons sugar

Steamed or boiled rice

1. Using a sharp knife, trim away any fat or gristle from the meat. Cut lengthwise with the grain into strips about 2 inches wide. Cut the strips, across the grain, into thin slices about ⅛ inch thick. (You may partially freeze the meat to facilitate cutting.) Place in a bowl, add the *Beef Marinade*, toss lightly to coat, and cover with plastic wrap. Let sit 1 hour at room temperature or refrigerate overnight.

2. Heat a wok or a skillet, add 3 tablespoons of the oil and heat until very hot. Add half the beef slices and stir-fry over high heat until the meat changes color and separates. Remove with a handled strainer or a slotted spoon, and drain. Wipe out the wok and reheat. Add 3 more tablespoons of oil and heat until very hot. Add the remaining meat and cook. Remove and drain. Wipe out the wok.

3. Reheat the wok, add the remaining 2 tablespoons of oil and reheat until very hot. Add the *Minced Seasonings* and stir-fry about 10 seconds, until fragrant. Add the snow peas and toss lightly over high heat for 1 minute. Add the *Sauce* and heat until thickened, stirring continuously to prevent lumps. Add the cooked beef slices, toss lightly to coat, and transfer to a platter. Serve immediately with steamed or boiled rice.

Stir-Fried Beef With Eggs

Hua Dan Niu Rou

6 Servings ⌣ Main Dish or Breakfast

THE STANDARD WESTERN version of steak and eggs can hardly be considered a "gourmet" item, but the Chinese rendition is a memorable and savory delicacy. The fluffy scrambled eggs contrast in taste and texture with the tender beef slices.

1½	pounds beef tenderloin or sirloin

Beef Marinade

1½	tablespoons soy sauce
1	tablespoon rice wine or sake
1	teaspoon sesame oil
1	tablespoon cornstarch
1	teaspoon sugar
2	slices gingerroot, the size of a quarter, smashed with the flat side of a cleaver

8	large eggs
¾	teaspoon salt
½	cup peanut, safflower or corn oil
3	tablespoons minced scallions
1	tablespoon minced scallion greens

1. Remove any fat or gristle from the beef, and discard. Cut the meat, across the grain, into slices ⅛ inch thick. (You may partially freeze the meat to facilitate cutting.) Cut each slice into pieces 1½ inches long and 1 inch wide. Place the pieces in a bowl, add the *Beef Marinade*, toss lightly, and let marinate for at least 2 hours. Discard the gingerroot slices, and drain the meat. Beat the eggs lightly until frothy, adding the salt.

2. Heat a wok, add 3 tablespoons of the oil, and heat the oil until very hot. Add half the beef slices, and cook over high heat for about 1 minute, stirring constantly, until the pieces change color. Remove with a handled strainer or slotted spoon, and drain. Wipe out the wok, reheat and add 3 more tablespoons of the oil. Heat until hot and add the remaining meat and cook. Remove and drain. Wipe out the wok.

3. Reheat the wok, add the remaining 2 tablespoons of oil, and heat until very hot. Add the minced scallions, and stir-fry for 10 seconds, until fragrant. Add the eggs, and stir-fry over medium-high heat until they begin to set. Add the beef slices, and toss lightly. Cook for a bit longer, and transfer the mixture to a platter. Sprinkle the minced scallion greens on top, and serve immediately.

Dry-Cooked Beef With Vegetables
Gan Pian Niu Rou Si
6 Servings ⌇ Main Dish

1½   pounds eye-of-round roast or top sirloin roast

Beef Marinade
  2   tablespoons soy sauce
  1   tablespoon rice wine or sake
  1   tablespoon water
  1   teaspoon sesame oil

1½   cups peanut, safflower or corn oil
  2   ounces rice stick noodles

Minced Seasonings
  3   tablespoons minced garlic
  1   tablespoon minced scallions
  2   teaspoons minced gingerroot

  2   teaspoons chili paste
  2   cups shredded carrots
1½   cups shredded celery

Beef Sauce
  3   tablespoons chicken broth, preferably Chinese Chicken Broth (page 345)
  2   tablespoons soy sauce
  1   tablespoon rice wine or sake
1½   teaspoons sesame oil
1½   teaspoons Chinese black vinegar or Worcestershire sauce
1½   teaspoons sugar
 ½   teaspoon Sichuan peppercorns, toasted in a heavy skillet over low heat for 2 minutes and pulverized

IN SICHUAN PROVINCE, *cattle are used as work animals, hauling salt and other provisions. Once old age inhibits their usefulness, they are slaughtered for consumption. The meat is extremely tough; accordingly, most Sichuanese chefs cook beef in very hot oil far longer than any Western chef would dare. The cooked meat in this dish is dry, crisp and tender, combining well with the spicy seasonings.*

1. Remove any fat or gristle from the beef, and discard. Cut the meat, across the grain, into slices ¼ inch thick. (You may partially freeze the meat to facilitate cutting.) Cut the slices into matchstick-sized shreds, and place them in a bowl.

Add the *Beef Marinade*, toss lightly, and let marinate for 20 minutes.

2. Heat a wok, add the oil, and heat the oil until nearly smoking, about 425 degrees F. Add the rice noodles, and deep-fry them until puffed and pale golden. This should happen almost immediately. Turn them over, and deep-fry for a few seconds on the other side. Remove, and drain the noodles on absorbent paper. Transfer them to a platter, and lightly break up the noodles with your fingertips. Leave a slight depression in the middle of the platter. Remove all ½ cup of oil from the wok.

3. Reheat the oil to 425 degrees F. Drain the beef, and add half of the shreds to the hot oil. Fry, stirring constantly, over high heat for 3½ minutes, or until the beef is golden brown and slightly crisp. Remove with a handled strainer or slotted spoon, and drain. Reheat the oil, and fry the remaining beef shreds in the same manner. Remove the oil from the wok, reserving 3 tablespoons. Wipe out the wok.

4. Reheat the wok, add the 3 tablespoons of oil, and heat until very hot. Add the *Minced Seasonings*, and stir-fry for about 5 seconds, until fragrant. Add the chili paste, and stir-fry for another 5 seconds. Add the carrot shreds and celery, and continue stir-frying over high heat for about 3 minutes, until they are tender. Add the *Beef Sauce* and the cooked meat shreds. Toss lightly to coat with the sauce. Pour the mixture over the rice noodles, and serve immediately.

Cinnamon-Flavored Beef

Gui Pi Niu Rou

6 Servings ⌣ Main Dish or Appetizer

2½   pounds eye-of-round roast or flank steak

Beef Marinade
   3   tablespoons rice wine or sake
   ¾   teaspoon salt
   2   slices gingerroot, the size of a quarter, smashed with the flat side of
       the cleaver

   4   strips dried tangerine or orange peel, about 2 inches long (fresh
       peel may be substituted)
   ¼   cup 1-inch pieces dried chili peppers
   7   tablespoons peanut, safflower or corn oil

Beef Seasonings
   1   tablespoon Sichuan peppercorns
   1   whole star anise
   1   cinnamon stick

Braising Liquid
1½   cups water
   3   tablespoons rice wine or sake
1½   tablespoons soy sauce
   3   tablespoons sugar

   2   tablespoons sesame oil
   1   teaspoon clear rice vinegar

SINCE ANCIENT TIMES, *the Chinese have felt cinnamon to be particularly appealing with beef. During the Han dynasty, beef was seasoned with gingerroot and cinnamon, then grilled or barbecued. These spicy beef slices are equally good served hot with rice or at room temperature on a bed of shredded lettuce as an appetizer.*

   1. Remove any fat or gristle from the beef, and discard. Cut the meat, across the grain, into slices about ¼ inch thick. (You may partially freeze the meat to facilitate cutting.) Cut the slices into pieces about 1½ inches long and 1 inch wide. Place the meat in a bowl, add the *Beef Marinade*, toss lightly, and let marinate for at least 3 hours, or overnight in the refrigerator. Soak the dried tangerine peel in hot water to cover for 30 minutes. Then cut it into julienne strips. Shake out the seeds from the chili peppers.
   2. Heat a wok, add 3 tablespoons of the oil, and heat the oil until very hot. Drain the beef slices, and discard the gingerroot. Add half the beef slices to the

hot oil, and fry for 3 or 4 minutes, stirring constantly, until the beef changes color and is cooked. Remove with a handled strainer or slotted spoon, and drain. Wipe out the wok, add 3 more tablespoons of the oil, heat the oil, and fry the remaining beef in the same manner. Remove and drain. Wipe out the wok.

3. Reheat the wok, add the remaining 1 tablespoon of the oil, and heat the oil until nearly smoking. Add the chili pepper pieces, and stir-fry over high heat, stirring constantly, until the peppers turn black. Remove the peppers with a slotted spoon, and set aside. Add the *Beef Seasonings* and the tangerine peel. Stir-fry over high heat for about 20 seconds; then add the *Braising Liquid*. Add the beef pieces, and heat the mixture until boiling. Reduce the heat to low, partially cover, and cook for 40 minutes, stirring occasionally. The sauce should be reduced to a third of its original amount. Uncover, turn the heat to high, and continue cooking the beef, stirring constantly, until the sauce has reduced to a thick glaze. Remove the cinnamon and star anise. Add the cooked chili peppers, the sesame oil and the rice vinegar. Toss lightly, transfer the mixture to a platter, and serve immediately.

Red-Cooked Oxtail

Hong Shao Niu Wei

6 Servings ⌣ Main Dish

3	pounds oxtail, separated into sections at the joints
2	tablespoons peanut, safflower or corn oil
1	medium-sized onion, diced

Braising Mixture

6	cups water
6	tablespoons soy sauce
3	tablespoons rice wine or sake
1	tablespoon sugar
3	scallions, smashed with the flat side of a cleaver
3	slices gingerroot, the size of a quarter, smashed with the flat side of a cleaver
2	strips dried tangerine or orange peel, about 2 inches long (fresh peel may be substituted)
1	whole star anise
1	cinnamon stick

Thickener

1	tablespoon water
2	teaspoons cornstarch

1. Rinse the oxtail sections, and drain. Blanch for 1 minute in boiling water, remove, and rinse in cold water. Drain thoroughly.

2. Heat a heavy 3-quart casserole or a Dutch oven, add the oil, and heat the oil until very hot. Add the onion, and stir-fry until soft and transparent. Add the oxtail sections, and brown lightly on all sides. Add the *Braising Mixture*, and heat until boiling. Reduce the heat to low, partially cover, and simmer for 3 hours, or until the oxtail is very tender and the braising mixture has reduced and become somewhat thick. Place the oxtails in a serving bowl, and strain out the seasonings from the braising liquid. Heat the strained liquid until boiling. Add the *Thickener*, and heat until the sauce has thickened, stirring constantly to prevent lumps. Pour the sauce over the oxtails, and serve immediately.

ALTHOUGH TAIPEI IS *just north of the tropical zone, the winters there can be extremely cold and raw, and there is little central heating. This hearty stew of oxtails slowly cooked in a fragrant soy-based liquid was a favorite cold-weather dish in our Chinese household. Accompanied by rice and a green vegetable, it makes a filling and inexpensive meal.*

Mongolian Barbecue

Meng Gu Kao Rou

6 Servings ⌣ Main Dish

THIS NORTHERN SPECIALTY *of barbecued meat slices and tender vegetables still hot from the fire, wrapped in a flaky bread or steamed bun, can be successfully duplicated at home with a heavy steel Genghis Khan grill (available in Asian markets) or on an ordinary hibachi or barbecue covered with several layers of heavy-duty aluminum foil pierced with holes. Boneless leg of lamb, cut into thin slices, also may be used in this dish, which is ideally served stuffed in Sesame Flat Breads (page 64) or steamed Lotus Buns (page 59). Few dishes are as simple or as appealing as this delicacy, especially for entertaining. (See photograph, page 176.)*

豪
古
烤
肉

2 pounds top sirloin roast or eye-of-round roast

Beef Marinade

½ cup soy sauce
¼ cup hoisin sauce
¼ cup rice wine or sake
¼ cup water
1 tablespoon minced garlic
1 tablespoon minced gingerroot
3 tablespoons sugar

3 tablespoons sesame oil
6 cups fresh bean sprouts, lightly rinsed
4 cups shredded scallion greens or leeks
1½ cups ginger water (Pinch 6 slices gingerroot, the size of a quarter, smashed with the flat side of a cleaver, in 1½ cups water repeatedly for 1 minute.)

1. Remove any fat or gristle from the beef, and discard. Cut the meat, across the grain, into slices about ⅛ inch thick. (You may partially freeze the meat to facilitate cutting.) Cut the slices into 2-inch squares, and place the squares in a bowl. Add the *Beef Marinade*, toss lightly, and let marinate for at least 4 hours, or overnight in the refrigerator.

2. Prepare a charcoal fire, and wait until the coals are red; then place the Genghis Khan grill over the charcoal grill. Or you may place the Genghis Khan grill over an electric hot plate. Heat the grill until water sprinkled on the surface evaporates immediately. Brush the surface with sesame oil. Arrange one-sixth of the slices of beef on the grill, wait 15 seconds, and sprinkle 1 cup bean sprouts and ⅔ cup scallions on top. Using chopsticks, toss the mixture, and pour ¼ cup of ginger water over all. When the meat and vegetables are cooked (about 2 to 3 minutes), remove. Repeat for the remaining meat and vegetables.

Lamb Shish Kebab

Kao Yang Rou Chuan

6 Servings ⌢ Appetizer or Main Dish

2   pounds boned shoulder or leg of lamb

Lamb Marinade

¼   cup soy sauce

2   tablespoons rice wine or sake

2   teaspoons sesame oil

1   tablespoon minced gingerroot

1   tablespoon minced garlic

1   teaspoon Sichuan peppercorns, toasted in a heavy skillet over low heat for 2 minutes and pulverized

1   teaspoon five-spice powder

¼   teaspoon freshly ground black pepper

6   10-inch bamboo skewers

1. Remove all but a thin layer of fat from the lamb. Cut the meat into 1-inch cubes. Place the lamb cubes in a bowl, add the *Lamb Marinade*, toss lightly, and let marinate for at least 3 hours, or overnight in the refrigerator. Before cooking, soak the bamboo skewers in cold water to cover for 1 hour. (This will prevent them from burning during cooking.)

2. Loosely thread an equal number of lamb cubes onto each skewer. Reserve the marinade for basting. Preheat the broiler.

3. Broil the meat about 4 inches from the source of heat for 3½ to 4 minutes on each side, turning once and basting occasionally. Cook the lamb until medium-rare. Serve the lamb with steamed Lotus Buns and sweet bean sauce.

I FIRST TASTED THIS delicious dish several years ago at the famous Peking restaurant known as the Sick Duck. The skewered meat offers a pleasant departure from the usual repertory of stir-fried platters. It is traditionally served with steamed Lotus Buns (page 59) and sweet bean sauce.

Spicy Lamb Kebabs

Kao Yang Rou

6 Servings 〜 Main Dish

THE FLAVOR OF GRILLED *lamb is complemented by a marinade with a bean- or hoisin-sauce base. At first glance, the dish might be considered a classic, but the addition of skewered peppers, onions and mushrooms makes it more contemporary. You may substitute chicken, pork, beef or turkey for an equally superb variation.*

2½   pounds boned leg of lamb, shank portion or precut lamb kebabs

Lamb Marinade

¾   cup sweet bean sauce or hoisin sauce
¼   cup rice wine or sake
3   tablespoons soy sauce
1   teaspoon sesame oil
2   tablespoons minced garlic
2   tablespoons sugar
1   tablespoon crushed red peppers

1   pound small white onions
1   pound fresh button mushrooms, ends trimmed
2   large red or yellow peppers, cored, seeded and cut into 1-inch squares
1   tablespoon peanut, safflower or corn oil (optional)

6   10-inch bamboo skewers, soaked in cold water to cover for 1 hour

1. Remove any fat or gristle from the lamb. If using a boned leg of lamb, separate the muscles of the meat and cut into cubes about 1½ inches square. Place the pieces in a bowl. Add the *Lamb Marinade* to the meat, tossing lightly to coat.

2. Peel the onions, and heat 2 quarts of water until boiling. Add the onions, and cook for about 2 to 3 minutes, until barely tender. Drain in a colander, and refresh under cold, running water. Drain again. Add the onions, mushrooms and bell pepper pieces to the meat, and toss lightly to coat. Cover with plastic wrap, and let marinate for at least 1 hour at room temperature, or overnight in the refrigerator. Thread the meat, onions, mushrooms and peppers alternately onto the skewers, starting and ending with the peppers. Reserve the marinade.

3. Prepare a medium-hot fire for grilling or preheat the broiler. Brush the grill with the oil, if using. Arrange the skewered meat and vegetables about 3 inches from the source of heat, and cook, about 3 minutes for medium-rare to 4 minutes for medium on each side, turning once, basting occasionally with the marinade. Arrange on a serving platter, and serve immediately.

Finger Lamb in Dipping Sauce

Zha Yang Pai

6 Servings ⌣ Main Dish

2½   pounds blade or rib lamb chops

Braising Liquid

- 6   cups water
- 2   tablespoons rice wine or sake
- 1   tablespoon soy sauce
- 4   scallions, smashed with the flat side of a cleaver
- 4   slices gingerroot, the size of a quarter, smashed with the flat side of a cleaver
- 2   2-inch strips dried tangerine or orange peel (fresh peel may be substituted)
- 1   whole star anise
- 1   teaspoon Sichuan peppercorns
- 1   cinnamon stick
- 1   teaspoon salt

Dipping Sauce

- ¼   cup soy sauce
- 1½   tablespoons rice wine or sake
- 1½   tablespoons Chinese black vinegar or Worcestershire sauce
- 2   teaspoons sesame oil
- 1½   teaspoons chili oil or chili paste
- 2   tablespoons minced scallions
- 1   tablespoon minced fresh cilantro
- 2   teaspoons minced garlic
- 2   teaspoons minced gingerroot
- 1½   tablespoons sugar

THE MONGOLIAN *custom of eating with one's hands offended many ancient Chinese, who considered it primitive. Later, this attitude seems to have softened considerably as "grab-your-own-lamb" dishes gained popularity in Peking restaurants. Perhaps the extraordinary flavor of these tender lamb chop pieces, seasoned with Sichuan peppercorns and orange peel and dipped in cilantro-ginger sauce, was partially responsible for the Chinese gourmands' change of attitude.*

1. Direct the butcher to cut the chops crosswise, through the bones, into pieces 2 inches long. Remove any excess fat, and discard. Blanch the lamb chop pieces in boiling water for 1 minute. Drain thoroughly.

2. Place the *Braising Liquid* in a heavy pot or casserole. Heat until boiling, reduce the heat to low, and cook for 20 minutes. Add the lamb, and heat until boiling. Reduce the heat to medium, and cook, uncovered, for 35 minutes, or until the lamb is tender. Remove the lamb, and arrange on a platter. Serve the lamb pieces with the *Dipping Sauce*.

Succulent Lamb in Sweet Bean Sauce

Jiang Yang Rou

6 Servings ⌒ Main Dish

STEAMED LAMB HAS been a popular Mongolian specialty since the Sung dynasty, when it was first introduced to Peking by the northern tribesmen. Over the years, it was refined by the Han chefs until it became a subtle delicacy with seasonings of sweet bean sauce and star anise. Serve these fragrant lamb slices on steamed Lotus Buns (page 59) or with rice.

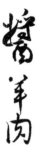

2½   pounds boned shoulder of lamb or boned leg of lamb, shank half

Seasoning Mixture

2   tablespoons soy sauce
1½   tablespoons sweet bean sauce
1   tablespoon rice wine or sake
1   tablespoon sugar
2   scallions, smashed with the flat side of a cleaver
2   slices gingerroot, the size of a quarter, smashed with the flat side of a cleaver
2   cloves garlic, smashed with the flat side of a cleaver
1   whole star anise, smashed with the flat side of a cleaver

Thickener

3   tablespoons chicken broth, preferably Chinese Chicken Broth (page 345)
1   teaspoon cornstarch

1. Trim all but a thin layer of fat from the lamb. Place the lamb in a bowl, and rub with the *Seasoning Mixture*. Let the lamb marinate for at least 1 hour or, if possible, overnight in the refrigerator. Place the lamb in a heatproof bowl or deep plate, and pour the seasoning mixture on top. Place the bowl in a steamer tray.

2. Fill a wok with water level with the bottom edge of the steamer tray, and heat until boiling. Place the steamer tray over the boiling water, cover, and steam for 1¼ hours over high heat, or until the lamb is just pink in the center. (Alternatively, if you do not have a steamer large enough to hold the bowl, you may cover the bowl with a double layer of heavy-duty aluminum foil and bake it in a preheated 475-degree oven for 10 to 12 minutes per pound.) Remove the lamb from the bowl, and let it stand for 10 minutes. Cut the lamb, across the grain, into thin slices, and arrange the slices on a platter.

3. Skim any fat from the liquid in the bowl, and strain out the seasonings. Discard the seasonings. Heat the sauce until boiling, and slowly add the *Thickener*, stirring constantly to prevent lumps. When the sauce has thickened, pour it over the lamb slices. Serve with steamed Lotus Buns or rice.

Stir-Fried Lamb With Scallions

Cong Bao Yang Rou

6 Servings 〜 Main Dish

2   pounds boned leg of lamb, shank half

Lamb Marinade
2½   tablespoons soy sauce
2   tablespoons water
1½   tablespoons rice wine or sake
1   tablespoon cornstarch
1½   teaspoons sugar

½   cup peanut, safflower or corn oil
5   cups shredded scallion greens or leeks
6   cloves garlic, very thinly sliced

Lamb Sauce
2   tablespoons soy sauce
2   tablespoons rice wine or sake
1   tablespoon sesame oil
2   teaspoons clear rice vinegar

THIS NORTHERN DISH has become popular throughout China. One can hardly discern any flavor of lamb, since the meat slices are redolent of garlic and scallions.

1. Remove any fat or gristle from the lamb, and discard. Cut the meat, across the grain, into slices about ⅛ inch thick. (You may partially freeze the lamb to facilitate cutting.) Cut the slices into pieces that are 1½ inches long and 1 inch wide. Place the pieces in a bowl, add the ***Lamb Marinade***, toss lightly, and let marinate for 30 minutes.

2. Heat a wok, add 3 tablespoons of the oil, and heat the oil until very hot. Add half the lamb, and stir-fry over high heat, stirring constantly, until the lamb changes color. Remove the meat with a handled strainer or slotted spoon, and drain. Wipe out the wok, add 3 more tablespoons of oil, heat the oil, and stir-fry the remaining lamb pieces in the same manner. Remove and drain. Wipe out the wok.

3. Reheat the wok, add the remaining 2 tablespoons of oil, and heat until very hot. Add the shredded scallions and the garlic. Stir-fry over high heat for about 30 seconds. Add the cooked lamb and the ***Lamb Sauce***. Toss lightly, and transfer the mixture to a platter. Serve immediately.

Sichuan Lamb

Chuan Shi Yang Rou

6 Servings ⌢ Main Dish

THIS TASTY STIR-FRIED *platter is distinctly Sichuanese in character, as evidenced by the pungent seasonings and the textural delicacies—wood ears and water chestnuts. Serve this spicy platter with a steamed green vegetable and rice.*

1½   pounds boned leg of lamb, shank half

Lamb Marinade
1   tablespoon soy sauce
1   tablespoon water
½   tablespoon rice wine or sake
1   tablespoon minced gingerroot
2   teaspoons cornstarch
1   teaspoon sugar

10   dried wood ears
1½   cups water chestnuts
½   cup peanut, safflower or corn oil

Minced Seasonings
2   tablespoons minced scallions
1   tablespoon minced garlic

1½   teaspoons chili paste

Lamb Sauce
¼   cup chicken broth, preferably Chinese Chicken Broth (page 345), or water
3   tablespoons soy sauce
1   tablespoon rice wine or sake
1½   teaspoons Chinese black vinegar or Worcestershire sauce
1½   tablespoons sugar
1   teaspoon cornstarch

1. Remove any fat or gristle from the lamb, and discard. Cut the meat, across the grain, into slices ⅛ inch thick. (You may partially freeze the lamb to facilitate cutting.) Cut the slices into pieces 1½ inches long and 1 inch wide. Place the pieces in a bowl, add the *Lamb Marinade*, toss lightly, and let marinate for 1 hour. Soften the wood ears for 20 minutes in hot water to cover; drain thoroughly. Cut away and discard the hard, bitter nib on the underside of the wood ears, and cut the wood ears into thin shreds. Plunge the water chestnuts into

boiling water for a few seconds to remove the tinny flavor. Refresh them in cold water, and slice thinly.

2. Heat a wok, add 3 tablespoons of the oil, and heat the oil until very hot. Drain the lamb pieces, and add half of the pieces to the hot oil. Stir-fry over high heat, turning constantly, until the lamb changes color. Remove with a handled strainer or slotted spoon, and drain. Wipe out the wok, add 3 more tablespoons of the oil, heat, and stir-fry the remaining lamb in the same manner. Remove, and drain. Wipe out the wok.

3. Reheat the wok, add the remaining 2 tablespoons of oil, and heat until very hot. Add the *Minced Seasonings*, and stir-fry for about 10 seconds, until fragrant. Add the chili paste, and stir-fry for another 5 seconds. Add the wood ears and water chestnuts, and stir-fry over high heat for about 20 seconds, until they are heated through. Add the *Lamb Sauce*, and stir-fry until the sauce begins to thicken. Add the cooked lamb pieces, toss lightly to coat with the sauce, and transfer the mixture to a platter. Serve immediately.

Vegetables

WINTER COMES HARD TO Taipei. The normally balmy air takes on a raw, chilling edge. The sky, which reflects the seasonal changes by its color, turns gray and threatening. Since central heating is virtually nonexistent, layers of clothing are donned and voluminous down quilts, unpacked from storage, are thrown over beds. In the mornings, seats are hard to come by at the *dou jiang* stands, as most of the city's residents combat the winter chill by downing a bowl of hot, filling soybean milk. At night, the shrill call of the sweet-potato vendor is heard as he roams the alleyways, peddling his hot snack. He wheels a portable charcoal stove filled with sizzling potatoes and carries a scale for measuring the weight and calculating the cost of each purchase.

Every evening, my Chinese surrogate sister and brother would pile out of the house at the sound of the sweet-potato call and buy a hot potato for their bedtime snack. I, on the other hand, had fallen into the habit of purchasing a whole catty of potatoes—more than two pounds. At first, my surrogate siblings were quite surprised, since I normally shunned large quantities of any food, being constantly on a diet. In time, they came to appreciate my ingenuity: I wrapped each potato in foil, bundled the lot in a towel and carefully tucked the hot package between my sheets. The Japanese have their hot bricks and the British their hot-water bottles, but I had my sweet potatoes. In the morning, the same potatoes—now slightly crushed by my nocturnal tossings—would be donated to the family's breakfast. They were sliced, fried to a crisp golden brown and served with the morning congee or rice.

In the winter marketplace, in addition to sweet potatoes, the stalls are heaped with other winter vegetables. Numerous green cabbages and winter bamboo shoots, the tastiest and most prized of the bamboo family, line the shelves.

Taiwan is an agricultural paradise. Because the northern half of the island suffers through cold temperatures several months of the year and the southern half is drenched in sunshine and humid heat, both tropical vegetables and those that grow best in cooler temperatures thrive. China, too, with its varied climate and fertile acreage, is a land of agricultural promise. The economy is largely agrarian, and has been since the beginning of civilization. The ancient Chinese were accomplished farmers, raising crops of beans, mallow, melons, turnips, gourds, Chinese leeks, cabbage, amaranth, garlic, water chestnuts and bamboo shoots.

Later, as China opened her doors to the outside world, a host of new vegetables was introduced: spinach and celery came from Nepal, and kohlrabi and garden peas were brought by the Europeans. Because of horticultural experimentation, the native vegetables also increased in numbers and varieties. As farming methods and transportation improved, so, too, did the availability of these products. Vegetables came to be obtainable year-round, and they were enjoyed by the wealthy and poor alike. Hence they came to assume a prominent role in the Chinese diet and in Chinese cuisine.

Vegetables served other purposes as well. Lotus root, rhubarb, kohlrabi and the licorice plant were believed to possess medicinal properties and were prescribed as tonics. Garlic, leeks and shallots were said to warm the body. During the Han dynasty (206 B.C. to 220 A.D.), these and other strong-smelling vegetables were hung from doors and gates in the summertime to ward off disease, poisonous insects and other evils. And most vegetables were used as offerings for the deities.

The Chinese classify vegetables according to three categories: root, leafy and fruit. Root vegetables include carrots, turnips, potatoes, taro, bamboo shoots, water chestnuts, lotus root and gingerroot. Members of the leafy category are Chinese cabbage, watercress, spinach, amaranth, "vegetable hearts," mustard greens and edible chrysanthemums. The fruit family includes tomatoes, cucumbers, eggplant, winter melon, peas and the many gourd varieties.

Stir-frying and steaming are the preferred cooking methods employed in hot vegetable dishes because these two processes preserve the vitamins, fresh flavors, crunchy textures and bright colors of each vegetable.

Many vegetables also appear in cold salads. For hygienic reasons, vegetables are rarely eaten raw. They are plunged into boiling water and refreshed immediately in cold water before being used in salads and other cold dishes. A great deal of attention is paid to combining foods with contrasting flavors, colors and textures: shredded ham, chicken or pork as well as dried jellyfish and shrimp are paired with bean sprouts, celery, carrots, peppers, green beans, cucumbers, eggplant or Chinese turnip. Noodles, cellophane noodles, agar-agar and vermicelli sheets are used as textural bases. The dressings are numerous and may vary from a delicate vinegar-sesame-oil creation to a hot and spicy peanut-butter or sesame-paste sauce. Since most parts of China experience a summer season of sorts, salads have become an ideal hot-weather dish. Their cool, crisp textures are pleasing to the palate, and their preparation is quite simple.

Pickled vegetables also enjoy a prominent position in the Chinese diet, as they have for many centuries. In ancient China, fresh vegetables were scarce, owing to seasonal agricultural factors and lack of adequate refrigeration. To preserve these and other foods, methods such as smoking, drying, steeping, pickling and salting were employed.

It is believed that the first Chinese pickles were salted and dried during the T'ang dynasty (618 to 907). Shortly thereafter, a vinegar-based brine was used to preserve vegetables. Even in these early times, a selection of vinegars was available: rice, peaches, wheat and grape juice were fermented to make vinegar, and kumquat leaves and peach blossoms were added to enhance the flavor. Water chestnuts, bamboo shoots and mustard greens were all pickled in this manner.

Salt and wine were used in fermenting some vegetables. Pickled cabbage, or sauerkraut, is the most notable example of this process. It is said that the oldest form of sauerkraut was invented by Chinese workers building the Great Wall during the Han dynasty. They subsisted on a diet of cabbage and rice and used rice wine to preserve the cabbage from summer to winter. When the Tatars overran China, they sampled the pickled cabbage and adapted it to their own tastes, substituting salt for rice wine. It was in this form that sauerkraut was introduced to Europe.

Pickles are served as a piquant garnish to rice and congee or as a pungent seasoning in cooked dishes. In modern China, most people eat large quantities of vegetables and pickles, for obvious reasons—they are flavorful, inexpensive and nutritious.

Deep-Fried Mushrooms With Pine Nuts

Song Zi Yang Gu

6 Servings ⌣ Appetizer or Side Dish

1½ pounds fresh button mushrooms
3 large eggs, lightly beaten
2 tablespoons soy sauce
¼ teaspoon freshly ground black pepper
2 cups all-purpose flour
3 cups coarsely chopped pine nuts
2 cups peanut, safflower or corn oil

Dipping Sauce
½ cup soy sauce
3 tablespoons Chinese black vinegar or Worcestershire sauce
1 tablespoon finely shredded gingerroot

1. Lightly rinse the mushrooms, and drain thoroughly. Pat dry. Mix the eggs with the soy sauce and black pepper. Put the flour, egg mixture and pine nuts in separate deep dishes. First dredge the mushrooms in the flour, shaking out the excess, then dip them in the eggs, again draining away the excess, and finally coat with the pine nuts. Arrange the coated mushrooms on a tray, and let them dry for 1 hour.

2. Heat a wok, add the oil, and heat the oil to 400 degrees F. Add a few of the coated mushrooms, and deep-fry, turning constantly, for 2½ minutes, until the mushrooms are tender and the pine nuts are golden brown. Remove with a handled strainer or slotted spoon, and drain on absorbent paper. Reheat the oil, and deep-fry the remaining mushrooms in the same manner, reheating the oil after each batch. Serve at room temperature with the *Dipping Sauce*.

F OR CENTURIES, NUTS *have been relished by the Chinese. Pine nuts have been cultivated since the T'ang dynasty, and they are added to numerous dishes for flavor and texture. In this dish, they provide a buttery, crisp accompaniment to the tender mushrooms. Serve the fried mushrooms as an hors d'oeuvre or first course with the tart dipping sauce.*

Celery Hearts in Mustard Sauce

Jie Mo Chin Cai

6 Servings ⌣ Appetizer or Side Dish

IN CHINESE RESTAURANTS *in the Far East, an empty stomach is never neglected for long. Small dishes of peanuts and pickled salads are served as soon as the diners sit down so that they may nibble while planning their order. This spicy dish is often served in Peking restaurants. (See photograph, page 82.)*

2	pounds celery hearts
1½	tablespoons powdered mustard
1	tablespoon boiling water
1	tablespoon rice wine or sake
1	teaspoon salt
2	teaspoons sugar
1	tablespoon sesame oil

1. Rinse the celery hearts, and peel away the tough skin, if necessary. Cut off the root ends and leafy tops. Cut the celery in half lengthwise and cut each half into 2-inch pieces. Blanch the celery pieces in boiling water for 1 minute. Refresh immediately in cold water, drain thoroughly, and pat dry. Place the celery pieces in a bowl.

2. Mix the mustard powder and the boiling water to a smooth paste. Add the rice wine, and combine well. Cover the mixture with a plate to allow the heat to bring out the flavors, and let it sit for 10 minutes. Add the salt, sugar and sesame oil to the mustard mixture, and stir until smooth. Add the dressing to the celery pieces, toss lightly to coat them, and refrigerate for 1 hour before serving.

Cantonese Pickled Vegetables

Yue Shi Pao Cai

6 Servings ⁓ Appetizer or Side Dish

1	daikon radish (Chinese turnip), about ½ pound
4	carrots, peeled
6	small pickling cucumbers or 2 English (gourmet seedless) cucumbers
1	tablespoon salt
½	cup sugar
½	cup clear rice vinegar
12	thin slices gingerroot, the size of a quarter, smashed with the flat side of a cleaver

P AO CAI OR PICKLED
vegetable salads, are found
all over China, but they differ
from place to place depending on
the local products and flavorings.
This sweet-and-sour version can
stand alone, but it is often used
as a colorful garnish for
sweet-and-sour shrimp or pork.

1. Peel the daikon, and cut off the root and stem ends. Cut the daikon lengthwise in half. Then cut each half lengthwise into thirds, and roll-cut each section into 1-inch pieces. Roll-cut the carrots into 1-inch pieces. Cut the cucumbers in half lengthwise. Remove any seeds, and cut each half lengthwise into thirds. Roll-cut the cucumbers into 1-inch pieces. Place the vegetables in a mixing bowl, add the salt, toss lightly, and let sit for 2 hours. Drain off any water that has collected, and pat the vegetables dry.

2. Combine the sugar and rice vinegar, stirring until the sugar has dissolved. Add this mixture and the gingerroot slices to the vegetables, and toss lightly to coat. Refrigerate for at least 3 hours, or overnight, before serving.

Sichuan Pickled Cucumber Slices

Si Chuan Ma La Huang Gua

6 Servings ⁓ Appetizer or Side Dish

1	pound small pickling cucumbers or English (gourmet seedless) cucumbers
1	tablespoon salt
½	cup finely shredded gingerroot, soaked in cold water for 20 minutes
1	fresh red chili pepper, seeded and cut into thin shreds
½	cup sesame oil
1	teaspoon Sichuan peppercorns
¼	cup dried chili peppers, seeded and cut into ¼-inch lengths
3	tablespoons clear rice vinegar
1½	tablespoons sugar

FROM ALL OUTWARD *appearances, this dish may seem quite simple, but the complexity of flavors in the sauce is unusual: simultaneously sweet, sour, hot and numbing. Contrasted with the cool crispness of the cucumbers, the overall effect is exquisite.*

1. Rinse the cucumbers, drain, and pat dry. Cut the cucumbers lengthwise in half, remove any seeds, and cut into slices about 4 inches long and 1 inch thick. Place the slices in a bowl, add the salt, toss lightly, and let sit for 30 minutes. Pour off any water that has accumulated. Rinse the cucumbers lightly, drain thoroughly, and pat dry. Place the cucumbers in a bowl, and add the shredded gingerroot and fresh chili pepper.

2. Heat a wok, add the sesame oil, and heat until nearly smoking. Add the Sichuan peppercorns, and stir-fry over high heat for about 30 seconds, until fragrant. Add the dried chili peppers, and stir-fry for about 30 seconds, until they turn black. Pour this mixture into the bowl containing the cucumbers, toss lightly, and let cool. Add the rice vinegar and sugar, toss to coat, and let the mixture sit for at least 6 hours in the refrigerator before serving.

Sichuan Pickled Salad

Si Chuan Pao Cai

6 Servings ⌣ Appetizer or Side Dish

1	pound Chinese cabbage (Napa)
1	daikon radish (Chinese turnip), about ½ pound
4	carrots, peeled

Pickling Mixture

10	cups warm water
¼	cup rice wine or sake
5	tablespoons salt
1½	tablespoons Sichuan peppercorns
12	slices gingerroot, the size of a quarter, smashed with the flat side of a cleaver
3	fresh red chili peppers, seeded and cut into ¼-inch lengths

1. Rinse the cabbage lightly, drain, and pat dry. Remove and discard the core, and cut the leaves into 2-inch squares. Lightly bruise the cabbage pieces by smashing them with the flat side of a cleaver. Spread the cabbage pieces out on a tray, and let them air-dry for 1 hour, turning once. Peel the daikon, and cut off the root and stem ends. Cut the daikon lengthwise in half. Then cut each half lengthwise into thirds, and roll-cut each piece into 1-inch pieces. Roll-cut the carrots into 1-inch pieces.

2. Pour the *Pickling Mixture* into a glass jar or a pickling crock. Stir to dissolve the salt. Add the Sichuan peppercorns, and let the liquid cool to room temperature. Add the gingerroot and the chili peppers. Add the vegetables, and stir again. The liquid should cover the vegetables. If not, add more water. Cover tightly, and let sit for 3 days at room temperature. Remove the vegetables, and serve. Refrigerate the marinade, and use it again, adding 2 tablespoons each of salt and rice wine every time, plus enough water to cover the vegetables.

A CCORDING TO MY *Sichuanese teacher, the flavor of this pickling marinade doesn't begin to "ripen" until the second use. In the Far East, starter marinades are available from small Sichuanese restaurants. For those of us in the West, perseverance is the key; just realize that your second batch will be better than the first. The traditional pickle is made with cabbage, carrots and daikon radish, but green beans and cucumbers may also be used.*

Cold Chinese Salad

Liang Ban Dou Ya Cai

6 Servings ⌒ Appetizer or Side Dish

THE LIGHT SESAME-OIL-based vinaigrette in this northern salad provides a piquant contrast to the fresh vegetable shreds, sliced shrimp and minced peanut topping. Shredded chicken or pork may be substituted for the shrimp. In a cold salad such as this, it is traditional and more refined to trim the ends of the bean sprouts, but this procedure is optional.

2	cups shredded English (gourmet seedless) cucumbers or small pickling cucumbers
2	cups shredded carrots
⅔	pound fresh bean sprouts
¼	pound medium-sized shrimp, shelled, deveined and cooked
3	tablespoons dry-roasted peanuts, coarsely chopped

Chinese Vinaigrette

¼	cup light soy sauce
3	tablespoons Chinese rice vinegar
2	tablespoons sesame oil
1	tablespoon rice wine or sake
1	tablespoon sugar
½	teaspoon salt

1. Combine the shredded cucumbers with two-thirds of the shredded carrots. Place the mixture in the center of a large platter. Arrange the remaining carrot shreds around the outer edge of the platter. Place the bean sprouts around the cucumber-carrot mixture.

2. Holding a cleaver or a large chef's knife parallel to the cutting surface, slice the shrimp in half horizontally. Arrange the shrimp, pink (uncut) side up, on top of the bean sprouts. Sprinkle the crushed peanuts over all. Before serving, pour the *Chinese Vinaigrette* on the salad. Toss lightly, and serve.

Three-Flavor Tossed Salad

Liang Ban San Si

6 Servings ～ Appetizer, Side Dish or Main Dish

1½   pounds boneless center-cut pork loin

Pork Marinade
- 2   tablespoons soy sauce
- 1   tablespoon rice wine or sake
- 1   teaspoon minced gingerroot
- 1   teaspoon minced scallions
- 1   tablespoon cornstarch
- ½   teaspoon sugar

1   pound green beans
2   ounces cellophane noodles (bean threads)

Cellophane-Noodle Seasonings
- 1   teaspoon sesame oil
- 1   teaspoon salt

6   tablespoons peanut, safflower or corn oil

Dressing
- ¼   cup soy sauce
- 2   tablespoons sesame oil
- 2   tablespoons clear rice vinegar
- 2   tablespoons rice wine or sake
- 1   tablespoon sugar
- 1½   teaspoons salt

2   dried red chili peppers, seeded and shredded

Although Peking is in the north of China, its summers are long and sultry. Cold vegetable dishes and salads, similar to this platter, are extremely popular in the hot weather. In this tantalizing dish, tender pork shreds, crisp-cooked green beans and smooth cellophane noodles are tossed in a tart sesame dressing. Serve the salad as the first course of a banquet or as a filling, one-dish lunch or dinner.

1. Remove any fat or gristle from the pork loin, and discard. Cut the meat, across the grain, into slices ⅛ inch thick. (You may partially freeze the meat to facilitate cutting.) Cut the slices into matchstick-sized shreds. Place the shreds in a bowl, add the *Pork Marinade*, toss lightly, and let marinate for 20 minutes.

2. Snap off the ends of the green beans, and cut the beans into 2-inch lengths. Cook the beans in salted boiling water for about 2 minutes, or until tender. Refresh immediately in cold water, and drain thoroughly.

3. Soften the cellophane noodles for 10 minutes in hot water to cover. Drain them; then cook for 5 minutes in boiling water. Rinse the cellophane noodles in cold water, drain thoroughly, and add the *Cellophane-Noodle Seasonings*. Arrange the cellophane noodles on a platter.

4. Heat a wok, add 3 tablespoons of the oil, and heat until very hot. Add half the pork shreds, stir-fry over high heat until they change color, and remove. Drain thoroughly. Wipe out the wok, reheat, and add 3 more tablespoons of the oil. Heat, and add the remaining pork. Cook until pork changes color, remove, and drain. Wipe out the wok. Arrange the green beans on top of the cellophane noodles and place the pork shreds in a mound on top of the green beans.

5. Reheat the wok, and add the *Dressing* and the chili peppers. Heat the mixture until boiling, and cook for 1 minute. Pour over the salad, and serve.

Stir-Fried Mushrooms & Hearts of Cabbage

Dong Cu Cai Xin

6 Servings ⌒ Side Dish

B ABY HEARTS OF CABBAGE *become succulent when cooked briefly. If cabbage hearts are not available, I like to substitute bok choy, roll-cutting it into bite-sized sections.*

1½	pounds hearts Shanghai cabbage or bok choy
12	small dried Chinese black mushrooms, soaked in hot water to cover for 20 minutes
1	tablespoon peanut, safflower or corn oil
2	tablespoons minced scallions, white part only

Sauce

1	cup chicken broth, preferably Chinese Chicken Broth (page 345)
2	tablespoons rice wine or sake
1	teaspoon sesame oil
1	tablespoon cornstarch
¾	teaspoon salt

1. Remove any wilted or old stems and leaves from the hearts of cabbage. Trim the stem end, cutting off the tip. Cut off the leafy end of the stalk, leaving about ½ inch of leaf. Cut the hearts lengthwise in half or quarters, depending on the thickness. Remove and discard the stems of the black mushrooms, and cut the large caps into halves and quarters.

2. Heat 2 quarts water until boiling, add the cabbage hearts, and cook until almost tender, about 7 or 8 minutes. Drain and refresh in cold water. Drain thoroughly.

3. Heat a wok or a skillet, add the oil, and heat until very hot. Add the minced scallions and black mushrooms and stir-fry about 15 seconds, until fragrant. Add the *Sauce* and heat until thickened, stirring constantly. Add the cabbage hearts, toss lightly to coat, and transfer to a serving platter. Serve.

Stir-Fried Lettuce With Straw Mushrooms

Cao Gu Pa Cai

6 Servings ⌢ Side Dish

1½	pounds leafy or Boston lettuce
2	15-ounce cans straw mushrooms, drained
2	tablespoons peanut, safflower or corn oil

Lettuce Seasonings

1	tablespoon rice wine or sake
½	teaspoon sesame oil
¾	teaspoon salt

Minced Seasonings

1	tablespoon minced scallions
2	teaspoons minced gingerroot

Oyster Sauce

½	cup chicken broth, preferably Chinese Chicken Broth (page 345)
2	tablespoons soy sauce
1	tablespoon oyster sauce
½	teaspoon sesame oil
1	teaspoon sugar
1½	teaspoons cornstarch

1. Discard any wilted leaves from the lettuce, and cut away any stem ends. Rinse the lettuce, drain thoroughly, and pat dry. Cut the leaves lengthwise into 1-inch strips. Blanch the straw mushrooms for 10 seconds in boiling water; drain, and refresh in cold water. Drain again.

2. Heat a wok, add 1 tablespoon of the oil, and heat until nearly smoking. Add the lettuce and the *Lettuce Seasonings*. Stir-fry over high heat for about 1 minute, until the lettuce is slightly wilted. Arrange the lettuce around the outer

LETTUCE HOLDS A SPECIAL place in the hearts of the Chinese. This leafy vegetable symbolizes prosperity because the Chinese name is similar in sound to the word for thriving. Consequently, it is often served at Chinese New Year celebrations.

edge of a platter.

3. Reheat the wok, add the remaining tablespoon of oil, and heat until very hot. Add the *Minced Seasonings*, and stir-fry over high heat until fragrant, about 10 seconds. Add the straw mushrooms, and toss lightly for about 15 seconds. Add the *Oyster Sauce*, and cook for about 1½ minutes, or until the sauce has thickened. Spoon the mushrooms and the sauce into the center of the platter, and serve immediately.

Stir-Fried Hot & Sour Cabbage
Suan La Bai Cai

6 Servings ⁓ Side Dish

CHINESE CABBAGE IS ONE *of the most versatile vegetables. It can be stir-fried, steamed, pickled or cooked in soups, and its taste lends a pronounced flavor to any dish. Fortunately, several varieties are now available in most supermarkets. For this spicy northern dish, I prefer to use Napa, which is found in both supermarkets and Chinese grocery stores.*

2	pounds Chinese cabbage (Napa)
1	tablespoon peanut, safflower or corn oil
1	tablespoon rice wine or sake
1	tablespoon sesame oil

Cabbage Seasonings

6	dried chili peppers, seeded and cut into ¼-inch lengths
1	tablespoon Sichuan peppercorns
2	tablespoons finely shredded gingerroot

Cabbage Sauce

1	tablespoon soy sauce
1	tablespoon rice wine or sake
2	teaspoons Chinese black vinegar or Worcestershire sauce
2	teaspoons sugar
1	teaspoon cornstarch
¾	teaspoon salt

1. Discard any wilted leaves from the cabbage, and cut away any stem sections from the leaves. Cut the leaves into 2-inch squares, and separate the hard pieces from the leafy pieces.

2. Heat a wok, add the oil, and heat until nearly smoking. Add the hard cabbage pieces, and stir-fry over high heat, stirring constantly, for 30 seconds. Add the rice wine, and continue stir-frying for another 30 seconds. Add the leafier

cabbage pieces, and stir-fry for about 1 minute, stirring constantly. Remove the cabbage, and set aside.

3. Reheat the wok, add the sesame oil, and heat until very hot. Add the *Cabbage Seasonings*, and stir-fry for about 1 minute, until the dried chili peppers have turned black. Add the gingerroot shreds, and stir-fry for 10 seconds, until fragrant. Add the cooked cabbage, and stir-fry for about 30 seconds. Add the *Cabbage Sauce*, and toss lightly over high heat. Cook until the sauce begins to thicken. Transfer the mixture to a platter, and serve immediately.

Spicy Steamed Eggplant
Zheng Qie Zi
6 Servings ～ Side Dish

2	pounds eggplant
1	teaspoon salt

Eggplant Sauce

¼	cup soy sauce
2	tablespoons sesame oil
1	tablespoon rice wine or sake
1	tablespoon clear rice vinegar
2	teaspoons chili oil or chili paste
1½	tablespoons minced garlic
1	tablespoon minced scallions
2	teaspoons sugar

THE CHINESE EGGPLANT, *unlike its American cousin, is long, thin and about the size of a zucchini. It is also an extremely versatile vegetable; its tender flesh absorbs flavors and is the perfect carrier for both spicy and delicate sauces. If Chinese eggplant are unavailable, use small, tender eggplant. This dish may be served hot or cold.*

1. Peel the eggplant, and cut off the ends. Cut the eggplant in half lengthwise, and cut each half into strips about 1 inch thick. Cut the strips into pieces 2 inches long. Place the eggplant in a bowl, add the salt, toss lightly, and let sit for 1 hour. Pour off any water that has accumulated.

2. Fill a wok with water level with the bottom edge of a steamer tray, and heat until boiling. Place the eggplant on a heatproof plate, place the plate in a steamer tray, and cover. Place the steamer tray over the boiling water, and steam the eggplant for 20 minutes, or until tender. Pour the *Eggplant Sauce* over the steamed eggplant, and serve.

Stir-Fried Broccoli in Oyster Sauce

Hao You Jie Lan Cai

6 Servings 〜 Side Dish

CHINESE BROCCOLI *differs from its Western relative in that the stems are longer, the florets are tiny and the flavor is slightly bitter. It is available year-round at most Chinese markets, but if you cannot obtain it, substitute Western broccoli.*

2	pounds Chinese broccoli
8	dried Chinese black mushrooms
2	tablespoons peanut, safflower or corn oil

Minced Seasonings

1	tablespoon minced scallions
1	tablespoon minced gingerroot
1	tablespoon minced garlic

Oyster Sauce

6	tablespoons chicken broth, preferably Chinese Chicken Broth (page 345), or water
3	tablespoons oyster sauce
2	tablespoons soy sauce
1	tablespoon rice wine or sake
1	teaspoon sesame oil
2	teaspoons cornstarch
1	teaspoon sugar

1. Peel away the tough outer skin of the broccoli, and separate the florets. Roll-cut the stems into 1-inch pieces. Soak the dried mushrooms in hot water to cover for 20 minutes. Remove and discard the stems; cut the caps in half.

2. Heat 3 quarts salted water until boiling. Add the broccoli stem pieces, and cook for ½ minute. Add the florets, and cook for 1½ minutes, or until both stems and florets are just tender. Refresh immediately in cold water. Drain thoroughly.

3. Heat a wok, add the oil, and heat until very hot. Add the *Minced Seasonings*, and stir-fry for 10 seconds, until fragrant. Add the mushroom halves, and stir-fry for about 5 seconds. Add the broccoli, and toss lightly over high heat until the broccoli is heated through. Add the *Oyster Sauce*, and heat until thickened, tossing lightly to coat the broccoli. Transfer the mixture to a serving platter. Serve immediately.

Vegetable Balls With Scallops

Gan Bei Liang Se Qiu

6 Servings 〜 Side Dish or Main Dish

1 pound fresh scallops

Scallop Marinade
1 tablespoon rice wine or sake
2 slices gingerroot, the size of a quarter, smashed with the flat side of a cleaver
½ teaspoon salt

1½ pounds carrots (preferably big ones), cooked in boiling water for 2 minutes and refreshed in cold water
1½ pounds English (gourmet seedless) cucumbers or small pickling cucumbers

Vegetable Sauce
2 cups chicken broth, preferably Chinese Chicken Broth (page 345)
1½ tablespoons rice wine or sake
1 teaspoon salt
½ teaspoon sugar

Thickener
1 tablespoon water
2 teaspoons cornstarch

1. Rinse the scallops lightly, and drain thoroughly. Holding a cleaver or a chef's knife parallel to the cutting surface, slice each scallop in half through its thickness. Cut each half into matchstick-sized shreds. Place the shredded scallops in a bowl. Pinch the gingerroot slices in the *Scallop Marinade* repeatedly for several minutes to impart their flavor. Add the marinade to the scallops, toss lightly, and let marinate for 20 minutes. Discard the gingerroot.

2. Peel the carrots and cucumbers, and cut off the ends. Using a melon baller, cut the vegetables into balls. (Alternatively, you may cut the vegetables into 2-inch diamond shapes.) Heat 3 quarts of salted water until boiling, and add the carrot balls. Cook for about 2 minutes over medium heat, add the cucumber balls, and continue cooking for 2 more minutes. The carrot and cucumber balls should be tender. Remove and drain.

3. Heat a wok, add the *Vegetable Sauce*, and heat until boiling. Add the carrot

THIS VEGETABLE PLATTER *is often served at Chinese New Year because the spheres of carrots and cucumbers are said to resemble money. (Foods that look like money are eaten then in hopes of achieving prosperity during the coming year.) Dried scallops, a savory delicacy used as a pungent seasoning, are traditional in this recipe, but I have adapted the original to create a more delicately seasoned platter.*

315

and cucumber balls, and cook for 30 seconds. Add the *Thickener*, stirring constantly to prevent lumps. When the sauce has thickened, add the scallop shreds. Stir to blend, taste the sauce for seasoning, and adjust if necessary. Transfer the mixture to a bowl, and serve immediately.

Dry-Cooked String Beans

Gan Bian Si Ji Dou

6 Servings ⁓ Side Dish

YARD-LONG STRING beans have become more readily recognizable to Americans as the demand for Chinese ingredients has increased. Now, these long beans are available seasonally in most Chinese markets, and the seeds are sold in major seed catalogues. Western string beans may be used in this recipe. Plump with soy sauce and rice wine, the beans are delicious hot or at room temperature.

2	pounds yard-long string beans
½	pound ground pork or beef

Meat Seasonings

1	teaspoon soy sauce
1	teaspoon rice wine or sake
½	teaspoon sesame oil

2	cups peanut, safflower or corn oil
5	tablespoons minced Sichuan preserved mustard greens, rinsed lightly and drained

Green-Bean Sauce

1½	tablespoons soy sauce
1	tablespoon rice wine or sake
1	tablespoon water
1½	teaspoons sugar

2	tablespoons minced scallion greens
1	teaspoon sesame oil

1. Snap off both ends of the beans. Cut the beans on the diagonal into 2-inch pieces. Rinse the beans, and drain thoroughly. Lightly chop the ground meat until fluffy. Place the meat in a bowl, add the *Meat Seasonings*, and stir vigorously in one direction to combine evenly.

2. Heat a wok, add the oil, and heat the oil to 400 degrees F. Add a batch of the beans, covering the wok with a dome lid as they are placed in the oil to prevent the oil from splashing. Deep-fry the beans for about 3½ minutes, stirring constantly, until they are tender and golden brown at the edges. Remove with a handled strainer or slotted spoon, and drain. Reheat the oil, and deep-fry the

remaining beans in the same manner, reheating the oil between batches. Remove the oil from the wok, reserving 2 tablespoons. Wipe out the wok.

3. Reheat the wok, add the 2 tablespoons of oil, and heat until very hot. Add the ground meat, and stir-fry until the color changes, mashing and chopping to separate. Push the meat to the side, and add the preserved mustard greens. Stir-fry over high heat for about 15 seconds, until fragrant. Add the fried beans and the *Green-Bean Sauce*, and return the meat to the center of the pan. Toss lightly to coat the beans with the sauce. Add the minced scallion greens and the sesame oil. Toss lightly, and transfer the mixture to a platter. Serve immediately.

Five-Treasure Vegetable Platter
Wu Se Su Cai
6 Servings ⁓ Side Dish

1	pound baby carrots
1	pound fresh asparagus
3	medium-sized tomatoes

Vegetable-Cooking Mixture

6	cups chicken broth, preferably Chinese Chicken Broth (page 345)
3	tablespoons rice wine or sake
2	teaspoons salt
1	15-ounce can straw mushrooms, drained and blanched briefly in boiling water
1	can baby corn ears, drained and blanched briefly in boiling water

Thickener

1	tablespoon water
2	teaspoons cornstarch
1	teaspoon sesame oil

Although Sichuanese cuisine is best known for its fiery, spicy seasonings, there are a number of more mild-flavored banquet dishes. This platter is such a dish. The vegetables used may be varied according to seasonal availability, with yard-long string beans substituted for asparagus when available. Although tomatoes are not indigenous to China (they were introduced in the 1700s), they are now a staple in the repertory of classic vegetable dishes. (See photograph, page 170.)

1. Peel the baby carrots, and trim the ends. Peel the asparagus to within a few inches of the tip, and break off the tough ends. Heat a quart of salted water until boiling. Add the asparagus, and cook for 7 minutes, covered. Drain, and refresh in cold water. Add the carrots to the boiling water. Cook the carrots for 4 min-

utes, uncovered. Drain, and refresh in cold water.

2. Cut out the stem of each tomato, and make a shallow cross in the skin at the opposite end, cutting through the skin only. Plunge the tomatoes into boiling water for 20 seconds, until the skin puckers, and refresh immediately in cold water. Drain, and peel the skin. Cut each tomato into quarters, and remove the seeds.

3. Pour two-thirds of the *Vegetable-Cooking Mixture* into a wok or saucepan, and heat until boiling. Add the asparagus and carrots, and cook for 2 minutes. Remove the vegetables with a slotted spoon, and heat the mixture until boiling. Add the straw mushrooms and baby corn ears, and cook for 1 minute. Remove with a slotted spoon, and again heat the mixture until boiling. Add the tomatoes, and cook for about 1 minute. Remove the tomatoes with a slotted spoon. Discard the liquid.

4. Place the straw mushrooms in the center of a large round platter. Arrange the tomatoes in a circle around the mushrooms. Arrange the remaining vegetables decoratively in individual piles around the tomatoes and mushrooms.

5. Pour the remainder of the vegetable-cooking mixture into a saucepan or wok, and heat until boiling. Slowly add the *Thickener*, stirring constantly to prevent lumps. Add the sesame oil, stir to combine, and pour the sauce over the vegetables. Serve immediately.

Stuffed Cucumbers

Niang Da Huang Gua

6 Servings ⌣ Side Dish

T HE TENDER FLESH OF
*the cucumber is a superb
match for the savory meat filling
in this eastern dish, which is
excellent accompanied by rice.
Zucchini may be substituted for
the cucumber for an equally
delectable variation.*

3	medium-sized English (gourmet seedless) cucumbers
2	tablespoons cornstarch
½	cup water chestnuts
1	pound ground pork or beef

Meat Seasonings

1½	tablespoons soy sauce
1	tablespoon rice wine or sake
1½	teaspoons sesame oil
1	tablespoon minced scallions
2	teaspoons minced gingerroot
1½	tablespoons cornstarch
½	teaspoon salt
3	tablespoons peanut, safflower or corn oil

Braising Mixture

2	cups chicken broth, preferably Chinese Chicken Broth (page 345)
1	tablespoon soy sauce
1	tablespoon rice wine or sake
½	teaspoon salt
½	teaspoon sugar

Thickener

1	tablespoon water
1½	teaspoons cornstarch

2	tablespoons minced scallion greens

1. Cut each cucumber lengthwise in half, and scoop out the centers and any seeds. Cut each half crosswise into thirds. Sprinkle the cucumber cavities with cornstarch. Plunge the water chestnuts into boiling water for a few seconds to remove the tinny flavor. Refresh them in cold water, and chop coarsely. Lightly chop the meat until fluffy. Place it in a mixing bowl with the water chestnuts and the *Meat Seasonings*. Stir vigorously in one direction, and lightly throw the mixture against the inside of the bowl to combine evenly. Stuff the cucumbers with the ground meat mixture, and smooth the surface with the underside of a spoon dipped in water.

2. Heat a wok, add the oil, and heat until very hot. Place a third of the cucumbers, meat side down, in the bottom of the wok. Fry over medium-high heat for about 1 minute, until golden brown. (The filling will remain in the cucumbers.) Remove with a slotted spoon. Fry the remaining cucumbers in the same manner, and remove. Add the *Braising Mixture* to the wok, heat until boiling, and add the cucumbers, meat side up. Cover the wok, and heat until the liquid boils again. Turn the heat to medium-low, and simmer for 15 minutes, or until the meat is cooked and the cucumbers are tender. With a slotted spoon, remove the cucumbers, and arrange them on a platter. Heat the braising mixture until boiling, add the *Thickener*, stirring constantly to prevent lumps, and heat until thickened. Pour the sauce over the cucumbers, sprinkle the tops with the minced scallion greens, and serve immediately.

Stuffed Peppers in Black Bean Sauce

Niang Qing Zhao

6 Servings ⌣ Side Dish or Main Dish

THE BLACK BEAN SAUCE *in this dish is quite subtle, yet substantial enough to complement the green peppers and meat filling. Raw shelled shrimp may be substituted for the pork for a flavorful variation.*

1¼	pounds ground pork or beef

Meat Seasonings

1½	tablespoons soy sauce
1	tablespoon rice wine or sake
2	teaspoons sesame oil
1	tablespoon minced gingerroot
1	tablespoon minced scallions
1½	tablespoons cornstarch

6	medium-sized green peppers, halved, cored and seeded
2	tablespoons cornstarch
3	tablespoons peanut, safflower or corn oil

Minced Seasonings

1	tablespoon fermented black beans, rinsed, drained and minced
1	tablespoon minced garlic
1	tablespoon minced scallions

Sauce

1	cup chicken broth, preferably Chinese Chicken Broth (page 345)
1½	tablespoons soy sauce
1½	tablespoons rice wine or sake
1	teaspoon cornstarch
¾	teaspoon sugar
½	teaspoon salt

1. Lightly chop the ground meat until fluffy. Place the meat in a mixing bowl, and add the *Meat Seasonings*. Stir vigorously in one direction to combine evenly. Lightly throw the mixture against the inside of the bowl.

2. Lightly dust the cavity of each green pepper with the cornstarch. Stuff a portion of the ground-meat mixture into each pepper. Using the underside of a spoon dipped in water, smooth the surface of the filling.

3. Heat a wok, add the oil, and heat until very hot. Place half the peppers,

filling side down, in the hot oil. Fry for ½ minute over high heat to sear the outside, until the filling is golden brown. (The filling will remain in the peppers.) Remove the peppers, and reheat the oil. Fry the remaining peppers in the same manner, and remove. Reheat the oil, add the *Minced Seasonings*, stir-fry for about 10 seconds (until fragrant), and add the *Sauce*. Add the green peppers, filling side up, and heat the mixture until boiling. Cover, reduce the heat to medium, and cook for about 10 minutes, until the meat is cooked and the peppers are tender. Uncover, turn the heat to high, and reduce the sauce to a coating consistency, about 2 minutes. Transfer the stuffed peppers to a platter, meat side up, and pour the sauce over the top. Serve immediately.

Spicy Stir-Fried Eggplant

Yu Xiang Qie Zi

Servings ⌒ Main Dish or Side Dish

1½	pounds eggplant
½	pound ground pork or beef

Meat Marinade

2	teaspoons soy sauce
1	teaspoon rice wine or sake
½	teaspoon sesame oil

2	cups peanut, safflower or corn oil

Minced Seasonings

2	tablespoons minced scallions
1½	tablespoons minced garlic
2	teaspoons minced gingerroot

2	teaspoons chili paste

Spicy Sauce

2	tablespoons soy sauce
1½	tablespoons Chinese black vinegar or Worcestershire sauce
1	tablespoon rice wine or sake
1	teaspoon sesame oil
1	tablespoon sugar

THE SPICY SAUCE IN THIS *dish is simultaneously sweet and tart. Its origin is traced to Sichuan, where the innovative chefs initially developed this sauce for the preparation of fish. They soon found that it complemented pork, chicken and eggplant as well.*

1. Rinse the eggplant, cut off the stems, and cut the eggplant lengthwise in half. Cut each half into slices ½ inch thick, and cut the slices into pieces 3 inches long and 1 inch wide. Lightly chop the meat until fluffy, and place it in a bowl. Add the *Meat Marinade*, toss lightly, and let the meat sit for 10 minutes.

2. Heat a wok, add the oil, and heat the oil to 400 degrees F. Add a third of the eggplant slices, covering the wok with a dome lid as they are placed in the oil to prevent the oil from splashing. Fry the slices for about 3 minutes, or until tender. Remove with a handled strainer or slotted spoon, and drain. Reheat the oil, and deep-fry the remaining eggplant in the same manner, reheating the oil between batches. Remove the oil from the wok, reserving 2 tablespoons. Wipe out the wok.

3. Reheat the wok, add the 2 tablespoons of oil, and heat until very hot. Add the ground meat and marinade, and stir-fry until the color changes, mashing and chopping to separate it. Push the meat to the side, and add the *Minced Seasonings*. Stir-fry for about 10 seconds, until fragrant. Add the chili paste, and stir-fry for about 5 seconds. Add the *Spicy Sauce*, return the meat to the center of the pan, and toss over high heat until the sauce thickens. Add the fried eggplant, toss lightly to coat with the sauce, and transfer the mixture to a platter. Serve immediately.

Stir-Fried Asparagus & Lettuce in Oyster Sauce

Hao You Shuang Cai

6 Servings ⁓ Side Dish

SINCE LETTUCE *symbolizes prosperity, it would not be unusual to serve this dish for an auspicious occasion, such as a birthday or a New Year's banquet. Accompany it with plenty of steamed rice and noodles for a delicious vegetarian main course. With meat or seafood, it also works well as a side dish. For convenience, the lettuce may be stir-fried in advance and served warm or at room temperature.*

1	pound leafy or Boston lettuce or trimmed, cleaned spinach or watercress
1½	pounds fresh asparagus
2	tablespoons peanut, safflower or corn oil

Lettuce Seasonings

1	tablespoon rice wine
¾	teaspoon salt

Minced Seasonings

2	tablespoons minced scallions, white part only
1	tablespoon minced gingerroot

½   pound fresh shiitake mushrooms, stems trimmed, caps cut in half

¼   pound snow peas, ends snapped and veiny strings removed

1½   tablespoons rice wine or sake

Oyster Sauce

¾   cup chicken broth, preferably Chinese Chicken Broth (page 345)

3¾   tablespoons oyster sauce

1½   tablespoons soy sauce

¾   teaspoon sesame oil

1¾   teaspoons cornstarch

1½   teaspoons sugar or to taste

1. Discard any wilted leaves and the stem end from the lettuce. Rinse the lettuce lightly, drain thoroughly, and pat dry. Cut the leaves lengthwise into 1-inch strips. Snap the asparagus stem ends off, leaving the tender section of the stems and the tips. Cut the asparagus into 1½-inch sections. Heat 1 quart of water in a pot until boiling, and add the asparagus. Cook about 5 minutes, until just tender, and refresh immediately in cold water. Drain thoroughly.

2. Heat a wok, add 1 tablespoon of the oil, and heat until nearly smoking. Add the lettuce and *Lettuce Seasonings*, and stir-fry over high heat for about 1 minute, until the lettuce is slightly wilted. Arrange the lettuce around the outside of a serving platter.

3. Reheat the wok, add the remaining 1 tablespoon oil, and heat until hot. Add the *Minced Seasonings*, and stir-fry about 10 seconds, until fragrant. Add the shiitake mushrooms and toss lightly over high heat for about 1 minute. Add the snow peas and the rice wine, and stir-fry over high heat for an additional minute. Add the *Oyster Sauce* and cook, stirring constantly, until thickened. Add the asparagus, toss lightly to coat, and portion the mixture into the center of the platter. Serve immediately.

Stuffed Pancakes

Shi Jin Liang Cai

6 Servings ⌢ Side Dish or Main Dish

THE FESTIVAL OF THE *Dead is a Chinese holiday celebrated 106 days after the winter solstice. On this day, ancestors' graves are visited, and offerings are presented to their departed souls. Traditionally, no fires are lit for three days before the holiday, so it has become known as the "cold foods" festival. Dishes like this one are prepared in advance and eaten cold or at room temperature. It is similar to a fresh spring roll, stuffed with fresh vegetables and pork, and complemented by a dab of hoisin sauce and chopped peanuts. Salted daikon radish is a condiment available in plastic bags in Asian markets.*

½	pound boneless center-cut pork loin

Pork Marinade

1	tablespoon soy sauce
1	tablespoon rice wine or sake
1	tablespoon water
1	teaspoon sesame oil
2	teaspoons cornstarch

18	Shanghai spring roll or *lumpia* wrappers
½	cup coarsely chopped dry-roasted, unsalted peanuts
1	tablespoon sugar
4-5	dried Chinese black mushrooms, soaked in hot water to cover for 20 minutes
7	tablespoons peanut, safflower or corn oil
1	cup shredded leeks or 1-inch scallion green pieces
3	cups fresh bean sprouts, rinsed

Pork Sauce

¼	cup chicken broth, preferably Chinese Chicken Broth (page 345)
1½	tablespoons soy sauce
1	tablespoon rice wine or sake
1	teaspoon sesame oil
2	teaspoons cornstarch
½	teaspoon sugar

Minced-Vegetable Seasonings

2	tablespoons minced salted daikon radish (Chinese turnip), rinsed and drained
1	tablespoon minced garlic

2	cups shredded Chinese cabbage (Napa)
2	cups finely shredded carrots

Vegetable Sauce

⅓	cup chicken broth, preferably Chinese Chicken Broth (page 345)
1	tablespoon rice wine or sake
2	teaspoons cornstarch
1	teaspoon sugar
1	teaspoon salt

½   cup hoisin sauce

1. Remove any fat or gristle from the pork loin, and discard. Cut the meat, across the grain, into slices ⅛ inch thick. (You may partially freeze the meat to facilitate cutting.) Cut the slices into matchstick-sized shreds. Place the shreds in a bowl, add the *Pork Marinade*, toss lightly, and let marinate for 20 minutes. Using your fingers, separate the spring roll wrappers, and fold in quarters. Arrange them in a steamer tray that has been lined with parchment paper. Fill a wok with water level with the bottom edge of the steamer tray, place the steamer over boiling water and steam for 5 minutes. Let the pancakes sit in the steamer, and serve them from it. Mix the peanuts and sugar. Drain the mushrooms, and cut off and discard the stems. Cut the caps into shreds.

2. Heat a wok, add 3 tablespoons of the oil, and heat the oil until very hot. Add the pork shreds, and stir-fry over high heat until they change color, about 1 minute. Remove with a handled strainer or slotted spoon, and drain. Wipe out the wok.

3. Reheat the wok, add 2 tablespoons of the oil, and heat until very hot. Add the shredded mushrooms, and stir-fry for about 10 seconds, until fragrant. Add the shredded leeks, and stir-fry for another 30 seconds. Add the pork, the bean sprouts and the *Pork Sauce*. Toss lightly over high heat until the sauce thickens. Transfer the mixture to a platter. Wipe out the wok.

4. Reheat the wok, add the remaining 2 tablespoons of oil, and heat until very hot. Add the *Minced-Vegetable Seasonings*, and stir-fry for about 10 seconds, until fragrant. Add the cabbage and carrot shreds. Toss lightly over high heat for 2 minutes, until the shreds are tender. Add the *Vegetable Sauce*. Stir-fry over high heat, stirring constantly until the sauce thickens. Transfer this mixture to another platter. To eat, spread a little hoisin sauce over a spring roll wrapper, sprinkle on some chopped peanuts, portion some of each stir-fried mixture on top, and roll up.

Vegetarian Dishes

THE KUANTU TEMPLE, A BUDDHIST-Taoist sanctuary founded in 1661, lies at the intersection of two rivers about an hour's drive from Taipei. Visitors can view several lavishly decorated temples containing gilded statues of Buddha and Matsu, the Holy Mother, or they can wander in the 320-foot-long Buddha Cave, which contains a small statue of the thousand-handed Goddess of Mercy flanked by her four fierce-looking protectors. Chinese from all parts of Taiwan flock here to sightsee, to pursue religious meditation and to partake of the superb vegetarian food prepared in the temple's kitchen and served in its famous restaurant.

On a recent visit to Taiwan, I and 14 fellow American food professionals had the honor of dining in the Kuantu Temple restaurant, where reservations are hard to come by. We feasted our way through a magnificent 12-course meal that included cold asparagus spears with mock ham; braised Chinese black mushrooms coated in sesame seeds; deep-fried oyster mushrooms in batter; vegetarian dumplings with shredded spring ginger; a mixed vegetarian platter with fresh broccoli spears, water chestnuts, *enoki* mushrooms, cucumbers and silver tree ears; and two soup pots—one with hairy seaweed and assorted vegetables and the other with steamed wheat gluten, pickled mustard cabbage, bamboo shoots and straw mushrooms. The meal ended with a huge platter of fresh sliced fruit and a cold, sweet soup garnished with fresh pineapple, watermelon and silver tree ears.

The quality and magnificence of the dishes was in no way diminished by the lack of meat. If anything, it was enhanced. Furthermore, we were all impressed by the level of sophistication that Chinese vegetarian cuisine has achieved.

To trace its creation and development, one must go back to the introduction of Buddhism and Taoism to China, for it was in the kitchens of these monasteries that vegetarian cuisine was conceived and refined. Although undocumented, it appears that Buddhism was first introduced to China from India before the first century A.D. The movement did not gain strength, however, until the Han dynasty (206 B.C. to 220 A.D.), when it was paired with Taoism, which was founded by Lao-tze, an eminent Chinese philosopher who preached simplicity and harmony with nature. The two religions had strong similarities in ideology and dietary practices: the Buddhists refrained from eating meat because they believed in reincarnation and abhorred killing any living animal; the Taoists abstained from eating meat and grains in order to achieve immortality and unity with the natural order of the universe. Both factions encouraged a diet of vegetables, herbs, plants, nuts and seeds. The only major difference in the dietary regimens of these two groups was that the Buddhists shunned garlic, onions, leeks, scallions and the like, believing that these spicy seasonings disrupted the internal tranquility of the body, whereas the Taoists credited many of these plants with medicinal value.

As Buddhism and Taoism became more widespread, the number of temples increased. Pilgrimages were made to the monasteries in observance of holidays and for religious meditation. In ancient China, these refuges also provided lodging and refreshment for travelers. Visitors sampled the food and slowly developed a taste for the cuisine. Gradually, restaurants and food stands offering vegetarian fare opened. While many of the pastries and snacks had once been eaten in observance of Buddhist festivals, they now became available on a seasonal basis in the marketplaces.

As the cuisine became more popular, the ancient chefs, particularly in eastern China, used their expertise and imagination to create an impressive repertory of delicate and sophisticated dishes. Imitations of chicken, goose, duck, ham and fish were refined and perfected to the point where one was hard-pressed to distinguish them from their models. Various ingredients were used to make these creations resemble the original foods as much as possible: mock duck and goose were made from fried bean curd sheets; mock shrimp balls were created with potatoes and carrots; turtles were fashioned out of mushrooms and cucumbers; mock eels were formed with seaweed, turnips, mushrooms and bamboo shoots; and imitation crab was created with tofu.

Protein-rich foods, such as soybeans and their by-products—tofu, soybean milk, bean milk sheets and bean curd sheets—figure prominently in vegetarian cookery. Wheat gluten (*mian jin*), the spongy material remaining after the starch in a flour dough has been removed, is another product available in several forms. Rolled into balls and deep-fried (*mian jin pao*), it is then stuffed with a variety of fillings; separated into chunks and steamed, with the resulting material (*kao fu*) braised and simmered, it is rolled into cylinders. This ingredient (*su chang*) is then used in stir-fried platters or braised and served cold in slices.

Naturally, vegetables themselves—fresh, dried, salted or pickled—play a substantial role in vegetarian cooking. Preserved vegetables also are used as seasonings, and condiments like pickled tofu (*dou fu ru*) and hot sauces and pastes with a vegetable base provide additional seasoning for bland dishes. Nuts of all types figure prominently in a meatless diet; other foods used in vegetarian cookery include seaweed (in its many forms), noodles and grains.

Today in the Far East, many Chinese still observe a reformed regimen of the Buddhist and Taoist dietary practices: some abstain from eating meat each day before noon, while others will eat no meat on the second and sixteenth days of each month. In China, Buddhist teachings and temples gradually are being restored after the repression of the Cultural Revolution, and in Taiwan, there are still a considerable number of Buddhist temples like the Kuantu and eateries that serve magnificent vegetarian fare in the memorable and refined style of the ancient Chinese master chefs.

素菜類

Crunchy Cashews

Zha Yao Guo

6 Servings ⌒ Appetizer

THE RONG SHING *Restaurant in Taipei is known for its superb Sichuanese cuisine. Once they are seated, diners are treated to a number of small snacks to munch on. These crunchy cashews were a favorite of mine. I would alternate mouthfuls of the cashews with sips of cold beer, becoming quite content even before the food was served.*

2	cups water
¼	cup honey
1	teaspoon salt
½	pound raw cashews
4	cups peanut, safflower or corn oil

1. Place the water, honey and salt in a saucepan. Stir to dissolve the honey. Add the cashews, and heat the mixture until boiling. Reduce the heat to medium and cook, uncovered, for 15 minutes. Remove the cashews from the liquid, drain thoroughly, and place them on a tray to air-dry for 1 hour, turning occasionally.

2. Heat a wok, add the oil, and heat the oil to 350 degrees F. Add the cashews, and deep-fry over high heat, turning constantly for about 3½ minutes, until the cashews are golden brown. Remove the nuts with a handled strainer or slotted spoon, and spread them out on brown paper to drain. (Do not use paper towels, as the nuts will stick.) Let cool completely, and serve.

Mock Shrimp Balls

Su Zha Wan Zi

6 Servings ⁓ Appetizer, Side Dish or Main Dish

Mock-Shrimp Mixture

3	cups firmly packed mashed boiled potatoes, still hot
½	cup minced raw carrots
¼	cup blanched, chopped water chestnuts
1	tablespoon minced scallions
2	teaspoons minced gingerroot
1	tablespoon rice wine or sake
1½	teaspoons sesame oil
1½	teaspoons salt
1	egg white, lightly beaten
¼	cup cornstarch plus more if necessary
4	cups peanut, safflower or corn oil

THESE GOLDEN FRIED *balls, with their pinkish hue, truly do resemble shrimp balls in appearance if not in flavor. They are delightfully crisp on the outside and tender inside, like fried potatoes, with the flavors of ginger, scallions and sesame oil. Served piping hot, they make a superb hors d'oeuvre or an unusual vegetable main dish.*

1. Make the *Mock-Shrimp Mixture*, stirring vigorously after the addition of each ingredient. Add the egg white, and stir vigorously in one direction until the mixture is smooth. Add the cornstarch, and stir again until smooth. If the mixture is very soft, add another tablespoon of cornstarch, and mix well. Refrigerate the mixture for about 1 hour.

2. Heat a wok, add the oil, and heat the oil to 350 to 375 degrees F. Shape the mock-shrimp mixture into balls about ½ inch in diameter, and carefully slide a batch of them into the hot oil. Turn up the heat to high, and deep-fry the balls, stirring constantly, for about 3½ minutes, until they are golden brown and cooked through. Remove with a handled strainer or slotted spoon, and drain on absorbent paper. Reheat the oil. Deep-fry the remaining balls in the same manner, reheating the oil between batches. Arrange the fried balls on a platter, and serve immediately.

Vegetarian Spring Rolls

Su Chun Juan

20 Spring Rolls ⌣ Appetizer or Main Dish

CHINESE BLACK mushrooms and Chinese garlic chives give these rolls a pronounced flavor. Serve the fried rolls with duck sauce or a sweet-and-sour sauce for dipping.

4	cups peanut, safflower or corn oil
2	cups 1-inch length Chinese garlic chives, scallion greens or leeks
3	cups fresh bean sprouts
½	teaspoon salt
2	tablespoons rice wine or sake
8-10	dried Chinese black mushrooms, soaked in hot water to cover for 20 minutes

Minced Seasonings

1	tablespoon minced gingerroot
1	tablespoon minced garlic
2	cups finely shredded Chinese cabbage (Napa)
1½	cups finely shredded carrots

Spring-Roll Sauce

3	tablespoons soy sauce
1	tablespoon water
1	teaspoon sesame oil
1½	teaspoons cornstarch
20	Shanghai spring roll or *lumpia* wrappers

Adhesive

1	egg yolk
3	tablespoons water
2	tablespoons flour

Duck sauce or sweet-and-sour sauce

1. Heat a wok, add 1 tablespoon of the oil, and heat until very hot. Add the Chinese garlic chives, and stir-fry for about 1 minute over high heat. Add the bean sprouts, salt and 1 tablespoon of the rice wine; continue stir-frying over high heat for 1 minute, until the bean sprouts are slightly limp. Place the mixture in a colander, and let it drain for 10 minutes; toss occasionally. Drain the mushrooms, cut off the stems and cut the caps into fine shreds.

2. Heat a wok, add 2 tablespoons of the oil, and heat until very hot. Add the *Minced Seasonings*, and stir-fry for about 10 seconds, until fragrant. Add the black mushroom shreds, and stir-fry for another 10 seconds. Add the cabbage and carrot shreds. Stir-fry for about 30 seconds, and add the remaining tablespoon of rice wine. Stir-fry for another minute over high heat, and add the *Spring-Roll Sauce*. Toss lightly over high heat until the sauce has thickened. Spread the mixture out on a tray, and let it cool for 15 minutes. Combine it with the bean-sprout mixture. Clean the wok.

3. Separate the spring roll wrappers, and place them on a counter. Place 2 heaping tablespoons of the stir-fried mixture on one wrapper toward the edge of the wrapper closest to you (**a**). Spread the filling out evenly over the wrapper to within 2 inches of each end. Spread some of the *Adhesive* on the opposite end. Gather in the sides (**b**), and roll up the wrapper to enclose the filling (**c**). Press to secure (**d**). Repeat for the remaining wrappers and filling.

4. Reheat the wok, add the remaining oil, and heat the oil to 375 degrees F. Add half the spring rolls, and deep-fry, turning constantly over high heat for about 5 minutes, until golden brown. Remove with a handled strainer or slotted spoon, and drain on absorbent paper. Reheat the oil, and deep-fry the remaining spring rolls in the same manner. Arrange the spring rolls on a platter, and serve immediately with duck sauce or sweet-and-sour sauce.

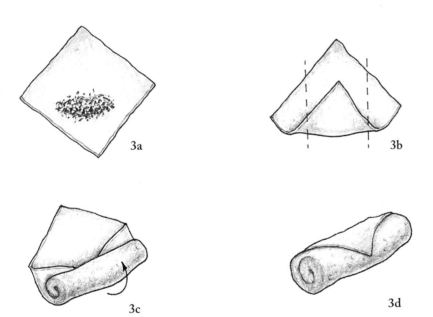

3a

3b

3c

3d

Mock Abalone in Oyster Sauce

Hao You Su Bao Yu

6 Servings ⌣ Side Dish or Main Dish

ONE CAN HARDLY DIS-CERN *the difference between the abalone mushrooms and real abalone in this flavorful meatless platter, in which the mushrooms are surrounded by spinach and drenched in oyster sauce. If abalone mushrooms are unavailable, substitute straw or button mushrooms.*

3 tablespoons peanut, safflower or corn oil
1 teaspoon minced garlic
1 pound fresh spinach, trimmed and cleaned

Spinach Seasonings
1 tablespoon rice wine or sake
1 teaspoon sesame oil
¾ teaspoon salt

Minced Seasonings
1 tablespoon minced scallions
2 teaspoons minced gingerroot

2 10-ounce cans abalone mushrooms, drained, thoroughly rinsed and briefly blanched

Oyster Sauce
½ cup water
2 tablespoons soy sauce
1 tablespoon oyster sauce
1 teaspoon sesame oil
1½ teaspoons cornstarch
1 teaspoon sugar
¼ teaspoon freshly ground black pepper

1. Heat a wok, add 1 tablespoon of the oil, and heat until nearly smoking. Add the minced garlic and the spinach. Toss lightly over high heat for 30 seconds; then add the *Spinach Seasonings*. Toss lightly, and continue cooking until the spinach is barely limp. Arrange the spinach around the outer edge of a platter.

2. Reheat the wok, add the remaining 2 tablespoons of oil, and heat until very hot. Add the *Minced Seasonings*, and stir-fry for about 10 seconds, until fragrant. Add the abalone mushrooms, and stir-fry for about 1 minute, until heated through. Add the *Oyster Sauce*. Toss lightly over high heat, and cook until the sauce has thickened. Spoon the mixture into the center of the platter, and serve immediately.

Two Winters

Chao Shuang Dong

6 Servings ⌣ Side Dish or Main Dish

12	small dried Chinese black mushrooms
1	19-ounce can winter bamboo shoots, plunged briefly into boiling water, refreshed and drained
1	cup peanut, safflower or corn oil
1	teaspoon minced garlic
1	pound fresh spinach, trimmed and cleaned

Spinach Seasonings

1	tablespoon rice wine or sake
¾	teaspoon salt

Minced Seasonings

2	teaspoons minced scallions
1	teaspoon minced gingerroot

Black-Mushroom Sauce

½	cup mushroom-soaking liquid
3	tablespoons soy sauce
2	tablespoons rice wine or sake
2	teaspoons sugar

Thickener

1	tablespoon water
1½	teaspoons cornstarch

1½	teaspoons sesame oil

THE TITLE OF THIS *colorful vegetable platter refers to the winter varieties of black mushrooms and bamboo shoots commonly used in the dish. The flavor and quality of these two vegetables are believed to be at their best during the colder months. Whatever the season, this dish will please both the eye and the palate. (See photograph, page 174.)*

1. Soften the dried mushrooms for 20 minutes in hot water to cover. Remove and discard the stems. Retain ½ cup of the mushroom-soaking liquid. Trim each bamboo shoot to a rectangle, and cut three V-shaped wedges lengthwise in each side. Then cut the bamboo shoots crosswise into slices about ⅛ inch thick.

2. Heat a wok, add 1 tablespoon of the oil, and heat until nearly smoking. Add the minced garlic, and stir-fry for about 3 seconds; then add the spinach and the *Spinach Seasonings*. Toss lightly over high heat until the spinach is slightly wilted. Arrange the spinach around the outer edge of a platter.

3. Reheat the wok, add the remaining oil, and heat the oil to 400 degrees F.

Add the black mushrooms and the bamboo slices, and deep-fry, stirring constantly, for about 1½ minutes over high heat. Remove with a handled strainer or slotted spoon, and drain. Remove the oil from the wok, reserving 1 tablespoon. Wipe out the wok.

4. Reheat the wok, add the tablespoon of oil, and heat until very hot. Add the *Minced Seasonings*, and stir-fry for about 10 seconds, until fragrant. Add the *Black-Mushroom Sauce*, and heat until boiling. Add the fried mushrooms and bamboo shoots. Cover, and cook for 1½ minutes over high heat. Uncover, and slowly add the *Thickener*, stirring constantly to prevent lumps. When the sauce thickens, add the sesame oil, toss lightly, and transfer the mixture to the center of the platter. Serve immediately.

Broccoli in Mock Crabmeat Sauce

Su Xie Jie Lan

6 Servings ⁓ Side Dish or Main Dish

THE MINCED TOFU *and minced carrot arranged on crisp stir-fried broccoli spears are meant to resemble flecks of crabmeat and pinkish roe.*

1½	pounds broccoli
1	square firm tofu, about 1 pound
½	teaspoon sesame oil
3	tablespoons peanut, safflower or corn oil

Minced Seasonings

2	teaspoons minced gingerroot
1½	teaspoons minced garlic

Broccoli Sauce

2	tablespoons rice wine or sake
1	teaspoon sesame oil
1	teaspoon salt

Mock Crabmeat Sauce

½	cup water
1½	tablespoons rice wine or sake
2	egg whites, lightly beaten
½	teaspoon sugar
½	teaspoon salt
¼	teaspoon freshly ground white pepper

Thickener

1	tablespoon water
1½	teaspoons cornstarch

1	tablespoon minced carrot

1. Peel away the tough outer skin of the broccoli, and separate the florets. Roll-cut the stems into 1-inch pieces. Heat 2 quarts salted water until boiling. Add the stem pieces, and cook for ½ minute. Add the florets, and cook for 2½ minutes, or until both stems and florets are just tender. Refresh immediately in cold water. Drain thoroughly.

2. Mash the tofu with a fork, and add the sesame oil.

3. Heat a wok, add 1 tablespoon of the oil, and heat until very hot. Add the *Minced Seasonings*, and stir-fry for about 10 seconds, until fragrant. Add the broccoli and the *Broccoli Sauce*. Toss lightly over high heat, and cook for about 1 minute. Transfer the mixture to a platter. Wipe out the wok.

4. Reheat the wok, add the remaining 2 tablespoons oil, and heat until very hot. Add the mashed tofu, and toss lightly over high heat for 30 seconds. Add the *Mock Crabmeat Sauce*, and stir. Cook for about 20 seconds, stirring constantly, until the mixture begins to bubble. Slowly add the *Thickener*, stirring constantly, and cook until thickened. Pour the mixture over the broccoli, and sprinkle the minced carrot over the top. Serve immediately.

Vegetarian Eight Treasures

Su Ba Bao

6 Servings ⌒ Main Dish or Side Dish

IN THE STIR-FRIED PLATTER *on which this vegetarian dish is based, pork cubes are one of the eight treasures. One hardly misses the pork in this spicy meatless version.*

1	square firm tofu, about 1 pound
3	tablespoons peanut, safflower or corn oil
¾	cup ½-inch-diced cucumber, cooked in boiling water until just tender, about 2 minutes, and drained
¾	cup ½-inch-diced carrot, cooked in boiling water until just tender, about 4 minutes, and drained
¾	cup ½-inch-diced water chestnuts, plunged briefly into boiling water and drained
¾	cup green peas, cooked in boiling water until just tender and drained
2	teaspoons chili paste

Sweet Bean Sauce

3	tablespoons soy sauce
2	tablespoons sweet bean sauce
1½	tablespoons water
1	tablespoon rice wine or sake
3½	tablespoons sugar

¾	cup dry-roasted unsalted peanuts

1. Place the tofu between two paper towels, and place a light weight on top. (This will compress the cake and remove excess water.) Let it sit for 30 minutes. Drain the tofu, and cut it into ½-inch dice.

2. Heat a wok, add 2 tablespoons of the oil, and heat until very hot. Add the tofu, cucumber, carrot, water chestnuts and peas; toss lightly over high heat, stirring constantly, until the ingredients are hot, about 1½ minutes. Remove, and set aside. Wipe out the wok.

3. Reheat the wok, add the remaining tablespoon of oil, and heat until very hot. Add the chili paste, and stir-fry for about 10 seconds, until fragrant. Add the *Sweet Bean Sauce*, and cook until the sauce begins to thicken. Add all the cooked vegetables and the peanuts. Toss lightly, and transfer the mixture to a platter. Serve immediately.

Assorted Vegetables Over Sizzling Rice

Shi Jian Guo Ba

6 Servings ⌒ Main Dish or Side Dish

12	Sizzling Rice Cakes (page 41)
10	dried Chinese black mushrooms
1	pound fresh oyster mushrooms, rinsed thoroughly and drained, or 2 10-ounce cans oyster mushrooms, plunged briefly into boiling water, refreshed and drained
2	cups peanut, safflower or corn oil

Minced Seasonings

1	tablespoon minced scallions
2	teaspoons minced gingerroot
1	cup fresh button mushrooms, quartered

Sauce Base

2	cups water
1	cup mushroom-soaking liquid
2	tablespoons soy sauce
1	tablespoon rice wine or sake
1½	teaspoons Chinese black vinegar or Worcestershire sauce
2	teaspoons sugar
½	teaspoon salt

Thickener

¼	cup water
2	tablespoons cornstarch
2	cups snow peas, ends snapped and veiny strings removed
1	teaspoon sesame oil

THE DISTINCTIVE SHAPE and texture of oyster mushrooms add a special touch to any dish, including this one. A selection of mushrooms and crisp snow peas are drenched in a hot-and-sour sauce and served over Sizzling Rice Cakes. Be sure to prepare the rice cakes well in advance.

1. Prepare the Sizzling Rice Cakes. Soak the dried black mushrooms in at least 1 cup of hot water for 20 minutes. Remove and discard the stems, and cut the caps in half. Retain 1 cup of the mushroom-soaking liquid. Cut the oyster mushrooms into quarters.

2. Heat a wok or a casserole, add 2 tablespoons of the oil, and heat until very hot. Add the *Minced Seasonings*, and stir-fry over high heat for about 10 seconds, until fragrant. Add the button mushrooms, and stir-fry for about 1 minute, stirring constantly. Add the black mushrooms and the oyster mushrooms, if using canned. Toss lightly over high heat for 30 seconds, and add the *Sauce Base*. Heat the mixture until boiling, and slowly add the *Thickener*, stirring constantly to prevent lumps. When the sauce has thickened, add the snow peas and the sesame oil. Toss lightly, and turn the heat to low.

3. Heat a wok, add the remaining oil, and heat the oil to 400 degrees F. Add half the rice cakes, and deep-fry, turning constantly, until the cakes are puffed and golden. Remove with a handled strainer or slotted spoon, and place in the bottom of a deep serving dish or bowl. Deep-fry the remaining rice cakes in the same manner. Pour the vegetable mixture over the rice cakes to create the sizzling sound. Serve immediately.

Wheat Gluten
Mian Jin
24 One-Inch Pieces

1   teaspoon active dry yeast
1   cup warm water
2   cups gluten flour or all-purpose flour

WHEAT GLUTEN IS AN ingredient that plays a major role in Chinese vegetarian cookery. Its spongy texture and mild flavor make it extremely versatile; it may be steamed, stir-fried, deep-fried or braised. Wheat Gluten is easily made, as demonstrated here, or it may be purchased dried, frozen or in cans at most Chinese grocery stores. Wheat Gluten will keep for up to a week when refrigerated, or it may be frozen.

1. Dissolve the yeast in the warm water. Place the flour in a bowl. Add the yeast mixture, and mix to a rough dough. Turn the dough out onto a lightly floured surface, and knead vigorously for about 5 minutes until smooth and elastic. Place the dough in a lightly greased bowl, cover with a damp towel, and let rise for 2 hours in a warm place free from drafts.

2. Punch down the dough, and knead lightly on a floured surface for 1 minute. Rinse the dough in running water, squeezing it repeatedly like a sponge. Continue rinsing and squeezing until the water runs clear. The dough should feel very spongy and be free of all starch. This is now the Wheat Gluten. Tear the gluten into 1-inch-square pieces, arrange the pieces on a lightly greased plate, and place the plate in a steamer tray.

3. Fill a wok with water level with the bottom edge of the steamer tray, and heat until boiling. Place the steamer tray over the boiling water, cover, and steam for 10 minutes over high heat. Remove the Wheat Gluten, and use as directed in the individual recipes.

Vegetarian Lion's Head

Su Shi Zi Tou

6 Servings ⁓ Main Dish or Side Dish

2	squares firm tofu, about 2 pounds
10	dried Chinese black mushrooms, softened in hot water to cover for 20 minutes
1	cup finely shredded carrots
¾	cup water chestnuts, plunged briefly into boiling water, refreshed in cold water and minced

Tofu Seasonings

1½	tablespoons soy sauce
1	tablespoon rice wine or sake
2	teaspoons sesame oil
1	tablespoon minced scallions
2	teaspoons minced gingerroot
1	teaspoon salt
¼	teaspoon freshly ground black pepper

3	large eggs, lightly beaten
½	cup cornstarch
1	pound Chinese cabbage (Napa)
¼	cup peanut, safflower or corn oil

Soup Base

4	cups water
2	tablespoons rice wine or sake
½	teaspoon salt

Lion's Head Coating

1½	tablespoons water
1	tablespoon soy sauce
1	tablespoon cornstarch

LION'S HEAD, THE CLASSIC eastern casserole, is a filling meal-in-one dish with its meatballs, cabbage and broth. This tasty vegetarian variation is a trifle more subtle than the hearty meat-filled original. Although Chinese cabbage is available year-round, it is at its best in late summer and early fall.

1. Place the tofu squares in the center of a dishtowel, gather the edges together, and twist to squeeze out as much liquid as possible. (The squares will crumble.) Place the tofu in a bowl. Drain the mushrooms, cut off the stems and discard, and mince the caps. Using a fork, mash the tofu until smooth. Add the mushrooms, carrots, water chestnuts and the *Tofu Seasonings*. Stir vigorously in

one direction until the ingredients are thoroughly combined. Add the eggs, and stir to combine. Add the cornstarch, and stir briefly to combine. Set the mixture aside.

2. Remove 4 of the outer cabbage leaves, rinse them lightly, and set aside. Cut the remaining cabbage into 2-inch squares, discarding the stem and keeping the harder pieces separate from the leafy ones.

3. Heat a wok, add 2 tablespoons of the oil, and heat until very hot. Add the harder cabbage pieces, and toss lightly over high heat for about 1½ minutes. Add the leafy pieces, and continue stir-frying over high heat for about 1 minute. Add the *Soup Base*, and heat the mixture until boiling. Cook for about 5 minutes, and transfer the mixture to an earthenware casserole or a Dutch oven. Wipe out the wok. Preheat the oven to 375 degrees F.

4. Reheat the wok, add the remaining 2 tablespoons of oil, and heat until very hot. Shape the tofu mixture into 4 oval-shaped balls, and dip them in the *Lion's Head Coating*. Carefully lower the coated balls into the hot oil, and fry on both sides over high heat until golden. Arrange the balls on top of the cabbage in the casserole. Arrange the 4 whole cabbage leaves on top, and cover the casserole. Bake the casserole for 1 hour. Remove from the oven, and serve.

Mock Sweet & Sour Pork

Su Tang Cu Rou

6 Servings ⌒ Main Dish

CHINESE VEGETARIAN cooks are fond of re-creating classic dishes using mock meat products. The fried Wheat Gluten and walnuts are used to replace the cubes of pork found in the traditional version of this dish. The Wheat Gluten has little flavor but absorbs the tastes of the other ingredients. The resulting vegetarian rendition is delicious.

½ recipe Wheat Gluten (page 338) or store-bought wheat gluten (available at well-stocked Asian markets)
1 cup pickled carrots (page 266), drained

Sugar Syrup
2 cups water
½ cup sugar

2 cups walnut halves
2 cups peanut, safflower or corn oil

Minced Seasonings
1 tablespoon minced scallions
2 teaspoons minced gingerroot

1 cup pineapple chunks, drained

Sweet & Sour Sauce

- ⅔ cup water
- ¼ cup ketchup
- 3 tablespoons clear rice vinegar
- 2 teaspoons soy sauce
- ½ teaspoon sesame oil
- 3 tablespoons sugar
- 2 teaspoons cornstarch
- 1 teaspoon salt

1. Make the Wheat Gluten and the pickled carrots. Place the *Sugar Syrup* in a saucepan. Heat the mixture until the sugar has dissolved. Add the walnuts, and heat until boiling. Reduce the heat to medium-low, and cook for 20 minutes. Remove the walnuts with a slotted spoon, and drain thoroughly. Discard the syrup.

2. Heat a wok, add the oil, and heat to 375 degrees F. Add the walnuts, and deep-fry over high heat, stirring constantly, until golden brown. Remove with a handled strainer or slotted spoon, and drain.

3. To make fried Wheat Gluten balls, reheat the oil. Add the Wheat Gluten pieces, and deep-fry over high heat for about 5 minutes, stirring constantly, until golden brown. Remove with a handled strainer or slotted spoon, and drain. Remove the oil from the wok, reserving 1 tablespoon.

4. Reheat the wok, add the tablespoon of oil, and heat until very hot. Add the *Minced Seasonings*, and stir-fry for about 10 seconds over high heat, until fragrant. Add the pineapple chunks and the pickled carrots. Toss lightly for about 1 minute, and add the *Sweet & Sour Sauce*. Continue mixing until the sauce has thickened, and add the fried walnuts and wheat gluten. Toss lightly to coat with the sauce. Transfer the mixture to a platter, and serve immediately.

Soups

Although my Chinese surrogate mother, Huang Su Huei, is a superb cook and has her own established cooking school in Taipei and three best-selling cookbooks to her credit, she rarely planned dinner parties in her home. Instead, she would entertain guests and family in the noted restaurants of the city, and we would feast on regional specialties from all parts of China. When asked for an explanation of why we never entertained at home, she curtly replied, "Too much trouble."

Her father's sixtieth birthday (an auspicious event in the Chinese culture), was another matter. She decided to prepare a banquet herself. Invitations were dispatched to the many relatives, and the serious planning began. After witnessing the extensive preparations involved, I easily understood why such dinner parties were not planned more frequently. They were, in fact, "too much trouble."

Plotting the menus, so it seemed, was the most painstaking chore; consideration was given to the seasonal products available and, more important, to the food preferences of her father, her husband, the children, me and the other guests (in that order). Foods traditionally reserved for such an event also had to be considered. Since noodles and steamed peach buns, both symbolizing longevity, are traditionally served on birthdays, they automatically became part of the menu. As soon as the other dishes were selected, calls were made to the chicken lady, directing her to set aside plenty of chicken

feet for the stock, and to the butcher, informing him of the date of the meal and indicating the type of meat and bones required.

The house was cleaned from top to bottom and the best china and linens were made ready. A few days before the dinner, Huang Su Huei and I journeyed to the best market in the city, selecting only the plumpest chickens, the choicest meat and the freshest-looking vegetables.

The actual cooking for the party began with the preparation of the stock. This brew, made from chicken feet, pork bones and trimmings, was the base for all the banquet's soups and sauces. My Chinese mother strongly maintained that the key to a superb dish was a superb stock (this same maxim was repeated to me by French chefs when I later trained in France), and she insisted on making the stocks herself.

The procedure was not overly complicated, but her actions were deliberate and meticulous: First, the bones were blanched in boiling water to clean them. They were then cracked at the joints to allow the marrow and flavors to be released. If a richer stock was required, pork loin would be added after it had been blanched and scored so that its flavors would emerge in the cooking. The bones (and meat) were then put in a big pot; water, scallions, gingerroot and Shaohsing (rice wine) were added; and the pot was set on the stove to boil. Once the liquid reached a boil, the heat was adjusted so that the broth would simmer and yield a clear stock. (Vigorous boiling results in a cloudy stock, referred to as a "cream stock.") After six hours of gentle simmering, the pot was emptied, and the fragrant liquid was strained through a fine-meshed sieve (and treated like liquid gold); the bones and meat, depleted of flavor, were discarded.

Since my Chinese mother was such an avid fan of soups, it was not unusual for her to plan two or three soup courses in a banquet menu. For her, as well as for most Chinese, soups are a vital part of any meal, be it a 12-course banquet or a simple family dinner. Whereas soups seem to play a rather restricted role in western cuisine, in China they have a much broader calling. During a multicourse banquet, light, savory and sweet soups are served as entremets to cleanse the palate and to signify the end of a series of courses. In a family-style meal, soup is served along with the other dishes to provide nourishment and to function as a beverage. The Chinese credit soups with aiding digestion and improving circulation, so they are often served toward the end of a full meal.

Soups have been present in the Chinese diet since ancient times. The earliest form of this dish, and one that is still popular today, is *keng*, a stewlike concoction made with meat, fish and vegetables. It was not unusual for this dish to be served at the beginning of a sumptuous banquet or with rice and millet as an everyday meal. During the Sung dynasty (960 to 1279), streets in the prosperous eastern city of Kaifeng were lined with small eateries that specialized in soups

of all kinds. The universal appeal of these soups was obvious: they were nourishing, inexpensive and delicious.

Some soups have been used for centuries to treat certain ailments. In ancient China, a broth made from bamboo leaves dotted with early-morning dew was believed to cure tuberculosis. Stocks simmered with assorted Chinese herbs were administered for a number of maladies. Even today, chicken soup, flavored with gingerroot in southern China and sesame oil in Taiwan, is prescribed daily for a month after childbirth to restore the body's energy.

As the regional chefs utilized the products of their provinces, delicious and unusual concoctions were added to the repertory of Chinese soups. Eastern chefs excelled at preparing soups with fish and seafood garnishes. Fujianese chefs, in particular, gained renown for their clear and delicate broths. The Cantonese distinguished themselves with flavorful stocks, often adding such exotic ingredients as snake, turtle and frogs' legs as garnishes. Soups from Sichuan, Hunan and Yunnan, the western provinces, were particularly varied, featuring both robust and refined seasonings. And northern chefs, who drew their expertise from all parts of China, contributed a broad range of masterpieces.

Chinese soups may be divided into two categories: light and heavy. Light soups are characterized by a clear broth with the addition of assorted garnishes of meat, fish, seafood and vegetables. Soups of this type are cooked briefly so that the ingredients

湯
類

maintain their original textures. Steamed soups, also included in this category, are made by putting the ingredients in a covered heatproof container and then steaming gently. The resulting broth is unusually clear and delicate.

Heavy soups are thickened with cornstarch or a flour-and-oil roux and garnished with meat, seafood, fish and vegetables. Included in this group are soupy stews, made by putting the ingredients in a heatproof casserole and simmering slowly so that the flavors marry.

In addition to their culinary significance, soups have, on occasion, provided inspiration for eloquent prose. Li Yü, a famous poet and essayist of the Ch'ing dynasty, articulated his devotion to soup in the following manner:

As long as there is rice, there should be soup. The relationship between soup and rice is like that between water and a boat. When a boat is stranded on a sandy bank, only water can wash it back to the river; rice goes down better with soup. I would go so far as to say that it would be better to go without all main dishes than to have no soup.

Homemade Chicken Broth

To my mind, taking the time to make a good, flavorful stock from scratch is a necessity in soup making and desirable for general purposes. The chicken broth, with its delicate flavor, may be used in any soup. In preparing it, the following points should be considered:

1. The bones should be cracked and broken with the blunt edge of a cleaver or by the butcher, to allow the marrow and rich flavors to be released into the liquid.

2. The bones and meat should be blanched briefly in boiling water to clean them so that the resulting broth will be as clear as possible.

3. Chicken feet make an excellent broth, as they contain natural gelatin and a great deal of flavor. If you can find them, use 3 pounds of feet in place of the roasting chicken or fowl called for in the recipe. If these are unobtainable, use a fryer or backs and necks.

4. Once the water and bones reach a boil, reduce the heat, and simmer the mixture slowly, uncovered, so that the broth will not become cloudy. Skim the liquid repeatedly to remove any impurities.

Chinese Chicken Broth

Qing Tang

6 Cups

1   whole roasting chicken or small fowl, about 3 pounds
10   cups water
⅓   cup rice wine or sake
3   slices gingerroot, the size of a quarter, smashed with the flat side of a cleaver

1. Using a heavy cleaver or a chef's knife, cut the chicken, through the bones, into 2-inch pieces as for Red-Cooked Chicken (page 181). Blanch them in boiling water for 1 minute. Rinse them in cold water, and drain thoroughly.

2. Place all the ingredients in a soup pot. Heat until the liquid is boiling. Reduce the heat to low, and simmer, uncovered, for 1½ hours. Periodically skim any impurities from the surface. Strain the broth through cheesecloth, removing the chicken pieces and reserving them for another use. The broth will keep, refrigerated in an airtight container, for up to 1 week. It may also be frozen.

Shrimp Ball Soup

Xia Wan Tang

6 Servings

1   pound medium-sized raw shrimp, shelled
½   ounce pork fat, chopped to a smooth paste (optional)

Shrimp-Paste Seasonings
1   egg white, lightly beaten
1   tablespoon rice wine or sake
1   teaspoon minced gingerroot
1   teaspoon minced scallions
3   tablespoons cornstarch
1   teaspoon salt

F EW SOUPS COMPARE IN *delicacy and beauty to this one. With its fluffy, pink shrimp balls, crisp snow peas and subtly seasoned broth, it will surely impress even the most sophisticated gourmet.*

Soup Base

6   cups chicken broth, preferably Chinese Chicken Broth (above)
2   tablespoons rice wine or sake
1   teaspoon salt

¼   pound snow peas, ends snapped and veiny strings removed

Thickener

¼   cup water
2   tablespoons cornstarch

1   teaspoon sesame oil
2   tablespoons minced Chinese ham, Smithfield ham or prosciutto

1. Devein the shrimp, rinse lightly, and drain thoroughly. Place the shrimp in a dishtowel, and squeeze out as much moisture as possible. Mince the shrimp to a paste with two cleavers or in a food processor fitted with the steel blade. Place the shrimp paste in a mixing bowl, add the pork fat, if using, and the *Shrimp-Paste Seasonings*, and stir vigorously in one direction to blend the ingredients. Lightly throw the mixture against the inside of the bowl to combine evenly. Refrigerate the shrimp paste for 1 hour; then shape it into 1-inch balls.

2. Heat a large pot, add the *Soup Base*, and heat until boiling. Add the shrimp balls, and heat the mixture until boiling. Lower the heat to medium, and cook for about 3 minutes, or until the balls rise to the surface. Skim the soup to remove impurities. Turn up the heat to high, and add the snow peas and the *Thickener*, stirring constantly to prevent lumps. When the soup has thickened to the consistency of heavy cream, add the sesame oil, stir lightly, and transfer the soup to a tureen. Sprinkle the minced ham over the soup, and serve immediately.

Stuffed Shrimp
& Cucumber Soup

Xia Gua Tang

6 Servings

1¼   pounds medium-sized raw shrimp, shelled

Shrimp Marinade

2   slices gingerroot, the size of a quarter, smashed with the flat side of a cleaver

2   scallions, smashed with the flat side of a cleaver

1   tablespoon rice wine or sake

½   teaspoon salt

Shrimp-Paste Seasonings

10   water chestnuts, plunged briefly into boiling water, refreshed in cold water and chopped to a coarse paste

1   teaspoon pork fat, minced to a smooth paste (optional)

½   egg white, lightly beaten

1   teaspoon minced gingerroot

1½   tablespoons cornstarch

½   teaspoon salt

2   English (gourmet seedless) cucumbers or 4-5 small pickling cucumbers

2   tablespoons cornstarch

Soup Base

6   cups chicken broth, preferably Chinese Chicken Broth (page 345)

2   tablespoons rice wine or sake

1   teaspoon sesame oil

1   teaspoon salt

¼   teaspoon freshly ground white pepper

1   tablespoon minced scallion greens

*C*HEFS FROM F*UJIAN* IN *eastern China are known for their clear soups and delicate broths, which often contain fish and seafood garnishes, since this eastern province borders the sea. This soup, with its delicate flavor and attractive appearance, illustrates the refinement of this regional cuisine. Pork fat is often added to the shrimp paste to give it body.*

1. Rinse the shrimp lightly, and drain thoroughly. Place the shrimp in a dish-towel, and squeeze out as much moisture as possible. Refrigerate the shrimp for 1 hour. Divide the shrimp into a ¾-pound portion and a ½-pound portion. Set the

½-pound portion aside. Deeply score the remaining shrimp down the back to within ¼ inch of each end, removing the vein and creating a pocket. Place the shrimp in a bowl. Pinch the gingerroot and scallions in the *Shrimp Marinade* repeatedly for several minutes to impart their flavors. Add the shrimp marinade to the ¾-pound portion of shrimp, toss lightly, and let marinate for 20 minutes. Discard the scallions and gingerroot.

2. Devein the remaining ½ pound of shrimp. Using 2 cleavers or a food processor fitted with the steel blade, mince the shrimp to a smooth paste. Place the shrimp paste in a mixing bowl, add the *Shrimp-Paste Seasonings*, and stir vigorously in one direction. Lightly throw the mixture against the inside of the bowl to combine evenly. Refrigerate the shrimp paste for 30 minutes.

3. Cut the cucumbers in half lengthwise, remove any seeds, and cut each half crosswise into three sections. Roll-cut each section into 1-inch pieces.

4. Lightly dust the pocket of one whole shrimp with cornstarch, and stuff the cavity with a heaping tablespoon of shrimp paste. Using the underside of a spoon dipped in water, smooth the surface of the shrimp paste. Repeat for each shrimp. Arrange the shrimp, stuffed side up, on a greased heatproof plate, and put the plate in a steamer tray.

5. Fill a wok with water level with the bottom edge of the steamer tray, and heat until boiling. Place the steamer tray over the boiling water, cover, and steam for 6 minutes over high heat. Remove the plate from the steamer tray.

6. Pour the *Soup Base* into a pot, and heat until boiling. Add the cucumber pieces, and cook for about 2 minutes, until the cucumber is just tender. Skim the surface to remove any impurities. Add the stuffed shrimp, and cook for 1 minute. Transfer the soup to a tureen, garnish with the scallion greens, and serve immediately.

Crabmeat & Corn Soup

Xie Rou Yu Mi Tang

6 Servings

¾   pound fresh lump crabmeat or frozen crabmeat, thawed

Crabmeat Marinade
1   tablespoon rice wine or sake
1   teaspoon minced gingerroot
½   teaspoon salt

2   egg whites, lightly beaten
1   tablespoon water

Soup Base
6   cups chicken broth, preferably Chinese Chicken Broth (page 345)
2   tablespoons rice wine or sake
1   teaspoon salt

1½   17-ounce cans creamed corn

Thickener
¼   cup water
2½   tablespoons cornstarch

1   teaspoon sesame oil

MOST AMERICANS ARE *familiar with the classic Cantonese corn soup because it appears on the menus of many American Cantonese restaurants. In this flavorful variation of the classic, the minced chicken breast of the original recipe is replaced by lump crabmeat. With the creamed corn, the overall effect is a memorable combination of flavors and colors.*

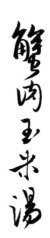

1. Pick over the crabmeat, discarding any pieces of shell or cartilage. If the crabmeat has been frozen, squeeze out any excess water. Shred the crabmeat, using your fingers. Place the crabmeat in a bowl, add the *Crabmeat Marinade*, toss lightly, and let marinate for 20 minutes. Beat the egg whites with the tablespoon of water until frothy.

2. Place the *Soup Base* in a large pot. Heat until boiling, and add the creamed corn. Heat again until boiling, and add the *Thickener*, stirring constantly to prevent lumps. Add the crabmeat, and simmer for 30 seconds. Turn off the heat, and slowly add the egg whites in a thin stream around the edge of the pot. Stir once or twice, add the sesame oil, toss lightly, and transfer the soup to a tureen. Serve immediately.

Chicken & Pickled Cucumber Soup

Hua Gua Dun Ji

6 Servings

IN THIS SIMPLE YET CLASSIC soup, the tender chicken and seasoned broth contrast beautifully with the crisp pickled cucumbers. This is one soup that should be served in the traditional Chinese manner—toward the end of the meal. The soothing broth aids digestion and refreshes the palate.

1	whole roasting chicken, 3½-4 pounds

Soup Base

6	cups water
¼	cup rice wine or sake
3	slices gingerroot, the size of a quarter, smashed with the flat side of a cleaver
3	scallions, smashed with the flat side of a cleaver
¾	teaspoon salt
½	cup canned Chinese pickled cucumbers
¼	cup brine from pickled cucumbers

1. Remove the fat from the cavity and neck of the chicken. Rinse the chicken lightly, and using a heavy knife or a cleaver, cut it through the bones into 2-inch pieces, as for Red-Cooked Chicken (page 181). Blanch the pieces in boiling water for 1 minute. Rinse in cold water, and drain thoroughly. Place the chicken pieces and the *Soup Base* in a heavy heatproof bowl or a pot. Place it in a steamer tray.

2. Fill a wok with water level with the bottom edge of the steamer tray, and heat until boiling. Place the steamer tray over the boiling water, cover, and steam for 1½ hours over high heat. Check the water level after 1 hour, and add more boiling water to the wok if necessary. (Alternatively, if you do not have a steamer large enough to hold the bowl, you may bake the soup, tightly covered, in a pre-heated 400-degree oven for 1¼ hours.)

3. Uncover the pot, skim any grease and impurities from the surface, and discard the gingerroot and scallions. Add the pickled cucumbers and the brine, cover, and steam for another 10 minutes. Transfer the soup to a tureen, and serve immediately.

Steamed Chicken in Yunnan Pot

Qi Guo Tang

6 Servings ⌒ Main Dish

1	whole frying chicken, about 3 pounds
8	dried Chinese black mushrooms
4	paper-thin slices (about 2 ounces) Chinese ham, Smithfield ham or prosciutto

Soup Base

4	cups boiling water
¼	cup rice wine or sake
½	teaspoon salt
½	teaspoon sugar
3	slices gingerroot, the size of a quarter, smashed with the flat side of a cleaver
3	scallions, smashed with the flat side of a cleaver

1. Using a heavy knife or a cleaver, cut the chicken, through the bones, into 2-inch pieces, as for Red-Cooked Chicken (page 181). Blanch them in boiling water for 1 minute. Rinse in cold water, and drain thoroughly. Soak the dried mushrooms in hot water to cover for 20 minutes. Remove and discard the stems. If the caps are large, cut them in half. Cut the ham slices into 2-inch squares.

2. Arrange the chicken pieces, mushrooms and ham in the bottom of a Yunnan pot 9 inches in diameter. Pour the *Soup Base* on top. Cover the pot, and place it in a steamer tray.

3. Fill a wok with water level with the bottom edge of the steamer tray, and heat until boiling. Place the steamer tray over the boiling water, cover, and steam for 1½ hours over high heat. Check the water level in the wok after 1 hour, and add more boiling water if necessary. (Alternatively, if you do not have a steamer large enough to hold the pot, you may bake the soup, tightly covered, in a preheated 400-degree oven for 1¼ hours.)

4. Remove the pot, skim any fat from the surface, and discard the gingerroot and scallions. Serve the soup directly from the pot.

APART FROM ITS spherical shape and unusual glaze, from outward appearances there seems to be little to distinguish a Yunnan pot from any other casserole. The truly distinctive feature is the cone-shaped chimney in the center of the vessel; it sprays the ingredients with a fine mist of steam, making them tender and juicy. Chicken, squab and a variety of meats and vegetables may be cooked in this unusual pot. Yunnan pots may be purchased at any well-equipped Chinese grocery store. (If a Yunnan pot is unavailable, you may use a tightly covered Dutch oven or casserole.)

Steamed Chicken in Melon Soup

Dong Gua Ji Tang

6 Servings ⁓ Appetizer or Main Dish

THE INSPIRATION FOR
this refined soup is an
age-old recipe that originated in
Suzhou, a city famous for its
stunning scenery, exquisite
cuisine and succulent
watermelons. In the original
recipe, a whole baby watermelon
is hollowed out and used as a
steaming vessel. I like to
substitute ripe cantaloupe or
Cranshaw melon, creating a
superb contrast in flavor to the
Chinese ham or prosciutto and
black mushrooms. Carve out
some of the tender melon as
you eat.

1	whole frying or broiling chicken, about 2½ pounds
10	dried Chinese black mushrooms, soaked in hot water to cover for 20 minutes, stems removed
6	paper-thin slices Chinese ham or prosciutto, about ¼ pound

Soup Broth

5	cups boiling water
½	cup rice wine or sake
6	scallions, smashed with the flat side of a cleaver
6	slices gingerroot, the size of a quarter, smashed with the flat side of a cleaver

6	small ripe cantaloupes, about 1 pound each

1. Remove any fat from the cavity opening and around the neck of the chicken. Rinse lightly, and drain. Using a heavy knife or a cleaver, cut the chicken, through the bones, into 1½-inch square pieces, as for Red-Cooked Chicken (page 181). Heat 2 quarts of water until boiling, and blanch the chicken pieces for 1 minute to clean them. Remove the pieces, rinse in cold water, and drain. Cut the mushroom caps in half, and cut the ham slices into 1-inch squares.

2. Place the chicken pieces, black mushrooms, Chinese ham and *Soup Broth* in a heatproof pot or 2-quart soufflé dish. Cover tightly with plastic wrap and place in the bottom of a steamer tray.

3. Fill a wok with water level with the bottom edge of the steamer tray, and heat until boiling. Place the steamer tray over the boiling water, cover, and steam 1½ hours over high heat, replenishing the water if necessary. Periodically skim off any grease from the surface of the soup. (Alternatively, if you do not have a steamer large enough to hold the pot, you may bake the soup, tightly covered, in a preheated 400-degree oven for 1¼ hours.) Remove the soup pot from the steamer. Discard the ginger and scallions. Keep the soup warm.

4. Using a sharp knife, cut a very thin wedge from the bottom of each melon so it will stand upright. Cut off the top quarter of each melon, rinse, drain, and set aside. Scoop out and discard the seeds from inside each melon, leaving all but ½ inch of the flesh around the shell. Place the melons in a steamer tray or trays

and ladle as much of the chicken-soup mixture into them as possible. Cover and steam for 12 to 15 minutes, or until the melons are soft but firm enough to hold their shape. Remove the melons and place in bowls. Pour the soup into the melons, and serve.

Bean Sprout & Sparerib Soup

Ya Cai Pai Gu Tang

6 Servings

1	pound spareribs
1½	tablespoons peanut, safflower or corn oil
1	tablespoon minced scallions
1	medium-sized tomato, peeled, seeded and diced
1	tablespoon soy sauce

Soup Base

6	cups chicken broth, preferably Chinese Chicken Broth (page 345)
3	tablespoons rice wine or sake
3	slices gingerroot, the size of a quarter, smashed with the flat side of a cleaver
1	teaspoon salt
½	pound soybean sprouts, rinsed lightly and drained

1. Direct the butcher to cut the spareribs into shorter lengths so that they are 1½ to 2 inches long. Separate the ribs, cutting between the bones. Blanch the ribs in boiling water for 1 minute. Rinse in cold water, and drain thoroughly.

2. Heat a wok, add the oil, and heat until very hot. Add the minced scallions, and stir-fry for about 10 seconds, until fragrant. Add the diced tomato, and stir-fry for 1 minute, stirring constantly over high heat. Add the soy sauce, toss lightly, cook for about 15 seconds, and remove the mixture.

3. Place the *Soup Base* in a large pot, and heat until boiling. Add the spareribs, and heat until boiling. Reduce the heat to low, and simmer, uncovered, for 30 minutes, skimming occasionally to remove impurities. Remove and discard the gingerroot. Add the tomato mixture and the soybean sprouts. Continue cooking for 20 minutes, skimming occasionally. Taste for seasoning, and adjust soy sauce if necessary. Transfer the soup to a tureen, and serve immediately.

ONE MIGHT ASSUME *from the mild and delicate flavor of this soup that it is from eastern or northern China. Surprisingly enough, it is from Sichuan province, in the west. My Sichuanese teacher was fond of serving this dish after several fiery main courses; its soothing broth and pleasing textures refresh the palate after the spicy seasonings. Mung bean sprouts may be substituted for soybean sprouts, but they should be added at the end and cooked for only 1 to 2 minutes.*

Duck Soup With Cabbage & Cellophane Noodles

Bai Cai Ya Tang

6 Servings

1	carcass from Peking duck or bones from a duck weighing about 2½ pounds
2	ounces cellophane noodles (bean threads)

Soup Base

8	cups water
3	tablespoons rice wine or sake
2	slices gingerroot, the size of a quarter, smashed with the flat side of a cleaver
2	scallions, smashed with the flat side of a cleaver
4	cups Chinese cabbage (Napa), stem sections removed and leaves cut into 2-inch squares

Soup Seasonings

1	teaspoon sesame oil
1	teaspoon salt
½	teaspoon freshly ground black pepper

WASTE IS AKIN TO blasphemy in the Chinese culture. The carcass of a Peking duck, for example, although stripped of its meat and skin, is never discarded. Instead, it is thrown into a pot of water with seasonings, cabbage and cellophane noodles and cooked at a ferocious pace. This dish is then served as the last course of a traditional Peking duck dinner. For those who don't happen to have the carcass of a Peking duck on hand, any cooked duck or turkey carcass will do nicely.

1. Using a heavy knife or a cleaver, cut the duck carcass, through the bones, into 2-inch pieces. Soften the cellophane noodles for 10 minutes in hot water to cover. Drain, and cut them into 6-inch lengths.

2. Place the duck carcass pieces in a heavy pot. Add the *Soup Base*, and heat until boiling. Reduce the heat to medium-low, and cook the soup for 45 minutes, uncovered. Skim any grease from the surface. Add the cabbage and the cellophane noodles. Cook for 30 minutes longer, and add the *Soup Seasonings*. Toss lightly to combine, and transfer the soup to a tureen. Serve immediately.

Hot & Sour Soup

Suan La Tang

6 Servings

6	dried Chinese black mushrooms
10	dried wood ears
½	pound boneless center-cut pork loin

Pork Marinade

1	teaspoon soy sauce
1	teaspoon rice wine or sake
½	teaspoon sesame oil
1	teaspoon cornstarch
2	squares firm tofu, about 2 pounds

Soup Base

6	cups chicken broth, preferably Chinese Chicken Broth (page 345)
2	tablespoons rice wine or sake
1	teaspoon salt
½	teaspoon sugar

Thickener

6	tablespoons water
3½	tablespoons cornstarch

Soup Seasonings

3	tablespoons soy sauce
3	tablespoons clear rice vinegar plus more if necessary
1½	teaspoons sesame oil
1	teaspoon freshly ground black pepper
2	tablespoons minced scallions
2	tablespoons minced gingerroot plus more if necessary
2	large eggs, lightly beaten

ALTHOUGH HOT & SOUR *soup has become (at least to my mind) a too familiar selection on Sichuan and Peking restaurant menus, its popularity continues. Perhaps it is the unique blending of flavors and textures that appeals to the American palate. Here is my version of this classic.*

1. Soak the dried mushrooms in hot water to cover for 20 minutes. Soak the wood ears in hot water to cover for 20 minutes. Remove any fat or gristle from the pork loin, and discard. Cut the meat, across the grain, into slices ¼ inch thick.

(You may partially freeze the meat to facilitate cutting.) Cut the slices into matchstick-sized shreds. Place the shreds in a bowl, add the *Pork Marinade*, toss lightly, and let marinate for 10 minutes. Remove and discard the stems of the dried mushrooms. Cut the caps into matchstick-sized shreds. Cut away and discard the hard, bitter nib on the underside of the wood ears, and cut the wood ears into matchstick-sized shreds. Cut the tofu into thin slices and then into matchstick-sized shreds.

2. Place the *Soup Base* in a large pot, and heat until boiling. Add several tablespoons of the hot broth to the pork shreds, and stir to separate; then add the pork shreds to the pot. Heat until boiling, and cook until the pork shreds change color, about 1 minute. Skim any impurities from the surface of the soup. Add the shredded mushrooms, wood ears and tofu. Heat the mixture until boiling, and slowly add the *Thickener*, stirring constantly to prevent lumps. Continue to skim the surface to remove impurities. When the soup has thickened, add the *Soup Seasonings*. Stir to blend, and taste for seasoning. If the soup is not spicy enough, add more vinegar and minced gingerroot. Remove the soup from the heat. Add the eggs, slowly pouring in a thin stream. Stir the soup once in a circular motion. Transfer the soup to a tureen, and serve immediately.

Spinach & Meatball Soup

Bo Cai Rou Wan Tang

6 Servings

¾   pound ground beef, preferably chuck

Meat Seasonings

1   tablespoon soy sauce
1   tablespoon rice wine or sake
1½   teaspoons sesame oil
1   tablespoon minced scallions
1½   teaspoons minced gingerroot
1½   tablespoons cornstarch
½   teaspoon salt

2   ounces cellophane noodles (bean threads)

Soup Base

6   cups chicken broth, preferably Chinese Chicken Broth (page 345)
1   teaspoon salt
¼   teaspoon freshly ground white pepper
½   teaspoon sesame oil

½   pound fresh spinach, trimmed and cleaned

I FIRST SAMPLED THIS SOUP a number of years ago in a Peking restaurant in Taipei. One of my Chinese teachers, a true gourmet, had decided that it was time to introduce me properly to authentic northern cuisine. He invited me to lunch and ordered some of his favorites. This soup was one of his selections, and I have been especially fond of it ever since.

1. Lightly chop the meat until fluffy, and place it in a mixing bowl. Add the *Meat Seasonings* to the ground meat. Stir vigorously in one direction to mix the ingredients. Lightly throw the mixture against the inside of the bowl to combine evenly. Shape the mixture into 1-inch balls. Soften the cellophane noodles for 10 minutes in hot water to cover. Drain, and cut them into 6-inch lengths.

2. Place the *Soup Base* in a large pot, and heat until boiling. Add the meatballs to the broth, and heat until boiling. Cook for about 10 minutes over medium heat, skimming any impurities from the surface. Add the cellophane noodles, and cook for another 5 minutes. Add the spinach, and cook for about 1 minute. Transfer the soup to a tureen, and serve immediately.

Vegetable Beef Soup

Luo Song Tang

6 Servings

WHILE VEGETABLE *beef soup cannot be counted as a bona fide classic in Chinese cuisine, it has become popular all over China. A Chinese friend of mine whose family hails from Peking remembers this as a childhood favorite. The Chinese title gives a hint to the dish's origin: Luo song is a slang expression for "Russian-style."*

1½	pounds chuck or stewing beef, cut into 1½-inch cubes

Soup Base

8	cups water
2	tablespoons rice wine or sake
3	scallions, smashed with the flat side of a cleaver
3	slices gingerroot, the size of a quarter, smashed with the flat side of a cleaver
1	tablespoon peanut, safflower or corn oil
2	medium-sized tomatoes, peeled, seeded and diced
½	cup diced onion
1	tablespoon soy sauce
3	cups Chinese cabbage (Napa), stem sections removed and leaves cut into 2-inch squares
2	medium-sized potatoes, peeled and diced
2	carrots, peeled and diced

Soup Seasonings

1	teaspoon salt
¼	teaspoon freshly ground black pepper
1	teaspoon sesame oil

1. Remove any fat or gristle from the beef, and discard. Blanch the meat in boiling water for 1 minute. Rinse in cold water, and drain thoroughly.

2. Place the beef cubes in a heavy pot, and add the *Soup Base*. Heat the mixture until the liquid is boiling, and reduce the heat to low. Simmer, uncovered, for 1½ hours, skimming occasionally to remove any impurities, until the beef is tender. Discard the gingerroot and scallions.

3. Heat a large soup pot or casserole, add the oil, and heat until very hot. Add the tomatoes and onion. Stir-fry for about 1 minute, until the onion is soft and transparent. Add the soy sauce, and stir-fry for about 30 seconds. Add the cabbage, potatoes and carrots. Toss lightly over high heat for about 1 minute. Add the cooked beef and broth. Heat the mixture until boiling, and reduce the heat to low. Skim any impurities from the surface. Cook, uncovered, for 1 hour. Add the *Soup Seasonings* and stir lightly to blend. Transfer the mixture to a tureen, and serve.

Egg Flower Soup

Dan Hua Tang

6 Servings

1	teaspoon peanut, safflower or corn oil
1½	ripe but firm tomatoes, stems and seeds removed, cut into ¼-inch dice
2	tablespoons minced scallion, white part only
3	tablespoons soy sauce
2	tablespoons rice wine or sake
5	cups chicken broth, preferably Chinese Chicken Broth (page 345)
1½	pounds firm tofu, cut into ¼-inch dice
1	teaspoon salt
¼	teaspoon freshly ground black pepper

Thickener

7	tablespoons water
5	tablespoons cornstarch
2	large eggs, lightly beaten
2	tablespoons minced scallion greens

THIS SOUP IS SO SIMPLE, *yet so good. I find it particularly soothing when I am feeling slightly blue. Serve this soup as a snack or accompanied by fried rice or noodles for a light, but filling lunch or dinner.*

1. Heat a heavy pot or a casserole, add the oil, and heat until very hot. Add the tomatoes and scallion, and stir-fry about 10 seconds, until fragrant. Add the soy sauce and rice wine, and continue stir-frying for a minute. Add the chicken broth, tofu, salt and pepper, and heat until boiling.

2. Add the *Thickener*, stirring constantly to prevent lumps. Skim off any impurities that may have risen to the surface. Turn off the heat, and slowly add the eggs in a thin stream, pouring in a circular manner around the pot. Stir once or twice. Pour into a soup tureen, or portion into individual serving bowls. Sprinkle the minced scallions on top and serve.

Five-Treasure Seafood Fire Pot

Wu Fu Hai Xian Huo Guo

6 Servings ⌒ Main Dish

I LIKE TO DESCRIBE THIS *soup pot as a Chinese-style fondue where assorted seafood and vegetables are dipped in a bubbling-hot broth, then in a pungent dipping sauce. The broth becomes even more flavorful as the meal progresses. At the end of the meal, the noodles are added, and the soup is drunk. I usually like to serve steamed Lotus Buns (page 59) or rice as a staple to round out the meal. If a fire pot is unavailable, you may substitute an electric wok.*

1½	pounds firm-fleshed, skinned fish fillets, such as haddock, scrod, red snapper or pickerel
¾	pound medium-sized raw shrimp, shelled and deveined
¾	pound sea scallops or bay scallops, rinsed and drained

Seafood Marinade

⅓	cup rice wine or sake
1	teaspoon sesame oil
1½	tablespoons minced gingerroot
1	teaspoon salt

1	pound Chinese cabbage (Napa), stems removed and leaves cut into 2-inch squares
1	tablespoon peanut, safflower or corn oil
4	cloves garlic, smashed with the flat side of a cleaver
3	tablespoons rice wine or sake

Soup Base

7	cups chicken broth, preferably Chinese Chicken Broth (page 345)
1	teaspoon salt or to taste

1	ounce cellophane noodles (bean threads)
½	pound fresh shiitake mushrooms, stems trimmed, cut in quarters
½	pound fresh spinach, trimmed and cleaned (optional)

Dipping Sauce

¾	cup light soy sauce
6	tablespoons rice wine or sake
2	tablespoons Chinese black vinegar or Worcestershire sauce
3	tablespoons minced scallions, white part only
2	tablespoons minced gingerroot
2	tablespoons minced garlic
2	tablespoons sugar

1. Holding a cleaver or a sharp knife at a 45-degree angle to the fish, cut the

fillets into paper-thin slices measuring about 2 inches long. Place in a bowl. Score each shrimp along the back so it will "butterfly" when cooked, and place all the shrimp in another bowl. If using sea scallops, holding the cleaver parallel with the cutting surface, slice the scallops in half through the thickness. Place the scallops in a separate bowl. Divide the *Seafood Marinade* evenly among the bowls with the seafood. Toss lightly, and arrange the seafood attractively on a platter, cover with plastic wrap, and refrigerate.

2. Separate the harder pieces of the cabbage from the leafier ones. Heat a Dutch oven or a casserole, add the oil, and heat until very hot. Add the garlic cloves and the harder sections of the cabbage, and stir-fry over high heat for about 1 minute. Add the rice wine, and continue cooking, adding the leafier sections of the cabbage. Add the *Soup Base* and heat until boiling. Reduce the heat to low, and simmer 20 minutes, uncovered.

3. Soften the cellophane noodles in hot water to cover for 10 minutes. Drain, and cut them into 6-inch lengths. Arrange the cellophane noodles, shiitake mushrooms and spinach, if using, on a platter. Place the platters containing the seafood and the vegetables on the table and portion the *Dipping Sauce* into 6 bowls, placing them at each setting.

4. Place a Mongolian fire pot in the middle of the table, setting it on a cutting board and asbestos pad. Prepare the coals for the fire and when they are red-hot, carefully arrange in the fire pot. Pour the soup into the fire pot and heat until boiling.

5. Each diner takes a portion of seafood, dips it into the hot stock until it is cooked, then dips the cooked food into the dipping sauce and eats. The mushrooms and spinach are placed in the hot broth and cooked until done. (The mushrooms will cook in 5 to 6 minutes, but the spinach will take only 1 minute.) Once all the ingredients have been eaten, the noodles are added and cooked, and the soup is consumed.

Steamed Chinese Cabbage Casserole

Gan Bei Dun Bai Cai

6 Servings ~ Main Dish

THE CHINESE CULINARY term "dun" refers to the process of steaming in a closed receptacle. In this case, the cabbage, black mushrooms, ham and shrimp are placed in a heavy pot, and broth is added. The pot is then covered and placed in a steamer, where the mixture gently cooks. In this manner, the flavors of the ingredients are allowed to mingle, and the resulting broth is clear and light.

1	large head Chinese cabbage (Napa), about 2 pounds
1	teaspoon dried shrimp (optional)
6	dried Chinese black mushrooms
4	paper-thin slices (about 2 ounces) Chinese ham, Smithfield ham or prosciutto

Soup Seasonings

2	tablespoons rice wine or sake
1½	teaspoons sesame oil
4	scallions, smashed with the flat side of a cleaver
3	slices gingerroot, the size of a quarter, smashed with the flat side of a cleaver
1	teaspoon salt
4	cups boiling chicken broth, preferably Chinese Chicken Broth (page 345)

1. Cut the cabbage head crosswise in half. Cut away and discard the stem. Cut the cabbage head halves lengthwise into strips about 2 inches wide, but don't separate the leaves. Rinse the dried shrimp, if using, and soak for 1 hour in hot water to cover. Drain, and mince. Soak the black mushrooms in hot water to cover for 20 minutes. Remove and discard the stems. Cut the caps into matchstick-sized shreds. Cut the ham into matchstick-sized shreds.

2. In the bottom of a heavy heatproof bowl or casserole, arrange the cabbage strips, cut edges up, tightly packed to line the bottom. Sprinkle the shredded ham and mushrooms and the minced shrimp on top. Combine the *Soup Seasonings* and the boiling chicken broth, and pour the mixture over the cabbage. Cover the bowl tightly, and place it in a steamer tray.

3. Fill a wok with water level with the bottom edge of the steamer tray, and heat until boiling. Place the steamer tray over the boiling water, cover, and steam for 1 hour over high heat. (Alternatively, if you do not have a steamer large enough to hold the pot, you may bake the soup, tightly covered, in a preheated 400-degree oven for 1 hour.) Remove the bowl from the steamer, skim any fat from the surface, discard the gingerroot and scallions, and serve immediately.

Eight-Treasure Mixed Soup Pot

Sha Guo Dou Fu

6 Servings ⌣ Main Dish

4	cups Chinese cabbage (Napa), stems removed and leaves cut into 2-inch squares
2	tablespoons peanut, safflower or corn oil
2	cloves garlic, smashed with the flat side of a cleaver
1	tablespoon rice wine or sake

Soup Base

6	cups chicken broth, preferably Chinese Chicken Broth (page 345)
2	tablespoons rice wine or sake
1	teaspoon salt
½	pound boneless center-cut pork loin

Pork Marinade

1	teaspoon soy sauce
1	teaspoon rice wine or sake
½	teaspoon sesame oil
1	teaspoon cornstarch
6	dried Chinese black mushrooms
1	ounce cellophane noodles (bean threads)
2	squares firm tofu, about 2 pounds
½	pound medium-sized raw shrimp, shelled

Shrimp Marinade

2	slices gingerroot, the size of a quarter, smashed with the flat side of a cleaver
2	teaspoons rice wine or sake
½	teaspoon salt
2	carrots, roll-cut into 1-inch pieces
¼	pound fresh spinach, trimmed and cleaned
¼	cup scallion greens, diagonally cut into ¼-inch pieces

A VESSEL OF CONSIDERABLE *importance in the preparation of Chinese soups and casseroles is a sandy pot, commonly referred to as a sha guo. This pot is made from a mixture of sand and clay, which is then fired at a very high temperature so that it can withstand direct heat. The pot also conducts heat evenly and efficiently. Tofu and fish heads are both often cooked in this kind of pot. If a sandy pot is unavailable, substitute any heavy casserole or a Dutch oven.*

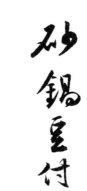

1. Separate the harder cabbage pieces from the leafier ones. Heat a wok, add the oil, and heat until very hot. Add the smashed garlic, and stir-fry for about 5 seconds, until fragrant. Add the harder cabbage pieces, and toss lightly over high heat, adding the tablespoon of rice wine. Stir-fry for about 1 minute, and add the leafier pieces. Stir-fry for about 1 minute more. Add the *Soup Base*. Heat the mixture until boiling, reduce the heat to low, and cook, uncovered, for about 30 minutes. Transfer the cabbage and liquid to a sandy pot, a casserole or a Dutch oven.

2. Meanwhile, remove any fat or gristle from the pork loin, and discard. Cut the meat, across the grain, into slices about ⅛ inch thick. (You may partially freeze the meat to facilitate cutting.) Cut the slices into 2-inch squares. Place the meat in a bowl, add the *Pork Marinade*, toss lightly, and marinate for 20 minutes. Soak the dried mushrooms in hot water to cover for 20 minutes. Soak the cellophane noodles in hot water to cover for 15 minutes. Drain, and cut them into 6-inch lengths. Remove and discard the stems of the mushrooms. Cut the tofu into 1-inch dice.

3. Devein and rinse the shrimp. Pat dry, and place in a bowl. Pinch the gingerroot slices in the *Shrimp Marinade* to impart their flavor. Discard the gingerroot. Add the shrimp marinade to the shrimp. Toss lightly, and let marinate 20 minutes.

4. Arrange the meat slices, tofu, black mushrooms, cellophane noodles and carrots separately, each in its own spot, over the cabbage, leaving a place for the shrimp and the spinach. Cover the pot, and cook for 20 minutes over medium heat. Uncover, arrange the shrimp and the spinach on top of the cabbage, and sprinkle the scallion greens over all. Cover, and cook for another 5 minutes. Serve directly from the pot.

Mongolian Beef Fire Pot

Shuan Niu Rou

6 Servings ⌒ Main Dish

ONGOLIAN FIRE POT *was introduced to Peking (and China) by the northern people of Mongolia. It soon became universally popular all over China, and regional variations resulted. Eastern chefs developed a "10-varieties hot pot," with meat and seafood garnishes, and the Cantonese created a "chrysanthemum fire*

| 1½ | pounds top sirloin of beef, cut across the grain into paper-thin slices |

Meat Marinade

1½	tablespoons soy sauce
1	tablespoon rice wine or sake
1	teaspoon sesame oil

1	pound Chinese cabbage (Napa), stems removed and leaves cut into 2-inch squares
2	tablespoons peanut, safflower or corn oil
2	cloves garlic, smashed with the flat side of a cleaver

Soup Base

6	cups chicken broth, preferably Chinese Chicken Broth (page 345)
2	tablespoons rice wine or sake
1	teaspoon salt
2	ounces cellophane noodles (bean threads)
2	squares firm tofu, about 2 pounds
1	pound fresh button mushrooms, rinsed, drained and stems trimmed
½	pound fresh spinach, trimmed and cleaned

Dipping Sauce (For One Person)

2	tablespoons soy sauce
1	tablespoon rice wine or sake
1	teaspoon Chinese black vinegar or Worcestershire sauce
½	teaspoon chili oil (optional)
½	teaspoon fermented tofu (optional)
½	tablespoon minced scallions
1	teaspoon minced gingerroot
1	teaspoon minced garlic
1	teaspoon sugar

1. Place the beef slices in a bowl, add the *Meat Marinade*, toss lightly, and arrange the slices attractively on a platter.

2. Separate the harder cabbage pieces from the leafier ones. Heat a wok, add the oil, and heat until very hot. Add the garlic. Stir-fry briefly. Add the harder cabbage pieces. Stir-fry about 1 minute over high heat, adding a tablespoon of the *Soup Base*. Add the leafy cabbage. Stir-fry another minute. Add the remaining soup base. Heat to boiling. Reduce heat to low. Simmer, uncovered, 20 minutes.

3. Soften the cellophane noodles for 10 minutes in hot water to cover. Drain, and cut into 6-inch lengths. Cut the tofu into 1-inch dice. Arrange the mushrooms, tofu, spinach and cellophane noodles attractively on platters. Make the *Dipping Sauce*. Place the platters containing the meat and vegetables on a table where a heated Mongolian fire pot has been set up. (Or use a pot and a hot plate or an electric skillet or an electric wok.) Put a bowl of dipping sauce at each place.

4. Pour the soup base into the fire pot, and heat until boiling. Each diner takes a slice of meat, dips it into the hot soup until the meat is cooked, then dips the meat into the dipping sauce and eats. The tofu, mushrooms and spinach are placed in the stock a little at a time and cooked until done. The diners may help themselves to these ingredients, once again dipping them in the sauce before eating. The tofu and mushrooms should cook in 5 to 6 minutes, but the spinach should take only 1 minute. Once all the ingredients have been eaten, the noodles are added, cooked, and consumed with the flavorful soup.

pot," made with edible chrysanthemum petals. Today, the traditional "rinsed lamb" fire pot, so named because the lamb is dipped into the hot broth, has inspired a "rinsed beef" rendition. This filling dish may be served as a meal in itself. Here is my adapted version. Fire pots are sold at many Asian markets and at many cookware stores. If one is unavailable, improvise with an electric wok.

Sweets

ON THE FIFTEENTH DAY OF THE eighth month of the lunar calendar, when the moon is reputed to be at its maximum brightness, Chinese people the world over gather to celebrate the birthday of the moon. Some honor this holiday, called the Moon Festival or Mid-Autumn Festival, by exchanging gifts with relatives, friends and business associates. Others present offerings to departed spirits and burn incense to "heaven and earth." And everyone eats moon cakes—often while gazing at the moon.

The Chinese bakeries, all of which manufacture these holiday cakes, start their preparations for this festival weeks in advance. The usual confections that line the shelves are cleaned off, and pyramid-shaped mountains of numerous varieties of moon cakes replace them. A scarlet paper banner on each pile proclaims the name of the cakes in bold, black Chinese characters: red bean paste, lotus seed paste and eight-treasure moon cakes are just a few; the selection is extraordinary. The cakes may be moon-shaped or molded into the form of a rabbit, fish, pagoda or horse and rider. While most are simply brushed with an egg glaze, producing a golden crust, it is not uncommon to find red, green and brown food coloring used—and, in rare instances, gold leaf. Some cakes contain a salty duck egg yolk in the center, which provides a savory contrast to the sweet filling. Savory moon cakes filled with pork and vegetables are also available. As with other foods, there are regional versions of moon cakes, with various fillings and crusts.

Aside from their taste appeal, moon cakes are especially popular because of their influential role in Chinese history; they were instrumental in delivering the Chinese from Mongolian rule during the latter part of the Yüan dynasty (1271 to 1368). Concealed within the cakes, messages and plans for an uprising were passed from household to household. As a result of the rebellion, the Mongolian rulers were successfully overthrown, and the event marked the beginning of the Ming dynasty (1368 to 1644).

Like moon cakes, a number of other pastries and cakes play a prominent role in the Chinese diet and culture. Along with fruits, these foods constitute the varied and extensive category of Chinese sweets. Many confections are traditional holiday specialties, prepared in observance of age-old festivals and customs: longevity peach buns are served on birthdays; red and white stuffed sweet rice balls are prepared for the Chinese New Year, and sweet *zong zi*, sweet rice dumplings wrapped in bamboo leaves, are reserved for the Dragon Boat Festival. Unlike western ones, Chinese cakes and pastries are not necessarily served as desserts; most commonly, they are served with tea as snacks and as entremets during a traditional Chinese banquet. Because their flavor and texture is usually quite different from those of the dishes that precede them, they serve to refresh the palate. Fruits—by themselves or in soups, sweet salads and other preparations—are served more often as desserts.

It appears that the concept of cakes was

introduced to ancient China from the West; yet once the Chinese chefs had mastered the foreign techniques, they applied them using local products to create a diverse repertory. As in western pastries, flour and eggs are the basic ingredients in many Chinese sweets. But unlike western confections, lard rather than butter or margarine is the usual shortening, and rice and vegetables are common ingredients. Pastes made from red beans, lotus seeds, dates or sesame seeds form typical fillings. Various nuts (walnuts, almonds and peanuts) and seeds (olive kernels, apricot kernels, sesame seeds and watermelon seeds) are also important.

The earliest Chinese cakes were made with honey and maltose, a malt sugar made from barley. The process of refining sugar cane was introduced from India during the seventh century, and it was later that the Chinese were able to produce the fine powdered sugar—they called it sugar frost—that is used today.

Cakes and pastries became very popular in ancient China and remain so to this day. Crullers, rice cakes and deep-fried puff pastries dusted with sugar are made in much the same manner today as they were ages ago. So are milk cakes and sweetmeats eaten in observance of the Festival of the Dead and sweet cakes prepared for the Buddhist holidays.

Whereas most westerners prefer sweet cakes and pastries for dessert, the Chinese, as mentioned above, are partial to ending their meals with fruit.

A wealth of fruits was available in different parts of China as early as the T'ang dynasty (618 to 907). Peaches and grapes, introduced from central Asia, flourished in the north, as did jujubes (Chinese dates), crab apples, grapes, quinces, loquats (the fruit of an Asian evergreen—a cross between a kumquat and an apricot), pears and plums. Tangerines, kumquats and oranges thrived in the warmer western provinces. The "Canton" orange, grown in Sichuan and Hubei, was a particularly popular strain. Later, this variety was introduced to Europe, where it spawned Seville, Valencia and navel oranges. Canton and the southern provinces produced lychees, longans (similar to lychees), rambutans (a type of Chinese strawberry) and bananas. These fruits were consumed fresh, candied in honey and sugar or preserved by drying. Some were used in savory dishes, but most were served at the end of a meal, demonstrating their early importance in the Chinese diet as a dessert.

Most fruits also retain a symbolic role and are used as offerings in Chinese ritual and worship. The apple signifies harmony and peace. The orange symbolizes abundant happiness and prosperity. The peach is emblematic of marriage and immortality and the plum of winter and longevity.

The recipes in this chapter represent a sampling of traditional and contemporary sweets.

Almond Bean Curd With Fruit

Xin Ren Dou Fu

6 Servings

DURING THE HOT AND
humid summers in
eastern, western and southern
China, cold fruit salads and
sweet soups garnished with fruit
are popular snacks. Pineapple,
mangoes and papayas—in
addition to lychees and loquats—
are traditionally served in this
classic salad. The milky white
squares of almond curd are said
to bear a resemblance to bean
curd; hence the title.

2½	tablespoons unflavored gelatin
3	cups water
¼	cup sugar
½	cup sweetened condensed milk
½	tablespoon almond extract
1	15-ounce can lychees in syrup
1	15-ounce can loquats in syrup
2	cups fresh fruit of choice, cut into balls or 1-inch squares
3	tablespoons kirsch (optional)

1. Soften the gelatin in ½ cup of the water. Heat the mixture slightly, stirring
constantly to dissolve the gelatin. Place the sugar, condensed milk and almond
extract in a mixing bowl, and stir to blend. Slowly add the remaining 2½ cups of
water, stirring to dissolve the sugar. Add the dissolved gelatin, and stir again.
Pour the mixture into a chilled 9-inch round or square pan. Place the pan in the
refrigerator, and let the almond curd chill for at least 4 hours, or until firmly set.

2. In a large bowl, combine the lychees and loquats in syrup with the fresh
fruit. Add the kirsch, if using, toss lightly, and let macerate for 1 hour in the
refrigerator. Cut the almond curd into 1½-inch diamond-shaped pieces, and
carefully fold them into the fruit. Serve immediately.

Steamed Pears in Honey

Mi Zhi Li Zi

6 Servings

1	cup dried jujubes (Chinese dates)
6	nearly ripe Anjou or Bosc pears
6	tablespoons honey

1. Soften the jujubes for 1 hour in hot water to cover, changing the water twice. Drain the jujubes, and remove the pits. Cut the jujubes crosswise into thin strips.

2. Cut a thin slice off the bottom of each pear so that it will stand upright. Cut a piece about 1 inch deep off the top of each pear, and set aside. Using a fruit corer or a sharp paring knife, remove the core of each pear, being careful not to cut through to the bottom.

3. Arrange the pears upright on a heatproof plate. Spoon a tablespoon of honey into each cavity, and add some of the sliced jujubes to each one. Place the reserved tops on the pears, and if necessary, fasten them securely with toothpicks. Place the plate in a steamer tray.

4. Fill a wok with water level with the bottom edge of the steamer tray, and heat until boiling. Place the steamer tray over the boiling water, cover, and steam over high heat for 30 minutes, or until the pears are tender when pierced with a knife. Serve the pears hot or cold.

IN ANCIENT CHINA, THE *sweetest pears were reputed to be grown in the northern province of Shanxi. There, the trees thrived in the moderate climate and fertile soil. Jujubes, also known as Chinese dates, flourished in this area too. This recipe, popular for centuries, combines the flavors of these two fruits.*

Candied Apple Fritters

Ba Si Ping Guo

6 Servings

1	cup all-purpose flour
½	cup cornstarch
2	large eggs, lightly beaten
1¼	cups ice water
4	medium-sized Delicious or Granny Smith apples
½	lemon
4	cups peanut, safflower or corn oil
1½	cups sugar
½	cup water
2	tablespoons untoasted sesame seeds

*S*NACKING IS VERY MUCH *a part of the daily routine in modern China. Concessions offering candy, fruits and nuts are everywhere for the enjoyment of natives and tourists alike. In Peking, caramelized crab apples are among the snacks available, and in restaurants, candied apple fritters, a more formal dish, are served frequently as a dessert. In the south, where tropical fruits thrive, an equally delicious variation using bananas is common. Few desserts are as appealing: slices of the fruit are batter-fried, tossed lightly in caramel and served immediately with ice water. The fruit is dipped in the water, and the caramel hardens immediately.*

1. Place the flour and cornstarch in a mixing bowl. Slowly add the eggs, and beat vigorously with a whisk to combine evenly. Add the 1¼ cups ice water, whisking again to prevent lumps from forming. Refrigerate the batter for 20 minutes.

2. Peel and core the apples. Rub the apples with a cut lemon half to prevent them from turning brown. Grease a large platter with oil. Prepare a bowl of ice water, into which the caramelized apples will be dipped.

3. Cut each apple in half, and cut each half into 4 wedges. Add the apple slices to the batter, and stir to coat the pieces.

4. Heat a wok, add the 4 cups of oil, and heat the oil to 350 degrees F. Slide a batch of the apple slices into the hot oil, and turn them over, removing any drips of batter from the oil. Deep-fry the slices for about 1½ minutes, turning constantly until pale golden. Remove with a handled strainer or slotted spoon, and drain. Reheat the oil, add the remaining apple slices, and deep-fry them in the same manner. Heat the oil to 425 degrees.

5. Place the 1½ cups sugar and the ½ cup water in another wok or a saucepan. Heat slowly until the sugar has dissolved, stirring occasionally; once the sugar has dissolved, however, do not stir. Continue cooking the mixture over medium heat, occasionally brushing down the sides of the pan with a brush dipped in water (this will prevent crystals from forming). When the mixture has turned a light golden color (310 degrees on a candy thermometer) and a chopstick dipped in the caramel spins a thin thread when lifted from the caramel, turn the heat to the lowest setting.

6. Quickly deep-fry all the apples a second time in the hot oil until they are golden brown and crisp, about ½ minute. Remove the apples with a slotted

spoon and place them in the caramel. Working quickly, sprinkle the sesame seeds on the apples, and carefully toss the apples so that they are evenly coated with the caramel. Transfer the apples to the greased platter, and serve immediately. Before eating, dip the apple slices in the ice water to harden the caramel.

Variation: Candied Banana Fritters **(Ba Si Xiang Jiao)**

Use 6 just-ripe bananas roll-cut into 1½-inch pieces in place of the apple slices. Proceed in the same manner as above.

Almond Cookies

Xing Ren Bing

25 Cookies

½	cup unsalted butter or shortening, softened to room temperature
¾	cup granulated sugar
1	large egg
1¼	cups all-purpose flour
½	teaspoon baking soda
½	teaspoon salt
1	cup finely chopped almonds
1	teaspoon almond extract
1	large egg, lightly beaten, for brushing on cookies
36	whole blanched almonds

1. Preheat the oven to 350 degrees F. In a mixing bowl, cream the butter and sugar for about 5 minutes. Add the egg, and continue beating until smooth. Sift together the flour, baking soda and salt. Slowly add the dry ingredients to the butter mixture, and mix until smooth. Add the chopped almonds and the almond extract. Mix until smooth.

2. Drop tablespoons of the cookie batter onto a lightly buttered baking sheet, spacing them about 1 inch apart. Dip your thumb in some flour, and make an indentation in the center of each cookie. Brush each cookie with the beaten egg, and place a whole almond in the center of each indentation. Bake for 10 to 12 minutes, until the cookies are golden brown and puffed. Let cool slightly; then transfer to a cooling rack. Serve when cooled.

W*HILE COOKIES, LIKE many western pastries, were not indigenous to China, once introduced, they were quickly embraced with a vengeance. Almond Cookies have now become a staple sweet in Chinese bakeries from Boston to Hong Kong. I like to use sweet butter, in place of lard, making a richer, but still crisp cookie.*

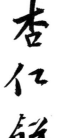

Walnut Cookies

He Tao Bing

30 Cookies

L IKE ALMONDS, WALNUTS *appear in both sweet and savory dishes. First introduced from the West during the T'ang dynasty, they are particularly popular in the south, where these cookies originated. The crisp wafers are excellent with tea.*

2¼	cups all-purpose flour
1	teaspoon salt
1	teaspoon baking soda
1	cup butter, softened to room temperature
1	cup light brown sugar, tightly packed
2	large eggs, lightly beaten
1½	teaspoons vanilla extract

Glaze

1	large egg, lightly beaten
1	tablespoon water
30	walnut halves

1. Sift together the flour, salt and baking soda. In a bowl, cream the butter and brown sugar until light, about 5 minutes. Add the eggs, and mix until they are evenly incorporated. Add the dry ingredients and the vanilla extract. Using a wooden spoon, mix to a smooth dough.

2. Drop the dough, by heaping tablespoonfuls, onto a greased baking sheet. Dip your thumb in flour, and make an indentation in the center of each cookie. Brush the cookies with the *Glaze* and place a walnut half in each indentation.

3. Preheat the oven to 350 degrees F. Bake the cookies for 10 to 12 minutes, until puffed and golden brown. Cool on a rack, and serve.

Date-Filled Crisps

Zao Ni Bing

24 Filled Cookies

Crust

4	cups all-purpose flour
¾	cup dried milk powder
1	tablespoon baking powder
1	teaspoon salt
3	large eggs
1¼	cups sugar
¾	cup butter, melted and cooled to room temperature
1	teaspoon vanilla extract

Filling

1	pound chopped pitted dates
4	cups hot water
½	cup butter
2	teaspoons freshly squeezed lemon juice
1½	teaspoons ground cinnamon

Glaze

1	large egg, lightly beaten
1	tablespoon water

½	cup pine nuts

*D*ATES ARE A POPULAR *fruit in China and are used in sweet pastries and soups. I like to make my own date paste, enriching the mixture with butter and cinnamon. It then becomes the filling for numerous steamed buns and pastries.*

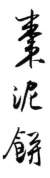

1. To make the *Crust*, sift together the flour, dried milk powder, baking powder and salt. Break the eggs into a mixing bowl, add the sugar, and beat vigorously until the mixture "ribbons" off the beaters, about 5 minutes. Add the melted butter, vanilla extract and the sifted dry ingredients to the egg mixture, folding after each addition. Mix to a rough dough, turn out onto a lightly floured surface, and knead briefly to a smooth dough. Form the dough into a long, snake-like roll, and cut it into 24 pieces.

2. To make the *Filling*, place the dates in a saucepan with the hot water. Heat until boiling, and reduce the heat to low. Let the mixture simmer for about 15 minutes, stirring occasionally, until the water has evaporated. Continue cooking and stirring until the paste is thick and sticky. Add the butter, and continue cooking, stirring constantly, until the mixture comes away from the sides of the pan. Remove from the heat, and add the lemon juice and cinnamon. Stir to

blend, and let cool. Divide into 24 portions.

3. Press each dough piece into a 3-inch circle with the edges thinner and the center thicker. Place a portion of the filling in the center of one circle, and gather up the edges of the dough to enclose the filling. Pinch the edges to seal. Roll the filled dough into a ball, and flatten it to a 2½-inch round. Make the remaining cookies in the same manner. Arrange the cookies on 2 lightly greased baking sheets, spacing them about 1 inch apart. Brush the surface of each cookie with the *Glaze*, and sprinkle a few pine nuts in the center.

4. Preheat the oven to 375 degrees F. Bake the cookies for about 30 minutes, until golden brown. Cool on a rack, and serve.

Moon Cakes

Yue Bing

24 Moon Cakes

Crust

4	cups all-purpose flour
¾	cup dried milk powder
1	tablespoon baking powder
1	teaspoon salt
3	large eggs
1¼	cups sugar
¾	cup butter, melted and cooled to room temperature
1½	teaspoons vanilla extract

Filling

1	cup chopped pitted dates
1	cup coarsely chopped walnuts or pecans
1	cup apricot preserves
½	cup sweetened flaked coconut
½	cup raisins

Glaze

1	large egg, lightly beaten
2	tablespoons water

ALTHOUGH MOON CAKES *are made with both sweet and savory fillings, the sweet variety seems to be more popular and more readily available in the United States. The moon cake, with its fillings of dried fruits and assorted sweetmeats, is especially relished by the Chinese. These filled cakes have a buttery outer crust and a delicious raisin-apricot filling.*

1. To make the *Crust*, sift together the flour, dried milk powder, baking powder and salt. Break the eggs into a mixing bowl, add the sugar, and beat vigorously until the mixture "ribbons" off the beaters, about 5 minutes. Add the melted butter, vanilla extract and the sifted dry ingredients to the egg mixture, folding after each addition. Mix to a rough dough, turn out onto a lightly floured surface, and knead briefly to a smooth dough. Form the dough into a long, snake-like roll, and cut it into 24 pieces.

2. Mix together the *Filling*, and stir to combine evenly. Divide into 24 portions.

3. Preheat the oven to 375 degrees F. Lightly grease 2 baking sheets. Using your fingers, press each dough piece into a 3-inch circle with the edges thinner and the center thicker. Place a portion of filling in the center, gather up the edges of the dough to enclose the filling, and pinch to seal. Roll the cake into a ball, and flatten it to a 3-inch round. Carve a crisscross design on top. Arrange the cakes about 1 inch apart on the baking sheets. Brush the surface with the *Glaze*. Bake the cakes for about 30 minutes, until golden brown. Cool on a rack, and serve.

Custard Tartlets

Dan Ta

24 Tartlets

SWEET AND SAVORY pastries, dumplings, breads and noodles all are included in dim sum, the extensive category of Cantonese snacks. There is no finer example of dim sum than the sweet tartlets below, and their flaky crust and creamy custard filling make them a superb snack with tea. In the traditional recipe, lard is used in the crust and the custard is made simply with egg yolks and water. This is my adapted version.

Crust

1	cup all-purpose flour
1	cup cake flour
½	cup butter, well chilled, cut into tablespoon-sized pieces
1	large egg, lightly beaten
¼	cup sugar
2-4	tablespoons ice water

Custard Filling

¾	cup sugar
3	egg yolks
2	large eggs
1	cup half-and-half
½	cup heavy cream
2	teaspoons vanilla extract

1. To make the *Crust*, sift together the two flours, and place them in a bowl. Add the butter, and cut it into the flour until the mixture resembles cornmeal. Add the egg and sugar. Stir to combine, and slowly add the ice water, adding up to 4 tablespoons if necessary. Mix to a rough dough, and turn out onto a lightly floured surface. Mix the dough briefly until somewhat smooth, and form into a ball. Cover with plastic wrap, and refrigerate for 1 hour.

2. To make the *Custard Filling*, place the sugar, egg yolks and eggs in a mixing bowl. Whisk lightly until the sugar is dissolved. Add the half-and-half, cream and vanilla extract, and mix well.

3. Form the dough into a long, snakelike roll about 2 inches in diameter, and cut it into 24 pieces. Using your fingers, press each piece into a 3-inch circle, and fit it into a 2½-inch tartlet tin. Refrigerate the crusts for 30 minutes. Arrange the tartlets on a baking sheet, and fill each shell with the custard filling.

4. Preheat the oven to 325 degrees F. Bake the tartlets in the lower third of the oven for 30 minutes, or until a toothpick inserted into the custard comes out clean. Let the tartlets cool for 10 minutes; then remove them from their tins, and place on a cake rack to cool further. Serve at room temperature.

Fried Caramel Crisps

Sha Qi Ma

20 Squares

3	cups all-purpose flour
½	tablespoon baking powder
4	large eggs, lightly beaten
4	cups peanut, safflower or corn oil

Caramel

½	cup honey
½	cup water
¼	teaspoon clear rice vinegar (optional)
1	cup sugar
1	cup raisins

FOR THIS CLASSIC Cantonese treat, strands of dough are fried until crisp, tossed in a light caramel and cut into squares. These squares are often sold in Chinese grocery stores, wrapped in plastic. To my mind, the flavor of the homemade variety is infinitely better. Three tablespoons of sesame seeds may be sprinkled on top of the squares as a garnish. Serve as a snack with tea.

1. Place the flour and baking powder in a mixing bowl, and stir to combine. Add the beaten eggs, and mix to form a rough dough. Turn the dough out onto a lightly floured surface, and knead for about 5 minutes, until smooth. Cover the dough with a towel, and let it rest for 30 minutes. Cut the dough in two. Using a rolling pin, on a lightly floured surface, roll out each half to a large rectangle about ⅛ inch thick. Cut the rectangle lengthwise into 2-inch strips. Cut the strips crosswise into matchstick-sized shreds. Dust the shreds with flour to prevent them from sticking together. Lightly grease an 8-by-12-inch lasagna pan.

2. Heat a wok, add the oil, and heat the oil to 375 degrees F. Add a batch of the shreds, and deep-fry, stirring constantly, until puffed and golden brown, about 5 minutes. Remove with a handled strainer or slotted spoon, and drain on absorbent paper. Reheat the oil, and deep-fry the remaining shreds in the same manner, reheating the oil between batches. Drain on absorbent paper.

3. Place the *Caramel* ingredients in a heavy wok or saucepan, and slowly cook over low heat, stirring until the sugar has dissolved. Turn up the heat to medium, and continue cooking, without stirring, occasionally swirling the mixture in the pan, until it is a light caramel, about 310 degrees on a candy thermometer. Add the fried strips and the raisins. Toss so that the strips will be coated evenly with the caramel and the raisins will be evenly distributed. Pour the mixture into the greased lasagna pan, and using the flat side of a cleaver, press the strips into a compact rectangle. Let the mixture cool, and cut it into 20 squares. Arrange them on a platter, and serve.

Eight-Treasure Rice Pudding

Ba Bao Fan

6 Servings

THIS SWEET PUDDING
*is one of the better-known
confections in the repertory of
Chinese sweet dishes. It is
generally served at a banquet or
a formal dinner for the Chinese
New Year, a wedding or any
other festive occasion. The
traditional sweet garnishes
include red and black dates,
red and green papaya shreds,
preserved kumquats and lotus
seeds. I have adapted the
standard recipe to use fruits
that are readily available.*

1¼   cups Red Bean Paste, homemade (recipe follows) or canned
2   cups sweet (glutinous) rice

Rice Seasonings
2   tablespoons butter
3   tablespoons sugar
1   teaspoon vanilla extract

4   slices candied orange peel
¼   cup raisins
5   maraschino cherries, cut in half

1. Make the Red Bean Paste.

2. Rinse the rice in cold running water until the water runs clear. Place the rice in a bowl, add cold water to cover, and let sit for about 2 hours. Drain the rice, and place it in a saucepan with 2 cups of water. Cook over high heat until the water boils, reduce the heat to low, cover, and cook for 20 minutes, until craters appear in the surface of the rice. Remove from the heat, and let sit, covered, for 10 minutes. Add the *Rice Seasonings*, and mix to blend evenly.

3. Lightly grease a heatproof bowl that is 7 inches in diameter and 3 inches deep. Cut the candied orange peel into small triangles. Arrange the raisins in the center of the bowl, and alternately place the candied orange peel and the maraschino cherry halves around the raisins in a decorative pattern. Spread half the sweet rice in the bottom of the bowl, being careful not to dislodge the decorative pattern. Pat the rice down firmly, and make a depression in the middle. Add the red bean paste, and spread it evenly over the rice. Pack the remaining rice on top, spreading it evenly. Smooth the surface of the rice with the underside of a spoon dipped in water. Place the bowl in a steamer tray.

4. Fill a wok with water level with the bottom edge of the steamer tray, and heat until boiling. Place the steamer tray over the boiling water, cover, and steam for 1 hour over high heat. Check the water level after ½ hour, and add additional boiling water if necessary. (Alternatively, if you do not have a steamer large enough to hold the bowl, you may double-wrap the bowl in heavy-duty aluminum foil, place it in a broiler pan containing several inches of water, and bake in a preheated 400-degree oven for 1 hour.) Remove the rice pudding, invert it onto a platter, and serve immediately. To reheat, steam for 15 minutes over high heat.

Red Bean Paste

Dou Sha

3 Cups

½   pound azuki beans
¾   cup sugar
¾   cup butter
2   teaspoons vanilla extract

1. Rinse the beans, and discard any discolored ones. Place the beans in a bowl, add water to cover, and let the beans soak for 12 hours. Discard any beans that float to the surface. Drain the beans, and place them in a pot with 3 cups of water. Cook over high heat until the water boils, reduce the heat to medium-low, and cook, uncovered, for 1½ hours, or until the beans are very soft and the mixture is almost dry.

2. Transfer the beans to a blender or a food processor fitted with the steel blade, and chop to a smooth puree. Return the mixture to a saucepan, add the sugar and the butter, and cook, stirring constantly, over medium heat, until the mixture is very thick and comes away from the sides of the pan, about 20 minutes. Remove from the heat, and add the vanilla extract. Let cool.

C ANNED RED BEAN PASTE *is insipid. Homemade, laced with butter and seasoned with cinnamon and vanilla, it is absolutely delicious.*

Steamed Bread Pudding

Bu Ding

6 Servings

AFTER READING THE
list of ingredients, one
suspects that this is not a
traditional Chinese recipe. The
Chinese title bu ding, a direct
transliteration from the English,
further strengthens this theory.
Origin aside, this steamed
pudding is guaranteed to please
even the most discriminating
palate; it was a favorite of my
Chinese sister and brothers, who
often devoured it for breakfast.
Like all bread puddings, this one
is creamy, buttery and full of
richness.

18	slices white sandwich bread, crusts removed
1¼	cups sugar
6	large eggs, lightly beaten
6	tablespoons butter, melted
2	teaspoons vanilla extract

Orange Sauce

1½	cups freshly squeezed orange juice
2	tablespoons Grand Marnier
¼	cup sugar
1½	tablespoons cornstarch

1. Place the bread slices in a bowl, and add hot water to cover. Let sit for 10 minutes. Drain the bread in a fine-meshed sieve. Squeeze the bread in your hands to remove as much water as possible. Place the softened bread in a bowl, and using a fork, mash it to a paste. Add the sugar, eggs, melted butter and vanilla extract, stirring well after each addition. Generously grease a 1½-quart ring mold with melted butter, and pour the pudding mixture into the mold. Cover the mold securely with a piece of aluminum foil, and place it in a steamer tray.

2. Fill a wok with water level with the bottom edge of the steamer tray, and heat until boiling. Place the steamer tray over the boiling water, cover, and steam the pudding for 1 hour over high heat. (Alternatively, if you do not have a steamer large enough to hold the mold, you may double-wrap the mold in heavy-duty aluminum foil, place it in a broiler pan containing several inches of water, and bake it in a preheated 400-degree oven for 1 hour.)

3. Remove the mold, and run a knife between the pudding and the mold. Unmold the pudding onto a platter.

4. Place the *Orange Sauce* in a saucepan, and heat slowly until thick, stirring constantly. Pour the sauce over the pudding, and serve.

Steamed Chinese Cake

Ma La Gao

6 Servings

2¼	cups all-purpose flour
2	teaspoons baking powder
1	teaspoon salt
½	teaspoon baking soda
6	large eggs
1½	cups light brown sugar, tightly packed
1	cup milk
2	teaspoons vanilla extract
2	tablespoons minced blanched orange peel
	Juice of 1 orange
½	cup butter, melted and cooled

*O*NE IS SURE TO FIND *this airy and delicate cake on any Cantonese dim-sum tray. Though most traditional recipes use only brown sugar as a seasoning, I prefer to add orange peel and vanilla extract for extra flavor.*

1. Sift together the flour, baking powder, salt and baking soda. Generously grease a 7-inch tube pan, making certain that it is thoroughly coated.

2. Break the eggs into a mixing bowl, and beat vigorously until light and lemon-colored, about 5 minutes. Add the brown sugar, and continue beating for another 3 minutes. Add the milk, vanilla extract, orange peel and orange juice, mixing well after each addition. Alternately fold in the dry ingredients and the melted butter. Pour the batter into the greased pan, and place the pan in a steamer tray.

3. Fill a wok with water level with the bottom edge of the steamer tray, and heat until boiling. Place the steamer tray over the boiling water, cover, and steam for 1 hour over high heat. Check the water level in the wok after ½ hour. Add more boiling water if necessary. (Alternatively, if you do not have a steamer large enough to hold the tube pan, you may double-wrap the tube pan in heavy-duty aluminum foil, place it in a broiler pan containing several inches of water, and bake it in a preheated 400-degree oven for 1 hour.) The cake should be light and springy to the touch. Remove the pan from the steamer tray, and let the cake cool. Unmold the cake onto a platter, slice it, and serve.

Metric Conversions

General Conversions

	American	British	Metric
Weight	1 ounce	1 ounce	28.4 grams
	1 pound	1 pound	454 grams
Volume	1 U.S. teaspoon	1 U.K. level teaspoon	5 milliliters
	1 U.S. tablespoon *(3 teaspoons)*	1 U.K. dessert spoon	15 milliliters
	1 U.S. cup *(16 tablespoons)*	⅚ breakfast cup *(8 fluid ounces)*	236 milliliters *(about ¼ liter)*
	1 U.S. quart *(4 cups)*	⅚ Imperial quart	1 scant liter
	1 U.S. gallon *(4 quarts)*	⅚ Imperial gallon	3¾ liters
Length	1 inch	1 inch	2.5 centimeters *(25 millimeters)*
	12 inches *(1 foot)*	12 inches *(1 foot)*	30 centimeters

Note: All conversions are approximate. They have been rounded off to the nearest convenient measure.

Selected Measurements

	American (SPOONS AND CUPS)	British (OUNCES AND POUNDS)	Metric
Flour *(all-purpose, unsifted)*	1 teaspoon	⅛ ounce	3 grams
	1 tablespoon	⅓ ounce	9 grams
	1 cup	4¼ ounces	120 grams
	3⅔ cups	1 pound	454 grams
Herbs *(fresh, chopped)*	1 tablespoon	½ ounce	15 grams
Meats *(cooked and finely chopped)*	1 cup	8 ounces	225 grams
Rice *(raw)*	1 cup	7½ ounces	215 grams
Seasonings: *scallions, garlic, gingerroot (chopped, sliced or minced)*	1 tablespoon	⅓ ounce	9 grams
	1 cup	5 ounces	140 grams
Spinach and Leafy Vegetables *(fresh, cooked)*	1¼ pounds, raw	1¼ pounds, raw	550 grams, raw
	1 cup, cooked *(squeezed dry, chopped)*		

Selected Measurements (continued)

	American (SPOONS AND CUPS)	**British** (OUNCES AND POUNDS)	**Metric**
Sugar	1 teaspoon	⅙ ounce	5 grams
(regular granulated or	1 tablespoon	½ ounce	15 grams
superfine granulated)	1 cup	6½ ounces	185 grams
Vegetables *(raw—chopped fine,* *such as carrots or celery)*	1 cup	8 ounces	225 grams

All conversions are approximate. The weights have been rounded off to the nearest useful measure. Weights and measures of specific ingredients may vary with altitude, humidity and variation in method of preparation.

Oven Temperatures

Fahrenheit	Centigrade	British Regulo Setting	French Setting
212°	*100°*		*1*
225°	*107°*	*¼*	*2*
250°	*121°*	*½*	*3*
275°	*135°*	*1*	*3*
300°	*149°*	*2*	*4*
325°	*163°*	*3*	*4*
350°	*177°*	*4*	*4*
375°	*191°*	*5*	*5*
400°	*204°*	*6*	*5*
425°	*218°*	*7*	*6*
450°	*232°*	*8*	*6*
475°	*246°*	*8*	*6*
500°	*260°*	*9*	*7*
525°	*274°*	*9*	*8*
550°	*288°*	*9*	*9*

About the Author

NINA SIMONDS HAS BEEN WIDELY
praised for her ability to make Chinese cooking
enticingly accessible to a Western audience.
Fluent in Chinese, she has
traveled all over China and the Far East.
She is also the author of *China Express*,
China's Food and *Chinese Seasons*.
She lives in Salem, Massachusetts.

Mail-Order Sources

Kim Man Food
200 Canal Street
New York, New York 10013
(212) 571-0330

**Oriental Food Market and
Cooking School, Inc.**
2801 West Howard Street
Chicago, Illinois 60645
(312) 274-2826

Uwajimaya
519 6th Avenue South
Seattle, Washington 98104
(206) 624-6248

Index